A FOUNDATION IN ECONOMICS

Graham Donnelly

unreel photograply

apply to lola owen on

0113 2678888

Stanley Thornes Publishers Ltd

Text © Graham Donnelly   1991

Original line illustrations © Stanley Thornes (Publishers) Ltd 1991

First published in 1991 by:
Stanley Thornes (Publishers) Ltd
Old Station Drive
Leckhampton
CHELTENHAM   GL53 0DN
England

British Library Cataloguing in Publication Data
Donnelly, Graham
   A foundation in economics.
   1. Economics
   I. Title
   330

ISBN 0–7487–0560–0

Typeset in Palatino and Rockwell by Northern Phototypesetting Co. Ltd
Printed and bound in Singapore by Chong Moh Offset Printing Pte Ltd.

Contents

Foreword

As the title suggests, this book aims to meet the needs of those professional and other students for whom economics is a principal component of their studies, usually at the foundation stage, though sometimes further on in their professional examination programme. It is recognised that many students will be studying economics for the first time so that each area is covered from first principles and taken up to the level required of all the main examining bodies.

One of the commonest complaints of students is that 'there is nothing in the book on that', usually because they are looking in the wrong place or, more likely, because the material is included in a form they do not recognise. This real concern is addressed in two ways. First, each chapter begins with questions which aim to point towards the key issues raised in that chapter. Second, the text is written with the type of examination question likely to occur very much in mind. While, therefore, a conventional text, it is hoped that it will also prove 'user-friendly' for the student studying alone or on an open-learning basis.

Despite being aimed specifically at the professional student, this book should also be a useful text for students of economic theory and its applications, whether at GCE A Level, first year undergraduate or those seeking an NVQ qualification at levels III/IV.

My thanks are due to the many people who have made helpful comments and suggestions during the writing of this text, to Carolyn for assisting in assembling it and for the inventor of the word processor without which this project would have taken much longer to complete.

Graham Donnelly 1991

Acknowledgements

We are grateful to the following for permission to reproduce questions from past examination papers:

Association of Business Executives; London Chamber of Commerce and Industry; Institute of Chartered Secretaries and Administrators; Chartered Association of Certified Accountants; Chartered Institute of Management Accountants; Institute of Company Accountants; Chartered Institute of Marketing; Institute of Purchasing and Supply; Institute of Actuaries; Institute of Financial Accountants.

Syllabus guide

The following table indicates whether particular chapters are relevant to the syllabuses of the examining bodies listed. In each case the syllabus under consideration is 'economics' or a similar title.

Key

ABE	Association of Business Executives
LCCI	London Chamber of Commerce and Industry
ICSA	Institute of Chartered Secretaries & Administrators
ACCA	Chartered Association of Certified Accountants
CIMA	Chartered Institute of Management Accountants
ICA (SCCA)	Institute of Company Accountants (formerly the Society of Company & Commercial Accountants)
Cert.M	Certificate in Marketing
IPS	Institute of Purchasing and Supply
I.Act	Institute of Actuaries
IFA	Institute of Financial Accountants

This list comprises many of the major professional bodies but is illustrative rather than exhaustive. Students of other bodies will find that the book covers their syllabus requirements equally well.

Chapter	ABE 1	ABE 2	LCCI 3	LCCI 2	ICSA	ACCA	CIMA	ICA (SCCA)	CERT M	IPS	I. ACT	IFA
1	X		X	X	X	X	X	X	X	X	X	X
2	X		X	X	X	X	X	X	X	X	X	X
3	X		X	X	X	X	X	X	X	X	X	X
4					X	X	X		X	X		X
5	X		X	X	X	X	X	X	X	X		X
6	X		X	X	X	X	X	X	X	X	X	X
7	X		X	X	X	X	X	X	X	X	X	X
8	X		X	X	X	X	X	X	X	X	X	X
9	X*		X*	X*	X	X	X	X	X	X		
10	X		X*	X*	X	X	X	X	X	X	X	X
11	X		X	X	X	X	X	X	X	X	X	X
12	X		X	X	X	X	X	X	X	X	X	X
13	X		X	X	X	X	X	X	X	X	X	X
14	X		X	X	X	X	X	X	X	X	X	X
15		X	X	X	X	X	X	X	X	X	X	X
16	X	X	X	X	X	X	X	X	X	X	X	X
17		X	X	X	X	X	X	X	X	X	X	X
18	X*	– X	X	X	X	X	X	X	X	X		
19		X	X	X	X	X	X	X	X	X	X	X
20		X	X	X	X	X	X	X	X	X	X	X
21		X	X	X	X	X	X	X	X	X	X	X
22		X	X	X	X	X	X	X	X	X	X	X
23		X	X	X	X	X	X	X	X	X	X	X
24		X	X		X	X	X	X	X	X	X	X
25		X	X	X				X				

* Second part of chapter only.

1 The nature and scope of economics

- *What are the three fundamental economic problems?*
- *How do the various forms of economic society attempt to solve these problems?*

What is economics?

Economics is one of a group of academic disciplines, also including political science and sociology, which are collectively known as the social sciences and are concerned with the study of the behaviour of society. The area of social activity with which economics is concerned is the allocation of scarce resources between the various demands made upon them. Indeed, the literal meaning of 'economics' is 'household management'. How individuals or societies decide on the allocative process will clearly depend on the nature of the individual and of society, the influence of cultural, historical, and sociological factors and the nature of the prevailing political system. It is thus impossible to study economics without some awareness of its interrelationships with other fields of human behaviour.

The social sciences use the scentific methods of observation, experimentation and research to study social behaviour. However, the success with which the social sciences are able to predict behaviour and the results of experiments are far inferior to that of the physical sciences, like physics or chemistry. In a physical science the results of an experiment will be identical each time it is carried out, provided the conditions remain the same. In the social sciences conditions are constantly changing and human behaviour is never entirely predictable so that even apparently identical experiments may not yield the same answer each time.

The methodology of economics

As with all the social sciences, the nature of the subject imposes limitations on the use of scientific methods in studying economics. These will be examined briefly before looking in detail at the subject matter of economics.

1 Measurement

It is very rare to get the exact terms available to the physical sciences in measuring quantity, distance, heat, etc. If you want to measure expenditure patterns, for example, you find that no two consumers exhibit identical behaviour. Even one consumer's behaviour will change over relatively short periods. When trying to measure relatively straightforward items like total exports or the level of earned income the data is by no means easy to obtain. Again, many of the things we wish to measure are abstract concepts like satisfaction or competition and these are extremely difficult to quantify.

2   Experiment

Experiments are vital in the physical sciences to prove hypotheses and to enable forecasts to be made when outside events follow the pattern of a controlled experiment. In economics, however, such conditions rarely apply. People cannot be expected to behave as predictably as a gas or liquid nor can their economic behaviour be divorced from previous conduct or current events in society. Instead, the economist must rely on past events and try to predict future patterns. Thus economics makes much use of statistical information and looks for the correlation between the data and actual events, e.g. the extent to which changes in income affect buying patterns in particular products.

3   Forecasting

Using statistical data some success can be had in forecasting future economic behaviour. However, such are the complexities of human behaviour patterns that economic forecasting remains fraught with dangers. The situation is aggravated by confusion between the causes and effects of particular events, e.g. a rise in income may lead people to buy more food but a greater interest in healthy eating may simultaneously be driving people to buy less. Again, if enough people are convinced that a share price will rise soon and buy the share now, the price will indeed rise. For this reason economists frequently preface forecasts of the consequences of a change in economic conditions with the phrase 'all things being equal'. In other words, when we forecast that an event will have a certain outcome we assume that no other factor will come into play to disturb this outcome.

4   Models

Models serve two useful purposes in economics.

First, they take the place of controlled experiments which, as we have seen, are very difficult to conduct in economics. A model enables an economic phenomenon to be simplified to an extent not possible in the real world. It is then possible to isolate the most important issues involved and so make predictions which will have some relevance to the real world. Thus we have models of the economy as a whole which enable predictions to be made about the impact of particular government policies on the level of economic activity.

Second, a model may be produced of a hypothetical situation which, although not found in the real world, can be used as a benchmark by which to judge real-life events. This sort of model is used to examine the behaviour of firms.

Whether a complicated structure or a simple illustrative diagram, the purpose of any model is to assist in the understanding of a concept or idea and much use will be made of tables and diagrams in this book with this aim in mind.

The problems of resource allocation

Scarcity and choice

Every economic society, from the household unit to the nation state, is confronted by the fundamental problem of how to allocate the scarce resources available to it in the face of insatiable demands for those resources. Scarcity in the economic sense means that, however plentiful a particular resource, supply of it is limited to the extent that if it were free total demand could not be satisfied. The resource is therefore able to command a price. In this sense all resources, with the exception of air, are scarce. In allocating its scarce resources, an economic society must deal with three fundamental problems:

1 **What shall be produced?** What goods and services, and in what quantities, shall society choose to produce with the limited resources at its disposal?

2 **How shall these goods and services be produced?** Which resources and what technical processes will be employed to produce these goods and services?

3 **For whom shall they be produced?** How is society to allocate the goods and services produced when the supply is never able to satisfy total demand?

Dealing with each of these problems involves choice. By deciding which goods and services to produce society will choose these at the expense of others. But it is not simply a choice between refrigerators and washing machines or between clothes and curtains. Society must decide whether to produce **consumer goods** or **capital goods**. Consumer goods are those which are produced for their own sake to add to the material well-being of individual members of society, such as food, clothing, a compact disc or a bar of chocolate. Capital goods are produced to aid in the production of consumer goods and services and include tools, machinery, lorries, factories and oil refineries. By using scarce resources to produce capital goods society chooses to go without consumer goods and services in the present to enable their production to be maintained or increased in the future.

In choosing how goods and services shall be produced society has access to four groups of resources. These are the 'factors of production':

1 **Land**   The natural resources which provide raw materials.

2 **Labour**   The human resources which actually make the goods and perform the services.

3 **Capital**   The capital goods which enable labour to work the raw materials.

4 **Enterprise**   The expertise which organises the other factors of production to enable production to take place.

Choices must be made as to which combinations of these factors will be used in the productive process and how that production will be organised.

Finally, choices must be made as to the distribution of the supply of goods and services available. A mechanism must be found for deciding which groups in society shall have priority in the receipt of goods and services. The allocation of rewards to the various factors of production for their part in the productive process must also be determined.

The need for choice can be simply illustrated by a **production possibility curve.** For the sake of simplicity, let us assume that a society can use its resources to produce only two goods, guns and butter. The result is shown in Figure 1.1 where the production possibility curve XY represents the maximum production that can be achieved by society. A number of possibilities exist:

1   Society may choose to produce only guns by producing at point X.

2   Society may choose to produce only butter by producing at point Y.

3   Society may choose to produce both guns and butter and produce at a point on the curve somewhere between X and Y, as at W or Z.

4   Society may not be using all its resources efficiently and so produces within its production possibility curve, e.g. at point U.

What is not possible is for society to produce at points outside its production possibility curve, because either the resources are not available or the state of technical progress prevents resources being used more effectively.

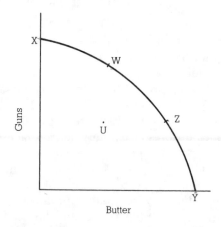

Figure 1.1 *Production possibility curve*

Opportunity cost

The production possibility curve outlines the dilemma facing any economic society. Every choice made involves the sacrifice of alternative uses of scarce resources. For society it may be guns or butter, more consumer goods or a better health service. Individual consumers must choose between a holiday or a new television, a cinema ticket or a pair of gloves. For the firm the installation of new machinery or increased advertising expenditure, increased production of existing lines or the development of new ones. In each case the choice made results in a cost; the cost of the alternative next best use to which the resources so used could have been put. This cost is known as **opportunity cost**. So the opportunity cost for an individual buying a new television is the new washing machine he or she could have bought instead. Of course, one could argue that the opportunity cost of buying the television is all the other expenditure choices that the individual might have made. However, many of these would not have been considered (say 6000 boxes of matches or a reconditioned engine for a car he or she does not own), so it is usual to measure opportunity cost in terms of the choice that was most closely considered as an alternative.

Note that we expect individuals, firms and governments to behave rationally in their choice so that opportunity cost is kept to a minimum. If an individual chooses to buy a new suite of furniture rather than an extra holiday the opportunity cost of choosing the furniture should be less than having the holiday.

REVISION TEST

1   How would you distinguish between a science and a social science?
2   Give examples of how economics is likely to be affected by (a) political science and (b) psychology.
3   Why is model-making a more successful tool for the economist than experimentation?
4   What are the two main purposes of model-making in economics?
5   What are the three fundamental economic problems?
6   Define scarcity in economic terms.
7   What are the four factors of production?
8   Distinguish between consumer goods and capital goods.
9   What function does a production possibility curve perform?
10   Define the term 'opportunity cost'.

The economic society

Underlying the principle of opportunity cost is the premise that all economic decision-takers, whether individual households, firms or governments, attempt to derive the maximum satisfaction from their use of resources. It is this desire to achieve optimum resource utilisation which drives individuals to seek an economic society larger than the individual household. The individual, self-sufficient household depends on its own resources to meet all its needs and cannot progress beyond the talents and abilities of its own members. By joining with other households to form a larger economic unit, however, it can enjoy the benefits which come from participation in a larger economic unit.

1 Exchange

In a larger economic unit the individual can exchange his excess produce for the produce of other individuals through the process of **barter**. He can exchange his resources for others, e.g. he can work for another individual in return for a wage rather than attempt to run his own business.

In a sophisticated society the number of exchanges is such that barter is inadequate to deal with the demands made upon it. In particular, it requires two difficult conditions to be met. First, the participants must be able to agree an exchange rate, e.g. how many chickens is a cow worth? Second, the participants to a barter must be able to find a double coincidence of wants, i.e. a person wishing to exchange a pig for a blue suit must find a person wishing to exchange a blue suit for a pig! So societies must eventually find a medium of exchange by which all goods and services can be valued and the process of exchange made easier; this is the principal function fulfilled by money.

2 Specialisation

In a society individuals do not have to attempt to perform every economic function themselves. People can abandon functions in which they have no gift or expertise and concentrate on those in which they can succeed. Specialisation speeds the process by which surpluses are accumulated and exchange can take place. The principle of specialisation applies equally well to the other factors of production. Land, for example, can be devoted to different types of farming or mineral extraction rather than always having to provide a variety of needs to individual households.

3 Division of labour

This takes the principle of specialisation even further and applies it within a particular industry. So workers become expert at certain tasks rather than every function within the factory farm or office. Taken to its ultimate conclusion this may result in workers spending an entire shift tightening nuts onto bolts or putting the orange creams into boxes of chocolates.

Like specialisation, the division of labour is both a result and a cause of the development of economic societies. The division of labour reduces the economic independence of the individuals and leads them to rely on exchange to meet the majority of their essential needs. So the members of society become increasingly interdependent.

Economic systems

Any economic society depends for its existence on the members of that society seeing the mutual benefits to be gained from exchange and specialisation. However, societies vary considerably in their perception of how best these benefits might be exploited. These differences manifest themselves in the way a particular society deals with such fundamental issues as:

1 The mechanisms by which scarce resources are allocated in society, both for production and distribution.

2 The nature of the relationship between the individual and society.

3 The role of government in the allocation of resources and the direction of economic activity.

The response to these issues determines the type of economic system under which a society operates. There are three main types of economic system:

Market economy

Within a free market or *laissez-faire* economy the questions of resource allocation are solved by the price mechanism. Resources are obtained under this system by those who are able and willing to pay for them, whether they want them for production or consumption. Support for this system is based on the view that each individual is best able to pursue his or her own best interests and, in so doing, will automatically benefit the rest of society as well. In its most pure form the market economy accords no role whatever for the state in the economy since government regulations direct the economy from its natural course and inhibit economic growth. Furthermore such regulations are inclined to encourage the self-interest of privileged groups to the detriment of the rest of society. Under the market economy, the allocation of resources is the result of endless individual decisions by producers and consumers in the market.

As a theoretical concept the market economy was highly popular in the early nineteenth century and economic liberals fought to free the economy of all government regulation. In practice, however, the market economy has a number of defects:

1 The price mechanism does not guarantee that resources will go to those individuals or firms which will use them most efficiently, e.g. rare minerals essential for some industrial processes might be squandered on luxury decorations by a very wealthy individual.

2 There would be no restriction on the production and sale of undesirable and dangerous goods, e.g. explosives, firearms or drugs.

3 Competition may lead to a waste of resources if companies spend enormous amounts on advertising which could be used for product development.

4 Competition may not persist in the market economy, e.g. if some companies are very efficient they may eventually drive rivals out of the market or absorb them and so attain a monopoly position.

5 Important goods or services may not be provided because they are insufficiently profitable, e.g. services to rural areas or aids for the physically handicapped.

6 Some services, such as the police, armed forces, etc. are essential to the nation as a whole and it is both undesirable and impracticable for them to be provided through the workings of the market.

7 A free market society will result in some members of the community being unable to

afford even the necessities of life, e.g. those too ill to work, the very old and other groups with insufficient earning power.

8   When the distribution of income is determined by the market the results may be socially unacceptable, e.g. wealth may be concentrated in the hands of the few.

While several of the points made above contain social or political criticisms of the free market economy, they are still economic arguments. Suppose that the price mechanism operates in such a way that much of the workforce is undernourished or lacking in resistance to disease, then the effect is to reduce the likelihood that labour resources will be used to their full potential. Similarly if all the wealth is concentrated in the hands of a tiny minority of the population there will be little chance of developing industries based on mass production.

Command economy

In the command or centrally-planned economy the questions of *what, how and for whom* are answered by a central planning authority under the direction of the state. The quantities of goods and services to be produced are determined by this central planning authority, which also decides their price. Similarly, the methods of production and the patterns of distribution are determined by central authorities. The problem of scarcity is resolved, not by the price mechanism, but by rationing and waiting lists. Individuals retain some control over the allocation of their income but they are unable to influence the production system by their actions. The various forms of communist state have command economies but such economic systems are not confined to communist regimes. During the Nazi period in Germany the production system was largely under the direction of the state.

The economic arguments in favour of a command economy are based on the view that greater efficiency can be achieved under this system than under a free market economy:

1   Central direction ensures that resources are allocated to those sectors of the economy where they can be used most productively, rather than to those willing to pay the most for them.

2   Wasteful competition is eliminated because firms are not permitted to duplicate services or use resources on extensive marketing campaigns.

3   An appropriate balance may be struck between the production of capital goods and consumer goods to ensure sustained expansion of the society's production possibility curve.

4   Since all production and distribution is controlled by the state, considerations of economic efficiency are not distorted by decisions based purely on the desire for profit.

5   Economic development is based on planning rather than on the often haphazard decision-making of individual producers and consumers.

Of course, the drive to introduce command economies has just as often been based on social or political grounds. So central control of the economy has been seen as a way of correcting the social deprivation and concentration of wealth which may follow from a free market economy. Furthermore, the state can take over the supply of essential services, rather than these being left to the whim of private suppliers whose motive is profit rather than meeting the needs of consumers.

Despite its apparent advantages, the command economy has a number of weaknesses which operate against its success in practice.

1   The absence of the price mechanism makes it extremely difficult to judge the wants of households so production is often geared to targets which take no account of likely consumption patterns.

2   The absence of the profit-motive and other rewards for individual performance may weaken the level of effort and initiative among workers.

3   The absence of competition weakens the drive for producers to improve products or efficiency.

4   Planning usually requires large bureaucratic structures which waste resources.

5   Large-scale economic planning proves difficult to implement because of the sheer complexities and scale of the task being undertaken.

Mixed economy

In practice the economy which is entirely dominated either by the free market or by central control does not exist. The allocation of resources to such areas as defence or law and order will always be reserved to the state in a free market economy while all command economies contain some elements of private enterprise. Such isolated exceptions to the normal pattern, however, do not alter the general character of the economy which remains either free market or command. The mixed economy is a quite distinct form of economic structure characterised by the following features:

1   There must be substantial elements of both free market and state-directed economic decision-making.

2   Such a balance is both welcomed and consciously strived after. In the other economic systems such mixed aspects are merely tolerated.

3   The workings of the price mechanism are regarded as the proper means by which most resources will be allocated. However, state intervention is seen as essential to remedy the defects of the market economy outlined above.

The central question surrounding the mixed economy is the determination of this balance between **private sector** and **public sector**. All mixed economies recognise the need for defence, policing, the administration of justice, the collection of taxes and the provision of social services to be provided by the public sector. Similarly, farming, the manufacture and distribution of consumer goods and the provision of retail services are generally seen as areas of economic activity to be undertaken by the private sector. There are, however, many areas of activity about which there is no agreement as to how they should be undertaken in a mixed economy. These include the provision of health and education, the ownership of key industries such as aircraft manufacture and defence equipment, the distribution of essential materials such as fuel or electricity and the maintenance of the communications network, whether roads, railways or telecommunications. Nor is there consensus as to how far the government should intervene in the working of the economy and to what extent it should leave market forces to resolve the central economic problems.

The extent to which one mixed economy differs from another depends largely on the political complexion of each society and how the government interprets its role in the economy. Thus a socialist government is likely to accord a greater role to the public sector than a government keen to promote free enterprise, while the views of socialist governments will themselves differ from country to country. The nature of the mixed economy will also reflect current economic conditions and external political factors. Typically, all mixed economies exhibit greater public intervention in the economy during periods of economic crisis or of external threat. Over the past 50 years the time of greatest public sector intervention in the mixed economy occurred during the Second World War and the period of reconstruction after it. In recent years there has been a steady move away from public sector activity in the mixed economy. This has been particularly notable in Britain during the Thatcher years when reliance on market forces has been stressed and the level of direct public sector economic activity has been drastically reduced, especially through the privatisation programme.

REVISION TEST

1   What is 'barter'?

2   What function does money perform in society?

3   What are the three principal characteristics of any economic society?

4   What is the difference between 'the division of labour' and 'specialisation'?

5   In what sense are all economies 'mixed'?

6   Name three of the main problems associated with a free market economy.

7   Are there any functions affecting the economy which the government of a free market economy performs?

8   How are resources allocated in a command economy?

9   What is the importance of the price mechanism in the free market economy?

10   Is the mixed economy closer to the free market economy or the command economy? Why?

Examination questions

1   How are the problems of scarcity and choice solved in a free enterprise economy?

(ABE1, December 1986)

2   How do different types of economic system organise the allocation of goods and factors of production?

(ABE1, June 1987)

3   Economics is described as a social science:
    a) What functions must economics fulfil to be a social science?
    b) What methods does economics use to fulfil these functions?
    c) What difficulties are involved in achieving these functions?
                                                            (ABE1, December 1987)

4   a) Explain the functions of price in a market economy.
    b) Can the price mechanism cope effectively with all related economic problems?
                                                            (ABE1, June 1988)

5   'In the market economy, emphasis is laid on the freedom of the individual both as a
    consumer and as owner of resources.'
    a) Explain this statement.
    b) Discuss the major defects of the market economy.
                                                            (LCCI Higher, November 1986)

6   Compare and contrast the principal characteristics of a free market economy with
    those of a planned economy.
                                                            (LCCI Intermediate, May 1986)

7   a) Give a definition of economics.
    b) Explain the term 'opportunity costs'.
    c) Explain why, in a mixed economy, the government might intervene.
                                                            (LCCI Intermediate, May 1987)

8   What are the advantages and disadvantages of the free market system as a means
    of allocating resources?
                                                            (ACCA, June 1987)

9   The role of central planning in China and the Soviet union has recently been called
    into question. In the light of this.
    a) Define the centrally planned economy.
    b) Explain the economic reasons which might have led a government to adopt a
        centrally planned economy initially.
    c) Describe the economic problems which have led to the decline in popularity of
        central planning.
                                                            (ACCA, December 1989)

10 What is a mixed economy? Explain how resources are allocated in a mixed
    economy.
                                                            (Cert. M., June 1987)

11 a) Define the major functions of an economic system.
    b) Critically comment on how your job as a purchasing officer might differ as a
        result of operating in a centrally planned economy as opposed to a competitive
        economy.
                                                            (IPS, November 1987)

12   If meteorologists are able to predict weather patterns with a high degree of accuracy, why do Economists find it so difficult to predict what is likely to happen to the economy?

(IFA, December 1988)

13   What do you understand by 'the economic problem'?
Explain how different societies use different systems to solve the problem.

(IFA, June 1989)

2 Markets and the determination of price

- *How do markets work to allocate resources?*
- *Do higher prices always lead to less being demanded?*

The market

The market economy is an economic system in which resources are allocated through the working of the market. But what is 'the market'?

We are all familiar with the idea of a market as a place where buyers and sellers come together to trade, and the term is most frequently used to describe that weekly or daily event when stalls are set up to sell greengroceries and other goods to the public. In fact, a market exists wherever buyers and sellers trade and, by their actions, determine price. The market need not have physical location since in many markets trading is done mainly by telephone or computer, e.g. the stock market or the foreign exchange market. Nor do buyers and sellers have to play an equal part in the determination of price. In the market for most consumer goods the prices are fixed by the shops while at an auction it is buyers who take the lead.

The market economy is made up of many markets; those for the various resources used in the economy, those for each consumer good or service and those for capital goods and assets. Many of these markets are closely linked, like those for stocks and shares or for compact discs and cassette tapes. All markets are inter-related in that the more resources are devoted to one market the less there will be available for another.

Market forces

This is another common term and refers to the fact that changes in the price or other market conditions of a particular good are the result of large-scale movements in the market by buyers or sellers which most individuals are powerless either to initiate or to oppose.

Let us take an example of market forces with which most of us are familiar. Throughout the year there are major sporting and entertainment events at which ticket touts can be seen charging very high prices for even the cheapest seats. The touts can charge these high prices because demand for tickets far exceeds the limited supply available and so tickets are sold to those prepared to pay, for example, as much as £1000 to see a Wimbledon final. In England in 1966 ticket touts were selling 15/- (75 pence) seats for the Football World Cup third place play-off for 10/- (50 pence). Why were they so generous? Because they had bought many tickets for this match in case England lost in their semi-final and would be playing in this game. Instead the match was between Portugal and the USSR and the demand for tickets was so low that touts sold tickets at a loss rather than be left with them after the match. The touts recouped this loss and more, of course, through the sale of tickets for the final.

From this example we see that market forces are the result of the interaction of demand and supply. So to understand how markets operate to determine price we must examine the factors which determine demand and supply. In so doing we shall simplify matters by using a model; the *perfect market*.

The perfect market

This is based on a number of assumptions:

1   Both the buyers and the sellers in the market behave rationally so that the buyer always seeks the lowest available price and the seller the highest.

2   All the units of the product being traded are identical in every respect. This means that there is no product differentiation by individual sellers through packaging or advertising.

3   In the absence of product differentiation, both buyers and sellers act solely on the basis of price.

4   There are many buyers and sellers in the market, none of whom are able to influence the price by his or her action alone.

5   There is perfect communication in the market so that all buyers and sellers have complete knowledge of prices throughout the market.

6   There are no transport costs in the market so each buyer can buy from any seller.

If these conditions exist any price differences within the market will be eradicated and a single market price quickly established.

Demand

In economics 'demand' means effective demand, i.e. the desire for a good or service together with the willingness and ability to pay for it. If a person is unable or unwilling to buy something at a particular price then that person's effective demand is zero. Price is therefore the major determinant of effective demand; generally the lower the price of a good the greater the quantity demanded of that good. Table 2.1 shows an individual consumer's demand schedule for a hypothetical product, Good X. Note that the demand schedule does not tell us how much the consumer is actually buying. It merely indicates how much the consumer will buy if the price is £10 or £8 or whatever. This tendency for the quantity demanded to rise as the price falls is based on two factors:

1   It is assumed that each consumer is seeking to derive the greatest satisfaction from his or her income. A fall in the price of the good makes it cheaper compared to other

goods so that the consumer may be expected to transfer some expenditure from other goods to this one.

2   A fall in the price leads to the consumer being able to buy more of the product without having to spend more of his or her income on it.

TABLE 2.1
Demand schedule for Good X

Price (£)	Demand
8	15
7	20
6	30
5	40
4	50
3	65
2	85

When the information from the demand schedule is plotted on a graph we get the downward-sloping demand curve shown in Figure 2.1. This is typical of the demand curve for almost all products in most circumstances.

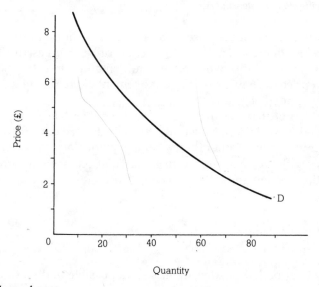

Figure 2.1 *The demand curve*

Clearly the individual's demand curve is of limited value. The demand curve for whisky of a teetotaller, for example, wouldn't tell us much about the level of demand for whisky. Of far greater use is the *market* demand curve which represents the sum of the demand curves of all the individual buyers in the market. Since the market demand curve reflects more accurately how demand responds to price changes, it will be the one we use from now on, except where stated.

Price changes and the demand curve

The demand curve represents the quantity which will be demanded at different prices. A change in price will result in a movement along the demand curve, as shown in Figure 2.2.

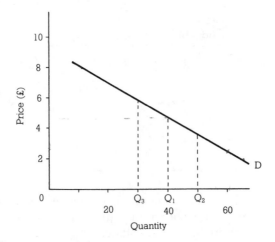

Figure 2.2 *Movements along the demand curve*

We begin by assuming that the price is £5. At this price the quantity demanded is 40 units, shown on the demand curve as Q_1. If the price changes to £4 the quantity demanded will be found by moving along the demand curve to Q_2 and 50 units. Similarly a rise in price to £6 will result in a movement along the demand curve to Q_3 and a quantity demanded of 30 units.

It is important to note that the demand curve can only relate changes in *price* to the quantity demanded. In so doing it is assumed that all other factors affecting demand are unchanged, i.e. *ceteris paribus* (other things being equal). Conversely, it is possible for demand to change without any alteration in price. This occurs when there is a change in one of the conditions of demand.

Conditions of demand

1   Taste

Over a relatively long period of 20 years or so it is possible to discern changes in the patterns of demand due to changes in the consumption habits of households. In the last 20 years in the UK there have been significant increases in the demand for wine, health foods and leisure activities and substantial decreases in the demand for bottled beers, tea leaves and cinema tickets.

2   Fashion

Changes in fashion are much more rapid than those in taste. A change in style will lead to the demand for particular types of clothes or hairstyles falling dramatically.

3 Income

If incomes rise people can buy more of a particular good without sacrificing their purchase of other goods and services. So, as incomes rise, consumers spend more on holidays and other leisure activities while keeping their expenditure on basic articles like bread, salt and sugar the same.

4 The distribution of national income

In societies where income and wealth is concentrated in the hands of a few, very rich people, patterns of demand will be different to those in societies where there is a fairly even distribution of national income. In the former case there may well be some demand for opulent goods like gold plated Rolls-Royces while the majority of the population cannot afford relatively cheap consumer durables like televisions or refrigerators. In the latter case there is likely to be a greater demand for consumer durables but much less demand for very expensive goods or the very cheapest of consumer goods.

5 The size of the population and its distribution

A growth in the population can be expected to lead to an increase in the demand for all goods. A change in the age distribution of the population will affect the demand for certain goods. Thus a fall in the birth rate will lead to a decrease in the demand for prams and cots. A change in the proportion of elderly people in the population will affect the demand for care facilities and sheltered accommodation.

6 Expectations of future shortages or gluts

If people expect shortages and consequent price rises to occur they may stock up and so increase demand now – so causing the very shortage they feared! If, on the other hand, consumers anticipate future gluts they may hold back from buying now, so causing a fall in demand.

7 The price of substitute goods

Substitute goods are goods that are alternatives to each other so that a rise in the price of one may lead consumers to switch to the other, e.g. different brands of tea or coffee. The degree of substitution may be weaker than this as when consumers switch from coffee to tea or from one leisure pursuit to another.

8 The price of complementary goods

Complements are goods that are generally bought together, e.g. torches and batteries, fountain pens and ink or cups and saucers. Such goods are described as being in **joint demand**. A rise in the price of one complementary good may adversely affect the demand for the other, as when higher petrol prices reduced the demand for large cars in the early 1970s.

A change in one of the conditions of demand, all other conditions and price remaining the same, will lead to a different quantity of the good being demanded at all prices; or at least at several prices. An increase in demand will therefore result in a new demand curve to the **right** of the old demand curve, as in Figure 2.3.

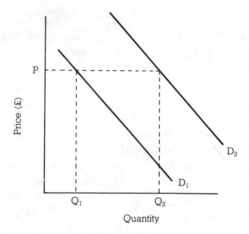

Figure 2.3 *Demand curve shift – right*

The shift to the right of the demand curve means that the quantity demanded at Price P rises from Q_1 to Q_2, and there are similar increases in the quantity demanded at all other prices. This may be due to a rise in household incomes, the product becoming more fashionable, a rise in the price of substitutes, etc.

When there is a decrease in demand a new demand curve to the **left** of the old one will result, as in Figure 2.4.

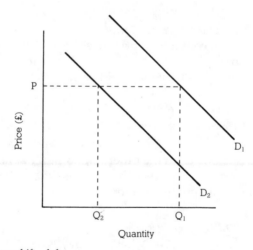

Figure 2.4 *Demand curve shift – left*

A leftward shift of the demand curve leads to the quantity demanded at Price P falling from Q_1 to Q_2 and so on. This leftward shift could be due to a fall in population, a rise in the price of complementary goods, expectations of future gluts, etc.

To summarise:

- Movements along the demand curve occur when demand is affected by a change in price.

- Shifts in the demand curve occur when demand is affected by changes in the conditions of demand.

Note that when demand is affected by changes in price we refer to **increases** and **decreases in the quantity demanded**. Alternatively the terms **extension** and **contraction of demand** may be used. When, however, demand is affected by a change in one of the conditions of demand we use the terms **increase** and **decrease in demand**.

REVISION TEST

1 Define the term 'market'.
2 How do market forces operate?
3 How are resources allocated in the market?
4 Give three of the conditions necessary for a perfect market.
5 On what factor alone is choice based in a perfect market?
6 For which of these products is an individual demand curve
   a) of most use and
   b) of least use?
   a Ferrari motor car   bread   postage stamps.
7 Name three factors likely to affect the demand for cars.
8 How does fashion differ from taste in its impact on demand?
9 Give an example of a substitute product for margarine.
10 Explain this sentence: 'A battery is a complementary product to a torch but a torch is not a complementary product to a battery'.

Supply

Supply refers to the amount of a good that a seller is prepared to supply at a particular price. Market supply is made up of the combined supply of all the individual suppliers operating in the market. As with demand, we shall find market supply more useful than the supply of an individual seller. When we look at the market supply schedule for Good X (Table 2.2), we see that the quantity supplied increases as the price rises. This is likely to be the case because a higher price, all things being equal, will result in higher

TABLE 2.2
Supply schedule for Good X

Price (£)	Supply
2	15
3	20
4	30
5	40
6	50
7	65
8	85

profits for the seller. In addition, a higher price will attract more suppliers into the market. When the information in Table 2.2 is plotted onto a graph the result is a supply curve which slopes upwards from left to right, as in Figure 2.5. As with demand, a change in price will result in a movement along the supply curve. Assume that the original price is £6 with a quantity supplied of 50 units. If the price rises to £7 there will be a movement along the supply curve to an output of 65 units. Similarly, a fall in price to £2 will result in a movement along the supply curve to an output of only 15 units.

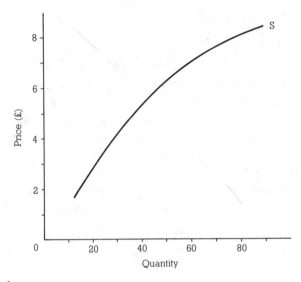

Figure 2.5 *The supply curve*

The supply curve can only relate changes in *price* to the quantity supplied. Again, as with demand, it is assumed that all other factors affecting supply are unchanged, i.e. other things being equal. It is, of course, possible for supply to change without any alteration in price when there is a change in one of the conditions of supply.

Conditions of supply

1   Natural events

Climatic or weather conditions will affect supply from one year to the next in agricultural products such as wheat or rice. Similarly affected will be goods derived from raw materials grown under natural conditions like wine or honey.

2   The prices of factors of production

Factors of production provide the resources used by suppliers in manufacturing or distributing their goods and services, and for which they must pay. A change in the price of any of these directly affects the costs of the firm and thus the amount which will be supplied at any given price. If, for example, the price of crude oil falls, an oil company will be able to produce a litre of petrol at a lower price than previously. So the company could maintain current production levels at a lower price without affecting its profits. Alternatively, the lower raw material costs will enable the company to expand output at current prices.

3   The state of technology
Technical improvements may enable large-scale increases in output with no increase in price. Major advances in electronics have led to better quality, superior products in the television and computer industries in the past decade while prices have actually fallen.

4   The prices of other goods
If the price of one good falls production of that good, all things being equal, will become less attractive. This may lead some firms to switch to the production of other goods, where this is practicable. Many UK breweries have, since the 1960s, switched much of their production of beers from bitter to the higher-priced, more profitable, lagers.

5   Goods in joint supply
Sometimes the supply of one good is directly related to that of another, e.g. beef and leather or oil and its by-products such as plastic. An increase in the supply of beef will lead to an increase in the supply of leather without any change in the price of the latter.

A change in any of the conditions of supply will, all things being equal, lead to a different quantity being supplied at all prices, or at least at several prices. An increase in supply will therefore result in a new supply curve to the **right** of the existing curve, as in Figure 2.6.

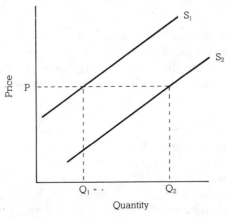

Figure 2.6   *Supply curve shift – right*

The shift to the right of the supply curve in Figure 2.6 means that the quantity supplied at Price P rises from Q_1 to Q_2 and there will be similar increases in the quantity supplied at all other prices. This may be due to a rise in production of a good in joint supply, a fall in the price of a factor of production, etc.

When there is a decrease in supply a new supply curve to the **left** of the existing one will result, as in Figure 2.7.

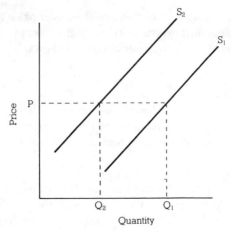

Figure 2.7 *Supply curve shift – left*

In Figure 2.7 a leftward shift in the supply curve will lead to the quantity supplied at Price P falling from Q_1 to Q_2 and so on. This leftward shift may be due to adverse weather or other natural conditions, a rise in the price of other goods which the firm is capable of supplying, etc.

To summarise:

- Movements along the supply curve occur when supply is affected by a change in price.
- Shifts of the supply curve occur when supply is affected by changes in the conditions of supply.

Note that when supply is affected by changes in price we refer to **increases** and **decreases in the quantity supplied**. Alternatively the terms **extension** and **contraction of supply** may be used. When, however, supply is affected by a change in one of the conditions of supply we use the terms **increase** and **decrease in supply**.

Determination of price

We have seen that the typical demand curve slopes downwards from left to right while the typical supply curve slopes upwards from left to right. When these two curves are placed on the same diagram they will intersect, as in Figure 2.8 where the data is taken from Tables 2.1 and 2.2. The two curves intersect where the price is £5 and both the quantity demanded and the quantity supplied are 40 units. This is the **equilibrium price** and is the only price which can be sustained in the market. To prove this we need only examine a situation in which the price is different to £5.

Suppose the price being charged by suppliers is £8. At this price 85 units are available from suppliers but only 15 units are demanded. Most of the suppliers face being left with their goods unsold so they will compete for the limited demand by lowering their price. This move will have two effects. First, some suppliers will leave the market rather than accept a lower price. Second, additional buying will be stimulated by the lower price on offer. This process will go on until the excess supply disappears and the quantity demanded equals that supplied, at price £5. Similarly a price of £3 is not sustainable because then there will be excess demand and buyers will compete to push up prices until equilibrium is restored.

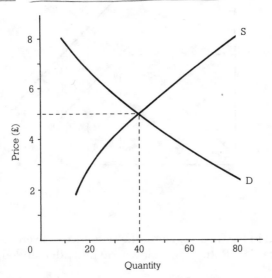

Figure 2.8 *Price equilibrium*

There will be no tendency for prices in the market to move away from the equilibrium price until there is a change in the conditions of either demand or supply. Suppose that Good X is a wool and that there is a shift in fashion towards more woollen products. The result will be an increase in demand and a rightward shift of the demand curve, as shown in Figure 2.9. The new demand curve cuts the supply curve at a higher price, P_2 instead of P_1, leading to a new market equilibrium whereby the quantity bought and sold has increased from Q_1 to Q_2. This new equilibrium does not occur immediately but follows from a sequence of events:

1   To begin with, demand rises at the original equilibrium price. There is now an excess of demand over the available supply.

2   Competition among buyers pushes up the price in the market.

3   A higher price draws new suppliers into the market and drives away some of the demand.

4   Eventually a new equilibrium price is established where once again the quantity demanded equals the quantity supplied.

The outcome of a rightward shift of the demand curve is thus:

a) A higher quantity demanded
b) A higher quantity supplied
c) A higher equilibrium market price.

A shift to the left of the demand curve would have the opposite effect on the market to

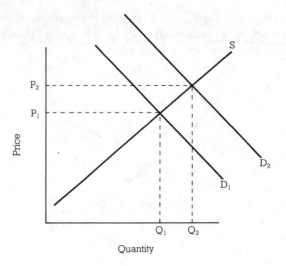

Figure 2.9

the above, as shown in Figure 2.10. Here, the sequence of events will result in a fall in the equilibrium price from P_1 to P_3 and a lower quantity demanded and supplied, from Q_1 to Q_3.

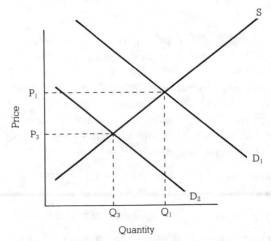

Figure 2.10

To see the effect of a shift in supply we go back to the original market equilibrium. Suppose that there are technical improvements in the production of wool so that more can be supplied at current prices. The effect will be a rightward shift in the supply curve, as in Figure 2.11. The new supply curve cuts the demand curve at a lower price, P_2 instead of P_1, with a higher quantity demanded and supplied of Q_2 in place of Q_1. Once again, this outcome is the result of a sequence of events:

1   To begin with, supply rises at the original equilibrium price. There is now an excess of supply over the amount buyers are willing to buy.

2   Competition among sellers leads them to lower prices to attract customers.

3   A lower price leads some suppliers to leave the market and also draws new buyers into the market.

4   Eventually a new equilibrum price is established where once again the quantity demanded equals the quantity supplied.

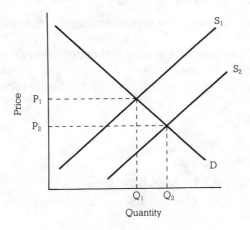

Figure 2.11

The outcome of a rightward shift of the supply curve is thus:

a) A higher quantity demand
b) A higher quantity supplied
c) A lower equilibrium market price.

A shift to the left of the supply curve would have the opposite effect on the market to the above, as shown in Figure 2.12. Here, the sequence of events will result in a rise in the equilibrium price from P_1 to P_3 and a decrease in the quantity demanded and supplied from Q_1 to Q_3.

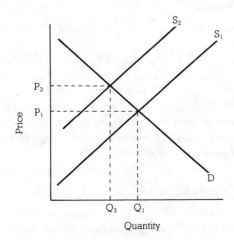

Figure 2.12

The role of price

In this chapter we have seen how, in a free market, market forces operate via the price mechanism. The outcomes of changes in the conditions of demand and supply are achieved through price changes and the impact these have on the quantities demanded and supplied.

The role of price in a free market is therefore:

a) To determine the allocation of scarce resources by bringing demand and supply into equilibrium.
b) To reflect changes in the pattern of consumer demand and lead sellers to respond by altering the level of supply.
c) To reflect changes in supply conditions and the impact these have on the market for a product.

REVISION TEST

1 Define 'equilibrium price'.
2 What is meant by the term 'joint supply'?
3 Give two examples of the conditions of supply which are likely to change only over a long period.
4 Trace the sequence of events following a shift in supply to the left.
5 The original equilibrium market price is accompanied by a quantity demanded of 100 units. Buyers increase their demand by 10 per cent but the consequent rise in price leads 8 per cent of them to leave the market. What is the total quantity demanded under the new equilibrium market price?
6 What would happen to the market if the highest price which any buyer is willing to pay is lower than the lowest price which any seller is willing to accept?
7 What is the difference between an increase in supply and an increase in the quantity supplied?
8 In each case state whether demand or supply has shifted, and in which direction:
   a) In the market for tea as the result of a rise in the price of coffee.
   b) In the market for televisions as the result of a new cheaper circuitry being invented.
   c) In the market for leather as the result of the expansion of beef output.
   d) In the market for petrol as the result of increased motor car sales.
   e) In the market for alcoholic drinks as the result of publicity on the dangers to health of excessive drinking.

Examination questions

1 Using diagrams explain why some tickets for an important sporting event such as a Wimbledon Final sell at exorbitant prices high above the stated selling price.

(ABE1, June 1986)

2 a) How is price determined in a competitive market?
   b) What is the difference between a shift in the demand curve and a movement
       along the demand curve?

(ABE1, June 1987)

3 What happens in response to an increase in the demand for a good (K) in terms of
   the price of another good (L) when the goods are:
   a) in joint demand
   b) in joint supply.

(ABE1, December 1987)

4 How will the *supply curve* of a commodity be affected by a change in tastes of
   consumers which leads them to buy more of that commodity?

(ICSA, June 1987)

5 If the price of a commodity falls what will be the effect on the demand for *other*
   commodities?

(ICSA, June 1988)

6 a) Explain briefly the difference between
        i) increases in supply and extensions in supply;
        ii) decreases in supply and contractions in supply.
   b) Explain the effect of the following changes on the demand for chocolate.
        i) A fall in the price of chocolate.
        ii) A health campaign which claims that chocolate makes you fat.
        iii) A rise in the price of chocolate substitutes.
        iv) A fall in consumers' income.
        v) An increase in the wages of chocolate workers.

(ACCA, December 1987)

7 In the last few years a number of eminent people have re-emphasised the role of
   market forces as the spur necessary to improve the performance and
   competitiveness of industry.
   a) Define the term market forces and explain how a system of market forces
       operates.
   b) Evaluate the claim that market forces do in practice act as a spur to improved
       performance and competitiveness.

(ACCA, December 1988)

8 a) With the aid of diagrams discuss the effects on the price and quantity of:
        i) coffee, as a result of failure in the harvest for coffee beans.
        ii) compact disc players, as a consequence of a significant reduction in income
             tax.
   b) Why do the prices of agricultural products fluctuate more than do the prices of
       manufactured goods?

(ACCA, June 1989)

9 What factors influence the demand and supply of petrol?

(Cert.M., November 1987)

10 Explain why an understanding of income as a determinant of demand is important to a marketer.

(Cert. M., December 1988)

11 a) Explain and illustrate the difference between a movement along and a shift in the demand curve.
   b) Using supply and demand analysis, illustrate the effect of:
      i) a fall in the price of pork on the market demand for beef.
      ii) an increase in taxation on whisky.
      iii) an increase in advertising expenditure for a specific commodity.

(IPS, November 1988)

3 Elasticity

- *Why does the demand for some products respond more to changes in price than others?*

- *What factors influence the ability of suppliers to respond to changes in demand?*

In the last chapter we saw that both the quantity demanded and the quantity supplied are directly affected by changes in price, all things being equal. Just as important, however, is the *extent* to which a given change in price will affect demand and supply.

Price elasticity of demand

Figure 3.1 illustrates the effect on demand of two products of a 20 per cent reduction in price. In Figure 3.1(a) a 20 per cent cut in price from £10 to £8 leads to an increase in the quantity demanded from 20 units to 22, a change of just 10 per cent. In Figure 3.1(b), on the other hand, the same price cut results in the quantity demanded rising from 20 units to 30, a rise of 50 per cent. These variations in the impact of a price change on demand can be attributed to differences in the responsiveness of demand of the two products to changes in price. Over the price range £9 to £10 the demand for the product

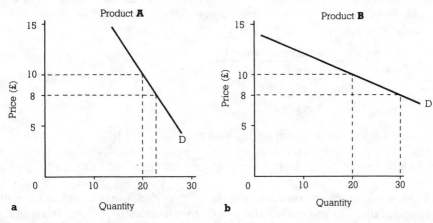

Figure 3.1 *Price elasticity of demand*

in Figure 3.1(a) is only weakly responsive to a change in price while the demand for the product in Figure 3.1(b) is highly responsive to a change in price. This responsiveness of demand to a change in price is known as price elasticity of demand.

The price elasticity of demand =

$$\frac{\text{Proportionate change in the quantity demanded}}{\text{Proportionate change in price}}$$

Since the quantity demanded rises as the price falls and falls when the price rises this formula will always produce a negative value, though the minus sign is generally ignored. When this formula produces an answer *greater than one*, demand is said to be **price elastic**. Where the answer is *less than one* demand is said to be **price inelastic**. If the answer is exactly one there is a situation of **unit price elasticity**.

Taking the examples from Figure 3.1 the price elasticity of demand for Product A is:

$$\frac{\dfrac{\text{Change in quantity demanded}}{\text{Original quantity demanded}}}{\dfrac{\text{Change in price}}{\text{Original price}}} = \frac{\frac{2}{20}}{\frac{2}{10}} = \frac{2 \times 10}{20 \times 2} = \frac{20}{40} = \frac{1}{2}$$

i.e. the price elasticity of demand is <1 and is therefore inelastic.

In the case of product B the price elasticity will be:

$$\frac{\dfrac{\text{Change in quantity demanded}}{\text{Original quantity demanded}}}{\dfrac{\text{Change in price}}{\text{Original price}}} = \frac{\frac{10}{20}}{\frac{2}{10}} = \frac{10 \times 10}{20 \times 2} = \frac{100}{40} = 2\frac{1}{2}$$

i.e. the price elasticity of demand is > 1 and is therefore elastic.

Note that if the price *rose* from £8 to £10 the elasticity of demand of each product would be different because the calculation would start from a different base, i.e. Product A would have a price elasticity of demand of 0.36 and B of 1.33. (Check to make sure that you see how these answers were obtained.) For this reason price elasticity is sometimes calculated by reference to base figures derived from the average of the old and new demand and price figures. Thus, in product A the following calculation of elasticity will result:

$$\frac{\dfrac{\text{Change in quantity demanded}}{\text{Average quantity demanded}}}{\dfrac{\text{Change in price}}{\text{Average price}}} = \frac{\frac{2}{21}}{\frac{2}{9}} = \frac{2 \times 9}{2 \times 21} = 0.43$$

This result will occur whether we start from a price of £8 or £10.

Note that while you may use either of these methods of calculation in an examination make sure you indicate clearly the basis for your calculation and which method is being used.

From Figure 3.1 it can be seen that the elasticity of demand of a product is reflected in the shape of the demand curve. The product with inelastic demand in Figure 3.1(a) has a steeper sloping demand curve than the product with elastic demand shown in

Figure 3.1(b). Indeed, the steeper the slope of the demand curve the more inelastic the demand. This is most clearly shown in the three special cases of price elasticity of demand where elasticity has a value of 0, 1 and infinity.

In the first case demand is perfectly inelastic and has a numerical value of zero. This is because there is no change in the quantity demanded, however large the change in price. The demand curve is therefore a vertical straight line, as in Figure 3.2.

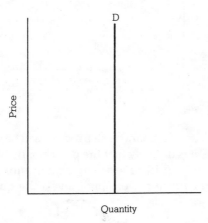

Figure 3.2 *Perfectly inelastic demand*

The second case represents a product which has unit price elasticity of demand over the entire price range. The numerical value of elasticity is always one and the demand curve is a **rectangular hyperbola**, as shown in Figure 3.3.

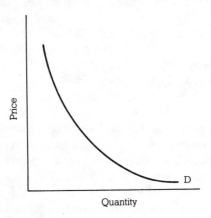

Figure 3.3 *Unitary elasticity of demand*

Thirdly, there is the case of perfectly elastic demand. At a certain price demand is infinite but at any price higher than this demand falls to zero. Thus a change from one price to the other will have an infinite effect on the quantity demanded. The numerical value of elasticity is therefore infinity and the demand curve is a horizontal straight line.

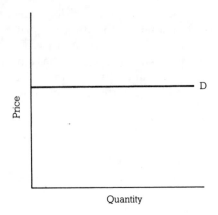

Figure 3.4 *Perfectly elastic demand*

In practice, the price elasticity of demand for a product will be somewhere between zero and infinity. Furthermore, it is unlikely that the price elasticity of demand for a product will have the same value at all price levels. The demand for salt, for example, is very price inelastic but if its price rose to very high levels the quantity demanded would eventually be affected.

The effect on revenue

The concept of elasticity is extremely important to suppliers since it indicates the likely effect of a change in price on the revenue they will receive.

In the case of the product with unit price elasticity of demand over the entire price range the revenue received by the firm will be the same whatever price is charged. So if the price is doubled the quantity demanded will halve while if the price is cut by a third the quantity demanded will rise by 50 per cent and so on. This must follow if the numerical value of elasticity is always **one.**

When demand for a product is inelastic an increase in price leads to a rise in the revenue received by a supplier. While the higher price results in the quantity demanded falling the revenue so lost is outweighed by the extra revenue gained from buyers who continue to purchase the product. So if previously ten units were sold at £10 each and nine are now sold at £12 suppliers gain £8 in revenue despite the loss of one customer. If, on the other hand, the price for a product with inelastic demand fell the revenue received by suppliers would also fall. This is because the gain in revenue resulting from an increase in the quantity demanded would be insufficient to compensate for the loss of revenue which would result from existing customers paying less for the product than before.

The opposite will apply when the demand for a product is elastic. Then, lower prices will result in an increase in the revenue received by suppliers while higher prices will reduce the revenue so received. This is because the quantity demanded changes more than proportionately to changes in price. The relationship between elasticity and revenue is shown in Table 3.1.

TABLE 3.1
Demand elasticity and the effect on revenue

Price (£)		Units sold		Total revenue	Elasticity of demand
14	✗	8	⇌	112	–
12		9		108	Inelastic
10		10		100	Inelastic
8		12		96	Inelastic
6		16		96	Unitary
4		25		100	Elastic
2		40		80	Inelastic

Factors determining price elasticity of demand

1 **The availability of close substitutes**   The easier it is to obtain a substitute, particularly a close substitute, the greater the elasticity of demand. Different brands of cigarettes, for example, are close substitutes and a rise in the price of one brand will lead many consumers to switch to an alternative. The demand for each brand is therefore highly responsive to changes in price, i.e. it is highly price elastic. The demand for cigarettes in general, however, is price *inelastic* since pipe tobacco, cigars and snuff are not *close* substitutes.

2 **The proportion of income spent on the product**   The smaller the proportion of consumers' income spent on a product the more inelastic the demand. So doubling the price of a box of matches would have a negligible impact on the quantity demanded. A doubling of the prices of overseas holidays, on the other hand, would have a significant impact on the number of holidays bought.

3 **The time period**   The longer the time period under consideration the greater the opportunity for buyers to find a substitute and adjust their expenditure plans. Thus a sudden rise in petrol prices may initially see little change in the quantity demanded. Later, however, demand may well prove less inelastic once commuters have had time to alter their travel arrangements, for example by car-sharing or greater use of public transport.

4 **The price of substitutes**   If the price of one product rises buyers will usually only switch to substitutes with a comparable price. The demand for the cheapest brand of tea may well prove inelastic if a price rise leaves it still somewhat cheaper than the nearest alternative.

The likelihood, therefore, is that the demand for cheap goods like bread or salt and necessities like water or electricity will be price inelastic. Goods distinguishable only by their brand name tend to have elastic demand. So also do luxury goods except that the most expensive luxuries can be afforded only by the very rich and a rise in the price of these has little impact on the quantity demanded.

Cross elasticity of demand

This is a form of price elasticity of demand which measures the responsiveness of demand to a change in the price of another good, whether it be a complement or a substitute. The numerical value of such a relationship is found by the formula:

$$\text{Cross elasticity of demand} = \frac{\text{Proportionate change in quantity demanded Good X}}{\text{Proportionate change in price Good Y}}$$

If the two goods are substitutes this formula will produce a *positive* answer since a rise in the price of Good Y will lead to a rise in the quantity demanded of Good X and vice versa. Where this answer is less than **one** cross-elasticity of demand will be inelastic and where it is greater than **one** cross-elasticity of demand will be elastic.

Where the two goods are complements the formula will produce a *negative* answer since a rise in the price of good Y will result in a fall in the quantity demanded of good X. If the relationship between the two goods is inelastic the answer will be less than minus one while if cross-elasticity of demand is elastic the formula will produce an answer in excess of minus one.

The closer the relationship between two products the greater the cross-elasticity of demand. A cut in the price of one brand of petrol, for example, will greatly affect the demand for all other brands because they are very close substitutes. Similarly, a sharp fall in the price of video-recorders will have an impact on the demand for its complementary product, the video tape.

REVISION TEST

1   Define the term 'price elasticity of demand'.
2   What is the price elasticity of demand of a product for which the demand curve is a horizontal straight line?
3   The price of a product is £8 and the quantity demanded is 40 units. Price is reduced to £7 and the quantity demanded rises to 50 units. Calculate the price elasticity of demand.
4   What would be the change in revenue as the result of the above price reduction?
5   What are the main factors affecting price elasticity of demand?
6   For a non-smoker is the demand for cigarettes elastic or inelastic?
7   When the price of one product rises the cross-elasticity of demand for the other is -1.3. What two conclusions may be drawn concerning the relationship of the two products?
8   'Cross-elasticity of demand measures the effect of a change in a particular condition of demand on the quantity demanded of a product'. Explain this statement.
9   Name another condition of demand which might be used as the basis of a cross-elasticity of demand.

10   The demand schedule for a product is as follows:

Price (£)	Demand
10	0
5	5
0	10

Draw the demand curve and calculate the price elasticity of demand at the three values given. Can you make any predictions about the elasticity of demand of any straight-line demand curves intersecting both axes?

Income elasticity of demand

Just as cross-elasticity of demand measures the impact on the quantity demanded of changes in the price of other goods, income elasticity of demand measures the impact of changes in household incomes. This is quantified by the formula:

$$\text{Income Elasticity of Demand} = \frac{\text{Proportionate Change in Quantity Demanded}}{\text{Proportionate Change in Household Income}}$$

Income elasticity of demand is complicated by the fact that there are four possible outcomes to this equation.

1   Positively income elastic

This occurs when a rise in income leads to a proportionately higher increase in the quantity demanded producing an answer to the equation **greater** than **one**. So, if income rises by 5 per cent and the quantity demanded of video tapes rises by 10 per cent demand is positively income *elastic*.

2   Positively income inelastic

Here a rise in income leads to an increase in the quantity demanded but proportionately less than the rise in income, yielding an answer **less** than **one**. So if income rises by 5 per cent and the quantity demanded of butter rises by only 2 per cent demand is positively income *inelastic*.

3   Negatively income elastic

The quantity demanded of some goods actually falls when income rises. These are the **inferior** goods which consumers give up for better goods as income increases. A doubling of income, for example, might enable a household to give up the purchase of cheap cuts of meat almost entirely. In this case the numerical value of the income elasticity of demand will be **greater** than **minus one**, i.e. demand will be negatively income *elastic*.

4 Negatively income inelastic

Where a rise in income leads the quantity demanded to fall but fall proportionately less than the rise in income the income elasticity of demand will be **less** than **minus one**. So a rise in income of 6 per cent may lead to a fall in the quantity demanded of bread of 3 per cent as the household replaces some of its bread consumption with more varied foods. In this example the income elasticity of demand for bread will be negatively income *inelastic*.

To summarise, luxury goods and services like dishwashers, holidays abroad and private health, tend to be positively income elastic as demand for these rises proportionately more rapidly than income for all but those on very low incomes. Basic goods such as milk, newspapers or green vegetables are likely to be positively income inelastic since demand tends to be constant across most income levels, again except for the very poor. Inferior goods are negatively elastic or inelastic, depending on the extent to which a given rise in income enables such goods to be abandoned.

Elasticity of supply

Elasticity of supply measures the responsiveness of supply to a change in price. Its numerical value can be found by the formula:

$$\text{Elasticity of Supply} = \frac{\text{Proportionate change in quantity supplied}}{\text{Proportionate change in price}}$$

Where this formula produces an answer **greater** than **one** supply is said to be elastic. If it produces an answer **less** than **one** supply is said to be inelastic. An answer of exactly **one** signifies unit elasticity.

The method of calculation is the same for that of price elasticity of demand. Similarly, the shape of the supply curve reflects the elasticity of supply; the steeper the slope of the supply curve the more inelastic the supply. Once again there are the three special cases where elasticity of supply has a value of zero, one and infinity.

In the first case supply is perfectly inelastic and has a numerical value of zero. This is because there is no change in the quantity supplied, however large the change in price. The supply curve is therefore a vertical straight line, as in Figure 3.5.

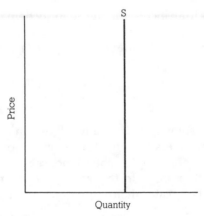

Figure 3.5 *Perfectly inelastic supply*

The second case represents a product which has unit elasticity of supply over the entire price range. The numerical value of elasticity is always one and the supply curve is represented by any straight line passing through the origin, as in Figure 3.6.

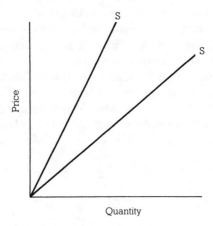

Figure 3.6 *Unitary elasticity of supply*

Thirdly, there is the case of perfectly elastic supply. At a certain price supply will be infinite but at any price below this supply falls to zero. Thus a change from one price to the other will have an infinite effect on the quantity supplied. The numerical value of elasticity is therefore infinity and the supply curve is a horizontal straight line, as in Figure 3.7.

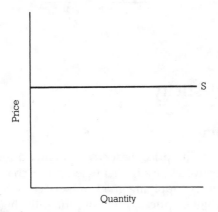

Figure 3.7 *Perfectly elastic supply*

Factors determining elasticity of supply

1 **The costs of factors of production** An increase in supply will require the use of more of at least some of the factors of production. If the cost of acquiring extra units of these resources is high this may affect the ability of the supplier to gain from an increasing production in response to a price rise. If, for example, the price of a

product rose by 10 per cent but output could only rise by 5 per cent before production costs prevented further expansion, supply would be inelastic.

2   **The time period**   The ability of suppliers to respond to changes in market conditions increases over time. A sudden rise in demand may find suppliers unable to respond immediately and for a time supply is perfectly inelastic. Within a relatively short time, however, suppliers will buy in more materials and adjust working schedules to increase production. Over a longer period suppliers may be able to change the scale of production through technical innovation and by building new plant so enabling an even greater expansion of supply. These two latter situations are distinguished as the short run and the long run and they will be examined at length in Chapter 6. But for now their impact on the elasticity of supply is shown in Figure 3.8.

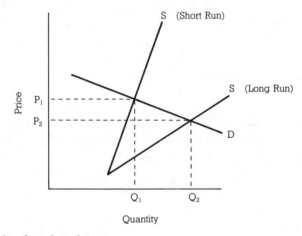

Figure 3.8   *Elasticity of supply and time*

Applications of elasticity

Price elasticity of demand

We have already seen that the price elasticity of demand for a product has a direct impact on the revenue received by a supplier when prices change. The conclusion to be drawn from this is that firms supplying goods or services which are demand inelastic are likely to benefit by higher prices, and consequently higher revenue, while the reverse is true for firms which supply products which are demand elastic. When the implications for each type of supplier are examined in more detail, however, the situation is somewhat more complicated.

Inelastic demand
Since they will benefit from market conditions in which prices are rising, suppliers who are in a position to influence the market should aim to reduce supply and push up prices. They will then enjoy the higher profits which follow from higher revenue

accompanied by falling production costs. Clearly there are limitations on this strategy. Prices can only be raised so far before buyers seek substitutes, however imperfect, and demand becomes price elastic. If this were not the case the prices of basic commodities could be pushed upwards indefinitely.

Elastic demand

Here the supplier should benefit by cutting prices since sales will rise faster than prices fall. However, the firm can only take advantage of this situation if its own supply is elastic so that costs do not rise rapidly as output is expanded. If not, lower prices and higher costs may combine to make an expansion of output unprofitable.

Cross elasticity of demand

If two products are close substitutes a rise in the price of one will cause a large-scale shift in demand to the other. Where, therefore, two or more firms supply very similar products it is in the interests of none to raise prices in isolation. In consequence such markets are characterised by price stability and collusion on prices among suppliers.

In the case of complementary products a high degree of cross-elasticity means that the demand for one product is highly dependent on the demand for the other. A rise in the price of the latter will therefore have a detrimental effect on the sales and revenue of the former. This dependency does not always work both ways. A rise in the price of petrol, for example, may well reduce the demand for big cars but a rise in the price of big cars is unlikely to have much effect on the demand for petrol.

Confronted by a high cross-elasticity of demand for its products, the aim of the supplier must be to reduce that high elasticity. If there are close substitutes available the firm may engage in marketing activities such as advertising and branding to differentiate its products from those of its rivals. Where it suffers from having a close complementary relationship with another firm's products the firm might try to loosen the link through diversification or the establishment of an independent market for its products. In the 1970s Lucas freed itself from a heavy dependence on the British motor car industry by branching out into other areas of the electrical industry.

Income elasticity

This poses the most complex issue of all for the supplier. As real incomes rise it is to be expected that the demand for inferior goods and services will decline, resulting in a negative income elasticity of demand for such products. Thus, industries providing such inferior goods and services could well find themselves in decline while the rest of the economy is expanding.

For the producers of basic necessities like tea or sugar the problem is zero income elasticity. As incomes rise the demand for their products barely changes so they do not benefit in the rising prosperity of the economy as a whole.

It is difficult to predict the effect of income elasticity over long periods but certain trends are likely. If higher incomes lead consumers to buy better quality, more expensive goods and services, one would expect to see those firms concentrating on the lower end of the market suffer a contraction of demand. This has indeed proved to be the case with many firms seeking to change their image and the type of good or service on offer in response to income-led changes in demand patterns. In recent years Kingfisher (formerly Woolworth) and the Co-operative Societies in retailing, Butlin's in the leisure industry and Volkswagon in the motor industry are obvious examples.

Elasticity and taxation

Governments are also concerned with the concept of elasticity and its application, notably in connection with the levying of taxes on goods and services, i.e. *indirect* taxes.

When the government imposes a tax on a good or service the initial impact is on the suppliers who are required to pay the tax. For the supplier the effect is therefore similar to a rise in costs and results in a shift in the supply curve to the left as the supplier passes the tax on to the buyer. This is shown in Figure 3.9.

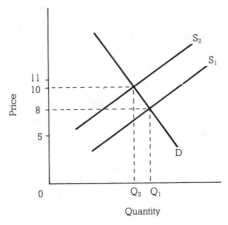

Figure 3.9 *Elasticity and taxation*

The imposition of a tax of £3 per unit leads, in Figure 3.9, to suppliers offering the same supply at £11 instead of £8. However, the effect of the higher price is to cause a contraction of the quantity demanded. The result is that the new equilibrium price of £10 is higher than the original price but less than it would have been if the entire tax had been borne by the buyer. Instead the burden of the tax is being shared between buyer and seller. The more elastic the demand the greater the proportion of the tax that will have to be borne by the seller. In the most extreme case, that of perfectly elastic demand, the entire tax must be borne by the seller or else the market will be lost. At the other extreme, perfectly inelastic demand, the entire tax will be borne by the buyer.

Elasticity of supply also has a bearing on the impact on the market of a particular tax. The more elastic the supply the greater the reduction in quantity supplied for each penny of tax borne by the supplier. So where both supply and demand are elastic the total output will contract proportionately much more than if both were inelastic.

Having possession of these facts the government may levy taxes for different purposes on particular goods and services.

1   The raising of revenue

If the aim of the tax is to raise revenue there are dangers in levying a tax on goods with elastic demand since the market will contract substantially and this may damage the viability of the industry. This situation will be exacerbated if supply is also elastic.

Instead, the government should levy the tax on goods with inelastic demand so that most of the tax burden is borne by consumers who will continue to buy the product. Clearly the taxation of necessities would be the favoured choice here but for the fact that the taxation of such goods as food and fuel is highly contentious. Traditionally, therefore, the most popular objects of such taxation have been non-essential goods which are inelastic in demand, i.e. tobacco, alcohol and petrol. Such goods are now heavily taxed and in the late 1980s the fear that demand might be becoming less inelastic was a contributory factor in the tendency for tax increases on these products to lag behind the rate of inflation.

2   Reducing demand

If the government wishes to reduce demand in the economy it is appropriate to levy taxes on goods with elastic demand such as luxury consumer goods. Clearly, the more elastic the demand the more effective the measure. However, manufacturers and suppliers will encounter difficulties through reduced income and profits unless they can find new markets, perhaps abroad.

REVISION TEST

1   Explain how a product could have positive infinite income elasticity of demand.

2   If incomes double and the demand for a product goes up by 10 per cent what is the income elasticity of demand?

3   What are the five possible categories of income elasticity which a product could have?

4   Which of these would be of most concern to a supplier and why?

5   What is the formula for calculating the elasticity of supply?

6   Why does supply become more elastic the longer the time period?

7   Draw a straight line supply curve through the origin of a graph and explain why the supply of such a product must have unit elasticity of supply.

8   Why would you expect the elasticity of supply to be greater for cassette tapes than for wheat?

9   If, as a supplier, you knew your product enjoyed unit elasticity of demand over the entire range of demand, would you operate a strategy of high, static or low prices?

10 Draw diagrams to show how (a) perfectly elastic demand and (b) perfectly inelastic demand result in respectively none or all of the burden of a tax falling on the buyer.

_____ **Examination questions** _____

1 a) What is meant by the term elasticity and, giving examples, explain the impor-
       tance of elasticity in relation to demand and supply?
   b) From the table of figures below calculate the price elasticity of demand for wine
       and explain the meaning of your answer.

	Period 1	Period 2
Price of wine	100	90
Quantity of wine demanded	100	120

                                                        (ABE1, June 1986)

2 a) What is price elasticity of demand?
   b) What are its implications for the pricing strategies of a firm and for tax revenue?
                                                        (ABE1, June 1987)

3 a) Explain how price elasticity of demand is determined.
   b) How can this necessary concept be used by business and government?
                                                        (ABE1, June 1988)

4 a) Define price elasticity and outline the factors which determine its value.
   b) Use the concept of price elasticity to analyse the effects of a rise in the price of
       petrol on different forms of transport.
                                                        (LCCI Higher, November 1985)

5 a) Explain the term *supply elasticity*.
   b) Due to an increase in tourist trade into an African country, the demand for
       wood carvings increases dramatically. Explain the factors which might help to
       determine supply elasticity for wood carvings.
                                                        (LCCI Intermediate, May 1986)

6 a) Explain the terms:
        i)   price elasticity of demand
        ii) income elasticity of demand
        iii) cross elasticity of demand
   b) Calculate the elasticities in each of the following situations and comment on
       the results:
        i)   The price of a textbook rises by 20 per cent and demand falls from 100 000
             copies to 90 000.
        ii) Wages rise by an average of 10 per cent and the demand for a major food
             product rises by 5 per cent.
        iii) The cost of a road journey between two major towns rises from £5 to £6 and
             the demand for rail travel on the same route rises by 25 per cent.
                                                        (LCCI Intermediate, December 1986)

7 a) Explain what you understand by the term 'elasticity of demand'.
   b) Explain the factors which might affect price elasticity of demand.

c) If product X rises in price by 20 per cent and the demand for Y rises by 50 per cent, calculate the cross elasticity of demand.

(LCCI Second Level, May 1988)

8   Explain the difference between price elasticity of supply and income elasticity of demand.

(ICSA, December 1986)

9   a) By use of appropriate examples, explain how economists measure the price elasticity of demand.
     b) Of what relevance is the price elasticity of demand to business people and governments?

(ACCA, December 1989)

10   What factors affect the price elasticity of demand? How might knowledge of price elasticity of demand influence changes in price of different products?

(Cert.M., June 1987)

11   Explain the terms:
     a) price elasticity of demand
     b) income elasticity of demand
     c) cross-elasticity of demand.
     Explain why marketers might need to consider the elasticity of demand.

(Cert.M., November 1987)

12   What are the determinants of the value of elasticity for any particular product of your choice?

(Cert.M., June 1988)

13   Explain why the government should take the elasticity of demand into account when placing a tax on a product.

(Cert.M., December 1988)

14   What are the main determinants of price elasticity of demand? Give examples.

(Cert.M., June 1986)

15   Explain the concepts of price elasticity and income elasticity and discuss their importance in marketing.

(Cert.M., November 1986)

16   Explain why the demand for petrol tends to be price inelastic. Discuss whether this is likely to be the case at all conceivable prices.

(IPS, November 1987)

17   a) Explain what is meant by the term price-elasticity of demand.
     b) Discuss the relevance of this concept to:

i) the pricing policy of any one product made by your firm or any other product with which you are familiar,

ii) the indirect taxation policy of the Chancellor of the Exchequer?

(IPS, May 1988)

18 a) Define the following terms:
   i) price elasticity of demand,
   ii) cross elasticity of demand,
   iii) income elasticity of demand.

   b) State the three main factors which influence the price elasticity of demand for a product.

   c)

Price of meat (pence per kg)	Demand for meat (kg millions)
130	20
120	30
110	50
100	65

Using the above table, calculate the price elasticity of demand when
   i) prices rise from 100 to 120 pence;
   ii) prices fall from 130 to 120 pence.

(I. Act., September 1989)

19 Provide a definition of 'price elasticity of demand'.
How might such a concept be helpful in the formulation of business policy?

(IFA, June 1989)

4 Consumer behaviour

- *How can we measure the satisfaction derived by consumers from the purchase of a particular product?*
- *Is the demand curve always downward sloping?*

Utility

In Chapter 2 we saw that the individual's demand curve for a particular good represents the amount of that good that he or she is prepared to buy at any given price over a given time period. The lower the price the greater the quantity demanded as the individual can buy more of the good using the same amount of income. At the same time a lower price may lead the person to switch some expenditure away from other goods, notably close substitutes. While such behaviour seems perfectly logical we must go further and analyse the factors behind it.

Because the income of consumers is limited the decision to spend their income in a particular way involves the sacrifice of all other patterns of expenditure. We assume, therefore, that each consumer acts in his or her own best interests and chooses a pattern of expenditure that will enable the greatest satisfaction possible to be derived from a given income. But in order to be sure that this is the case we need to be able to compare one expenditure pattern with another. This in turn requires that we can quantify the satisfaction gained from a particular expenditure. The term **utility** is used to measure the benefit or satisfaction a person derives from the consumption of goods and services.

Utility theory is a model since none of us consciously attempts to assign units of utility to our expenditure with the precision that will be used here. Furthermore, utility theory makes a number of assumptions which do not necessarily hold true in the real world.

1. The consumer always acts rationally.

2. The consumer is one of many buyers.

3. The consumer knows the prices of all goods.

4. The consumer has a fixed money income.

5. The consumer's tastes remain fixed.

It is important also to distinguish between total utility and marginal utility. **Total**

utility measures the total satisfaction that a person derives from the consumption of a particular good or service. **Marginal utility** measures the satisfaction gained from consuming one extra unit of the good or service. This might best be illustrated by a simple example, as in Table 4.1.

TABLE 4.1
The measurement of utility

Cream buns consumed	Total utility	Marginal utility
1	15	—
2	25	10
3	27	2
4	24	−3

In Table 4.1 we are measuring the satisfaction gained by a consumer through the purchase of cream buns. Suppose that the first bun is both highly enjoyable and satisfies any hunger that the consumer might have. On this basis let us give the bun a utility of 15 units. A second bun is also highly enjoyable but there is no hunger to satisfy so the utility to the consumer is likely to be somewhat less, say 10 units. The marginal utility is therefore 10 units while total utility has now risen to 25 units. A third bun is very much less satisfying since the person has nearly had his fill and so we accord it a utility of only 2 units. When we get to a fourth bun we see that the marginal utility is now **minus** 3. This is because, far from giving the consumer any satisfaction, it actually makes him feel sick and so diminishes his total utility. Note that we cannot assume that this pattern of utility will apply to all consumers; a Billy Bunter or similar over-eater may well still enjoy a positive marginal utility after six buns!

Value

The important point here is that, all things being equal, marginal, if not total, utility *must* decline as consumption increases. Were this not the case a very thirsty man would derive as much satisfaction from a fiftieth glass of water as he does from the first – clearly a nonsense. It is important to remember that it is marginal utility, not total utility, which determines the **value** of a product to the consumer. So while the thirsty man would give a considerable sum for that first glass of water he would not give the same value to successive glasses. Instead the point will be reached quite quickly when he would prefer to allocate further expenditure to other goods rather than to water. A different situation would apply if the good in question were precious stones or oil paintings by Rembrandt. Then the value of each successive unit of the good would decline very slowly. Since value is measured in society in monetary terms the difference in the value of water compared to precious stones is reflected in the price of each. Of course prices are determined by the market generally and so the price paid for a particular unit of a good does not necessarily reflect the value placed on it by each individual. A man who hasn't eaten for two days pays the same price for a loaf of bread as somebody doing their regular shopping, despite their valuing the bread differently.

If we plot the marginal utility data in Table 4.1 onto a graph, as in Figure 4.1, we see that the marginal utility curve is similar in shape to a demand curve, except that it may go below the horizontal axis. The emphasis is, however, different. While the demand curve shows that the quantity demanded rises when the price falls, the marginal utility curve shows that the price must fall if the consumer is to buy more of the product.

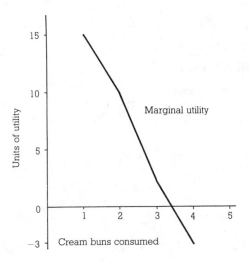

Figure 4.1 *Marginal utility curve*

Consumer surplus

We saw above that two customers will still be charged the same price for a loaf of bread despite the fact that they may place different values on it. This is true of any situation where all units are sold at the prevailing market price. Suppose that a person is prepared to pay £30 for a pair of shoes but they are currently priced at £25. That customer will still pay £25 and receive the benefit of £5 of 'free' utility. The difference between the amount that a consumer would be willing to pay for a good or service and the amount actually paid is known as the **consumer surplus**. In a market all those consumers who would be prepared to pay more for the product than the market price enjoy some consumer surplus, as shown in the market demand curve in Figure 4.2.

Consumer equilibrium

If the objective of the consumer is to derive the maximum satisfaction possible from his income he should aim to maximise his total utility. This will be achieved if he allocates his expenditure so that equal utility is derived from the last penny spent on each good or service consumed. So if the price of Good X is £100 and the price of Good Y is £1, the utility-maximising position or consumer equilibrium will be achieved when the marginal utility of Good X is 100 times that of Good Y, i.e.

$$\frac{\text{Marginal Utility Good X}}{\text{Price Good X}} = \frac{\text{Marginal Utility Good Y}}{\text{Price Good Y}}$$

In this case:

$$\frac{100}{£100} = \frac{1}{£1}$$

This may also be expressed in the formula:

$$\frac{\text{Marginal Utility Good X}}{\text{Marginal Utility Good Y}} = \frac{\text{Price Good X}}{\text{Price Good Y}}$$

Using the same example this gives:

$$\frac{100}{1} = \frac{£100}{£1}$$

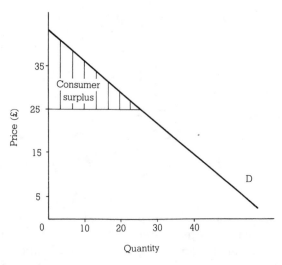

Figure 4.2 *Consumer surplus*

Thus consumer equilibrium requires that the ratio of the marginal utilities of the goods bought is equal to their relative prices. This is known as the principle of equal marginal returns.

The consumer equilibrium so established will be disturbed by a change in the relative prices of the goods and services bought. A rise in the price of Good X to £200, for example, will result in the marginal utility of Good X, per penny spent, falling. To restore equilibrium the consumer must buy more of Good Y and less of Good X, so lowering the marginal utility of Good Y and raising that of Good X. This process must continue until the marginal utility of Good X is 200 times that of Good Y.

We can therefore predict that, all things being equal, a rise in the price of a product will lead to the quantity demanded by each consumer falling. Conversely, a fall in the price of the commodity will lead to a rise in the quantity demanded by each consumer. In other words, the demand curve for a product normally slopes downwards from left to right.

Similar changes in consumption patterns would naturally follow changes in the income or tastes of consumers.

Upward sloping demand curves

Having established that the typical demand curve is downward sloping we shall now examine those cases where the demand curve slopes upwards, i.e. that the quantity demanded goes up when the price rises and goes down when the price falls. There are three types of good which follow this pattern.

1   Giffen goods

A Giffen good is a special form of inferior good. Demand for the typical inferior good falls when incomes rise but responds normally to changes in price. Demand for a Giffen good also falls when incomes rise but has an upward sloping demand curve. The Giffen good effect was first noted by Sir Robert Giffen during the potato famine in Ireland in the 1840s. People on very low incomes were living on a diet of the cheapest food, potatoes, with small quantities of other foods. They could not switch to substitutes when the price of potatoes rose because their incomes were not sufficient to enable them to buy sufficient quantities of other foods to live on. Instead they had to spend all their income on potatoes to survive, now buying more than before, as in Table 4.2.

TABLE 4.2
Giffen good

Price per unit Potatoes	Demand Potatoes	Price per unit Meat	Demand Meat
5	10	20	2
6	11	20	1
7	12	20	0
9	10	20	0

Examples of the Giffen good effect are still found in the Third World today, notably following drought and famine conditions, where people devote a very high proportion of their income to one commodity. Note that the demand curve for a Giffen good will not slope upwards indefinitely. If prices rise above a certain level even the poorest members of the community will have no alternative but to cut their consumption and the demand curve will then become downwards sloping.

2   Goods of ostentation

These are goods which at least some people buy because they are expensive. The higher price is regarded as denoting luxury, exclusivity and quality; in short, the product is a status symbol. Were the price to fall to the point where many people could afford it, the demand curve would resume its normal shape, as in Figure 4.3. Typical goods of ostentation include luxury cars, exclusive creations in clothing and jewellery and ocean-going yachts.

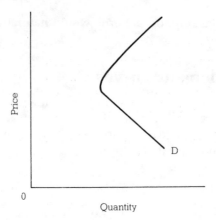

Figure 4.3 *Goods of ostentation*

3   Speculative goods

In certain markets the commodities are not bought purely as consumption or capital goods. Rather they are bought partly or exclusively with the intention of selling them at a later date at an enhanced price. Among such items are stocks and shares, antique furniture, property and works of art. The most extreme example is the very old bottle of wine which is never bought to be drunk but to be sold later at a profit; indeed the wine may have ceased to be drinkable but this cannot be checked without destroying its commercial value!

Once prices in such markets move upwards the quantity demanded rises as speculators anticipate further upward movements. Similarly a decline in prices leads buyers to leave the market as they fear the decline in price will persist. The Stock Exchange is an example of such a market in operation.

REVISION TEST

1   Define 'marginal utility'.

2   Give an example of a product which people regularly consume to the point where total utility falls.

3   Distinguish between 'utility' and 'value'.

4   Distinguish between 'value' and 'price'.

5   What are the principal assumptions made under utility theory?

6   Explain the principle of equal marginal returns.

7   A household spends all its income on two goods, X and Y. If the marginal utility of X is 6, the price of X is £10 and the price of Y is £4 what must the marginal utility of Y be for the consumer to be in equilibrium?

8   What happens to the marginal utility of a good if a person buys less of it, all things being equal?

9   Does money have a diminishing marginal utility?

10 In what way does a Giffen good differ from an inferior good?

Indifference curves

Marginal utility theory is frequently criticised on two counts. First, it attempts to measure utility with a precision that bears no relationship to the way that individual consumers make their buying decisions. Second, it assumes that the conditions of demand are constant and is unable to analyse the consequences of changes in both prices and incomes on demand. Indifference curve analysis is an attempt to address these issues.

We begin by looking at an indifference schedule (Table 4.3). For simplification we assume that a consumer spends all of his or her income on just two goods, in this case food and clothing. The indifference schedule shows all those combinations of these two goods which yield the same satisfaction to the consumer. Thus 25 units of food and 15 of clothing give the same satisfaction to this consumer as 10 units of food and 20 of clothing. You will notice, however, that each successive loss of clothing requires a greater number of units of food to compensate for this loss. This accords with the law of diminishing marginal utility by which the more of a commodity one consumes the lower will be the value placed on an extra unit of that commodity.

TABLE 4.3
Indifference schedule

Units of food	Units of clothing
40	13¾
35	14
30	14½
25	15
20	16
15	17
10	20
5	25

When the data in Table 4.3 is reproduced graphically as an indifference curve the result is the U-shaped curve shown in Figure 4.4. Of course, this indifference curve is specific to one consumer; each of another ten consumers would probably produce a different curve. Furthermore, for each consumer there will also be indifference curves for combinations of other goods or groups of goods. For example, we could combine one good like food with the income spent on all other goods.

If each of the points on the indifference curve in Figure 4.4 gives the same satisfaction to the consumer which of them will be chosen? In practice, the consumer has less choice than one might suppose. To see why we must first consider both the consumer's income and the price per unit of both food and clothing. Suppose that the consumer has an income of £80 and that the price of food is £1 per unit while that of clothing is £4. Assuming that all income is spent, the consumer can buy either 80 units of food or 20 units of clothing or some combination of the two goods amounting to a value of £80. All these combinations can be depicted as a straight line, known as a **budget line**, drawn from 80 units of food to 20 units of clothing.

When, in Figure 4.5 we draw the consumer's budget line on the same diagram as the indifference curve shown in Figure 4.4, only those points of the indifference curve inside or tangent to the budget line represent combinations which can be afforded given current income. In this case the one combination which meets this criterion is that of 16 units of food and 16 units of clothing. This, therefore, is the combination which must be chosen by the consumer under conditions of consumer equilibrium.

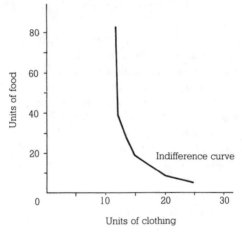

Figure 4.4 *Indifference curves*

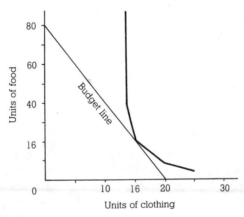

Figure 4.5 *Consumer equilibrium*

The consumer equilibrium portrayed in Figure 4.5 remains valid so long as there is no change either in the income of the consumer or the prices of either good.

Effect of income changes

If the consumer's income rises the effect will be to push the budget line to the right so that several of the points on the indifference curve now fall within the budget line. Given that all the combinations available yield the same satisfaction, however, the consumer will not be tempted to switch to a more expensive combination of the two goods. But if the consumer still wishes to spend all the income received he or she can now move to a new indifference curve which enables more of both goods to be consumed. Figure 4.6 illustrates the position where a series of income increases pushes the budget line successively outward and each time brings a new indifference curve into the range of the consumer. The line joining the tangental points a, b, c and d is the income consumption line and shows how the pattern of consumption between the two goods changes as income rises. If, on the other hand, income were to fall, the consumer would be forced to adopt a lower value indifference curve commensurate with a contracting budget line.

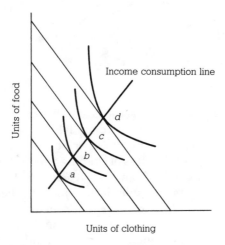

Figure 4.6 *Effect of increases in income*

Effect of price changes

Figure 4.7 shows the effect of a fall in the price of one of the products under consideration, in this case clothes. The budget line moves outward, but only along one axis, and becomes less steep. Since the consumer can now buy more goods with the same income the effect is to raise his or her real income and so enable access to a new indifference curve, IC". The line joining the tangental points a and b is the price consumption line and shows the impact on consumption patterns of the two goods of price changes. Clearly, a rise in prices would have an effect similar to that of a fall in income.

Income and substitution effects

The changed demand patterns depicted in Figure 4.6 were due simply to a change in income and such changes are therefore referred to as the **income effect**. When there is a change in price, as in Figure 4.7, there are likely to be two factors determining the changes in demand. Firstly, the fall in price has the effect of raising the real income of the consumer who can now buy more goods than before. Any changes in demand which result from this change in real income are again due to the income effect. Secondly, the fall in price makes this product more attractive compared to other goods and so the consumer may switch expenditure to this product; this is called the **substitution effect**.

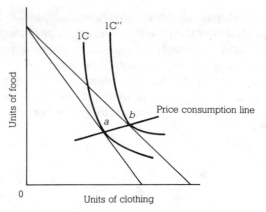

Figure 4.7 *Effect of price changes*

By using indifference curve analysis it is possible to differentiate between the income and substitution effects resulting from a fall in price. In Figure 4.8 we again assume that all income is spent either on food or clothes. Initially the consumer is in equilibrium at point *a* and buys OW units of clothing and OV units of food. A fall in the price of clothes shifts the budget line from AB to AC and enables the consumer to move to indifference curve IC". The new equilibrium point is *b* where OX units of clothing and OY units of food are bought. However, the consumer could also have reached indifference curve IC" through a rise in income shifting the budget line outwards to A' B'. Had this been the case the new equilibrium point would have been at *c* and OZ units of clothes would have been bought. So we can say that part (WZ) of the rise in consumption of clothing following the price fall was due to increased real income, i.e. the income effect. The remainder (ZX) was due to the substitution effect.

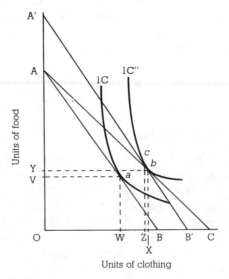

Figure 4.8 *Income and substitution effect*

The substitution effect will always be positive and will normally be accompanied by a positive income effect. In the case of Giffen goods, however, the income effect will be negative and this may well outweigh the positive substitution effect.

REVISION TEST

1 What are the main weaknesses of marginal utility theory?
2 Define the role of an indifference curve.
3 Why is a straight line indifference curve impossible?
4 What is a budget line?
5 What does it mean if the indifference curve cuts the budget line in two places?
6 What would be the effect on the budget line of a halving of all prices?
7 Why might the path of the income consumption line vary depending on the products under consideration?
8 Explain the term 'substitution effect'.
9 How can a change in price cause an 'income effect'?
10 Why is indifference curve analysis of little value to a marketing manager?

_____ Examination questions _____

1 How does a consumer with a fixed income, all of which he spends, react to a fall in the price of one commodity? (ICSA, June 1986)

2 Does the introduction of a new product affect only the demand for close substitutes or can it also affect the demand for all other products? (ICSA, December 1988)

3 Explain the following:
a Why the demand curve for a good or service is normally downward sloping.
b) The notion of consumer surplus.
c) What you understand by the concept, 'consumer equilibrium'. (ACCA, June 1988)

4 Explain the precise relationship between utility, value and price. (CIMA, November 1988)

5 Distinguish the 'income' and 'substitution' effects of an increase in a worker's wage rate on the number of hours a week that he would wish to work. (SCCA, November 1987)

6 Will a decrease in the price of a product always lead to an increase in quantity demanded owing to both the income and the substitution effects? (Cert.M., June 1986)

7 Explain the statement that the consequences of a price change will depend upon the relative strengths of the income and substitution effects. (Cert.M., December 1988)

8 Why do demand curves slope downwards to the right?
Are there any exceptions to this general principle? (IFA, December 1988)

5 Market failures and distortions

- *Is the free market unable to satisfy all the objectives of society?*
- *Why does government interference with prices often cause the very problems it seeks to prevent?*

Market failure

Two features underlay our examination of the operation of market forces in the last three chapters. First, the market was assumed to be perfect so that all changes in the market were determined by the decisions of individual producers and consumers implemented via the price mechanism. Second, any defects in the working of the market were largely ignored. This model was necessary in order to understand how the forces of demand and supply interact free from the complications of powerful individuals operating within the market and government and other pressures from without. In looking at the real world, we are concerned here with the problems posed by market imperfections and defects in the operation of the market and how these might be remedied.

Market imperfections

In theory the free market gives rise to a situation of **consumer sovereignty**. The freedom of individual consumers to decide what they want to buy is reflected in the market demand for particular goods and services. This in turn influences the output decisions of suppliers through the working of the price mechanism. Although price is determined by the interaction of demand *and* supply it is demand which is dominant. If consumers exhibit a change in taste or fashion, suppliers which do not respond to such changes by altering their products will go out of business. By the same token, suppliers who try to introduce products without determining the demand for such products face the risk that demand will not materialise and that they will suffer losses.

Consumer sovereignty relates, however, to the perfect market. Any market imperfections inevitably shift power away from the consumer to the supplier and negate the principle of consumer sovereignty. Under imperfect market conditions suppliers are able to exert their influence over the consumer through a variety of factors:

1 **Product differentiation** Individual suppliers use advertising, packaging and other means of attracting customers to their product other than through price. Consumers therefore cease to dominate the relationship between consumer and producer.

2 **Monopoly power** The perfect market assumes many small suppliers, none of whom are able to influence the price by individual action. The existence of large firms leads to prices being fixed by suppliers rather than being determined by market forces.

3 **Consumer ignorance and immobility**   The perfect market requires that consumers have both perfect knowledge and perfect mobility. Without these the consumer cannot make fully informed decisions and so cannot be sovereign.

Since the perfect market does not exist consumer sovereignty is an impossibility. Instead, the imperfect markets of the real world are ones in which individual consumers are usually at a disadvantage in their dealings with much more powerful suppliers.

Defects in the operation of the market

The operation of market forces ensures that resources go to those willing and able to pay for them. The system makes no judgements as to which consumers have the greatest need of particular goods nor which will use them most effectively; price is the only resource allocative criterion. So a poor man may have not one decent pair of shoes while a rich man has a dozen pairs. Nor do market forces differentiate as to the worth of particular goods and services; harmful drugs are just as likely to be produced as medicines. Such consequences of the price mechanism as a way of allocating resources are inevitable whether the market is perfect or imperfect.

Quite clearly, the operation of market forces cannot accommodate the needs of those without the economic power to make their needs effective. This is a direct consequence of a system in which the needs of each consumer are transmitted to the market in isolation. Suppose a person buys a piece of land and decides to dam a stream running through it, so depriving the owners of the adjacent piece of land of their water supply. Under a free market system the only remedy open to these owners is to buy water which previously came to them as of right. The market system, in other words, takes no note of the costs and benefits to society as a whole of the actions of individual buyers and sellers.

Cost and benefits

When a commodity is purchased the buyer encounters both a cost and a benefit. The cost is the resources used in obtaining the commodity and thus the foregone next best alternative to which those resources could have been put. (You will recognise this as a restatement of the principle of opportunity cost.) The benefit is the satisfaction obtained by the buyer through the purchase of this commodity. So, if a person buys a pen the cost is the resources allocated to this purchase measured in monetary terms (the price) and the benefit is the facility to write so acquired.

The cost and benefit in the case of the pen considered above are **private**; they relate directly only to the buyer. However, the acquisition or use of goods and services may also result indirectly in costs and/or benefits to other members of society. In the earlier example of the person who bought some land and dammed a stream on it there was the cost to other landowners resulting from their being deprived of water. Similarly, if a chemical processing firm builds a new, larger plant the private cost to it is obvious. But when in consequence the firm expands its activities people in the area experience the costs involved with greater industrial activity, e.g. more waste discharged into rivers, a higher level of pollution in the atmosphere, etc. People may also receive benefits as the result of the resource allocation of others. Suppose a family have a firework party in their garden. People living nearby will at least derive the benefit of seeing the rockets. Of course, if they dislike fireworks this would count as a cost! The costs and benefits encountered by other members of society in this way are known as **social costs** and **benefits**.

Externalities

Often, the social costs or benefits relating to a particular use of resources are so minor that they are usually ignored. But where the social costs are significant any attempt to measure the real cost of the activity in question must take some account of this. The difference between the private and social costs (or benefits) of a use of resources is termed the **externality**.

In modern times the most frequently cited externality in respect of industrial activity is pollution. So, to the private cost of an industrial activity which causes pollution must be added the social costs arising from increased illness in the community, damage to crops, reduced leisure facilities resulting from polluted rivers, etc. These social costs can be measured by adding up the resources employed in dealing with the pollution and its effects. In consequence the total cost to society of a particular output is higher than that actually measured by the firm. If these social costs were included the supply curve would be to the left of the market supply curve resulting in a lower quantity supplied and a higher price. The behaviour of individual consumers also results in this type of externality, e.g. the problems caused to society as a whole by alcohol or drug abuse.

The externality may, of course, involve a social benefit. Where, for example, a company produces safety harnesses to protect children in cars, the social benefits arising from reduced health care and insurance payments should be added to any direct benefit received by the firm. Effectively, the total utility received by society is greater than that indicated by the market demand curve. If this factor could be taken into account both the quantity demanded and the price would be higher than those resulting from market forces. Again, where people look after elderly relatives instead of putting them into state care the cost to society is less than would otherwise be the case, i.e. the benefit to society is greater than the benefit payments to families looking after the elderly.

The effect of externalities is to cause a misallocation of resources. Where the externality derives from a social cost the supply of the good or service exceeds the level giving optimum value to society. Less than the optimum level is being provided, however, when the externality involves a social benefit.

REVISION TEST

1 Explain the theory of consumer sovereignty.

2 Name the main factors which make consumer sovereignty impossible to achieve in the real world.

3 Why do not all consumers get what they want, even under a system of consumer sovereignty?

4 Define the term 'social cost'.

5 Define the term 'private benefit'.

6 A woman pays £20 to have her car converted to take unleaded petrol. What are the implications in terms of private and social costs and benefits?

7 Explain how an economic activity could have both social benefits and social costs.

8 What is an 'externality'?

9 How, in a diagram, would you show the effect of social costs on the supply of a product?

10 How do externalities cause a misallocation of resources?

Government intervention in the market

We have seen that the free market poses problems both because it contains imperfections and because the pure operation of market forces may have undesirable consequences for society as a whole. How the government deals with the results of market imperfection, such as monopoly power and restrictive trade practices, will be examined in a later chapter. In the remainder of this chapter we shall concentrate on the ways in which the government interferes with the working of market forces to achieve its own objectives.

The government has social as well as economic goals and the two are invariably intertwined. While, therefore, interference with market forces is sometimes justified on the grounds of economic efficiency social considerations are rarely totally absent. In other cases intervention may be based purely on social or political grounds. The greater the externality present in the supply of a particular good the more likely it is that the government will consider it appropriate to intervene. The main forms of intervention are:

1   Public goods

Here, the government takes over the responsibility of providing the supply of a good or service itself. Such a step is taken in a free market economy when to allow market forces to operate would present society with potentially enormous externalities. So the government is always held to be responsible for maintaining the nation's defences, providing a police force and administering justice rather than allowing such services to be supplied through the price mechanism.

In the case of other goods and services, however, the debate is not settled as to whether the state or the free market is best able to realise the maximum benefit. Supporters of the state provision of health and education, for example, argue that the large social benefits which accrue from a healthy, well-educated population will not be achieved if these services are left to the operation of market forces. Opponents argue that the free market is able to produce similar benefits but at a lower cost to society as a whole. Clearly, the debate is beset by political argument and the number of public goods will be higher in a mixed economy than in a free market one, and higher still in a command economy.

2 Legislation

The state may choose to make the provision of certain goods and services illegal where the social cost is regarded as unacceptable. These would include addictive drugs, poisons, pornographic material exploiting the young and so on. Again, there may be political debates within society as to which goods should come within this category, as when Islamic countries banned Salman Rushdie's book *The Satanic Verses* in 1989 while many other countries permitted its publication.

On the other hand the government may use legislation to enforce the purchase of certain goods and services. In Britain, for example, the wearing of crash helmets by motorcyclists is compulsory and all motorists are required to have third-party insurance.

3 Price regulation

The government may intervene in the market either to fix a maximum price or to fix a minimum price.

Maximum price fixing

Here the government intervenes in the market by imposing a price ceiling. Such a policy might be adopted when there is a shortage of an essential commodity and prices threaten to rise to a level beyond the reach of substantial numbers of consumers or because the government wishes to make a product cheap enough for more households to be able to afford it. There are three possible consequences of the institution of a maximum price:

a) The maximum price is the same as the market price and therefore has no effect on the market.

b) The maximum price is above the market price (as in Figure 5.1). In this case the maximum price is irrelevant since supply and demand interact to produce an equilibrium price acceptable to both the market and the government.

c) The maximum price is below the market price. This is shown in Figure 5.2 where the maximum price is P and the market price is E. The imposition of the maximum price deters producers, reducing the quantity supplied from Q to Q_1. At the same time the lower price leads the quantity demanded to expand from Q to Q_2. There is thus an excess quantity demanded of Q_2-Q_1.

In a situation in which supply and demand can no longer be brought into equilibrium by market forces, some way must be found of allocating the available

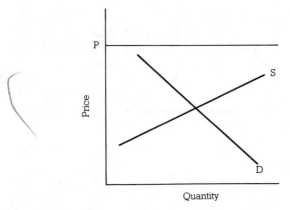

Figure 5.1 *Maximum price regulation*

supply among those wishing to buy it at the new price. Suppliers may operate a 'first come, first served' policy with those at the back of the queue losing out. Alternatively they may adopt some form of rationing by giving each customer a quota or by favouring some customers at the expense of others. Of course, the government may itself take the lead in rationing through the issue of coupons, as happened during the Second World War in the UK.

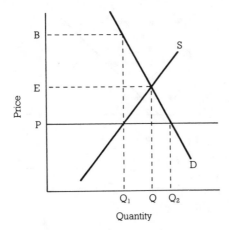

Figure 5.2 *Maximum price regulation*

However scrupulous the attempt to ensure an equitable distribution of supply there is always the risk that a **black market** will become established. The black market is that market in which the commodity is sold illegally at prices above the maximum price. In Figure 5.2 the quantity supplied is, as we have seen, Q_1. If this quantity were sold for a price high enough to remove excess demand it would be sold at price B. Since many consumers would be prepared to pay this or even higher prices it is inevitable that much of the supply will be sold or resold at prices above the maximum price.

Unless it is rigorously controlled, therefore, the effect of maximum price legislation is to destabilise the market. In so doing it enables supply to be sold at prices even higher than the market price which would prevail in the absence of price controls. At best it leads to the wastage of resources associated with queuing and the administration of a rationing system. At worst, it may lead to the racketeering and crime common in Europe during and immediately after the Second World War. In modern times the tickets for major sporting events are frequently priced below the market price and the ultimate buyer often pays many times the face value of the ticket to touts operating in the 'black market'.

Minimum price fixing

In this case the government seeks to assist suppliers by imposing a minimum price on the market. Such a policy might be adopted when a glut threatens to force prices below the minimum at which suppliers can make a profit. Again, there are three possible consequences of the institution of a minimum price.

a) The minimum price is the same as the market price and therefore has no effect on the market.

b) The minimum price is below the market price (as in Figure 5.3). In this case the minimum price is irrelevant since supply and demand interact to produce an equilibrium price acceptable to both the market and the government.

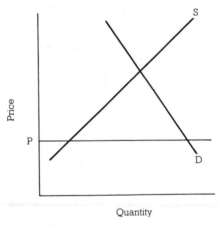

Figure 5.3 *Minimum price regulation*

c) The minimum price is above the market price. This is shown in Figure 5.4 where the minimum price is P and the market price is E. The imposition of a minimum price encourages suppliers to increase the quantity supplied from Q to Q_1. At the same time the higher price deters consumers and the quantity demanded con-tracts from Q to Q_2. The result is an excess quantity supplied of Q_1-Q_2.

Once again we have a situation in which supply and demand can no longer be brought into equilibrium by market forces. Suppliers will find that stocks build up and they will be tempted to find ways of selling off these surpluses at prices below the official minimum, especially if that price matches what they could expect in a free market. A government or international governing organisation may seek to deal with

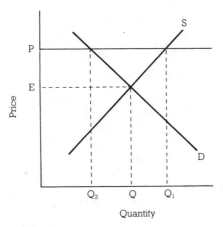

Figure 5.4 *Minimum price regulation*

this problem in one of two ways. Either it reduces the total supply by setting each producer a production quota or it guarantees to buy up any excess production which cannot be sold at the minimum price. The former approach has been adopted by the Organisation of Petroleum Exporting Countries (OPEC) and the latter by the European Economic Community (EEC) in respect of some agricultural products.

4   Price stabilisation

Throughout history the production of many essential, primarily agricultural, commodities has been subject to uncertainties connected with variations in weather and climate and other unpredictable events. Such uncertainties result in the production levels, and therefore prices, of these commodities being extremely volatile from one year to the next. In years when there is a glut prices are very low and, because demand is generally price inelastic, farmers suffer a dramatic fall in revenues. In years of shortage the very high prices lead to many consumers suffering severe hardship.

Because of the political problems inherent in the difficulties outlined above, governments have frequently intervened in the markets for agricultural products. The aims of such intervention have been to secure an adequate supply of the commodity for the population while at the same time ensuring that farmers do not suffer as a result of any over-production which might follow. These ends may be achieved by the government adopting a policy of price stabilisation and the maintenance of buffer stocks.

Suppose that, in a given year, the market for a particular agricultural good is as shown in Figure 5.5. The supply and demand curves intersect at a market price of P and an output of Q. Let us assume that the government considers this to be an equitable price and guarantees it in future years. In the following year good climatic conditions result in a bumper harvest and shift the supply curve to the right to S_1. Without government intervention the price would fall to P_1 so the government buys enough of the available supply to maintain the price at P. Provided the amount bought is put into storage it can be used as a **buffer stock**. So, if in later years the harvest is very bad and supply is unable to satisfy demand, the government can release this stock onto the market and keep the price at the guaranteed price.

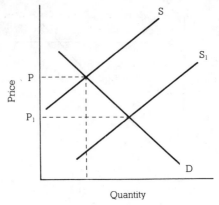

Figure 5.5 *Price stabilisation*

The danger of such a scheme is that the implicit encouragement to suppliers to increase production may lead to over-production and ever-expanding buffer stocks; a problem familiar under the Common Agricultural Policy of the EEC. In addition, suppliers are subsidised at the expense of consumers if improved production techniques lead merely to large stocks rather than benefitting consumers through lower prices.

5   Indirect taxes

The government may impose an indirect tax, such as value added tax (VAT), with the sole aim of raising revenue. However the imposition of such a tax has the effect of shifting the supply curve to the left since the impact on the supplier is similar to that of a rise in costs. The effect on the market is shown in Figure 5.6 where the imposition of a tax raises the equilibrium price from P_1 to P_2 and reduces the quantity demanded and supplied from Q_1 to Q_2. While consumers pay the new price suppliers do not, of course, receive this price; they receive the net of tax price (P_3).

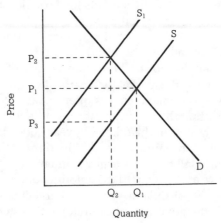

Figure 5.6 *Effect of taxing a product*

So the government may also place a tax on products when it wishes to discourage consumption of them, as with the high level of taxation on tobacco and alcoholic drinks. Clearly the effectiveness of such a policy depends on the elasticity of demand of the product in question (see Chapter 3). Where demand is very inelastic the imposition of a tax will increase government revenue without significantly affecting the total demand for the product. Such a policy is very much more successful when demand for the product is highly price elastic.

6 Subsidies

When suppliers are paid a subsidy the effect is the opposite of the imposition of an indirect tax. In this case suppliers experience the equivalent of a fall in costs and can supply more than before at the prevailing price. This is shown in Figure 5.7 where the granting of a subsidy results in the suppliers receiving a payment of XY per unit at the prevailing market price. They are therefore prepared to supply more at this price and the supply curve shifts to the right (S to S_1), leading to the establishment of a new market equilibrium in which the market price has fallen from P_1 to P_2 while the quantity demanded and supplied has increased from Q_1 to Q_2. Both consumers and suppliers benefit. Consumers now pay a lower market price and while suppliers receive a lower price than before they benefit both from receiving a subsidy of XY in addition to the market price and from selling more units.

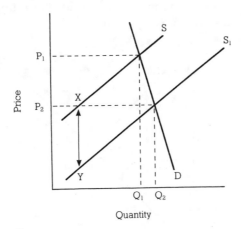

Figure 5.7 *Subsidy to a supplier*

When a new market equilibrium is established the effect is that the subsidy is shared between consumer and supplier. Assume, for example, that the original market price was £15 and that suppliers now receive a subsidy of £3 per unit. If the new market price is £13 consumers have gained from a reduction of £2 in the market price while suppliers now receive £16 per unit (£13 + £3). This division of benefit between consumer and supplier must occur unless demand is:

a) Perfectly elastic so that suppliers receive the entire benefit of the subsidy, *or*
b) Perfectly inelastic in which case buyers receive the entire benefit of the subsidy.

Subsidies are granted to suppliers for three main reasons:

1 To encourage greater production of essential goods such as fuel or raw materials for industry.

2 To reduce market prices and thus protect consumers from the full effects of market forces on essential goods such as food.

3 To protect suppliers from a slump in the market which has driven prices below the level adequate to sustain firms in the industry.

Underlying all these aims is the principle that the total supply under pure market conditions will not be sufficient to realise the social benefits which a greater supply, and probably lower prices, will bring.

The government may choose alternatively to subsidise the consumer. This might take the form of issuing coupons to be used in part-payment for particular goods or cash payments or tax relief attached to particular kinds of expenditure. The effect of such assistance is similar to that of a rise in income and is shown in Figure 5.8. A subsidy of XY per unit has an effect similar to a rise in income and results in a shift in the demand curve to the right (D to D_1). There will then be an increase in the quantity demanded and supplied from Q to Q_1 and a rise in the market price from P to P_1. Once again the benefits will be shared by consumer and supplier. The consumer pays a higher market price but against this will be set the value of the subsidy. The supplier receives a higher price than previously and sells more of the product.

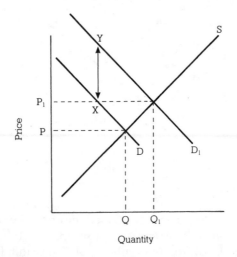

Figure 5.8 *Subsidy to a consumer*

Subsidies to consumers are usually adopted when the aim of the government is to assist particular sections of the population to buy essential goods or services, e.g. medical prescriptions and housing.

Price controls and subsidies compared

We have seen that the government has several policies at its disposal should it wish to assist consumers by reducing the price they have to pay to acquire a particular good. We can trace the effect of each of these policies by reference to, say, the housing market. Suppose the government is concerned by the high rents for private rented accommodation and seeks to intervene in the market to assist tenants. First, it can introduce maximum price legislation in the form of rent controls. The probable effect is that the supply of such accommodation will contract and, while some tenants will benefit through lower rents, many will either lose their accommodation or be forced to pay even higher rents than before. In the latter case this would take the form of key deposits and other illicit payments demanded by landlords in addition to the rent. The restrictions on rent levels in the UK through most of the post-war period were a major factor in the decline of this form of housing since the 1940s.

Second, it may subsidise private landlords, either through tax relief on rented income or a direct payment for each unit of accommodation provided. This would have the effect of increasing the supply of private accommodation available for renting and so reduce the market price for such housing. This policy will have the desired effect, therefore, though the government may find itself subsidising the landlord as much or more than the tenant.

Third, it may subsidise the tenant through the provision of housing credits or other direct payments. This policy will increase the demand for rented accommodation and so push up the market price and stimulate some expansion of this type of accommodation. Again, it will have the desired effect since tenants will pay a lower rent than before once the subsidy is taken into account. Both landlord and tenant will benefit but the government may target the assistance it gives more accurately than when a blanket subsidy is given to landlords.

The policy option preferred by the government is likely to vary with the prevailing social conditions, the probable response of the market to each of the options and its own political objectives.

REVISION TEST

1. Give examples of goods which tend to be public goods in any economic society.
2. What are the *economic* grounds on which legislation against the addictive drugs can be justified?
3. Explain the term 'black market'.
4. Explain how minimum price legislation is likely to lead to a waste of resources.
5. What are buffer stocks?
6. Use a diagram to show how the consumer bears all the incidence of a tax when demand is perfectly inelastic.
7. If the imposition of a tax of £2 per unit leads to a rise in the market price of £0.50 what proportion of the tax is borne by the supplier?
8. Give two reasons why agricultural products are more likely to be subsidised than manufactured goods.

9 With the aid of a diagram show how the market would respond to a subsidy being given to suppliers when demand is perfectly elastic.

10 Under what circumstances would maximum pricing be a more effective policy than subsidies to deal with high prices?

_____ **Examination questions** _____

1 a) Illustrate how the allocation of resources is affected by externalities.
   b) How can government intervention help to deal with the problem?
   (ABEI, June 1988)

2 Consider the view that price controls are an inefficient method of helping poor people because they always lead to shortages.
   (LCCI Higher, May 1986)

3 a) Governments frequently subsidise the price or cost of producing certain goods or services. Comment upon the effect of such subsidies on price and output.
   b) Why do governments choose to subsidise certain goods and to tax others?
   (LCCI Higher, November 1987)

4 The government of a small island state wishes to encourage further output of its staple agricultural product. In the long run there is a possibility that some of the commodity could be produced for export, but at present it is only for domestic use. The market situation is as follows:

Price per unit	Output	Demand
10	100	500
20	200	400
30	300	300
40	400	200
50	500	100
60	600	0
70	700	0
80	800	0

The government is uncertain how to promote production and faces a choice between a direct subsidy and an intervention price.
a) Explain the difference between a subsidy and an intervention price.
b) What would be the effect on the market of a guaranteed intervention price of 35p per unit?
c) What would be the effect on the market of a direct subsidy of 10p per unit?
   (LCCI Higher, November 1987)

5 Explain using diagrams, the effect of each of the following:
   a) The government introduces a maximum price for petrol.
   b) A national airline agrees with other major airlines to establish a minimum price for a particular route.
   c) The equilibrium price for a staple food product is £1 per kilo and the government imposes a 20p per kilo tax on the sale of this product.
   d) The government establishes a buffer stock system and a minimum price to suppliers of a major crop. The crop is in abundance following a good harvest.
   (LCCI Intermediate, December 1986)

6 a) Define and explain the concept of consumer sovereignty.
   b) Does the existence of the large corporation affect the sovereignty of the consumer? Give reasons for your answer.
   (ACCA, December 1987)

7 Many governments impose controls on the rents of private property with the object of assisting lower-paid workers. What are the likely consequences of such policies?
   (ACCA, June 1987)

8 What sources of 'market failure' exist in a free market economy? What, if anything, might government do about them?
   (SCCA, November 1987)

9 What problems might arise in an industrialised economy were the government to allow an unrestricted 'free play of market forces'?
   (SCCA, May 1989)

10 To what extent do you consider the market to be an adequate allocator of resources as compared with non-market approaches to resource allocation. Explain the significance to the Purchasing Officer of operating under free market conditions.
   (IPS, May 1989)

6 Production and costs

- *Why do large-scale organisations tend to be more efficient than small-scale ones?*

- *How do changes in output affect the cost of producing one unit?*

Production

Production takes place when scarce resources are used to make goods or provide services. This production is the **output** while the scarce resources used are the **inputs** or **factors of production**.

There are four factors of production:

1 **Land**   This term is used loosely to describe not only land itself but also all those raw materials which are extracted or otherwise obtained from the land, the seas, etc.

2 **Labour**   This consists of the workforce, whether manual or skilled, who contribute by their efforts to the productive process.

3 **Capital**   Land and labour are natural factors of production but capital is that factor which must be produced itself before it is available. It thus includes tools, machinery, plant, buildings and vehicles.

4 **Enterprise**   In order for the factors of production to produce anything, they must be organised. This organisation is provided by the **entrepreneur** who employs the labour, rents the land and invests in the capital required.

In practice the factors of production are a little more complex than the descriptions given above. The entrepreneur usually puts his own labour into the business as well as his enterprise. Labour itself is never just that. All workers possess some education and skills, the result of investment in their future potential at some time in the past. They are therefore part labour and part **human capital**. Animals can be labour, as in the case of a working horse, or capital like a prize bull or dairy cow.

All output involves aspects of the four factors of production. But any given level of output can be produced in more than one way, i.e. by using different combinations of the factors of production, especially through varying the quantities of capital and labour. A trench can be dug by a dozen men using pickaxes and shovels or by one man and a mechanical digger; cars can be painted by men or by robots. In short, production may be **capital intensive** or **labour intensive**. The term **isoquant** is used to describe the different combinations of factors which can produce a given output.

TABLE 6.1
Alternative ways of producing ten units of output

Units of labour	Units of capital
30	2
20	3
15	4
12	5
10	6
9	7
8	9
7	12

Table 6.1 reflects the fact that the factors of production are not perfectly inter-changeable. Machines must have workers to operate them so capital cannot replace labour indefinitely. Similarly, increasing the number of workers will not enable tasks to be performed effectively if these tasks require the force of a steam-hammer or the precision of a laser. Given that there are a number of ways in which the desired output can be achieved, which of these will be chosen? The entrepreneur will generally be drawn to the cheapest available. So, if labour is cheap, production will be labour intensive. If, on the other hand, labour is expensive the entrepreneur may well look for the opportunity to replace labour with capital. When the prices of the two factors of production used in Table 6.1 are known, say £20 per unit of capital employed and £5 per unit of labour, we can see the relative merits of the choices available. This is shown in Table 6.2, where a combination of four units of capital and 15 of labour is the cheapest of all the suitable combinations.

TABLE 6.2
Cost of alternative production methods

Labour (£5 per unit)	Capital (£20 per unit)	Total Cost (£)
30	2	190
20	3	160
15	4	155
12	5	160
10	6	170
9	7	185
8	9	220
7	12	275

From our brief look at isoquants we have seen that, while there may be several ways in which to produce a given output, the costs to the producer in each case will be different. If the relative prices of the factors of production were to change then a different combination may well become the cheapest available. But the combinations of the two factors at each end of the isoquant will never be the cheapest because of the fact that these combinations are using excessive amounts of one factor or the other to try to make up for the lack of the other factor.

The Law of Diminishing Returns

The lack of perfect interchangibility of the factors of production illustrated by the isoquant also presents problems when an attempt is made to increase output.

TABLE 6.3
The Law of Diminishing Returns

Units of capital	Units of labour	Total product	Average product	Marginal product
1	1	6	6	—
1	2	13	6½	7
1	3	18	6	5
1	4	20	5	2
1	5	21	4¼	1

In Table 6.3 there is one fixed factor (capital) and one variable factor (labour). Average product is found by dividing total product by the units of labour employed and marginal product is the addition to total output made by employing one more unit of labour. It is assumed that the entrepreneur is unable to add to his capital equipment in order to increase output – he is totally reliant on labour for any increase in inputs. So output rises through the addition of more and more labour to a fixed unit of capital. Initially this inability to add to capital is not too serious as the second worker contributes more to total production than the first. This may be due to the fact that the two workers can divide up the tasks to be done between them and so improve efficiency. In addition, the capital equipment may not have been fully used by one worker, leaving slack in the system which has now been taken up. However, the producer will find it impossible to sustain this growth in output by adding further units of labour. Instead there is a rapid fall in the extra output generated by each successive worker, i.e. the marginal product. Indeed it is likely that the marginal product will fall to zero as the producer has encountered the **Law of Diminishing Marginal Returns**, sometimes referred to as the **Law of Variable Proportions**. This law states that 'As successive units of a variable factor are added to a fixed quantity of other factors the rate at which output is increased must eventually decline'. In Table 6.3 marginal product declines almost immediately, to be followed more slowly by a decline in average product. Eventually, even total product may decline if the entrepreneur is foolish enough to employ so many units of the variable factor that they get in each other's way. The Law of Diminishing Returns is a law because it must be true. If this were not the case we could add more and more labour to a fixed amount of land without reducing the marginal product until all the world's food production were grown on one acre of land.

The Law of Diminishing Returns is not a theory without relevance to the real world. The population explosion in Africa and Asia has resulted in more and more labour attempting to farm the limited land available. The extra food so produced has often proved insufficient to meet the needs of the workforce growing it. In Europe we have seen the law in action in the fall in the catches of the North Sea and Atlantic Fishery fleets as these waters have been overfished. However much a business attempts to plan its future output a sudden change in market conditions is likely to find it unable to respond with a balanced increase in the use of resources. There may be a shortage of skilled labour in the area or it may not be possible to obtain new machinery immediately; in short, if one of the factors is fixed in supply the Law of Diminishing Returns will come into play.

Short run and long run

For the producer the **short run** is that period during which at least one factor of production is fixed and where the law of diminishing returns consequently applies. The **long run** is that period necessary for all the factors of production to become variable. Suppose that a producer finds that there is an increase in demand for his products which is likely to be sustained for the foreseeable future. In the short run he may be able to use more labour and materials with the same amount of capital equipment. In the long run he may vary all his factors of production by installing new machinery as well as taking on more labour and using more materials. The long run is not a set period of time, it will vary in length from industry to industry and from one firm to another within an industry. The long run for the oil tanker business, for example, is much longer than that for the clothing industry because of the much greater time scale involved in building new oil tankers compared to installing clothing machines. It is important to remember that the long run is essentially a planning period during which the producer has yet to commit itself to a particular scale of production. Once the producer has put the plans into effect it is back in the **short run** with fixed factors of production. Imagine the oil tanker company which orders a new ship in the expectation that it will be able to expand its operations in five years' time when the new ship is built. As soon as the new ship is delivered the firm is back in the short run since it again has a fixed number of ships, albeit in that there is one extra. The longer the long run is, the more difficult it is for the firm to plan effectively – it may even be necessary to scrap plans for growth if circumstances change during the long run period in question.

Not only does the long run have the advantage that it is possible to vary factor inputs in a way that is not feasible in the short run but it is also possible to change the whole scale of production rather than make piecemeal changes. This is shown in Table 6.4.

In Table 6.4 a producer increasing all the factors of production to scale is able to benefit from proportionately greater increase in output. The units of output are increasing at a faster rate than are the units of input and so the firm is experiencing the phenomenon of **increasing returns to scale**. Note that this is a phenomenon rather than a law because there is nothing inevitable about increasing returns to scale as there is with the law of diminishing returns. Nor is there any guarantee that increasing returns, once established, will go on indefinitely. As the table shows, the marginal product will eventually level off and, at this point, the producer will encounter **constant returns to scale**. Beyond a certain point marginal output may actually fall, as is the case in Table 6.4 when output reaches 76 units. The producer is now faced with **decreasing returns to**

TABLE 6.4
Returns to scale

Units of capital	Units of labour	Total product	Average product	Marginal product
1	1	6	6	—
2	2	14	7	8
3	3	24	8	10
4	4	42	10½	18
5	5	60	12	18
6	6	76	12.7	16
7	7	86	12.3	10
8	8	94	11¾	8
9	9	98	10.9	4
10	10	100	10	2

scale. If he wishes to enjoy the benefits of increasing returns to scale he must confine his output to between zero and 60 units. As we shall see producers will not necessarily choose to do this.

Economies of scale

Increasing returns to scale are also known as 'economies of scale' because increases in the scale of production usually bring economies to the producer in the form of more efficient production methods. Economies of scale may be classified into four main groups:

1 *Technical economies*
   a) Labour. As production grows it is possible to use specialisation and the division of labour to increase labour productivity. Larger producers are able to employ a wider range of labour skills to facilitate this process.
   b) Land. Larger fields are quicker to cultivate and reduce the waste associated with the borders between fields.
   c) Capital. Large scale production permits a more efficient use of capital for a number of reasons:
      i) Some capital equipment cannot be used efficiently below a certain level of output. Most mass production techniques like the use of a conveyor belt are impracticable at low output levels.
      ii) Capital is usually indivisible so a machine lying idle half the day is almost as costly to run as one running at full capacity.
      iii) Large-scale production enables different plants to specialise in particular areas of production.
      iv) Economies of dimension mean that large lorries need only one driver, just as a small van does.

2 *Financial economies*
The larger the firm, the lower tends to be the cost of borrowing. Blue chip companies

(those with the highest credit rating) can usually borrow at base rate plus one per cent while smaller companies will be paying much higher rates than this for credit. Larger companies also have access to the stock market to raise loans or float a share issue.

3   Marketing economies

Large producers benefit both from the lower costs associated with buying in bulk and the ability to dictate terms to suppliers to a degree no small firm could hope to do. Furthermore, advertising costs for the large firm are spread over a greater number of units of production, so reducing their unit cost. Similarly the sales offices of large companies will generally get larger orders per sales representative.

4   Management economies

In small companies decision-making is usually in the hands of the entrepreneur or a small group of managers. They cannot be expected to develop the highest levels of expertise in all the various management skills. In large companies, on the other hand, the efficiency of the management function is enhanced by the employment of specialist managers in such areas as production, marketing, finance, personnel and industrial relations.

Diseconomies of scale

We have already seen that increasing returns to scale may eventually give way to decreasing returns to scale if increased output results in a declining marginal product. These decreasing returns are the result of efficiency falling rather than rising with output and are also termed diseconomies of scale.

1   Managerial diseconomies

As a firm gets larger the managers are called upon to deal with more complicated problems within an increasingly more complex organisational structure. Not many managers will be able to cope as well as they did when the operation and their sphere of responsibility was smaller.

2   Administrative diseconomies

These are associated with the bureaucratic structures of many large companies where long lines of communication and complex administrative procedures delay effective action. Often the non-productive administrative parts of the large company grow faster than the production and distribution parts.

3   Over-specialisation

As they grow firms can become depersonalised. Workers may be trapped in repetitive, mundane jobs with only a limited interest in the success of the company and no identification with the aims of management. In such circumstances industrial relations are likely to deteriorate. At the same time the interests of the management team may diverge, resulting in a lack of decisiveness and a weakening of the ability to attain corporate objectives. All of these developments are likely to result in a reduction in efficiency.

The firm may also experience external economies and diseconomies of scale. These derive, however, from the environment within which the firm operates rather than through the internal operations of the firm itself. They will be examined elsewhere.

Replication

In theory, a producer should stop expanding a particular operation when increasing returns to scale have been maximised and constant returns to scale have set in. The producer should then *replicate*, i.e. build an identical operation elsewhere. In practice replication is not always appropriate. From Table 6.4 we saw that the *average* product may not be maximised until after the firm is producing under conditions of diseconomies of scale. In this case the average product at a total output of 98 units is still higher than it would be in a new plant where less than 42 units were produced. So even if management is prepared to replicate it would not make sense to do so until an output of over 130 units can be sold.

REVISION TEST

1 How is it that the West Indian plantation owners of the eighteenth century regarded their slaves as both labour *and* capital?

2 Define an isoquant.

3 How long is the long run?

4 Explain the term 'marginal product'.

5 Why is it the 'Law of Diminishing Returns' but not the Law of Increasing Returns to scale?

6 Why is it difficult for a taxi company to achieve economies of scale?

7 In what areas of its operation might they be possible?

8 Under what circumstances might a producer obtain increasing returns to a fixed factor?

9 What factors should a firm take into account when considering whether to replicate its operations?

10 Explain how an individual might combine elements of three of the factors of production in his or her person.

Costs

A firm incurs costs in producing a given output through the payment it must make for the factors of production involved in the production process. These costs will include not only purchased costs such as raw materials and hired costs like wages, but also the implicit costs involved in the use of the entrepreneur's capital or labour.

Costs may be divided into **fixed costs** and **variable costs**. Fixed costs (FC) are those which do not vary with output. They include interest charges on and depreciation of capital machinery, rent, rates, insurance and standing charges, all of which will have to be paid whether the firm is producing or not – at least in the short run. Variable costs

(VC) are those costs which do vary with output such as wages, raw materials and fuel. Together fixed costs and variable costs equal **total costs** (TC). In Figure 6.1 fixed costs are represented by a horizontal straight line as they do not vary with output. The variable cost line rises with output while the total cost line follows the same shape as variable costs but starts from the level of fixed costs.

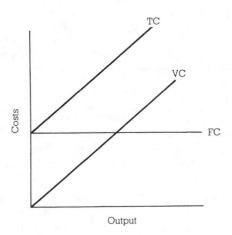

Figure 6.1 *Costs*

Relating costs more closely to production we see that fixed costs derive from the use of fixed factors of production and variable costs from the use of variable factors of production. Thus fixed costs can only occur in the short run. In the long run all factors of production are variable and so all costs must be variable. Although variable costs vary directly with output they do not vary *proportionately* with output. This is because, in the short run, the onset of diminishing returns will result in variable costs rising faster than output. In the long run variable (i.e. total) costs may rise slower than output under conditions of increasing returns to scale or faster than output under conditions of decreasing returns.

Average cost and marginal cost

Just as important as total cost are average cost and marginal cost. Average total cost (ATC) is found by dividing the total cost by the total product or output. Similarly, values may be found for average fixed cost (AFC) and average variable cost (AVC). Marginal cost (MC) is the addition to total cost resulting from the production of one extra unit of output. To illustrate the importance of average cost and marginal cost the data in Table 6.3 is revamped to include costs in Table 6.5. Table 6.5 shows that, as marginal product falls marginal cost rises. This is perfectly logical since these two developments are alternative ways of describing the same process. Efficiency is declining and this manifests itself as a falling rate of output per unit of input or, put another way, a rising rate of input per unit of output. In the same way, average cost will rise as average product falls.

TABLE 6.5
Short run cost schedule

Total product	Average product	Marginal product	Fixed cost (capital) (£)	Variable cost (labour) (£)	Total cost (£)	Average cost (£)	Marginal cost (£)	
6	6	–	30	10	40	6.7	–	
13	6½	7	30	20	50	3.8	1.4	(10÷7)
18	6	5	30	30	60	3.3	2	(10÷5)
20	5	2	30	40	70	3.5	5	(10÷2)
21	4¼	1	30	50	80	4.0	10	

Short run average cost curves

In Figure 6.2 the AFC line follows a predictable downward path as output is increased because a constant amount of fixed costs is being distributed over a growing number of units of output. The shape of the AVC, ATC and MC lines, however, is 'U'-shaped in each case. To see why, let us first examine the MC line. When output is increased MC falls at first due to a more efficient use of the factors of production as we saw in Table 6.5. Soon, however, further increases in output encounter the problem of diminishing returns and the MC line turns upwards. As long as MC is below AVC the AVC line will slope downwards, and this applies whether MC itself is falling or rising. Once MC exceeds AVC, however, the AVC line will also turn upward. So the point where MC crosses AVC is the lowest point of the AVC line. MC acts the same way on the ATC line so that MC crosses ATC at its lowest point. Note that the ATC line is a different shape to the AVC line because of the effect of AFC.

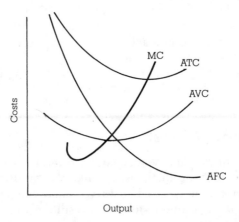

Figure 6.2 *Short-run cost curves*

This relationship between average cost and marginal cost is a very important one and is perhaps best illustrated by a simple example. If the average cost is £10 and the next unit is produced for anything less than £10 the average cost must fall. If this unit is produced for any amount more than £10 the average cost must rise. Only if the marginal unit is produced for exactly £10 will average cost be unchanged. Thus MC will intersect AVC (and therefore ATC) at the point where AVC has ceased to fall but not yet begun to rise, i.e. at its lowest point.

Long run cost curves

In the long run, as we have seen, the difference between fixed costs and variable costs disappears and the AVC line becomes the AC (i.e. ATC) line. However, the relationship between MC and AC persists with MC crossing AC at its lowest point. The AC line, while still 'U'-shaped, is more shallow in the long run because the firm has the opportunity to take advantage of increased returns to scale. Only if output is planned to be expanded indefinitely will decreasing returns to scale inevitably cause the AC curve to rise.

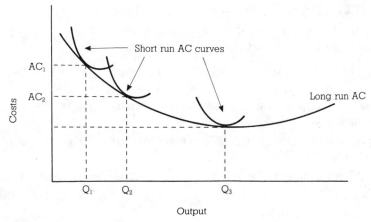

Figure 6.3 *Long-run average cost curves*

Figure 6.3 shows the relationship between short- and long-run average cost curves. The long run average cost curve represents the lowest cost attainable by the firm for any given output. At the output Q_1 the average cost is AC_1 and this is the lowest average cost achievable for that output. If the firm now chooses to produce Q_1 it will be producing in the short run, not the long run. This is because the long run is only a planning period and once production begins the firm will again have fixed factors of production. At an output of Q_1 the short- and long-run average cost curves touch at what is the minimum average cost in both the long and the short run for that output. Only if the firm deviates from this planned output in its new short run will average cost rise above the long-run minimum, though this of course is more likely to happen than not. If the firm decides to produce at Q_2 in the long run it will experience greater economies of scale with a minimum average cost of AC_2. The firm will also now operate along a different short-run average cost curve, though with similar constraints if output varies from Q_2. In Figure 6.3 the optimum output is at the minimum point of the average cost curve, Q_3, where increasing returns to scale are maximised. If, once this point is reached, it were possible to increase output without any change in long-run average cost the firm would enjoy a whole range of optimum outputs and would be producing under conditions of constant returns to scale.

The achievement of an optimum output position assumes that the firm is able to establish an output level which enables it to exploit to the full the available economies of scale and so produce at the lowest possible average cost. This output level is the **minimum efficient scale of production** and firms which produce a lower output will be experiencing higher unit costs. In Figure 6.3 this is the situation facing firms which operate within the output range of Q_1 to Q_3. It might be thought that such firms could not compete with those which are able to attain the optimum output level and, in theory, this should be the case. In practice industries are rarely so competitive that only those firms achieving the maximum economies of scale and producing at the minimum average cost level can survive. It is far more likely that firms within an industry will be operating at different cost levels and enjoying different degrees of success as a result.

REVISION TEST

1   If, with an output of 15 units, total cost is £70 and average fixed cost is £2.5, what is the total variable cost?

2   Explain how a firm's electricity bill could be part fixed cost and part variable cost.

3   What sort of cost is incurred by the entrepreneur putting his own capital into the business?

4   Explain the precise relationship between a firm's marginal cost curve and its average variable cost curve.

5   Why is the long-run average cost curve shallower than the short-run curve?

6   At which point on a 'U'-shaped long run average cost curve is the firm enjoying constant returns to scale?

7   What is meant by the term 'minimum efficient scale of production?'

8   Draw the long run average cost curve for the firm whose output range falls entirely under:
     a) Increasing returns to scale,
     b) Constant returns to scale,
     c) Decreasing returns to scale.

Examination questions

1   What is the distinction between fixed costs and variable costs in both the short run and the long run, and why is the distinction important?

(ABE1, June 1986)

2   Explain and illustrate the difference between cost behaviour in the short run and cost behaviour in the long run.

(ABE1, December 1987)

3   Explain why unit costs alter as output expands.

(LCCI Higher, Spring 1984)

4   **a)**   Explain how the Law of Diminishing Returns determines the shape of a firm's
           cost curve.
     b   Distinguish between short-run and long-run average cost curves.
                                                           (LCCI Higher, Spring 1985)

5   What, if anything, can a firm do to change the diseconomies of scale facing it?
                                                              (ICSA, December 1987)

6   A local entrepreneur has built up a successful business which is still growing. He is
    aware that the increasing scale of operations has a number of cost advantages but is
    finding the administration of the organisation increasingly difficult. He asks you as
    a student of economics to explain the relative merits of expanding the size of his
    business further. Write him a brief report on this subject.
                                                                 (ACCA, June 1988)

7   In advanced industrial societies, more capital is combined with a given amount of
    labour in agricultural production than in the lesser developed countries. With
    reference to the Law of Diminishing Returns, explain why this makes economic
    sense.
                                                                 (ACCA, June 1989)

8   What diseconomies and consequent problems may be associated with large-scale
    production?
                                                                   (CIMA, May 1989)

9   How does the determination of short-run costs differ from that of costs in the long
    run?
                                                              (CIMA, November 1989)

10 Explain how the long-run average cost curve of a firm may be affected by increasing
    returns to scale, constant returns or decreasing returns to scale.
                                                               (Cert.M., June 1984)

11 How are firms able to obtain economies of scale?
                                                             (Cert.M, November 1986)

12 Consider how a firm should decide whether to expand its existing plant to meet an
    increase in sales or to build an additional plant.
                                                               (Cert.M., June 1987)

13 Explain what is meant by the law of variable proportions.
                                                               (Cert.M., June 1988)

14 Discuss the major economies of scale and apply your analysis to an industry with
    which you are familiar.
                                                            (Cert.M., December 1988)

15   Explain how the short-run behaviour of a firm is likely to be constrained when it seems to add additional units of variable factors of production to a constant amount of a fixed factor.

(IFA, December 1988)

16   If large firms derive benefits from their size, explain why a point is often reached in the scale of production when long-run average costs start to increase.

(IFA, June 1989)

7 Revenue and profit

- *Why do economists and accountants differ in their view of what constitutes profit?*

- *How does the firm know when it is operating at its most profitable output?*

Revenue

The revenue of the firm is the proceeds it receives from the sale of its goods or services. The **total revenue** (TR) is thus the total output multiplied by the price (to simplify matters we are assuming that all output is sold). **Average revenue** (AR) is found by dividing total revenue by output and is therefore equal to price so long as all units are sold at the same price. **Marginal revenue** (MR) is the addition to total revenue obtained from the sale of one extra unit of output. Revenue is a much simpler concept than is cost since we are not concerned with short- and long-run differences nor with fixed and variable revenue.

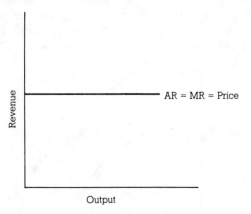

Figure 7.1 *Revenue*

In Figure 7.1 all output is sold at the same price so demand for the product is perfectly elastic. Average revenue is therefore equal to price. Since marginal revenue is the addition to total revenue of selling one extra unit and every extra unit sold yields the same price, marginal revenue must equal both price and average revenue.

TABLE 7.1
Revenue schedule

Output	Price (£)	Total revenue (£)	Average revenue (£)	Marginal revenue (£)
5	20	100	20	—
6	19	114	19	14
7	18	126	18	12
8	17	136	17	10
9	16	144	16	8
10	15	150	15	6
11	14	154	14	4
12	12	144	12	−10
13	10	130	10	−14
14	7	98	7	−32

However, revenue is not so straightforward that any number of units of output can always be sold at the same price. In Table 7.1 the firm can only sell more of its output by lowering the price. Thus average revenue falls with price as output is increased. The effect on marginal revenue is even more marked. As output is increased the addition to total revenue of each extra unit sold is less than the price of that unit. So, when output is increased from 10 to 11 and price reduced from £15 to £14, marginal revenue is only £4. This is because the firm has lost revenue on the units that were previously sold at £15 but are now sold at £14. As the table shows, it is possible for marginal revenue to become zero, and even negative. If marginal revenue does become negative total revenue will actually fall. Whether marginal revenue is positive or negative depends on the price elasticity of demand for the product. When demand is price elastic MR will be positive and when demand is price inelastic MR will be negative. The product in Table 7.1 therefore varies from price elastic to price inelastic as output is increased.

The data in Table 7.1 is produced in diagrammatic form in Figure 7.2. Here, marginal revenue is zero when the MR line crosses the output axis. At this point total revenue is maximised and it declines as marginal revenue becomes negative.

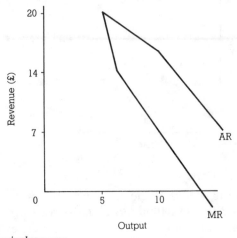

Figure 7.2 *Declining marginal revenue*

Profit

The simplest definition of profit is that it is the residue left to the firm after total costs have been deducted from total revenue, i.e. TR − TC = Profit.

These costs are payments to the factors of production for their contribution to the productive process. It can be deduced, therefore, that any residue which remains after these payments have been made is the reward to the entrepreneur for his own contribution to the business. Certainly this would be the case in the accounting method of calculating profit. The economist, however, makes an allowance for those hidden costs which are the result of the entrepreneur using his own resources in the business without taking a reward for them. Thus there are the wages which the entrepreneur could have earned had he worked for someone else, the rent he would have received if he had given his land over to somebody else to work and the interest he could have earned if he had deposited his capital with a financial institution rather than invested in his own business. These are the **implicit** wages, rent and interest the entrepreneur has given up and which must be compensated for by income from the firm if he is not to be financially worse off. So the economist includes in costs an estimate of the 'profit' which the entrepreneur must receive merely to cover these foregone incomes and make it worthwhile to stay in business. If, in the economist's terms, the firm is breaking even it is actually earning sufficient to cover all costs, including that reward which is necessary to keep the entrepreneur in business. In the accountant's terms, of course, the firm is making a profit. The payment necessary to keep the entrepreneur's own factors of production in their present use is known as **normal profit** and any profit received in excess of normal profit is **super-normal profit**. These different views of profit can be summarised in a simple example:

Accountant's estimate		Economist's estimate	
Revenue	£10 000	Revenue	£10 000
− Costs	£7 000	− Costs	£7 000
		− Normal Profit	£3 000
Profit	£3 000	(Super-normal) Profit	Nil

As the economist and the accountant are working from different viewpoints their results are the same in the sense that the firm has achieved exactly the same results whatever the method of profit calculation. It is important to remember that normal profit depends on the expectations of the entrepreneur and is not a fixed amount. So the normal profit for an entrepreneur whose principal concern is to be his or her own boss will be different to that for someone whose sole motive for setting up a business is to make money. So, if in the example above, the normal profit required by the entrepreneur were £4000 the firm would be making a profit in accounting terms but a loss in economic terms. In these circumstances the entrepreneur may well feel that, while the firm is making a profit, it is not worthwhile carrying on in the business. So the economist's view of profit is more likely to reflect how well or how badly the entrepreneur *feels* the business is doing whatever the paper profit.

The nature of profit

So far we have seen that part of the profit received by an entrepreneur is actually made up of factor rewards which the entrepreneur could have received in other ways if the business had never been set up. But most entrepreneurs expect, and frequently get, higher profits than can be explained by implicit factor rewards. These extra profit payments are a reward for the essential contribution made by the entrepreneur to the success of the business:

a) The organisation of the other factors of production, without which production would be at best haphazard and at worst non-existent.
b) The entrepreneur is an innovator who introduces new products or new ways of supplying existing products.
c) The entrepreneur is a risk-taker who is willing to back his ideas with his own capital and reputation.
d) The entrepreneur is not guaranteed a return on his efforts and must meet the payments due to the other factors of production before receiving a profit.

However high the expectations of an entrepreneur the profits received may well exceed these and then the firm is receiving super profits. Sometimes super-normal profits are the result of a combination of low expectations and entrepreneurial efficiency but just as often they are the consequence of monopoly power within the trade or industry, a subject to which we will return shortly.

REVISION TEST

1   Must average revenue always equal price?
2   Under what circumstances does AR = MR?
3   If output increases from 16 to 20 and total revenue from £64 to £70 what is now (a) the price and (b) the marginal revenue?
4   Complete the equation TR − TC =
5   Define 'Normal Profit'.
6   How is it possible for two entrepreneurs to earn the same profit in accounting terms and yet for one to think he has made a loss?
7   What is meant by 'implicit interest'?
8   In what ways does the entrepreneur differ from the typical senior director in a large company?

Equilibrium of the firm

The above analysis shows that all firms will strive to make sufficient profits in accounting terms to at least achieve their normal profit position. But will they be concerned to go further and achieve the largest profits possible, i.e. **maximise their profits**? Let us assume that this is the case and begin by examining a situation where profit maximisation is essential.

Perfect competition

The existence of perfect competition depends on a number of strict conditions prevailing in the market within which the firms operate:

1   All units of the good or service produced in the market are identical. This means that buyers will be influenced by no factors other than price.

2   All buyers and sellers have perfect knowledge of what is happening in the market so that no one buyer or seller has an advantage in terms of the information available to him or her.

3   Neither buyers nor sellers are individually able to influence the market price by their activities. So no one person deals in large enough quantities to affect the prevailing market conditions by their actions.

4   Buyers must have perfect mobility within the market so that they are not concerned with transport costs in deciding where to buy.

5   There must be perfect mobility of factors of production so that entrepreneurs can move freely from one market to another.

Of course, these conditions are impossible to find in the real world. Perfect competition is a model which keeps unpredictable behaviour to a minimum and from which we can deduce some of the characteristics of the behaviour of firms in real-life situations.

If the aim of the firm under perfect competition is to maximise its profits it must know at which output this optimum position will be attained. This is the output at which marginal revenue equals marginal cost. If MR>MC it will pay the firm to increase output since the extra revenue gained from producing one more unit will be greater than the extra cost incurred by producing that unit. If, however, MR<MC the firm will increase profit by reducing output as the loss in revenue from producing one less unit will be smaller than the reduction in costs. This point is illustrated in Table 7.2. As output is increased from 10 units to 11 MR = MC and profits reach a maximum. Any further increase in output will lead to MC being greater than MR and profits falling as a result. You will note that profits are actually the same when output is 10 units but not until output is 11 do we know that further expansion of profits is unattainable. The firm has then achieved **equilibrium output**.

The same principles apply even if a firm is making a loss. Then it should be striving to **minimise its losses**. Once again this will occur at the equilibrium output where MR = MC.

Short run equilibrium

We have seen that the perfectly competitive firm is unable to influence prevailing market conditions by its actions. This means that however much the firm produces it will always be able to sell that output at the existing market price. Since average revenue is equal to price it will be represented on a graph as a horizontal straight line parallel to the output axis, as in Figure 7.1. Similarly marginal revenue must also equal price as each extra unit sold yields the same revenue as the last. In Figure 7.3 this revenue line is combined with the firm's short-run cost curves. The firm's equilibrium

TABLE 7.2
Equilibrium output

Output	Price	Total Revenue	Average Revenue	Marginal Revenue	Marginal Cost	Average Cost	Total Cost	Profit
	(£)	(£)	(£)	(£)	(£)	(£)	(£)	(£)
1	30	30	30	—	—	17	17	13
2	29	58	29	28	2	9½	19	39
3	28	84	28	26	2	7	21	63
4	27	108	27	24	3	6	24	84
5	26	130	26	22	4	5.6	28	102
6	25	150	25	20	5	5½	33	117
7	24	168	24	18	6	5.6	39	129
8	23	184	23	16	7	5¾	46	138
9	22	198	22	14	8	6	54	144
10	21	210	21	12	9	6.3	63	147
11	20	220	20	10	10	6.6	73	147
12	19	228	19	8	11	7	84	144

output position is Q_2 where MR = MC. It is also the case that MR = MC at output Q_1 but this cannot be the equilibrium output since it does not include all the units between Q_1 and Q_2 whose production would add to profits. So we can see that the profit maximising (or loss minimising) output is where:

MC = MR, the MC curve having cut the MR line from below.

While the intersection of MR and MC determines at which output profits will be maximised it does not indicate how much these profits will be. This is ascertained by reference to the average revenue and average cost curves. At the profit maximising output the difference between AR and ATC represents the average profit (or loss) per unit produced and this average profit multiplied by the output yields the total profit because:

(AR − ATC) × output = (AR × output) − (AC × output) = TR − TC.

In Figure 7.3 this profit is shown by the rectangle *wxyz*. This profit is super-normal profit because the firm's normal profit is included in its total cost.

In the short run the firm may also be making a loss, as in Figure 7.4. Here the firm must make a loss since there is no output where TC is less than TR. MR = MC is thus the loss minimising output. Why produce at all if a loss will result? The answer lies in the fact that this is the short run where some costs are fixed and so must be met whether the firm produces or not. It will therefore pay the firm to produce as long as the losses which result are less than they would be if no production had taken place at all. The critical point is where AR = Minimum AVC. If AR < Minimum AVC production adds to losses while if AR > Minimum AVC losses will be reduced by entering into production. So:

AR (Price) = Minimum AVC = the firm's shutdown point

In Figure 7.4 AR is above AVC and therefore the firm will reduce its losses by producing where MR = MC. Nonetheless it will still have to bear the loss represented by the shaded area *wxyz*.

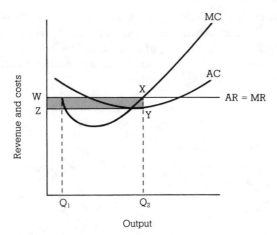

Figure 7.3 *Short run equilibrium I*

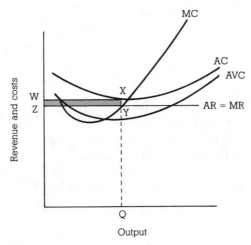

Figure 7.4 *Short run equilibrium II*

Long run equilibrium

In the long run all costs and all factors of production are variable so existing firms are free to leave the market and new ones enter it. Suppose that in the short run firms in the market were making super profits. In the long run new firms will be drawn into the market from less profitable ones. Now while individual firms are faced by a perfectly elastic demand curve (the AR line), the industry as a whole will face a conventional downward-sloping demand curve. The entry of new firms into the market will result in a shift in supply to the right so that the supply curve cuts the market demand curve at a lower price, as in Figure 7.5(a). This lower price is now the one received by firms in the market. With AR reduced and AC unchanged super-normal profits will be eradicated and when equilibrium is restored all firms will be earning only normal profit.

Where, on the other hand, firms are making losses in the short run they will shut down in the long run. This will shift the supply curve to the left, as in Figure 7.5(b), and push up the price, and thus the AR line, of individual firms. With AC unchanged those firms which remain in the industry will find their losses reduced and equilibrium will be restored when all firms are earning normal profits.

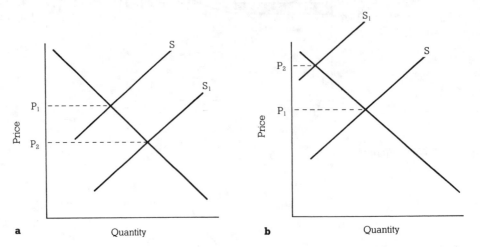

Figure 7.5 *Long run equilibrium*

The long-run position of the firm under perfect competition is shown in Figure 7.6. The equilibrium output is Q and here MR = MC = AC = AR. The firm is breaking even in that it is making neither losses nor super-normal profits. Since AC = MC average costs are at a minimum and resources are being used as efficiently as possible within the limitations imposed by the way production is organised. The industry is now also in equilibrium with no incentive for firms either to join or leave it.

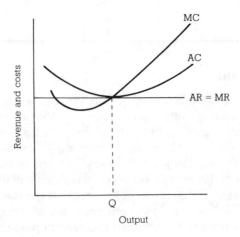

Figure 7.6 *Long run equilibrium*

One other point worth mentioning is the relationship between the firm's MC curve and its supply curve. Under perfect competition the firm's price, and therefore its AR and MR, are dictated to it. The firm produces where MR = MC so its output will be found where the prevailing market price intersects its MC curve. Any change in the market price will result in the AR = MR line crossing the MC curve at a different point and lead to a change in output, as in Figure 7.7. Since the firm's supply curve is the amount it will produce at different prices the MC curve and the firm's supply curve must be one and the same thing.

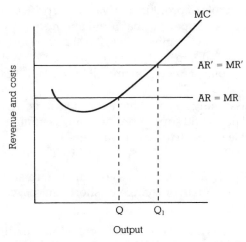

Figure 7.7 *Supply curve under perfect competition*

REVISION TEST

1 Name three of the characteristics of a perfectly competitive market.
2 Profit maximisation under perfect competition is where MR = ?
3 What is meant by the term 'homogenous product'?
4 Why does the firm under perfect competition face a perfectly elastic demand curve?
5 Why is the minimum AVC important for a firm in the short run?
6 If all firms are earning normal profits in the long run does this mean that they are all earning the same profits in accounting terms?
7 At which output does a firm maximise its profits?
8 A firm finds that if it produces 12 units it reaches its minimum AVC (£2). Its TR would then be £24. Should the firm produce in the short run?
9 Perfect competition never exists in the real world but can you think of any markets where the conditions come close to perfect competition?
10 Define free entry and exit to and from the market.

Examination questions

1   What are the conditions necessary for a firm to maximise its profits?
(ABE1, December 1986)

2   a)   Under what conditions might perfect competition exist?
    b)   Explain the conditions necessary for the equilibrium of the firm and industry in perfect competition.
(LCCI Higher, Autumn 1984)

3   a)   Explain the main role of profit in a private enterprise economy.
    b)   Distinguish between super-normal profit and normal profit.
    c)   Clive Richards decided to give up a £12 000 a year post as an architect, and to use his savings of £4000 to start up his own practice. At the end of the first year of trading his surplus, after deducting all his costs, is £24 000.
    Calculate:
    i)   His profit assuming he could have earned 8 per cent on his £4000 savings.
    ii) His normal profit and super-normal profit, assuming that Clive has decided he needs at least £8000 to stay in business.
(LCCI, Intermediate, Autumn, 1986)

4   Why will a firm which is making excess or super-normal profits in conditions of perfect competition maintain or change its short-run cost curve in the long run?
(ICSA, June 1986)

5   Explain carefully what is meant by 'normal profits' and discuss whether the level or rate of normal profits must be the same in every industry.
(ICSA, December 1987)

6   Explain how a producer operating under conditions of perfect competition can make super-normal profits. Is it possible for these to continue in the long run?
(ICSA, June 1988)

7   a)   What is the difference between fixed and variable costs?
    b)   What factors should a firm take into account before deciding whether to close down?
(ACCA, June 1987)

8   Explain why a firm in perfect competition may continue in the production of goods which it can only sell at a loss and why it cannot continue to do this indefinitely.
(ACCA, December 1988)

9   Describe the function of the entrepreneur and explain in detail the complex nature of his reward.
(CIMA, November 1989)

10 To what extent are accountants and economists at odds over how to measure 'costs'?
(SCCA, November 1988)

11 Explain why a firm will eventually go out of business if it cannot cover its costs.
(Cert.M., June 1986)

8 Monopoly power

- *Why is monopoly always regarded as inefficient?*
- *What are the limitations on monopoly power and how can the monopolist get round them?*

Monopoly

We have seen that the perfect competitor has no control over the market. The firm is subject totally to market forces and is unable to influence the market price by its actions. The monopoly is the opposite to the perfect competitor. It is the only supplier and therefore dominates the market by its activities. Indeed a *perfect* monopoly would be the exact opposite of the perfect competitor with absolute control over both the supply and the price charged for that supply. In fact the perfect monopoly is unattainable. Even if a firm supplied a product which was essential to life, such as water in the desert, it could not raise the price indefinitely without demand falling as some consumers could simply no longer afford it. A policy of raising the price indefinitely would mean that eventually the only person who could afford to buy the product would be the monopolist himself!

In the real world there is neither perfect competition nor perfect monopoly. All firms possess some monopoly power in that they exert control over the market within which they operate to a greater or lesser extent. To begin with let us consider the strongest form of market power; the monopoly. The monopolist is the sole supplier and can control either the price charged or the total output, but not both. This is because the demand curve for the market is also the demand curve for the firm. The monopolist either sets the price and sells the quantity demanded at that price or it determines the output and takes whatever price that point on the demand curve can command. Any increase in output, therefore, can only be sold if the monopolist is prepared to lower its price.

The equilibrium of the monopolist

The monopolist's AR line corresponds to its demand curve and is downward sloping with AR falling as output is increased. The MR line will also be downward sloping and be beneath AR because, when the firm lowers its price to sell one extra unit, it must cut its price to existing customers too, so the sale of the extra unit adds less to total revenue than its own price. The cost curves of the monopolist, on the other hand, are similar to those of the perfect competitor with a 'U'-shaped average cost curve cut at its lowest point by the marginal cost curve. The monopolist also shares with the perfect competitor a profit-maximising output where MR = MC. In Figure 8.1 the monopolist has a profit-maximising output of Q where MR = MC. Super-normal profits are shown by the rectangle *abcd*.

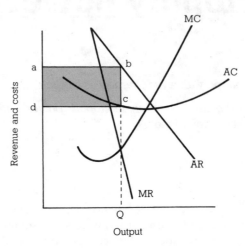

Figure 8.1 *Equilibrium of the monopolist*

Monopoly and perfect competition compared

Despite some similarities there are several important differences in the profit-maximising equilibrium of monopoly compared to that of perfect competition:

1 There is not the same distinction between short-run and long-run equilibrium in monopoly as there is under perfect competition. At first sight the situation in Figure 8.1 might be thought of as short-run because of the existence of super-normal profits. In fact these super-normal profits will persist in the long-run because they are not eroded by the entry of new firms into the industry. Despite the super-normal profits to be made firms are unable to enter the industry because of barriers to entry such as:

   a) *Costs of entry* Many major industries have built up a huge and complex infrastructure over the years which would provide insurmountable difficulties for a new firm. The problems facing a firm attempting to set up in competition with British Gas, for example, would be enormous.

   b) *Patents and licences* Sometimes a monopoly is protected by law from competition, such as the franchises given to television and radio companies.

   c) *Intimidation* Profits built up and retained over the years can be used in a price war to see off new rivals. A monopolist may even resort to sabotage to prevent new competition.

   d) *Economies of scale* An established firm may have achieved major economies of scale which enable it to produce at much lower costs than any new or smaller firm. The likeliest long-run change for the monopolist is that it will be able to exploit more efficient production methods, thereby reducing average costs and increasing profits.

2   If the monopolist is making losses in the short run it will leave the industry in the long run and the industry will disappear.

3   Under monopoly the effect of an increase in demand will be that a higher output is produced at a higher price. Under perfect competition the same situation will prevail in the short run. In the long run, however, the entry of new firms into a perfectly competitive industry will result in a shift of the supply curve to the right so that the long run price reverts to the level it was before the increase in demand, though at a greater level of output.

4   The profit-maximising output of the monopolist is lower than its most efficient output (where AC is at a minimum). This is because MC cuts MR before it cuts AC. Thus the monopolist produces at a higher average cost than a firm operating on a similar basis under perfect competition.

5   Since the monopolist will at least break even its AR (price) will be equal to or higher than its AC at its profit-maximising output. Since its AC is higher than that of a comparable firm under perfect competition its AR, and therefore its price, must also be higher than that of the firm under perfect competition.

6   These last two points mean that, all things being equal, the output of a monopolist will be lower and its price higher than that of a firm under perfect competition.

On the face of it, therefore, there are strong arguments against monopoly when compared to perfect competition. Most of these stem from the fact that the super-normal profits of monopolies persist in the long run.

1   **Monopoly is less innovative**   Without competition the monopolist lacks the incentive to innovate in order to stay ahead of its rivals and so tends towards technical stagnation.

2   **Monopoly is less efficient**   The most efficient output is that where average cost is at a minimum and the monopolist's profit-maximising output is *never* at this point. The existence of super-normal profits also enables the monopolist to tolerate diseconomies of scale and other inefficiencies within its cost structure.

3   **Monopoly is against the interests of consumers**   Consumers suffer because prices are higher and total output lower than would be the case under perfect competition. In addition, the super-normal profits earned by the monopolist are received at the expense of the consumer.

The first criticism of monopoly assumes that the perfect competitor will have a much greater incentive to innovate. This is because the perfect competitor can only make super-normal profits in the short run and so has a recurring incentive to establish a market advantage through lower costs. While this hypothesis cannot be tested in the real world one must have doubts about whether this would always be the case. It is difficult to see the incentive to innovate when, in a relatively short time, the firm's rivals will copy its success and cancel out any advantage. The monopolist, on the other hand, knows that barriers to entry will prevent new firms breaking into the industry, while patent laws limit the extent to which potential rivals can copy its products or processes. So increased profits resulting from innovation will not be wiped out in the long run. In any case the monopolist, with its reserves accumulated from past super-normal profits, would seem to have far greater resources available for innovation. On balance, therefore, the monopolist would seem to have a greater incentive to innovate than the perfect competitor.

The second criticism of monopoly is only unquestionably valid if we are comparing a monopolist with a perfect competitor operating under *the same technical conditions*. If the monopolist has introduced new low-cost methods of production and achieved greater economies of scale it will be producing *more* efficiently than could a firm under perfect competition. The misallocation of resources by the monopolist in producing at less than the optimum output is thus outweighed by the increased absolute efficiency achieved through technical progress and the reduction in average costs. The lower costs so achieved will even be able to accommodate the existence of diseconomies of scale within the monopolist's structure.

The third criticism is the most difficult to refute. Where the monopolist is operating under the same technical conditions as the perfect competitor the monopolist's price will be higher and output lower. Any improvements in the production process which result in lower average costs will not be passed on to the consumer but will result in higher super-normal profits for the monopolist. However, the position of the monopolist in relation to the consumer is not quite as powerful as it might appear at first sight. While the firm may be the only one operating in the industry it will have competition from other industries which provide a close substitute. So the Post Office receives competition from telecommunications, British Coal from gas and electricity and so on. The monopoly will balance its desire for higher profits with the need to ensure that customers do not find even unsatisfactory alternatives more attractive. Nonetheless, it is this area of monopoly which stands up least well against perfect competition.

REVISION TEST

1 Define the term 'monopoly'.

2 Draw the demand curve of a perfect monopoly, explaining the reason for its shape.

3 Why is the long-run average cost curve of the monopolist likely to be shallower and lower than that of the perfect competitor?

4 Explain the term 'barriers to entry'.

5 Why do monopolies tend to suffer from diseconomies of scale?

6 How may the consumer be better off if an industry is a monopoly rather than operating under perfect competition?

7 Explain how the MR line tells us whether demand for a monopolist's product is price elastic or price inelastic.

8   Why is the difference between long run and short run of less importance to the monopolist than the perfect competitor?

9   Which barriers to entry encourage, and which discourage, innovation?

10 Must the monopolist always make super-normal profits?

Price discrimination

We have seen that the limiting power of the monopolist is that it can control either the price or the output, but not both. If the monopolist wishes to increase sales it must cut its price, even to those who would be prepared to pay the higher price. But what if it were possible to charge each buyer the maximum price he or she would pay? The monopolist would then greatly increase its revenue, and therefore its profits. The practice of charging different prices to different buyers is known as *price discrimination*. Its effect can be seen in Table 8.1.

TABLE 8.1
Price discrimination

Before discrimination

Price (£)	Sales	TR	AR	MR
10	10	100	10	—
9	13	117	9	4¼
8	15	120	8	1½
7	16	102	7	−18

After discrimination

Price (£)	Marginal sales	TR	AR	MR
10	—	100	10	—
9	3	127	9.7	9
8	2	143	9.5	8
7	1	150	9.4	7

Table 8.1 shows that without price discrimination the maximum attainable revenue is 120. When price discrimination is introduced the monopolist charges each customer willing to pay 10 that price, those willing to pay 9 that price and so on. The result is that total revenue can be increased indefinitely by further price reductions and the firm will be able profitably to expand output as long as MR>MC. The MR curve replaces the AR curve as the firm's demand curve and the AR curve shifts to a higher position than before. The effect of price discrimination is that a discriminating monopoly will produce a higher output and receive a higher total revenue than a single price monopoly. Of course, price discrimination is not confined to monopolies. Any firm with some monopoly power will be able to practice price discrimination.

Conditions necessary for price discrimination

Price discrimination is not always a practical proposition. Two conditions are necessary in order for the firm to be able to put it into practice.

First, the different markets must be clearly separated so that the seller is able to control what is offered to each buyer. The markets may be differentiated by place, as with the home market and export market; by time, as with off-peak as opposed to standard tickets on trains, or by age as with cheaper cinema tickets for children and senior citizens.

Second, the seller must be able to prevent resale from one buyer to another otherwise customers charged the lower prices could buy more than they needed and sell the surplus to customers who would normally be charged higher prices. Price discrimination is therefore more successful when:

1   The firm is selling in self-contained markets where distance or accessibility prevent buyers from moving between markets. Thus a shop with branches in London and Newcastle can charge a few pence less per item in the Newcastle shop since Londoners would not find it worth their while to travel north to save such a small sum.

2   The firm is providing a service rather than a tangible good so that resale is impossible, or at least very difficult. Price discrimination is therefore common in hairdressing, medical treatment and transport.

3   The firm is selling capital rather than consumer goods, especially when the capital goods are fixed in location. Thus discrimination is more likely in the installation of central heating or fitted kitchens than in electric fires or domestic appliances.

Price discrimination is clearly beneficial to the monopolist since it enables profits to be increased, and because it benefits the monopolist we might assume that it must harm the consumer. This view is supported by the fact that, using discrimination, the monopolist manipulates the market to extract the highest possible price from every consumer. However, it can be argued that discrimination adds to the total satisfaction of consumers since some who would not otherwise have obtained the product now do so while those who pay higher prices would have done so anyway. It is also the case that resources are used more efficiently by a discriminating monopoly than a single-price one as output more nearly equates to what it would be if the market were a perfectly competitive one.

Monopolistic competition

In the real world even the imperfect monopoly examined in the previous sections is rare. Most markets are populated by a number of firms, all of which have some control over the market, albeit sometimes a very limited one. All these firms enjoy a degree of monopoly power in line with their control of the market and the form of market in which this monopoly power is at its weakest is that of monopolistic competition. Monopolistic competition describes a market in which there are many sellers, all producing goods or services which are similar but capable of being differentiated by customers. Each of the many firms in the market will be too small to dominate it so its actions will have only a marginal influence on the behaviour of other firms and of consumers. The differentiation between sellers may be one of location, time or convenience as much as any identifiable difference between products. In Figure 8.2 two garages are located on an arterial road, one each side of the dual carriageway. Since cars cannot get from one side of the road to the other for several miles in either direction each garage can ignore competition from the other. However, if one raised its prices so much that it became economical for a motorist to drive on to the next intersection and turn round (twice) to go to the other garage, it would clearly lose some custom. It would not lose customers in a hurry or those too low on petrol to consider a long detour. Both garages must beware that if they raise their prices too much motorists will fill up before or after they travel on the road. Other examples of monopolistic competition are local shops which stay open at different times and small-scale manufacturers like high-quality tailors or jewellers.

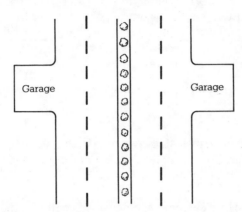

Figure 8.2 *Monopolistic competitors*

The demand (AR) curve of the monopolistic competitor, like that of the monopolist, slopes downwards. If it raises its price some of its customers will switch to other sellers. However, it will not lose all its customers as it will enjoy some product loyalty or advantages of location or time, even if it is charging more than its rivals. Similarly a cut in prices will attract some, but not all, of the customers of other firms in the market. Because no firm is large enough to dominate the market, existing firms will be powerless to prevent new firms entering the market in the long run if the profits are attractive enough. So equilibrium for the firm varies from short run to long run.

Figure 8.3(a) illustrates the short-run equilibrium of the firm under monopolistic competition. You will recognise it as identical to that of the monopolist shown in Figure 8.1. However, the existence of super-normal profits means that new firms will be attracted into the industry in the long run. These new firms will take customers away from existing sellers so that they now sell less than before at each price. The result is that the demand curve for each firm is pushed downward so that it must lower its prices in order to retain the same share of the market. Super-normal profits are thereby eroded and the new equilibrium is found where AR = AC so that all firms break even and make only normal profits, as shown in Figure 8.3(b). There will be no incentive for firms to leave the industry while normal profits are being made.

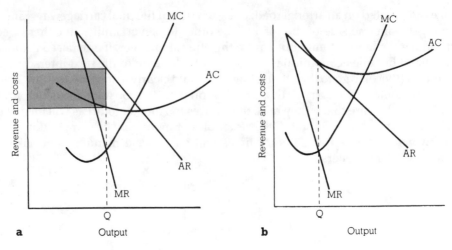

Figure 8.3 *Equilibrium under monopolistic competition*

Characteristics of monopolistic competition

1 The long-run equilibrium of the industry resembles that of perfect competition whereby all firms break even.

2 As firms are liable to lose customers to new firms entering the industry they tend to suffer from excess capacity, i.e. productive resources are being under-utilised.

3 Like a monopolist the firm produces below the optimum output but it may be too small to exploit economies of scale. Resources are therefore used less efficiently than under perfect competition.

4 Product differentiation means that the customer has more choice than under either monopoly or perfect competition.

Oligopoly

In the modern world industry and commerce are dominated by large firms with monopoly powers approaching those of the monopolist. The term **oligopoly** is used to describe a market dominated by a few firms. Typically there will be between three and six suppliers in the market but there may be as few as two so that the oligopoly is referred to as a **duopoly**. Two types of oligopoly may be distinguished. First, there are those industries in which the firms produce identical or extremely similar products such as the oil or tobacco industries, or the clearing banks. Second those industries where the firms sell differentiated products such as the chocolate or newspaper industries.

The tendency is for industries in the latter category to evolve into the former as with the motor industry since the 1950s.

The behaviour of oligopolistic firms is too complicated to be examined purely in terms of the maximisation of profits and monopoly power; it will be considered in some depth in the next chapter.

REVISION TEST

1 What would be the effect of a successful advertising campaign on the average revenue line of a monopolistic competitor?

2 What are the two conditions necessary for the monopolist to practice price discrimination?

3 Why is it easier to practice price discrimination with a service than a commodity?

4 What happens to the monopolist's MR line when it introduces price discrimination?

5 Define 'monopoly power'.

6 Give three ways in which monopolistic competition differs from perfect competition.

7 Is the industry or profession within which you work characterised by monopoly, monopolistic competition or oligopoly?

8 Define 'excess capacity'.

9 What is a duopoly?

10 Why might a firm leave a monopolistically competitive industry in the long run?

Examination questions

1 What barriers operate to prevent the entrance of a company into a new market?
(ABE1, December 1985)

2 The theories of perfect competition and monopoly are based upon assumptions which do not prevail in the real world. What, then, is the purpose of building such models?
(ABE1, June 1987)

3 Explain the major differences existing between monopoly and perfect competition as market situations.
(LCCI Higher, spring 1985)

4 a) Explain what you understand by monopolistic competition.
 b) Distinguish between the long- and the short-term equilibrium position of a firm operating in such a situation.
(LCCI Higher, November 1985)

5 a) Explain the short- and long-run equilibrium positions of a firm operating under conditions of monopolistic competition.
   b) Assess the extent to which monopolistic competition is wasteful.

(LCCI Higher, Spring 1987)

6 a) Explain the equilibrium of the firm under conditions of monopolistic competition.
   b) State the consequences for the firm's profits of the following:
      i) An increase in interest rates.
      ii) A successful advertising campaign.

(LCCI Higher, Spring 1986)

7 How does a profit-maximising monopolist decide the quantity of goods to produce and the price to be charged?

(ICSA, June 1986)

8 'The price charged by a monopolist is always higher than the price that would be charged were the same goods produced under conditions of perfect competition.' Discuss.

(ICSA, December 1986)

9 How will a monopolist adjust price and/or output if there is a decrease in the demand for his product?

(ICSA, June 1988)

10 Under conditions of perfect competition, a firm's price is likely to be lower and its output higher than under monopoly conditions. Explain the reasons for this.

(ACCA, December 1987)

11 What market conditions are necessary to enable a company to practice price discrimination? How may it do so?

(CIMA, November 1988)

12 What is a market? State the conditions necessary for a perfect market and describe the factors which cause imperfections.

(CIMA, November 1989)

13 What, to the economist, is meant by 'profit'? How will profits differ between a perfectly competitive industry, a monopolist, and an industry where monopolistic competition prevails?

(SCCA, May 1988)

14 What is 'price discrimination'? What factors will make it easier for a firm to engage in it?

(SCCA, November 1987)

15 Explain why the marginal cost curve of a firm is assumed to be its supply curve if it is in a competitive industry but not if it has monopoly power.

(Cert.M., June 1987)

16 Explain what is meant by price discrimination. Consider the conditions necessary for its successful implementation.

(Cert.M., June 1987)

17 Examine the argument that, under perfect competition, price is lower, output is higher, and resources are more optimally allocated than under monopoly.

(Cert.M., November 1987)

18 What are the theoretical assumptions and predictions in the model of monopolistic competition?

(Cert.M., June 1988)

19 How might a producer who wishes to adopt a policy of price discrimination segment his market?

(Cert.M., December 1988)

20 'Price discrimination is an effective strategy in the market place and one which is frequently used by suppliers.'
Consider the conditions necessary for its successful implementation giving examples of where it has been applied.

(IPS, May 1988)

21 Compare and contrast the long-run equilibrium position of the firm under conditions of perfect competition and that of monopoly.

(IFA, December 1989)

9 Oligopoly and alternatives to profit maximisation

- *Why do large companies often compete on everything but price?*
- *What other objectives might a firm pursue apart from profits?*

Oligopoly

In the last chapter oligopoly was briefly introduced as a market form in which a few firms dominate production and pricing policy. In isolation the oligopolistic firm's equilibrium might be expected to resemble that of the monopolist; but the oligopolist does not operate in isolation. Since each firm is large enough to exercise considerable control over the market its actions will impinge on the operations of its rivals to a degree far greater than under monopolistic competition. Any new marketing initiative or product development by one firm which results in a doubling of its market share may be of minor significance under conditions of monopolistic competition but it will have an enormous impact in an oligopolistic market. So any such innovation by an oligopolist is likely to provoke a rapid response from the other firms in the industry in order to protect their market share. Before embarking on any action, therefore, a firm must try to gauge the likely response of other firms in the industry to see whether the intended action is worthwhile. One example might be a new advertising campaign:

1 The campaign may not work so that the firm has wasted resources without increasing sales or market share. Other firms need take no action to preserve their market share.

2 The campaign increases sales for a short time but then the other firms retaliate by increasing their own advertising expenditure. Eventually market shares return to their original position so that all firms have lost through an increase in costs.

3 The extra advertising expenditure leads to higher sales but the extra costs incurred are not matched by the extra revenue so generated. This may be due either to the relative ineffectiveness of the campaign or to retaliation by other firms in the market reducing its impact. The firm has increased sales at the expense of profits.

4 The campaign results in both higher sales and higher profits. Other firms are either unable or unwilling to respond effectively.

Of these four outcomes only the last is satisfactory. In two of the other three cases the response of other firms in the industry has contributed to the ultimate failure of the company's policy. In one case the firm fails on its own so retaliation by other firms was unnecessary.

Game theory

Considering the potential damage to the firm's aims of retaliation by its competitors, it is not unreasonable to assume that an oligopolistic firm will be ever-mindful of the likely reaction of its competitors to any action it is contemplating. So much use has been made of game theory to try to predict the behaviour of oligopolists. Game theory, in this context, involves the study of rational strategies in small group situations. Predictions are then made as to the behaviour which will be followed if each firm acts rationally in its desire to achieve its objectives. Game theory relies on the participants being aware in advance of the likely result of their actions and assumes that they will act rationally in choosing their course of action. Neither condition can be relied upon always to hold true in the oligopolistic market.

When judged by their behaviour, oligopolistic markets display a tendency towards price stability with a marked lack of price competition between the participants. This is hardly surprising. When price wars do break out they are often disastrous, each firm able through its vast resources to sustain price cuts for a long period during which profits are reduced or even wiped out. Nor will a firm wish to raise prices for fear that other firms in the market will not raise theirs and so attract its customers. With each firm aware of the potential dangers of price competition it will have a vested interest in the maintenance of stable prices.

The kinked demand curve

This is an attempt to represent diagrammatically the tendency for the oligopolist to be driven by self-interest towards stable prices. It is assumed, as is usually the case, that the competing firms are selling similar but not identical products. This product differentiation means that the product of one firm is not a perfect substitute for those of its rivals. If the firm cuts its price it will attract some, but not all of the customers of the other firms. Similarly, if it raises its price it will lose some, but not all, of its customers to its competitors. Thus far the situation resembles that of monopolistic competition. However, unlike those of the monopolistic competitor, the actions of the oligopolist will have a marked impact on the other firms in the industry and will provoke a response. If we start with a stable market in which all the firms are making satisfactory profits there are two possible scenarios.

1   One firm raises its price. As the other firms sell very similar products they need take no action to improve their position. Customers will switch from the dearer product to those of the other firms and these firms will see their revenue and profits rise at the expense of the price-raising firm.

2   One firm lowers its price. The other firms will experience a slump in sales as their customers switch to the cheaper product. Faced with a fall in revenue and profits,

they will cut their prices to restore their competitiveness. The result is that all firms have the same market share as before but with a lower total revenue and profits.

So if one firm raises its price it will lose out while if one firm lowers its price all the firms in the industry will eventually lose. This situation results in the individual firm having a 'kinked' demand curve, as shown in Figure 9.1.

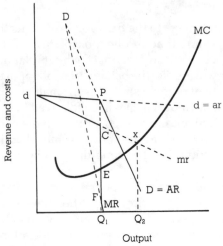

Figure 9.1 *The kinked demand curve*

In Figure 9.1 DD represents the firm's demand curve when all sellers move prices together; dd is the demand curve when one firm changes its price independently of the others. The prevailing market price is at P and it is at this price that firms tend to stick. If the firm raises its price demand curve dd will operate as demand for the firm's product proves price elastic. If, on the other hand, the firm cuts its price demand curve DD operates. Other firms cut their prices too and so the firm finds demand unresponsive to its price cut.

Note that MR is also kinked and is a straight line between points C and F. In consequence, there is a wide range of possible MC curves which would all cut the MR line at output Q_1. So even a considerable variation in costs would leave the most profitable level of output at Price P and Quantity Q_1. This point reinforces the argument that oligopolies tend towards stable prices.

Despite the plausibility of the kinked demand curve it has received little support from empirical testing. This is due to the fact that the theory is unable to incorporate many of the variables inherent in the complicated interactions of oligopolistic firms.

1   The theory assumes that the oligopolists are supplying products which are close substitutes. This may not be the case, and even if it is firms are likely to try to increase product differentiation through design and advertising.

2   An increase in price by one firm may lead the others to follow suit rather than take no action, as the theory would predict. This may be because rising costs force all firms to raise their prices or because the firms have an agreement to increase prices together.

3   The tendency for prices to be stable may be nothing to do with a kinked demand curve. Firms might be reluctant to change prices because of the administrative costs involved or because they have incomplete information about the price elasticity of demand of their products.

4   The theory assumes that the prevailing price has already been established but does not show how this would have come about.

Oligopolistic pricing

There are a number of ways in which the prevailing price within the oligopoly may become established.

1   Price leadership

Here one firm sets a price and the others follow it. This might indicate a situation where one firm is much more powerful than the others and is able to exert price leadership as a **dominant firm**. The other firms will always follow it for fear of sparking off a price-war in which the dominant firm would ultimately win. Thus Sealink, with over a third of the total traffic, has tended to take the lead in determining cross-channel passenger fares.

However, price leadership may be undertaken by a firm other than the dominant one. This will occur when one firm is regarded by all the others as having a special insight into prevailing market conditions. This is known as **barometric-firm** leadership. In 1989 it was Lloyds, the smallest of the 'Big Four' clearing banks, which took the lead in introducing interest-paying current accounts, the others following almost immediately. Just as frequently the lead on pricing will alternate between two or three equally powerful firms, as in the UK petroleum industry.

2   Price collusion

This is where the firms act together to fix prices. Such collusion may be an informal arrangement whereby the members consciously keep their prices in step with each other. Often this type of arrangement will be marked by regular meetings by the participants to discuss price and output policies. Alternatively, there may be a formal cartel with a binding, written agreement to ensure adherence to a minimum price.

The more co-ordinated and effective the price agreement the nearer the firms will come to joint profit maximisation whereby the combined profits of the oligopolists are those that would be earned if the market were controlled by a profit-maximising monopoly.

3   Entry-limit pricing

While price collusion will aim to ensure that prices are higher than they would be under open competition, the cartel may stop short of imposing a price which maximises joint profits. This is because high profits may attract new entrants into the market and reduce both the market share and the profits of existing firms. Thus the **limit price** is the highest price which existing firms feel they can charge without attracting new entrants.

In each case the effect is that a market price is established to which all the members of the oligopoly adhere. In such circumstances not every firm can be maximising its profits. In fact, it is far more likely that none of the oligopolists is either maximising its profits or producing where MR = MC since each will be able to make super-normal profits without operating at their equilibrium output. In setting their prices, therefore, most oligopolists use **cost-plus pricing**. The firm calculates its average variable cost and adds to this a percentage to cover fixed costs and provide a profit margin. The price agreed by the cartel must enable every member to obtain its minimum acceptable cost-plus price.

Cartels

Cartels are often highly formalised structures under the name of a trade association or similar term. It is the role of the trade association to ensure that agreements on prices are adhered to by the members. Typically, the cartel price will be geared to providing some profit to the weakest member and so will give substantial profit margins to the stronger, more efficient firms.

More unusually, the cartel will have an output agreement whereby each firm is allocated an output quota in order to restrict total market output and protect the price level. In its most extreme form this sort of agreement could lead to the establishment of a marketing board to distribute the members' output. The industry would then have the external appearance of a monopoly.

However well-organised the cartel it faces two major threats, one external the other internal.

Externally, the attractive profits made by the cartel may lure new firms into the industry. One defence against this likelihood, as we saw above, is the use of entry-limit pricing. The other is the existence of **barriers to entry** which prevent new firms entering the industry. These include:

1 **Economies of scale**   Existing large firms are likely to enjoy scale advantages denied to a new, smaller firm attempting to enter the industry.

2 **Restrictive trade practices**   Members of the cartel may put pressure on distributors by dealing only with those who agree to take the products of cartel members to the exclusion of other suppliers. Alternatively they may offer 'loyalty' rebates to dealers who deal exclusively with cartel members to deter them from giving new firms a trial order. To impose retailer loyalty they may go so far as to impose minimum retail prices and withdraw supplies from retailers who cut prices. They may also prevent new firms from obtaining raw materials or essential components by putting pressure on suppliers.

3 **Marketing campaigns**   The members of the cartel will be able to sustain a price war longer than a newcomer with limited reserves. They may therefore cut their prices drastically in order to see off a newcomer. Alternatively, they may mount a very expensive advertising campaign to force up the new firm's costs as it tries to respond in kind.

The internal threat to the cartel comes from the fact that each member is driven by two contradictory ambitions. On the one hand it sees the wisdom of co-operation within the cartel to protect profits and exclude potential new competitors. On the other, it retains a competitive instinct and will seek opportunities to gain an advantage over its rivals. If in Figure 9.1 the oligopolist could cut its price without attracting retaliation it would have the demand curve dd below P. It would then be able to attract customers away from its rivals with the MC curve cutting the MR line at point x and an output of Q_2. So firms will be tempted to evade cartel agreements on prices and output, particularly if they are the more efficient members of the cartel with low costs and under-utilised capacity. This evasion is likely to take the form of 'under the counter' discounts to customers and increases in production without notifying the cartel. Should they come to light, such practices will inevitably provoke retaliation and may well strain the cartel to breaking point. This is especially the case in a declining industry where excess capacity may start a scramble among cartel members to hang on to their market share which results in price agreements and output quotas breaking down completely.

While it is not inevitable that a cartel will collapse, it is always subject to considerable strain from the pressures outlined above. In consequence many industries display long periods of price collusion punctuated by bursts of fierce price competition. In the mid-1970s the three large mass-production bakeries engaged in a lengthy price war as they fought for a shrinking market. By the time the situation had stabilised one of the firms, Spillers-French, had withdrawn from the industry entirely. Some of the best examples of cartel behaviour are found in the oil industry. The Organisation of Petroleum Exporting Countries (OPEC) includes many of the world's major oil producers and sets both prices and output quotas for its members. Despite its success in forcing up oil prices after 1970, it has not been able to prevent member countries breaking rank and producing above their quotas, so pushing world prices down. Within the UK the major petroleum companies have frequently subsidised price wars between distributors with each company paying large discounts to its own distributors.

Non-price competition

We have seen that oligopolies are characterised by stable prices as firms seek to avoid potentially destructive price wars, not always successfully. But the firms' competitive instincts remain and these tend to be channelled into non-price forms of competition, especially when the firms have agreements on price levels.

Advertising

The importance of advertising in oligopolistic markets stems from the need to accentuate product differentiation in the absence of price differentiation. The role of advertising in this context assumes greater significance if the actual differences between the products of the competitors become less obvious. This is likely to be the case as an oligopoly develops and each firm imitates the successes of its rivals. In the motor industry, for example, each major producer offers a model in the main size and price categories, frequently very similar in specification, etc. to those of its rivals. Advertising enables such differences as there are to be highlighted.

Advertising also promotes brand loyalty, particularly important in such industries as tobacco, detergents and convenience foods where product differentiation relies almost exclusively on a strong brand image.

Branding

By producing under a variety of brand names the firm can convince customers that they have a far greater choice than is actually the case, particularly if subsidiary company names are used on the labelling rather than that of the parent company. Indeed, such practices may be essential if, following a takeover, the firm is to retain those customers who had a strong brand loyalty to the products of the firm it has acquired.

The use of several brand names for relatively similar products may be a way of taking a larger share of the market, especially if consumers exhibit a low degree of brand loyalty. The more brands the firm has the greater the likelihood that a customer who changes brand will switch to one of this company's brands. So we see the soap-powder duopoly of Unilever and Procter & Gamble marked by brand names which run well into double figures.

Sponsorship

This is probably the fastest growing form of non-price competition. By sponsoring sports, charities and the arts the large firm can obtain both free and good publicity. Such sponsorship has proved particularly attractive for the tobacco companies who are barred from advertising cigarettes on television in the UK. In addition, it is relatively cheap as the company's name or brand will be in the public eye for a fraction of the cost that advertising time of the same proportions would entail.

Promotions

There is a whole array of incentives which may be offered to the public to induce them to change to, or persevere with, a particular brand. These include competitions, free gifts and introductory offers (which may include a lower price for a limited period). One of the most common promotions is the offer linked to the collection of labels or packet-tops. This may take the form of a cash refund or a joint-marketing promotion whereby another product is obtained at a reduced price.

REVISION TEST

1   Is oligopoly more like monopoly or monopolistic competition? Give two areas in which this is so.

2   How would you describe an industry with 10 firms, one of which controls 90 per cent of total output?

3   Why is the impact of the actions of one firm on its rivals greater in oligopoly than in monopolistic competition?

4   Why is game theory considered particularly pertinent to oligopoly?

5   What causes the kink in the 'kinked demand curve'?

6   Is the market demand curve under oligopoly kinked?

7   Give three examples of how a firm can increase product differentiation.

8   What is the difference between dominant-firm and barometric-firm price leadership?

9   Define the term 'cartel'.

10   How would you distinguish between branding and design as ways of achieving product differentiation?

Alternatives to profit maximisation

The theory of the firm is based on the assumption that the firm's objective is the maximisation of profits. Under perfect competition this will indeed be the case since the firm can only survive by achieving its profit maximising output. In the real world, however, imperfections in the market permit firms to survive and make large profits without maximising their profits. In oligopolistic markets, as we have seen, firms may well sacrifice any attempt to maximise profits for the assured profits which will arise from membership of a cartel. Freed from the need to maximise its profits the firm may well consider the attainment of other objectives. This tendency is further reinforced by the fact that in large companies the managers are not the owners and so have an interest in profits only to the extent that they are accountable to shareholders for the success of the company.

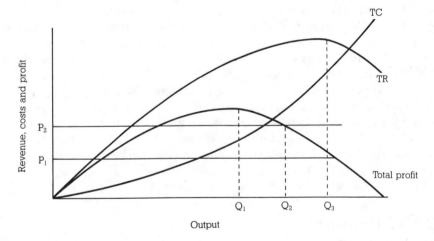

Figure 9.2 *Sales maximisation*

Sales maximisation

Managers who are concerned with growth and prestige may pursue this objective, especially if, as under oligopoly, there are limitations on their ability to pursue profit maximisation. The theory of sales maximisation assumes that the firm will seek the maximum level of sales consistent with its own minimum acceptable level of profit. Under *pure* sales maximisation the firm will produce an output where marginal revenue is zero and total revenue is at a maximum. If this level of output would cause profits to fall below their acceptable minimum the firm must reduce output to remedy the shortfall; it is then operating under *constrained* sales maximisation. A comparison of the firm's output under conditions of both forms of sales maximisation and profit maximisation is shown in Figure 9.2.

In Figure 9.2 the output under profit maximisation is represented by Q_1. The constrained sales maximisation output with a minimum profit requirement of P_2 is Q_2 while Q_3 represents the pure sales maximisation output with a profit requirement of P_1. Not only is output higher under sales maximisation than under profit maximisation but price is lower since the higher output can only be sold at a lower price.

Pure sales maximisation is unlikely to occur in practice because firms could expand their sales indefinitely by increasing marketing expenditure until higher costs reduced profits to their minimum acceptable level. The constrained sales maximisation which does occur will be accompanied by a much higher expenditure on marketing than would be the case under conditions of profit maximisation.

Growth maximisation

Clearly both the managers and the owners of a large company have an interest in their firm's success, though for different reasons. The manager is concerned with increasing the sales of the company to add to his personal status and to enhance his career prospects. The owner-shareholder wishes to see the capital value of the company grow, and with it his or her personal wealth and dividend income. The aims of these two groups may lead to conflict if the managers wish to plough profits back into the business to finance further expansion while the shareholders want more of the firm's profits to be distributed as dividends. The firm's growth resolves this dilemma by enabling the aims of both managers and owners to be achieved. It can be argued, therefore, that the objective of the firm is growth maximisation.

It is important to note that in order to keep both managers and owners content the firm must seek a balance between operational growth and capital/dividend growth. Too much emphasis on the former may restrict profit distribution and make disgruntled shareholders susceptible to a takeover bid; too little retention of profits will make the firm unable to undertake the capital investment necessary for continued growth. So the objective of the firm will be to maximise **balanced growth**.

Behavioural theories

The theory of growth maximisation recognises that a large company is likely to contain factional interests with different objectives rather than one aim like profit maximisation or sales maximisation. But it also believes that all a firm's energies can be directed towards one goal, that of growth.

Behavioural theories regard the firm as being made up of a number of diverse interests, including shareholders, managers, workers and customers. Each group has its own objectives and these are likely to be in conflict with those of other groups. The aims of the shareholders, for example, are likely to be very different to those of the workforce with regard to the distribution of rewards within the firm. The objectives of the company at any one time will reflect the current strengths of the different groups within the organisation. If the company wins a large order from a powerful new customer demanding firm delivery dates, the bargaining power of the workforce will increase against other interests in the company.

Against such a background of diverse interests and conflicting objectives there is little scope for the maximisation of any one objective. Rather the various interests within the organisation will set minimum acceptable objectives which they will seek to achieve through negotiation with other interests. The result is **satisficing** whereby the firm is satisfied by the achievement of a number of limited objectives. When one group is unable to achieve even its minimum objectives the resultant conflict could well inhibit the ability of the firm to achieve any of its objectives. The role of senior management is therefore to ensure that satisficing takes place through a process of negotiation and compromise.

REVISION TEST

1   Why does the perfect competitor have no alternative but to maximise profits?
2   Why should a firm be more concerned with profit maximisation in the long run than the short run under conditions of monopolistic competition?
3   Explain why market conditions may well lead oligopolists to choose not to pursue profit maximisation.
4   Price discrimination may assist the firm in achieving which two objectives?
5   Under what circumstances would the pursuit of sales maximisation lead to a firm making a loss?
6   What is the difference between pure and constrained sales maximisation?
7   Do the salary structures of sales staff compared to accountants within large companies reflect a greater interest in a particular objective? If so, which one?
8   Define the term 'satisficing'.
9   Why is it likely to be difficult to make any predictions using behavioural theory?
10   If the manager can safely ignore the interests of shareholders what form is growth maximisation likely to take?

Examination questions

1   Examine the view that profit maximisation is the sole objective of the firm.
(ABE1, December 1986)

2   In what circumstances might firms *not* pursue maximum possible profits? What other goals might they have?
(ABE1, June 1987)

3   i) What economic functions does the entrepreneur perform in a capitalist economy?

ii) In the large organisation where no individual dominates, who performs these functions?
(ABE1, December 1986)

4   A firm has the following cost and revenue schedules:

Output/Month (000s)	Total Cost (£000)	Total Revenue (£000)
1	37	80
2	70	130
3	90	160
4	110	190
5	150	210
6	200	185

a) What is the profit maximising level of monthly output?
b) The rent of the firm's factory is increased by £12 000. What will be the profit maximising price?
c) Suppose the firm is a sales maximiser and subject to a profit constraint. What would be the level of output and the new price?
d) Under the conditions outlined in (c), explain the type of profit which the firm would be earning.

(LCCI Higher, May 1987)

5   A firm operating under conditions of monopolistic competition has the following total cost and total revenue functions:

Output (units)	Total Cost £	Total Revenue £
0	375	0
1000	450	800
2000	600	1600
3000	775	2150
4000	1000	2400
5000	1250	2450
6000	1600	2100
7000	2100	1550
8000	2750	800

a) Using graph paper, plot the total cost and total revenue functions.
b) From the graph, identify the profit maximising level of output.
c) What is the profit maximising price?
d) If the firm continues to operate at the profit maximising output, explain what is likely to happen to the industry in the long run.
e) The firm now changes its objectives and decides to maximise sales revenue rather than profit. What will be the new level of output and price?
f) Explain what has happened to profit at the new level of output.

(LCCI Higher, May 1988)

6   'Prices of commodities produced under conditions of oligopoly are not necessarily the same but we would expect them generally to move together.' Discuss.

(ICSA, December 1986)

7 Why do oligopolists in an industry tend to increase prices at the same time as each other?

(ICSA, December 1988)

8 Faced with increasing costs, the world's big five car manufacturing companies are considering raising the prices of their cars.

What factors would they, as individual firms, take into account in deciding whether or not to raise prices?

(ACCA, June 1988)

9 In terms of both pricing and research activity, how are firms in oligopolistic industries likely to behave?

(SCCA, May 1988)

10 Why is the kinked demand curve said to be characteristic of oligopolistic markets?

(Cert.M., December 1988)

11 In oligopolistic markets discuss whether prices tend to respond slowly or quickly to changes in market conditions.

(Cert.M., November 1986)

12 What can economic theory tell us of the advantages of product branding and why might a firm develop a brand name for an individual product?

(Cert.M., June 1986)

13 In what ways can retailers compete other than by price?

(Cert.M., November 1987)

14 'In some situations price competition is far less important than various aspects of non-price competition.'

Comment on this statement giving examples from any industry with which you are familiar.

(IPS, November 1987)

15 As the purchasing manager of a group of petrol stations, you find that the price to your company of petrol fluctuates over a period of time, and yet the price offered to motorists at the pumps tends to be relatively stable.

Using appropriate economic theory explain the reasons for this.

(IPS, November 1988)

10 The growth of firms

- *Why do many firms seek to diversify their activities?*
- *Why do some firms grow while others remain small, however successful their activities?*

Most UK industries, whether manufacturing or service, began by being populated by a large number of small firms. Yet today many are oligopolistic, a few large companies dominating production and distribution. These oligopolies are the result of a long process by which the number of firms in the industry have been thinned out as some have disappeared and others have merged with or been taken over by the more successful companies. As an industry evolves, therefore, growth is essential to a firm's survival. Without it, the firm will find its competitive position weakened as rivals increase their hold on the market; eventually it will either suffer a declining market share or succumb to a takeover. Growth also offers the firm a greater opportunity to satisfy the aspirations of the diverse interests within its organisation, to the detriment of none of them.

Factors promoting growth

The willingness to grow is not sufficient. Conditions both within and outside the organisation must be favourable to growth if this is to be achieved. The principal factors promoting growth include:

1 **Profitability** If the firm is to grow it must be able to raise the necessary funds to finance the operation. The firm's profitability will determine its ability to raise these funds, whether internally or externally. Profitable firms are more likely to have built up reserves for future expansion and to be able to obtain fresh capital from investors.

2 **Efficiency** In a competitive environment growth will involve attracting customers from the firm's rivals. This will result in both higher costs through greater expenditure on marketing and lower average revenue through reduced prices. Clearly, the more efficient firms within an industry will be better equipped to cope with these costs of growth.

3 **Management competence** If the opportunities for growth are to be exploited to the full the firm must have a management capable of recognising growth opportunities

and implementing them. As growth occurs the management team becomes more experienced at handling growth opportunities, a process assisted by the acquisition of new expertise as the management team itself grows. In theory, therefore, the limitations imposed on growth by the competence of management should recede as the firm expands.

4   **Economies of scale**   The attainment of economies of scale gives the firm a competitive edge over smaller rivals and stimulates the growth of sales. The resultant expansion may be responsible for the attainment of further economies of scale so promoting another round of growth. The ability of economies of scale to promote growth depends, however, on the market potential being sufficient to justify new technical processes being introduced.

Thus far, we have considered only **organic growth**, i.e. growth achieved through the build-up of the firm's own productive resources and the expansion of its markets. Growth may also take place by merging or taking over other firms through the process of integration.

Integration

Integration typically takes one of two forms.

First, one firm may acquire a controlling interest in another, submerging that firm's identity into its own. This is a **takeover**.

Second, two firms may combine to form a new company which controls the assets and operations of both constituent firms. This is a **merger**.

Generally, the purpose of both forms of integration is the same and so the term 'merger' will be used to cover both types except where stated.

Integration can be divided into three broad categories: horizontal, vertical and conglomerate integration.

Horizontal integration

This involves the merger of two companies in the same industry and at the same stage of the industrial process, whether it be extraction, manufacture, distribution or whatever, e.g. when Nestlé merged with Rowntree in 1988. Where the two firms are in related but different industries the integration is sometimes referred to as lateral. The great oligopolistic firms which dominate so many industries today are frequently the result of a series of horizontal integrations.

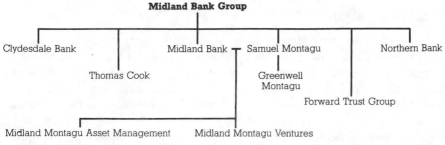

Figure 10.1 *Horizontal integration*

Motives for horizontal integration

Underlying the desire for the growth horizontal integration brings are a number of rational arguments for such mergers.

1 **Economies of scale**   Many horizontal mergers are prompted by the recognition that advances in production techniques within the industry have produced potential economies of scale which can only be realised by larger business units. Such motives underlay the mergers in the aircraft industry in the 1960s and 1970s. The size of the market may also prompt horizontal integration to achieve marketing economies of scale. The 1986 merger of Vantona Viyella with Coats Paton simultaneously created the largest UK-based textile company and enabled Vantona to benefit from Coats Paton's strength in international markets.

   In a declining industry merger activity may be the only way of preserving already established scale economies and reducing excess capacity. This accounted for the spate of mergers in the shipbuilding industry in the 1960s.

2 **Market domination**   When two companies in the same market sector merge the enlarged company inevitably increases its share of the market. Taken to its ultimate conclusion such merger activity will eventually give rise to a monopoly in the industry. For this reason some firms merge to resist market domination by a more powerful rival, particularly when an overseas company is threatening to take control of the home industry. Much of the political support given to the British Aerospace consortium bid for Westland Helicopters in 1985 arose from doubts for the future of an independent British helicopter industry if the American Sikorski bid was successful.

3 **Price stability**   The existence of fewer companies within the industry makes it easier to impose price agreements so merger activity is a way of reducing the level of price competition in the market.

4 **Entry into new markets**   Firms may well find it less costly to buy into a market through the acquisition of an existing company, rather than attempt to develop and market a whole new range of products itself. In 1988, for example, the newly privatised TSB expanded the range of its financial services through the acquisition of long-established merchant banking and credit company interests rather than starting from scratch in these areas.

Vertical integration

This occurs when firms in different stages of production or distribution within the same industry merge. **Backward** vertical integration occurs when a firm merges with another in a previous stage of the production or distribution process, e.g. a manufacturer merging with a supplier of raw materials. **Forward** vertical integration is when a firm merges with another further on in the chain of production and distribution, e.g. a wholesaler taking over a retailer. The major oil companies are one example of firms involved in most stages of the production and distribution process within their industry.

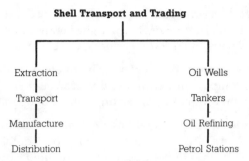

Figure 10.2 *Vertical integration*

Motives for vertical integration

The reasons for a vertical merger are frequently similar to those for a horizontal one, though with a different emphasis.

1 **Economies of scale** Backward vertical integration may provide a solution for a company whose supplier is not large enough to cope with its demands or is unable to maintain the same rate of technical innovation. In the 1960s the major motor manufacturers absorbed some of the smaller suppliers of vital components.

2 **To guarantee supplies or distribution outlets** The appearance of monopoly among a firm's suppliers may encourage the firm to buy up that supplier to guarantee its own supplies and deprive competitors of theirs. A similar motive could lead to a firm buying up its distributor.

3 **Diversification** Vertical integration offers scope for expansion when that part of the industry in which the firm is operating has limited potential for further expansion or when other areas appear to offer greater scope for growth. In 1987 the major banks bought up stockbroking firms to enable them to deal on the stock market on their own behalf. In fact, the events of the October Crash later that year called into question the wisdom of such moves.

Conglomerate integration

Such integration occurs when firms in apparently unrelated industries merge.

Motives for conglomerate integration

However random conglomerate mergers might appear, there is usually a clear rationale behind such mergers.

1 **Diversification** This is the principal motive for conglomerate mergers and is usually associated with growth. Where further expansion in the firm's current activities is seen as difficult to achieve diversification is an attractive proposition. Breaking into a new market is often fraught with problems, however, and might more easily be achieved through the acquisition of an established firm which already has the productive capacity, technical expertise and established market. Such mergers have become increasingly common as the opportunities for further

mergers within a growing company's original industry dry up. A recent example is the way that British American Tobacco (BAT) has branched out into insurance with the takeover of Eagle Star in 1984 and Farmers, the US insurers, in 1988.

2   **Faster growth**   The takeover of a company in a new, rapidly expanding industry may well provide a company with funds to invest a better rate of return than it could expect from further investment in its existing sphere of operations.

3   **Marketing economies**   Conglomerate merger may give a firm the opportunity to build up an apparently unconnected range of products which can be marketed jointly. In the 1970s the Imperial Group contained tobacco manufacturers, breweries, food snacks and convenience food producers and fast food restaurants.

4   **Asset growth**   During buoyant economic conditions and a rising share market the assets of many companies can become under-valued. There is thus an opportunity for a company with liquid funds to make speculative gains by acquiring one of these under-valued companies, especially if it feels it will be able to develop the assets in a more profitable way. A recent example of this phenomenon was the takeover fever which gripped the London Stock Exchange during the 1986/87 'bull market'.

REVISION TEST

1   Why is it necessary for the firm to grow if it is to ensure its survival?
2   Name three of the main factors conducive to the growth of the firm.
3   Explain the term 'organic growth' as applied to the firm.
4   What is lateral integration?
5   Why does horizontal integration eventually cease in an industry before it becomes a monopoly?
6   Explain how, for different reasons, economies of scale can be the motivation for both horizontal and vertical integration.
7   What are the main reasons for conglomerate integration?
8   During the last petrol shortage a motorist bought his own petrol station. What sort of integration was this?
9   Explain the term 'costs of growth'.
10   Why does conglomerate integration place greater demands on management than horizontal integration?

The survival of the small firm

The advantages enjoyed by large firms and the relentless progress of merger and takeover activity have led to large firms dominating British industry and commerce. Nonetheless in 1987 the hundred largest private sector companies contributed a similar proportion of total UK manufacturing output as they had done in 1970 – approximately 40 per cent. There has thus been a slowing down in the process by which British industries are becoming dominated by giant conglomerates.

De-merging and management buy-outs

In part, this slowing down in industrial concentration is due to a growing awareness of the diseconomies of scale which can afflict large companies and has resulted in more firms selling off interests which are not central to the company's future. Very often these sales have resulted in management buy-outs (MBOs) whereby the parent company sells a particular part of the business to the management responsible for running that area of the firm's activities. MBOs have grown in value in the UK from £40 million in 1980 to over £3 billion in 1987. The largest to date was the £718 million MBO of MFI/Hygena by which the Asda/MFI conglomerate formed in 1986 was demerged. The MBO is a way of restoring the link between ownership and management that is often lost in large companies. It also enables management to concentrate on the areas in which they have specialist knowledge.

In other cases conglomerates have voluntarily broken themselves up or retreated from areas in which they could not make an acceptable return. Recent examples include the break-up of the Bowater-Scott paper syndicate in 1986, Goodyear Tire's retreat from the oil industry in 1987 and Ellerman's sale of its Tolly Cobbold brewery to Brent Walker in 1989.

'Small is Beautiful'

Given the scale advantages enjoyed by large firms it is perhaps surprising that 95 per cent of British manufacturing firms are classified as small firms, i.e. they have less than 200 employees. Together they account for some 16 per cent of net output and 19 per cent of employment in manufacturing. In addition, many service industries, notably farming and some branches of retailing, are dominated by small firms. Even in industries where large firms predominate there are many examples of successful small firms co-existing with these much bigger companies. The reasons for the survival of so many small firms fall into two groups.

1   There are those factors which arise out of the diseconomies of scale experienced by large firms.
   a)   In a small firm there is not the divorce between control and ownership that occurs in large companies with the resultant conflicts over objectives. The management of a small firm is much more likely to be able to pursue clearly defined objectives.
   b)   Entrepreneurial activities are less likely to be frustrated in the small firm by red tape, management inertia and a bureaucratic administration.
   c)   Industrial relations tend to be better in small firms where managers and workers have a closer working relationship.

2   There are those factors which derive from the economies of small scale enjoyed by small firms.
   a)   There are many people for whom running their own business is more important than any financial rewards that might be derived from it. They will put more effort into the business than could reasonably be expected from any employee and the competent ones will survive, though many will fail however much effort they make.

b) Small firms are much more willing to take risks and to try new ideas. So while large companies are responsible for the majority of minor innovative changes, small firms are responsible for many major innovations. They thus often dominate the initial development of new industries.
c) In the retail services such as hairdressing, dry cleaning and taxi hire, and in some production processes like photographic developing, economies of scale will be achieved at low operation levels. Occasionally a technological breakthrough will change production methods and an industry will shift from being dominated by small firms to large-scale production or vice versa.
d) The industry may provide specialised or personalised goods of high quality which do not permit the development of technical economies of scale, such as bespoke tailoring or high quality jewellery.
e) The market may be too small or localised to enable the growth of large firms, as in the case of some areas of precision engineering.
f) In some large-scale industries like the motor industry small firms can survive by providing high quality, specialist products, e.g. Aston-Martin, Morgan or Lotus.
g) Small firms tend to be more flexible and willing to respond rapidly to meet their customers' needs. This gives them an edge over larger rivals.
h) Some small firms survive by acting as sub-contractors to larger firms, particularly in specialist areas of the market, e.g. the building trades.

In addition to all these reasons many firms are small because they choose to stay that way. The management may resist growth for fear of losing control of the business or 'getting in above their heads', or they may have achieved the limit of their ambitions with the firm as it is.

REVISION TEST

1 Why is the true entrepreneur most often found in the small firm?
2 Why do the professions tend to be dominated by small firms?
3 Why will even some very successful firms always remain small?
4 Which theoretical objective of the firm might lead a company to seek de-merger?
5 What advantages does the MBO hold over a manager setting up in his own business?
6 To what extent would you expect the normal profit expectations of a small firm to be different to those of a large corporation?
7 Under what circumstances could an oligopoly be populated by small firms?
8 Name two areas of management in which small firms tend to have an advantage.
9 Define the term 'economy of small scale'.
10 Give three examples of the advantages associated with small-scale production.

_____ **Examination questions** _____

1 Does the existence of economies of scale mean that the market has no place for small firms?

(ABE1, June 1987)

2 In view of the advantages claimed for large scale production, why do so many small firms continue to flourish?

(LCCI, Intermediate, November 1987)

3 In many countries small firms still predominate.
   a) Explain the reasons for the continued existence of so many small firms.
   b) John Ayesu runs a small shop. His annual takings (revenue) are £10 000 and his annual costs are £6000. Explain why an economist might, nevertheless, regard John's shop as being unprofitable.

(LCCI, Intermediate, May 1986)

4 What is 'vertical integration'? Citing examples, discuss why firms engage in it.

(SCCA, May 1988)

5 Distinguish between horizontal mergers and conglomerate mergers. What 'public interest' considerations do these types of merger raise?

(SCCA, May 1988)

6 Explain how it is possible for both large and small firms to co-exist in the same industry.

(Cert.M., November 1987)

7 Explain the main methods by which firms can grow. Distinguish between 'internal' and 'external' growth.

(Cert.M., June 1988)

8 In the past year there have been a number of mergers and acquisitions. Using examples, distinguish between horizontal and vertical integration and those leading to conglomerates. Indicate the economic advantages and disadvantages which might be expected to flow from such structures.

(IPS, May 1988)

9 a) Company A and Company B operate in the same expanding market and both would like to see growth in their level of business activity and profits. Company A has particularly low marginal costs and has achieved strong profit growth in recent years. Company B's profits have been sluggish due to higher marginal costs and relatively lower sales than Company A. However, it has particularly good research facilities.
       Ignoring acquisitions, mergers or capital issues, discuss the scope for growth for both companies and the methods by which they may achieve it.
   b) Two companies, C and D, operating in different sectors, agree to merge. Discuss what advantages the merger may have for each company.

(I.Act., September 1987)

11 State regulation of monopoly power

- *Are monopolies always harmful?*
- *How has the government's privatisation programme affected the structure of the UK economy?*

Economic theory shows that, all things being equal, monopoly is less efficient in the use of resources than is perfect competition. At the same time monopoly may exploit its power over the market to restrict choice and make large super-normal profits at the expense of the consumer. Unfortunately, the argument that the consumer is best served by competition raises a dilemma. Perfect competition cannot exist in the real world and competitive industries are prone, as we have seen, to evolve into oligopolies with considerable monopoly power. While there is no simple answer to this problem we can justify attempts by the state to lessen the impact of monopoly power where it causes resources to be used inefficiently or the consumer to be exploited.

Monopoly power and inefficiency

When we compared monopoly and perfect competition earlier we found that the perfect competitor is more efficient than the monopolist when they are producing *under the same technical conditions*. In fact, the monopolist or oligopolist is likely to have achieved economies of scale and a level of technical progress which are unattainable in industries dominated by small firms, whether under perfect competition or not. In short when we compare the efficiency of the monopolist with that of the hypothetical perfect competitor we are not comparing like with like. A marginally inefficient monopolist will still be using resources more efficiently than a perfect competitor producing at optimum efficiency.

In the real world comparisons of the relative efficiency of monopoly and competition are likely to be even more difficult. Under both monopolistic competition and oligopoly there may be a duplication of services and excess capacity, a situation much less likely to occur under monopoly. In addition, oligopolistic firms expend vast resources on marketing their products while an industry dominated by monopolistic competition may be unable to achieve the economies of scale of a monopoly. However, the absence of competition means that profits are the only spur to efficiency for the monopoly and, if large profits can be made while wasting resources, wastage is likely to result. Government intervention against a monopoly can be justified, therefore, to stop the wastage of scarce resources vital to the whole community.

Monopoly power and the consumer

The relationship between producer and consumer is at the heart of economics. Under perfect competition the consumer is king, the producer responding to his wishes through the action of market forces. But in the real world the consumer is likely to be an unequal partner when negotiating with the supplier. Where supply is under the control of a monopoly the consumer has no choice. Where the market is dominated by oligopolistic firms competition may well be illusory with the firms acting jointly to fix prices and perhaps output.

Again the issue is clouded by the fact that firms with monopoly power will be able to use large profits in further capitalisation and research and development which will help the consumer through better quality, low-cost goods in the long run. The advances in consumer electronic goods in the past 20 years, for example, do not reflect badly on the achievements of an oligopolistic market. Nor does price competition help the consumer if it takes the form of occasional price wars which force some firms out of the market, ultimately strengthening the control of those who remain. Nonetheless, the existence of price-fixing agreements and other restrictive practices which prop up inefficient firms and guarantee exorbitant profits to the efficient are worthy areas of state intervention.

Monopoly power and market concentration

It is inevitable that competition will lead to the more efficient firms gaining a greater share of the market and perhaps absorbing weaker competitors. However, the erection of barriers to entry by monopolies and oligopolies prevents new firms from entering the market and so reversing the trend towards greater concentration. In such circumstances the government must consider whether it ought to allow the process by which industries are concentrated in fewer and fewer firms to continue.

Another area of concern is the behaviour of conglomerates. Conglomerate growth by diversification does not increase the market concentration of any one industry but it does increase the concentration of economic power in general. Such diversifying firms may influence market behaviour detrimentally in a number of ways. By entering new markets they exclude the emergence of new independent firms which otherwise might have sprung up. They may use the resources accumulated from their primary sphere of activity to finance short-run price cutting and extensive advertising in their new operations and so gain market leadership in more than one industry.

Controlling monopoly power

There are a number of options available to the government to deal with the abuse of monopoly power.

1   Where a monopoly already exists the government may:
   a) Break up the monopoly, forcing the company to divide into a number of smaller independent firms. This was the policy adopted in the USA to end the monopoly of giant corporations like Standard Oil.
   b) Break down the power of the monopoly by withdrawing patent rights and encouraging new firms to start up with financial assistance.
   c) Impose price controls to protect the consumer, as the British government did in the nineteenth century in the case of the railways.
   d) Take the monopoly into public ownership and run it as a nationalised industry, as with the telephone system in 1911. The government can then ensure that pricing and output policies have due regard for the interests of the economy as a whole and of that industry's consumers.

2   To prevent a monopoly from developing the government may supervise merger activity and prevent mergers taking place where they are likely to lead to situations of market dominance.

3   Where potential competition still exists the government may:
   a) Enact legislation against price-fixing agreements and other cartel practices.
   b) Supervise prices.
   c) Outlaw the practice of manufacturers dictating to retailers the terms under which their goods may be sold.

Government control of monopoly power in the UK

Britain was some way behind other countries, notably the United States, in taking steps to deal with monopoly power. In the first half of the twentieth century a number of natural monopolies were nationalised but no steps were taken to limit the extent of concentration in industry or commerce. Indeed, mergers were often actively encouraged by the government to enable the development of economies of scale or to reduce over-capacity in declining industries.

Since 1948, however, successive governments have sought to supervise merger activity and combat restrictive practices by oligopolistic firms. The effect of the legislation, much of which was brought together under the Fair Trading Act 1973, can be summarised under three main headings.

Monopoly

By 1950 most of the natural monopolies had been brought under state control and the issues relating to these will be examined shortly. Elsewhere in the economy government legislation has consistently recognised that it is not necessary for a firm to control 100 per cent of the industry in order to enjoy market domination. Thus a monopoly is defined under the Fair Trading Act as a situation in which a quarter of the supply of goods in an industry or market is controlled by one firm or a group of firms acting together to restrict competition. Monopoly situations may be referred for investigation to the Monopolies and Mergers Commission (MMC) by the Secretary of State for Trade and Industry or by the Director-General of Fair Trading. It is then the role of the MCC to determine:

1   Whether a monopoly position exists.

2   If it does, the behaviour and importance of the dominant firm.

3   The effect on the public interest.

4   In the light of the above, what measures should be taken.

In deciding the question of the public interest the MMC examines how the monopoly came into existence; whether, for example, it was the result of a conscious takeover policy by the dominant firm. The Commission also looks at the level of innovation, the technical efficiency and the scale of production to see if monopoly can be justified on these grounds.

On the whole monopolies have been criticised in the reports of the MMC more for discriminatory or other restrictive practices rather than for technical inefficiency or excessive profits. The recommendations of the Commission have usually proposed a change in behaviour and have led to firms giving voluntary undertakings to the government to stop those practices which give offence. The Commission has never recommended the breaking up of the company and even when it suggested price and profit controls, as it did in the cases of British Oxygen, Unilever and Proctor & Gamble, the government chose not to implement the recommendations.

Mergers

The Department of Trade & Industry has had the power to refer any merger in the following categories to the MMC:

1   Where the assets involved exceed a certain level (currently £15 million).

2   Where the merger would lead to a monopoly situation as defined under the Fair Trading Act.

The MMC will then consider the merger as it affects the public interest and make recommendations accordingly. The merger may be referred up to six months *after* the merger has taken place. It is clearly in the interests of companies considering potentially contentious mergers, therefore, to approach the Department of Trade before embarking on a merger which might have to be undone at a later date.

The Department of Trade & Industry is required to examine each proposed merger on its merits and if economic considerations point in favour of a merger it may be decided not to refer that merger. Among the factors that will be considered are; the tendency towards either price leadership or parallel pricing in the industry, the degree of merger activity in the industry, barriers to entry and the likely effects of the merger on efficiency, employment and the balance of payments.

Only about 3 per cent of all eligible mergers have been referred to the MMC, so the legislation has had only a marginal impact on the level of merger activity. In the cases it has considered the MMC has taken a cost-benefit approach and has tended to oppose mergers only when they can be shown to be against the public interest. However, merger policy has reduced the number of horizontal mergers since 1970.

Since referral is rare the mere fact of referral has frequently been sufficient to make firms abandon merger plans. On the other hand the practice has increased of companies avoiding referral by consulting the Office of Fair Trading and making such changes to their structures as are necessary to ensure the merger will be acceptable, e.g. the Guinness takeover of Distillers in 1986 was made acceptable by the companies disposing of interests, continued ownership of which would have made referral, and possible disallowance by the MCC, much more likely.

Restrictive practices

The law on restrictive trade practices has been strengthened over the years so that cartel behaviour in both the manufacturing and service sectors is illegal in the following areas, unless the industry or firm concerned can satisfy certain stringent criteria applied by the Restrictive Practices Court.

1   Price-fixing agreements by the firms within an industry, whether formal or informal.
2   Trade agreements to restrict output or distribution.
3   Discrimination against categories of customer.
4   Restrictions by manufacturers or producers on the freedom of distributors to set their own prices, i.e. resale price maintenance.

In addition, the Director-General of Fair Trading may conduct enquiries into the behaviour of industries and refer cases of anti-competitive practice to the MMC for investigation and recommendation. Among recent investigations were the credit card companies in 1987 and the major breweries in 1988. If the Secretary of State accepts the recommendations of the MMC, the firms may be required to change their pricing or output policies or even to divest themselves of some of their activities. Despite the strong legislative stance, it has proved difficult to eradicate informal parallel pricing policies. Oligopolistic industries continue to concentrate on non-price competition with aggressive price-cutting a rare phenomenon. As far as the consumer is concerned much greater strides have been made in the field of consumer protection legislation. The individual consumer is now better protected by the law when dealing with unscrupulous traders or seeking recourse for misinformation, faulty goods or inadequate service.

REVISION TEST

1   Why is monopoly likely to be a greater force for economic progress than perfect competition?
2   How does the motivation for efficiency differ between an oligopolist and a perfect competitor?
3   What are the main options available to a government to deal with an existing monopoly?
4   Explain the term 'parallel pricing'.
5   How is a monopoly defined under current legislation on monopolies?

6 Explain the view that legislation on monopolies and mergers is really legislation on oligopoly.

7 Why has legislation in the UK been more equivocal in the treatment of monopoly than of restrictive practices?

8 Outline the role of the MMC.

9 In what sense could government merger policy be seen as an attack on market forces?

10 Apart from government policy, what other factors may have led to a reduction in horizontal mergers in recent years?

Public ownership of industry

The economic factors underlying the nationalisation programme of the period just after the Second World War have been partly obscured by the fact that it was also a political programme. However, it is possible to advance four distinct economic arguments in favour of nationalisation.

1 **The natural monopoly**   The nature of some industries is such that they can only operate efficiently as monopolies, competition tending to result in a wastage of resources through the duplication of services and excess capacity. By the late nineteenth century the railways in Britain had become regional monopolies and the gas and electricity companies followed a similar pattern early in the present century. As natural monopolies such industries must be subject to some form of state control to protect the consumer. One possibility is the state regulation of private firms; another is public ownership.

2 **National economic efficiency**   The phrase 'on the commanding heights of the economy' has been used to describe those industries which are vital to the effective running of the economy as a whole. These would include industries which provide essential raw materials such as steel, fuel and power such as coal, gas or electricity, or communications such as the railways or postal services. Inadequacies in the performance of any of these industries is liable to be detrimental to the effectiveness of the economy as a whole. Where, therefore, private sector ownership is unable or unwilling to provide the capital investment necessary to maintain the efficiency of such industries public ownership may be necessary. This argument was advanced in favour of the nationalisation of both the railways and the coal industry.

3 **Economies of scale and rationalisation**   In the early post-war period many major industries were badly in need of structural reorganisation to achieve their full potential and the private sector was not supplying the funding necessary for this restructuring to take place. Nationalisation was therefore considered appropriate to fund the reorganisation of the gas industry, the new capital programme of electricity and the modernisation of the coal industry and the railways. Similar arguments were used in the 1970s concerning the rationalisation of the shipbuilding industry and the provision of funds for aircraft manufacture and development.

4 **National economic strategy**   In the late 1940s it was argued that the government

should control a substantial sector of industry to assist the implementation of its strategy for the economy as a whole. It was felt that, by controlling part of the economy directly, the government could adopt measures to counter harmful influences elsewhere in the economy. Thus the government could increase public sector investment when that in the private sector was falling, protect jobs when unemployment was rising and restrain price rises during periods of inflation.

In addition, arguments in favour of nationalisation have often included the social principle whereby the service provided is important to all members of the community and should be available to all, even if this means that some consumers will be subsidised, e.g. rural communities. This argument is similar to those used in favour of the state provision of health, education and social welfare. In practice the duty to the consumer was stressed in the charters of all the nationalised industries.

Pricing and output policy in the public sector

A public sector organisation supplying goods or services need not have the commercial constraints of firms in the private sector with their emphasis on profit. Instead the government may insist on such objectives as uniform pricing to all consumers, the subsidisation of certain groups or the maintenance of quality. Clearly, the setting of such objectives may not be compatible with the organisation making a profit, or breaking even.

In the UK a compromise over this issue was suggested in the 1967 White Paper on the nationalised industries. This recognised that profit maximisation was neither desirable nor appropriate for the public sector but expected some degree of financial responsibility in relation to prices, investment and profits. In particular, it suggested that pricing policy be linked more closely to the cost of the goods and services actually provided. This may be achieved through the use of marginal cost pricing as in perfect competition. The effect of such a policy is shown in Figure 11.1.

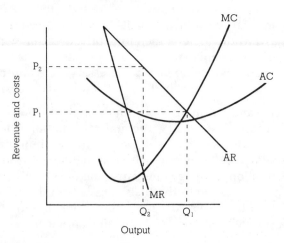

Figure 11.1 *Marginal cost pricing*

Marginal cost pricing by a monopoly, such as a nationalised industry, will result in a situation similar to that in Figure 11.1, where the firm produces an output of Q_1 at a price of P_1. The AR line can be said to measure the value to the consumer of extra units of the product while the MC line measures the cost of producing these extra units. At an output less than Q_1 the benefit to the consumer is greater than the cost of that output while at outputs greater than Q_1 the cost is greater than the benefit so the units will be unsaleable. The equilibrium output of the monopoly under marginal cost pricing will be higher than that of a profit-maximising output (Q_2) while the price will be lower. The nationalised industry will still be earning super-normal profits, though these will be less than for a profit-maximising firm. The existence of such super-normal profits can be justified on the grounds that the industry will need to be able to find the resources for future innovation and product development.

While marginal cost pricing is attractive in principle, the very nature of the nationalised industries makes its implementation difficult in practice. Neither short-run nor long-run marginal cost pricing ensures that average cost is covered by average revenue and therefore that the industry is breaking even. If, over the industry's likely output range, MC is falling continuously it will be below AC. So when MC equals price (AR) AC>AR and a loss results. Such a situation may well arise in a nationalised industry where, due to its capital-intensive nature, it faces high fixed costs in the short run and increasing returns to scale in the long run.

Despite the potential difficulties, a number of the nationalised industries went some way towards marginal cost pricing after 1967. This process was assisted by the 1967 White Paper's acceptance of the principle of price discrimination which enabled the adoption of much more flexible pricing policies.

Privatisation

During the 1970s government policy towards the nationalised industries required them to move towards greater profitability and the self-financing of more of their capital needs. The Conservative government elected in 1979 went further and decided that improved efficiency and a better use of resources could be best achieved by a return of these industries to the private sector.

Privatisation takes three main forms:

1 **Liberalisation**   The promotion of competition in certain areas of activity by the removal of statutory monopolies or other legal barriers to the entry of firms into the industry.

2 **Transfer of ownership of assets**   The partial or total sale by the government of its ownership of a public corporation or public company by the issue of shares.

3 **The extension of private provision of public services**   Here the private sector takes over the provision of services previously required to be provided by a public authority, e.g. the operation of a refuse collection system or the running of hospital laundries.

The case for privatisation

The arguments in favour of privatisation are of two types. First, those which stress the inadequacies of the nationalised industries and other state-run commercial activities and, second, the improvements in economic performance likely to result from their being provided in the private sector.

1   The nationalised industries possess monopoly power and are thus prone to be inefficient, lacking in the will to innovate and restrictive of consumer choice. The privatisation of such industries would increase competition and so force them to be both more efficient and more responsive to consumer needs.

2   A number of these industries have made huge losses and have had to be bailed out by the government, at the taxpayers' expense. Once privatised they could no longer rely on this source of support and would have to manage themselves more effectively in consequence.

3   Frequent changes in government policy have prevented the nationalised industries from maintaining consistency in the pursuit of their commercial objectives, so inhibiting their performance relative to that of comparable private sector industries.

4   Political interference in their policy-making has weakened the independence of managers in the nationalised industries and deterred many able industrialists from joining these industries. In the private sector managers would have the same incentives as other managers and would have the same opportunities for success.

5   Trade unions have been able to exploit the monopoly power of these industries to gain excessive wage rises and overmanning. A return to the private sector would ensure that the workforce, as well as the management, is subjected to the pressures of market forces.

There are also broader arguments in favour of privatisation which relate to improvements in the working of the economy as a whole following the reduction of the public sector.

The reduction of state activity in the economy
Privatisation is part of the government's strategy to shift the balance in the economy away from the public sector. State enterprise is seen by its opponents as bureaucratic, impersonal, unresponsive to the needs of those it serves and unable to command the loyalty of either employees or consumers. Such a view has always been popular with large sections of the electorate who have little faith in state enterprise and little sense of ownership of such industries.

The reduction of the public sector borrowing requirement
It is claimed that, by reducing the level of borrowing required by the government, there is a reduction in inflationary pressures. At the same time the lower demand for funds from the public sector stimulates the level of private sector investment as firms are no longer crowded out of the market by government borrowing activity. The public sector borrowing requirement (PSBR) is reduced by privatisation in three ways:

1   The operating deficits of loss-making public enterprises are removed, or at least reduced.

2   The future borrowing of those bodies which are privatised will no longer figure as part of the PSBR.

3   The receipt by the Exchequer of the proceeds of the sale of public assets increases government revenue during the year in which the privatisation takes place and thus reduces the need for borrowing to meet a given level of expenditure.

The creation of a wider share ownership

Most of the major privatisation share flotations have encouraged participation by the general public with the offer for sale favouring small investors, particularly employees of the industry being privatised. It is hoped that this stimulus to share-owning will reverse the decline in the number of private shareholders and, by blurring the distinction between company ownership and workforce, contribute to an improvement in industrial relations throughout the economy.

The case against privatisation

The arguments against privatisation are based on doubts about the validity of the case put forward by supporters of privatisation together with fears for the provision of public services once they are privatised.

1   Privatisation will not end the monopoly power of the nationalised industries, it merely passes this power from the public to the private sector, e.g. the natural monopolies of gas, electricity, telecommunications.

2   With control of the industry passing into private hands the public loses any say it previously had in the administration of the industry through its elected representatives. This is of particular concern where the industry provides an essential service and yet could be controlled by interests outside the UK.

3   The sale of corporations which provide public services make it very likely that such services will suffer if their provision threatens the profitability of the new private sector company. A similar concern arises when private companies take over services previously performed by government departments or local authorities.

4   The huge stock market flotations required to launch these industries onto the private sector impose strains on the functioning of the stock market, perhaps taking funds away from share issues by private sector companies. In addition, to ensure that the issue is not a flop, the government may be tempted to sell the shares too cheaply. A number of the privatisation issues did appear to come into this category while the BP issue of 1987 was a major flop, coming onto the market just after the October crash.

5   The argument that privatisation will create a nation of worker-shareholders is not borne out by events. The tendency is for shares in these new public companies to end up in the hands of the big financial institutions, however much small shareholders participate in the original share issue.

6 The once and for all benefit to government revenues resulting from the sale of assets is more than offset by the overall cost to the Exchequer of the privatisation programme. This cost consists of:
   a) The loss to government revenue once contributions from the profits of the nationalised industries cease.
   b) The capital loans made by the government to the industry while it was in public hands but written off as part of the privatisation package, e.g. Rolls-Royce and Jaguar.
   c) The loss of revenue when the shares have been sold too cheaply.
   d) The administrative and underwriting costs incurred with every privatisation issue.

7 The reduction of the public sector lessens the government's ability to influence the economy by direct action to give a lead to other industries. Private companies, for example, are unlikely to show the same loyalty to British goods.

The extent of the privatisation programme

However valid many of the doubts expressed about the wisdom of the privatisation programme, its progress has been rapid over the past decade.

1 **Liberalisation** Legislation has been enacted to increase competition in bus transport, telecommunications, postal services, electricity, gas and optical services; all areas where previously the government had enforced public monopolies.

2 **Extension of private provision of public services** The main progress here has been in the transfer of cleaning, catering and maintenance functions from central and local government agencies to private contractors. However, the government has promoted the private provision of vocational training and health care through contracting arrangements in the former and tax incentives to the elderly in the latter.

3 **Transfer of ownership and assets** It is in this area that the most obvious progress has been made. Among the major industries sold, in whole or in part to the private sector are British Telecommunications, Cable and Wireless, British Aerospace, British Gas, British Airways, British Airports Authority, British Steel, National Bus Company and the water authorities. In addition Rolls-Royce, Jaguar and Rover have all been returned to the private sector while the government's holding in British Petroleum has been further reduced. Future plans include electricity and the railways, though there is considerable public disquiet about control of the latter going into private hands.

The impact on the economy of the privatisation programme has been dramatic:

1 The state-owned industrial sector has been reduced by 40 per cent.

2 The total revenue for the government resulting from the sale of assets has been £22.5 billion. This has been largely responsible for the public revenue surpluses enjoyed by the government in the late 1980s and early 1990s.

3   Over 750 000 jobs have been moved from the public sector to the private, contributing to a decline in the public sector workforce of one million since 1979.

4   There are now as many shareholders as there are trade unionists. However, the wider share ownership hoped for by the government has not materialised. Over half of the seven million or so private shareholders own shares in only one company while the vast majority hold shares only in privatisation issues.

REVISION TEST

1   What is a 'natural monopoly'?

2   Explain the phrase 'on the commanding heights of the economy'.

3   Why are the railways considered suitable candidates for nationalisation in many mixed economies?

4   Explain the rationale behind marginal cost pricing for a public sector monopoly.

5   Why is marginal cost pricing not always practicable in a nationalised industry?

6   What are the three main forms of privatisation?

7   Give three of the deficiencies of nationalised industries which privatisation is claimed to cure.

8   How do taxpayers gain, and how do they lose, when an industry is privatised?

9   In which of the nationalised industries would you expect competition to increase as a result of privatisation?

10   Name four of the main arguments against privatisation.

Examination questions

1   A recent major act of the British government was to transfer a nationalised enterprise into private ownership. Identify and examine the economic factors which that government must take into account.

(ABE1, June 1986)

2   'Monopolies are not in the public interest.' Discuss, with reference to the government policy relating to control of monopolies.

(ABE1, December 1986)

3   a) What is monopoly power and what are its disadvantages for the economy?
    b) Describe the policies pursued by the government to restrict monopolies.

(ABE1, December 1987)

4   a) 'Monopolies are normally considered to be less desirable than competitive structures.' Comment.
    b) Examine the circumstances in which a monopolistic market may be preferable to a competitive one.

(LCCI Higher, November 1987)

5   Discuss the main problems in the private enterprise system that public enterprise is designed to solve and outline other solutions to these problems.

(LCCI Higher, May 1988)

6   a) By means of a diagram, identify the profit maximising position of a firm operating under conditions of monopoly.
     b) State with reasons whether perfect competition is always preferable to monopoly.
     c) What are the main measures which a government might use to deal with problems of monopoly?

(LCCI Higher, November 1986)

7   a) With the use of diagrams, distinguish between perfect competition and monopoly.
     b) Explain the methods used by governments to deal with problems caused by monopoly.

(LCCI Intermediate, November 1987)

8   For what economic reasons might a government encourage the creation of a privately-owned monopoly?

(ICSA, December 1987)

9   a) Examine the case for and against monopoly.
     b) If a monopoly was charged with operating in the public interest what price should it charge? And why?

(ACCA, June 1987)

10   State enterprises have lost favour in recent years. In the USA this has resulted in deregulation and in Britain it has resulted in privatisation. With these developments in mind explain:
     a) The case for privatisation.
     b) The case against privatisation.

(ACCA, December 1987)

11   In many countries public utilities (e.g. gas, water) are government-owned. Evaluate the case for transferring their ownership to the private sector.

(SCCA, November 1988)

12   In the UK, and to a lesser extent in some other western industrialised countries, a number of state-owned industries have been 'privatised' in recent years. Discuss the economic rationale for such transfers of ownership.

(SCCA, May 1988)

13   a) Describe the three main forms of imperfect competition.
     b) Discuss the means by which the United Kingdom government has sought to control the power of monopolies and encourage competition in industry.

(I.Act., September 1988)

14 a) Discuss the advantages and disadvantages of the nationalisation of major industries in the United Kingdom.

b) State the additional problems that arise when attempts are made to privatise existing nationalised industries.

(I.Act., September 1989)

12 The theory of distribution

- *When production takes place how is the reward to each factor of production determined?*
- *Which two components make up the reward to any factor of production?*

Marginal revenue product

In previous chapters the theory of the firm was examined. We saw that the firm makes profits or losses on a particular output depending on the relationship between costs and revenue. If the cost of producing one more unit (the marginal cost) is not matched by the revenue received from the sale of that unit (the marginal revenue) then the firm will not gain by producing it. In the theory of distribution we examine the costs of production in another way, i.e. as the rewards paid to the factors of production for their contribution to the productive process. In other words, each cost is seen as consisting of payments made for the use of land, labour, capital and enterprise. To see how costs can be broken down this way let us begin with a simple example.

Suppose that a firm producing electrical components receives an order for 4000 units at a price of £2 to be delivered as soon as possible. If it is assumed that the firm will maximise profits on this order and produce where marginal revenue is equal to marginal cost, it is possible to produce a simple financial breakdown of the operation:

Marginal Revenue		*Marginal Cost*
Extra revenue received from the sale of one more unit:		Extra payments for raw materials, fuel, wages, maintenance, equipment, etc. to produce one more unit
£2.00	=	£2.00

The payments which make up the marginal cost detailed above can be grouped together by factor of production as follows:

Land: payment for the use of land and the purchase of raw materials, i.e. **rent**.
Labour: payment for the hire of workers, whether salaried or wage-earning, i.e. **wages**.
Capital: payment for the use of capital goods such as plant, machinery and tools, i.e. **interest**.
Enterprise: payment for the expertise of the entrepreneur, i.e. **profit**.

It should therefore be possible to calculate the marginal cost of each factor of production. Suppose, for example, that the total labour cost of producing these 4000 units is £3600, i.e. 45 per cent of the total extra cost. The marginal cost of labour will then be £0.90 per unit. Now if the marginal cost of labour is 45 per cent of the total, labour should be contributing 45 per cent of the extra production and of the extra revenue earned as follows:

Marginal cost of labour = £0.90 = 45 per cent of marginal cost
Marginal product of labour = 1800 units (45 per cent of production)
Marginal revenue product of labour = $\dfrac{1800 \times £2}{4000}$ = £0.90

From the above it can be seen that, if we can ascribe a proportion of the extra production to a particular factor, we can calculate that factor's contribution to marginal revenue, i.e. the **marginal revenue product** (MRP).

At its profit maximising equilibrium the competitive firm should use each factor to the point where the MRP of the factor is equal to the MC of that factor. This theory of factor rewards is known as marginal productivity theory and predicts that:

> *The rate of reward offered to a factor will be equal to the marginal product of that factor when the market is in equilibrium.*

Unless this is the case the firm is not using the factors of production to their optimum level. Suppose, in the above example, that the marginal revenue product of labour is less than £0.90. In order for marginal revenue to be equal to marginal cost the marginal revenue product of another factor must be more than its marginal cost. Thus the firm would improve its efficiency and its profitability by using less labour and more of the other factor, if this is feasible. Similarly, if the marginal revenue product of labour is greater than £0.90 that of another factor will be less than its marginal cost and so the firm should switch its production methods to use more labour at the expense of other factors.

Limitations of marginal productivity theory

The application of marginal productivity theory is extremely difficult in practice for a number of reasons.

First, it is almost impossible to measure the marginal revenue product of any factor in a given situation. In a modern industrial or commercial operation it is frequently too difficult a task to separate out precisely the contribution to production made by any one factor. In the case of the electrical firm quoted above the order will be met without any extra rent payments yet the site on which the factory is built must have made some contribution to the extra output generated. Even if it were possible to make the necessary calculation it may well prove impracticable to use the combination of factors which would produce a situation in which the MRP of each factor is equal to its marginal cost.

Second, the theory assumes that all units of a factor are identical and therefore equally efficient. This is clearly not the case with either labour or land.

Third, it is assumed that changes can occur in one sector of the economy in isolation. In fact, if there is a general decline in economic activity the demand for factors will drop even in those industries where factor rewards have fallen.

Fourth, not all firms are profit-maximisers operating in a perfectly competitive market and relying on the achievement of optimum efficiency to break even. In the real world the typical firm will use some factors of production inefficiently and still be able to make profits.

So the theory of distribution based on marginal productivity theory cannot survive in the absence of a perfectly competitive environment. Rather than each factor receiving a reward commensurate with its contribution to output, the factors of production are generally in competition with each other for the rewards available; the final distribution depending to some extent on the monopoly power of the factors involved.

Factor markets

Demand for a factor

Of the four factors of production three, land, labour and capital, are hired by the other; enterprise in the form of the entrepreneur. In return for their services these factors earn rent, wages and interest. Any surplus after these payments have been made represents the enterpreneur's profit. If this surplus is not sufficient to cover the entrepreneur's expected or normal profit he makes a loss while if it more than covers normal profit he makes super profits. The entrepreneur's demand for the other factors is known as a **derived demand** since the factors are not wanted for their own sake but for what they can contribute to production and ultimately to profits.

Let us assume that it is possible to isolate the contribution of one factor to the productive process. The marginal product of a factor is then the addition to total product resulting from the use of one extra unit of that factor while all other factor inputs are held constant. Since we are treating only one factor as a variable the law of diminishing returns will eventually come into play and the marginal product will fall as extra units of the factor are added. The MRP will show a similar decline, and this decline will be much steeper if price is also reduced as output is increased.

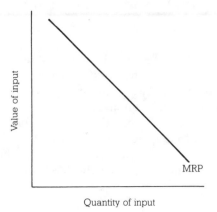

Figure 12.1 *Marginal revenue product*

Figure 12.1 shows a typical MRP line sloping downwards from left to right. The MRP resembles a demand curve and it *is* the demand curve for the factor. The lower the price of the factor, i.e. its reward, the greater will be the demand for that factor as producers will substitute this factor for other, more expensive, ones. So if labour is expensive firms might be expected to seek more capital-intensive forms of production. In addition, a fall in factor prices will enable the producer to expand output without any increase in costs.

The supply of a factor

The supply of any factor will vary with the reward offered to that factor, i.e. with its price. An increase in price will attract more of the factor into the market from other uses and will lead to more units of the factor entering the market for the first time. Thus, the higher the rate of interest available from manufacturing industry, the greater the incentive for owners of capital to shift funds from the commercial sector and the greater the loss for those who have chosen so far not to make their capital funds available for investment. Similarly, the higher the wage in a particular occupation the greater the likelihood that labour will transfer to that occupation from other labour markets and the greater the incentive for people outside the labour market entirely to enter this occupation. So the supply curve of a factor is similar in behaviour to that of the supply curve for a commodity.

Of course, the ability of units of a factor to move from one market to another depends on the mobility of that factor. Owners of land in the north of Scotland cannot make it available for commercial rents in the City of London; workers cannot transfer to labour markets for which they are not qualified.

Price determination in the factor market

From the above discussion it is apparent that the price of a factor of production will, in a competitive market, be found by the intersection of the demand and supply curves for the factor, as in Figure 12.2.

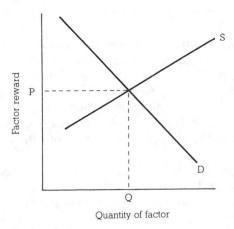

Figure 12.2 *Price determination for a factor*

The position facing an individual firm operating within a perfectly competitive market is rather different to that set out in Figure 12.2. A perfectly competitive firm is, you will recall, one which is unable to influence the market price by its actions and the same conditions apply to it whether it is acting as a buyer or a seller. So the firm will find that it can obtain as much of a factor as it wishes at the prevailing market price, i.e. it will find that the supply curve of the factor is perfectly elastic, as in Figure 12.3. Since each extra unit of the factor can be obtained at the same price as the last unit, the supply curve of the factor is also its marginal cost curve.

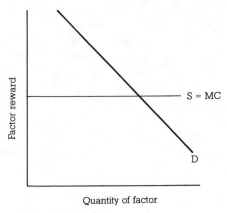

Figure 12.3 *Factor price for the perfect competitor*

The situation is rather different when there is imperfect competition in the factor market. Then each firm will influence the market price by its actions and so will be unable to obtain extra units of the factor without raising the reward offered. The supply curve of the factor facing the firm slopes upwards and to the right like a market supply curve. In an extreme case the firm may be a **monopsonist**, i.e. the sole buyer of the factor. This firm cannot obtain extra units of the factor by attracting them from other firms; it must offer sufficiently high rewards to attract new units of the factor into the market. The situation confronting the monopsonist or other firm with monopsonistic power is illustrated in Figure 12.4.

When the monopsonist offers higher rewards to attract new units of the factor it must also raise the reward to those units currently being employed. British Rail, for example, cannot raise the wages offered to new signalmen while leaving existing signalmen at the old rate of pay. The marginal cost of employing extra units of a factor is therefore above the supply curve. Suppose a monopsonist employs 1000 workers at £200 per week each and then attracts a new worker by offering a wage of £210. The marginal cost of labour for the monopsonist will be, not £210, but £210 + (1000 × £10) = £10 210!

For the monopsonist, like the perfect competitor, the profit-maximising use of a factor will be where the MRP of the factor is equal to its marginal cost. In Figure 12.4, therefore, the monopsonist will employ Q_1 units of the factor at the reward R_1. This contrasts with the competitive market situation in which the supply curve is also the marginal cost curve and so Q_2 units of the factor would be employed at the reward R_2.

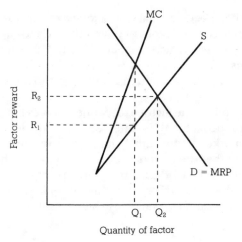

Figure 12.4 *Factor price and the monopolist*

So under monopsonistic market conditions both the rewards offered to a factor of production and the number of units of the factor employed will be lower than under a perfectly competitive factor market.

REVISION TEST

1 Explain how the income received by the owner of a small business could consist of elements of all the factor rewards.

2 What is the marginal physical product of a factor?

3 'The MRP of a factor is equal to its MC.' Explain.

4 A firm is in its profit-maximising equilibrium. If the MRP of labour is below its MC what statement can be made concerning the other factors of production?

5 Why is the MRP line for a factor downward-sloping?

6 A perfect competitor employs 50 units of a factor at £3 each. If an extra 10 units are employed what will be the total cost to the firm of using this factor?

7 Define the term 'monopsonist'.

8 A monopsonist employs 10 workers. The wage rate is raised by 10 per cent to attract an extra worker. By what percentage has the total wage bill risen?

9 What is the marginal cost in the above situation?

10 What factors, other than geographical ones, contribute to the immobility of land as a factor of production?

Economic rent and transfer earnings

When factor rewards are determined by market forces all units of the factor receive the market rate, irrespective of whether or not individual units could have been obtained at a lower rate. In Figure 12.5 Q units of the factor are employed at the reward R but most of these units would have been available at a lower reward. It is therefore possible to distinguish between two distinct types of payment made to each unit of the factor.

First, there is the payment which must be made to the unit to retain it in its present use – **transfer earnings**.

Second, there is the payment made to a unit over and above its transfer earnings – **economic rent**.

In Figure 12.5 each unit of the factor except one receives both types of payment. The exception is the unit of the factor at the intersection of the demand and supply curves. This unit enters the market at the equilibrium rate and therefore earns only transfer earnings. Clearly the higher the reward required by a unit of the factor the greater will be the proportion of the reward that is transfer earnings. The firm employing these units is unable to avoid making these economic rent payments since it cannot distinguish those units which would be available at a lower reward.

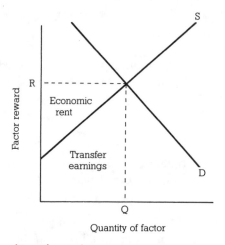

Figure 12.5 *Economic rent and transfer earnings*

The term 'economic rent' owes its origins to the nineteenth century economist David Ricardo. He argued that, as land was fixed in supply with no alternative uses, its reward was determined by the demand for land. So if food prices rose the profits earned by farmers would also rise. This in turn would push up the demand, and thus the rent, of the most productive farming land, giving the owners of such land economic rent payments. He thereby showed that high rents were the consequence of high food prices rather than the cause, as was generally believed in the 1840s. A comparable example today is the tendency for rents in city centres to be much higher than elsewhere in a country. These rents reflect the ability of hotels, shops and entertainment in city centres to charge higher prices for their services and so compete for land rather than site-owners being able arbitrarily to charge whatever rent they wish.

The term, economic rent, should not be confused with **commercial rent** which is the payment made for the use of land and property. Economic rent is now applied to any factor of production which receives surplus payments. For the entrepreneur economic rent takes the form of super profits, just as normal profits can be equated with transfer earnings.

The supply elasticity of factors

While the reward to most units of a factor is made up of both transfer earnings and economic rent, the ratio of one to the other depends on the responsiveness of the factor to changes in the reward offered, i.e. the elasticity of supply of the factor. Figure 12.6 shows the two extremes. In Figure 12.6 (a) supply of the factor is perfectly inelastic and all earnings are economic rent since the factor is available even if the reward is zero. In Figure 12.6 (b) the supply of the factor is perfectly elastic and all earnings are transfer earnings since no supply would be available below the market price. Thus the more elastic the supply of a factor the greater the proportion of earnings will be transfer earnings and the smaller the proportion will be economic rent.

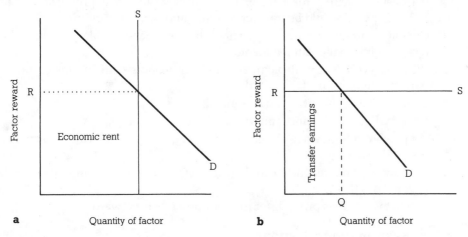

Figure 12.6 *Supply elasticity of factors*

It is possible to find cases of where almost all a factor unit's earnings are economic rent as, for example, when waste land is hired out for a fair or a film star receives £1 million to appear in a film. There are also cases where the factor unit receives only transfer earnings. Capital funds, for example, will not be available for investment unless the borrower matches the market interest rate while labour in most industries can only be employed at the standard wage rate.

Quasi-rent

The elasticity of supply of a factor is likely to vary between the short and long runs. In the short run the supply may be fixed and perfectly inelastic but be able to respond to changes in the level of rewards in the long run. The supply of qualified doctors, for example, is fixed at any one time but higher doctors' salaries may lead to an increase in the number of medical students and supply becoming more responsive to changes in factor rewards in the long run.

It is therefore possible for factors to earn economic rent payments in the short run only for these to disappear in the long run. Economic rent payments which persist only in the short run are known as **quasi-rent**. Such payments include higher labour rewards made when there is a temporary shortage of qualified labour. Another example is the payment made to a piece of capital equipment which has no other use and will not be replaced when it wears out. The more perfect the factor market the greater the likelihood that economic rent payments will be eliminated in the long run and that all factor payments will be transfer earnings.

REVISION TEST

1   Define the term 'transfer earnings'.

2   If the demand curve for a factor shifts to the right what is the effect on the economic rent payments made to existing employed units of the factor?

3   If the supply curve for a factor has unit elasticity what proportion of the factor's reward would be transfer earnings and what economic rent?

4   Give an example of where a person on a large wage or salary could still be receiving economic rent payments.

5   Why are economic rent payments unlikely to persist in the long run in a perfectly competitive factor market?

6   Explain what is meant by 'quasi-rent'.

7   Under what circumstances are super profits a form of quasi-rent?

8   If a person's entire wage consists of transfer earnings how would that person respond to a wage cut?

9   Under what circumstances could a factor reward be negative and to how many factors does this apply?

10 In what ways does profit differ from the other factor rewards?

_____ **Examination questions** _____

1   Examine the relationship between economic rent, transfer earnings and quasi-rent.
(ABE1, June 1988)

2   a) Assuming that each unit of output of labour can be sold for £4 complete the following schedule:

No. of Men	Total units produced	Average units produced per man	Marginal product (physical)	Average revenue product	Marginal revenue product
(a)	(b)	(c)	(d)	(c)*£4	(d)*£4
1	10				
2	25				
3	45				
4	65				
5	80				
6	92				
7	102				
8	110				
9	116				
10	120				

b) Draw a graph showing the average revenue product and marginal revenue product.

(ABE1, December 1987)

3 What effect would an increase in the marginal physical productivity of labour have on employment at the level of the firm or plant?

(ICSA, June 1987)

4 How will an increase in the marginal physical productivity of labour affect a firm's cost curves?

(ICSA, December 1987)

5 How will an increase in the price of capital equipment affect the level of employment in a firm?

(ICSA, June 1988)

6 a) What is the difference between the economist's concept of rent and the every-day use of the term to refer to the rent of a television, rent of a car, rent of rooms and so on?
   b) Explain how the rent of land in fixed supply is determined.

(ACCA, December 1989)

7 Firm Y seeks to maximise its profits. It is labour intensive and pays workers the 'going rate' of £x per week. What economic principles underlie the decision as to how much labour it should employ?

(SCCA, November 1988)

8 Explain the statement that the division of income between transfer earnings and economic rent depends upon the elasticity of supply.

(Cert.M., December 1988)

9 Explain how the layman's use of the term rent differs from the concept of 'economic rent'.

(IFA, December 1989)

13 The determination of wages

- *Why are some members of the workforce able to command large economic rent payments, even over a long period?*

- *What effect does the intervention of a trade union have on the market for labour?*

The market for labour

The market for labour is the most complicated and diffused of all the factor markets. There are several distinct markets for each factor but, in the case of labour, the complexities of the workforce make for a large number of different markets with movement between them hindered to a greater or lesser extent by the existence of barriers to mobility, most of which do not apply to the other factors of production.

Labour mobility

In a perfect labour market labour would respond quickly to variations in wage rates between occupations and regional differences in pay. The fact that labour is often lacking in mobility is therefore a principal cause of imperfection in the labour market. The immobility of labour takes two forms:

1 Geographical immobility

This occurs when labour does not move from one area to another to obtain work or to take advantage of higher wages. Its main causes are:

a) Lack of perfect knowledge in the labour market so workers are not always aware of opportunities elsewhere.
b) Variations in housing costs which make movement from poorer areas to more prosperous ones difficult.
c) Family and social ties which make people reluctant to leave their 'roots'.
d) Cultural and linguistic differences may restrict the extent to which people can move from one region to another, a notable problem within the EC.
e) Other non-monetary factors may make people reluctant to move, e.g. the quality of life in a rural area compared to an inner-city area.

2   Occupational immobility

This occurs when labour is unable to move from one occupation to another in response to higher wage rates. Its main causes are:

a)   Lack of perfect knowledge in the labour market concerning the nature of and opportunities in other occupations.

b)   Lack of natural ability to perform certain jobs, e.g. those requiring the ability to work at great heights or a high degree of manual dexterity.

c)   Specialisation between occupations so that workers may not have the experience or necessary qualifications to enter the occupation, e.g. a plasterer cannot become a dentist overnight nor vice versa.

d)   Current members of an occupation may prevent entry from outside through such barriers to entry as the pre-entry closed shop imposed by some trade unions and the stringent examinations of some professional bodies.

The greater the difficulty experienced by labour in transferring from one occupation to another the more inelastic the supply of labour to particular occupations and the greater the opportunity for economic rent earnings. The reverse also applies; where few skills or qualifications are required for an occupation the supply of labour will be highly elastic and only transfer earnings will be received by many of the workers.

The demand for labour

As we saw in the last chapter, the demand for labour is a derived demand and is related to its marginal revenue product. However, in many markets there is control over the demand for labour. The purchasers of labour may amalgamate for the purposes of wage negotiations and act as one, as with the Road Haulage Association. Alternatively, there may be only one purchaser of labour, as is the case with some nationalised industries such as British Coal and the British Railways Board. In either case a monosponistic position prevails and both the wage rate and the number of workers employed will be lower than would be the case in a perfectly competitive labour market as we saw in the last chapter in Figure 12.4.

The supply of labour

We have already seen that the supply of labour depends upon the mobility of labour into a particular occupation. The greater the difficulty experienced by labour in transferring to an occupation the more inelastic will be the supply of labour to that occupation and thus the greater the opportunity for economic rent earnings. The reverse also applies; where few skills or qualifications are required the supply of labour to a particular use will be highly elastic and only transfer earnings will be earned by many of the workers, especially where the demand for labour is dominated by a monopsonist. For such workers trade unions offer the means by which monopoly power may be acquired comparable to that enjoyed by workers with highly specialised skills or qualifications.

The effect of a union entering a particular labour market will depend on whether the market is competitive or monopsonistic. In a perfect market the existence of a union will almost inevitably mean claims for higher wages to push them above their competitive level and perhaps to establish a uniform minimum wage. The effect is illustrated in Figure 13.1. If the union succeeds in establishing a minimum wage of W_2 which is above the market wage of W_1 the supply curve of labour will become a horizontal straight line until Q_3. At Q_3 the original supply curve applies again for wage rates above W_2. The effect on employment, however, is that the higher wage leads to the demand for workers falling from Q_1 to Q_2 so that unemployment in the industry occurs for some union members. The union is thus confronted by the dilemma facing all monopolists; it can control either output (the number of workers available) or price (the wage rate) but it cannot control both simultaneously.

Note that the government faces a similar difficulty if it tries to introduce a minimum legal wage above the market rate. Such a wage rate will tend to lead to a reduction in the quantity of labour demanded and many of the workers which the government has set out to protect will either be out of work or tempted into retaining their jobs by working for less than the legal wage.

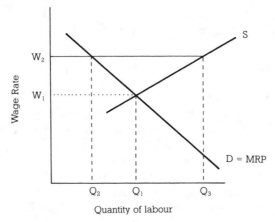

Figure 13.1 *Trade unions and wage rates*

The entry of a union into a monopsonistic labour market is rather more complicated and is shown in Figure 13.2. Before the entry of the union the market wage rate is W_1 and the quantity of labour employed is Q_1. With the introduction of a union minimum wage the supply curve becomes perfectly elastic until Q_2. While it is perfectly elastic the supply curve is the monopsonist's marginal cost curve though at wage rates above W_2 the marginal cost curve jumps to its original line. The firm will employ Q_2 workers since at this point the marginal cost of labour is less than its MRP while beyond Q_2 the marginal cost of labour is above its MRP. The introduction of a union has therefore raised both wages and employment in the industry as the marginal cost of labour is now lower than it was previously between Q_3 and Q_2. If, however, the union attempts to raise wages above W_3 it can only do so at the expense of employment in the industry.

Whether operating in a competitive market or a monopsonistic one, the trade union clearly exercises monopoly power over the sale of labour and will attain a monopoly position if the entire workforce is in the union. Where the industry is dominated by a

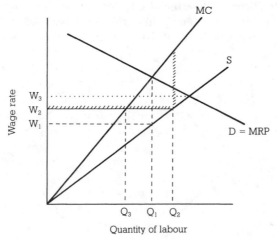

Figure 13.2 *Bilateral monopoly*

monopsonistic employer and a monopolistic trade union the situation is referred to as a **bilateral monopoly**.

Trade union objectives

The above analysis of wage determination shows that the trade union is faced with a dilemma. There is a risk that, in seeking to better the wages and working conditions of its members, it may put some of their jobs at risk. A more desirable outcome for the union will be to use the negotiating process to improve wage rates while protecting or even increasing employment levels. Unions have developed a number of sophisticated negotiating techniques to achieve both these ends but their success in exploiting them depends on the relative strengths of the union and the employer. Union negotiating techniques can be grouped under two headings; those which aim to shift the supply curve of labour to the left and those which aim to shift the demand curve to the right. Collectively they are frequently termed restrictive practices and their effect can be seen in Figure 13.3.

In Figure 13.3 (a) the effect of shifting the supply of labour to the left will be a reduction in the number of available workers at any given wage rate and this will force the wage rate up. The main measures which shift the supply curve to the left are:

1 **The closed shop** This is an agreement between union and management that all workers in the workplace must belong to the union. A pre-entry closed shop requires prospective workers to gain membership of the union before they can obtain employment at the workplace in question. Alternatively a union shop may operate by which all new workers are required to join the union within a set period of being employed by the company. The closed shop prevents non-union workers undercutting the union-negotiated wage and also controls the entry of workers into the industry.

2   **Pre-entry qualifications**   These include apprenticeships and a long series of examinations both of which limit entry into the industry and raise the status, and
therefore bargaining power, of established members of the workforce.

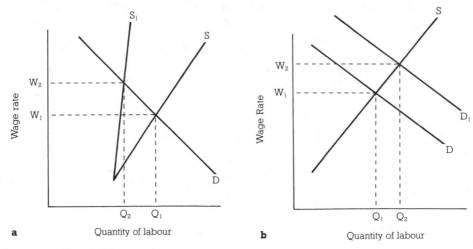

Figure 13.3 *Shifts in labour market curves*

In Figure 13.3 (b) the union's position is even stronger. The demand for labour has
increased and market forces have pushed the wage rate up from W_1 to W_2. The union
can now aim to establish W_2 as the minimum wage as a platform for future pay
negotiations. It can also aim to make the demand curve for labour as inelastic as
possible so that future pay rises do not jeopardise its members' jobs significantly.
Among measures which shift the demand curve to the right are:

1   **Reductions in working hours**   Reduced hours, whether on a daily or a weekly
basis, lead to a need for more workers, all things being equal, or enable existing
workers to receive overtime payments for the same hours worked.

2   **Staffing and safety rules**   Agreements which lay down strict rules on staffing
levels are likely to increase the demand for labour.

3   **Demarcation**   The existence of several unions within one industry emphasises the
individuality of particular skills and so maintains the demand for particular occupational groups within the industry.

Of course, in order for these measures to be implemented the union must secure the
establishment of union rights within the workplace, including agreement that time be
allowed for union meetings and that unpaid officials receive time off for union duties.

REVISION TEST

1   Why is the market for labour more fragmented than that for either land or
capital?

2   Name two factors contributing to the occupational immobility of labour.

3 Name three factors contributing to the geographical immobility of labour.

4 How is economic rent affected by the existence of a perfect market?

5 How does the existence of a union affect a market in which labour is purchased competitively?

6 Explain what is meant by a bilateral monopoly.

7 What is the likely market structure of the industry within which a monopsonist operates? And why?

8 How do union-negotiated pay structures effectively abolish economic rent payments?

9 What would be the effect on the wages of plumbers of a fall in the wages of building workers due to a rise in the supply of building workers?

10 What will be the effect on the demand for labour of the introduction of a minimum wage above the equilibrium level?

The effectiveness of trade unions

The analysis of wage determination shows that the aims of the firm and the trade union are likely to conflict. The aim of the firm is to make profits and, to this end, it will wish to keep costs, including labour costs, to a minimum. To the same end it will wish to retain the greatest possible flexibility in the use of factors of production if it is to pursue an efficient output policy. Thus it may wish to replace labour by capital or vice versa at short notice. The aim of the union, as we have seen, is to protect the jobs of its members and to improve their pay and working conditions.

These conflicting aims are reconciled through the process of **collective bargaining** by which the two sides of industry attempt to resolve their differences and effect a compromise acceptable to both. Sometimes the process of collective bargaining takes place at national level through the mechanism of a bilateral monopoly. Frequently, however, there will be local agreements at the individual firm or plant level. Both employers and unions have a vested interest in settling a dispute amicably since failure to do so will have unpleasant consequences for all concerned. For the firm there is the threat of lost production, reduced profits and possibly the loss of customers. For the workforce there is the likely loss of earnings in the short run and the possible loss of jobs in the long run. The collective bargaining process therefore allows both parties to **satisfice**, i.e. achieve at least their minimum objectives. During any negotiations there are several possible solutions which will enable satisficing to occur. It is the character and astuteness of the various parties involved which determines how far one side or the other is nearer to their ideal outcome when an agreement acceptable to both sides is formulated.

If negotiations are unable to effect an agreement the system of collective bargaining breaks down and both sides will have to resort to means aimed at forcing the other to back down. Both union and firm have a variety of tactics at their disposal. The union can impose an overtime ban or a work-to-rule or withdraw labour by strike action while the firm may send the workforce home, use non-union labour or threaten total closure. A prolonged dispute settles down into a war of attrition; the workers enduring lost earnings and the firm lost output until one side or the other gives in.

Success of union action

Whether in negotiation or through industrial action, the ability of a union to achieve its aims depends upon a number of factors.

1   The ability of the union to present a united front

The union membership may be deeply divided as to the appropriateness of industrial action in a given situation. In these circumstances there is a danger that union solidarity will waver during a protracted dispute. The 1984/85 miners' strike in Britain was weakened from the outset by the fact that the union was divided.

2   The possession of sufficient funds for a long campaign

The funds available in the event of a strike vary considerably from union to union so some workers may be forced to return to work if the firm can hold on until strike funds are depleted. Even where the union can give generous strike pay for a long period the lost earnings will soon mount up and may harden calls among members for a return to work.

3   The ability of the union to control the supply of labour

The existence of a closed shop agreement will enhance the effectiveness of a strike or other industrial action. This is because once a policy is adopted all members of the union must comply with it. Even where there is not a closed shop agreement non-union workers may find it impossible to break a strike in the face of intimidation.

4   The elasticity of demand for labour

This measures the responsiveness of the number of workers employed to changes in wage rates. The more inelastic the demand for labour the smaller the impact of higher wages on employment and thus the greater the bargaining power of the union. The demand for labour tends to be *inelastic* when:

a)   Capital is not easily substituted for labour.
b)   Demand for the final product is inelastic so higher wages can more easily be passed on as higher prices.
c)   Labour is a very small proportion of total costs.

5   The determination of the firm

Sometimes a firm will put up token resistance to a strike but be willing to give in fairly quickly if a prolonged strike is likely to be more costly than giving in. This is most obviously the case when labour productivity is rising and higher wages can be paid without harming the rewards to other factors of production. A firm may prefer also to grant concessions to the union rather than risk being unable to fulfil a vital contract. Against this the firm must consider the implications for the long-term conduct of industrial relations of giving in too readily in the short term. The firm may even see the strike as critical to the long-term viability of its operations and here resistance to union demand could go so far as closing down the firm.

6 The degree of support of other unions

The attitude of other unions will depend very much on the nature of the dispute. While they will not wish to weaken the effectiveness of the action they may have little sympathy with a particular dispute, especially if it places the jobs of some of their own members at risk. Support is most likely to be forthcoming when the dispute is over union recognition or when the justice of the union's case is universally acknowledged in the union movement. In these cases support is likely to take the form of contributions to funds, a refusal to handle the goods of the firm in dispute and possibly even support on the picket lines.

Trade union members are reluctant to cross the picket line of another union, even when they are not party to the dispute. So a company may well have its entire operation brought to a standstill because of a dispute involving only a small section of the workforce.

7 The impact of the action on the community

At first sight it would seem that unions operating in the major utilities and services would be in the strongest position because of the disruption likely to occur as a result of industrial action. The potential dangers inherent in a strike in some of these industries, such as gas or water, is so great, however, that the government would be forced to implement contingency plans which would effectively neutralise industrial action. Thus the army took over certain ambulance duties during the 1989/90 strike.

The attitude of the public is also critical. The public may have considerable sympathy with the union, despite the inconvenience to which they are subjected, as in the British Rail strikes of 1989. Even where there is little sympathy for the union cause the public may favour concessions if it is being subjected to a great deal of inconvenience.

8 Government legislation on industrial action

Where the government has passed legislation concerning the conduct of industrial relations, the firm may be able to use the legal system to prevent the union embarking on a particular course of action. In the UK, for example, the 1980s saw a succession of acts which placed restraints on the power of trade unions in such areas as picketing, the practice of a closed shop, the calling of strikes without a ballot and the election of officials.

But perhaps the most important factor of all is the extent to which both parties to a dispute feel that the union will be successful. The confidence with which both employer and union enter a dispute is inevitably influenced by the economic conditions pertaining to the industry in particular and to the whole economy in general. Throughout most of the 1980s the high unemployment levels in much of British industry seriously weakened the bargaining position of the trade unions and strengthened the willingness of employers to take a firmer line in negotiations. By the end of the decade, however, the shortage of workers led to many unions being once more prepared to take a stronger line in pay negotiations, especially in the public sector.

Trade unions and real earnings

The theory of wage determination predicts that a *long-term* improvement in wages can only be sustained by increases in labour productivity. An increase in the marginal productivity of labour will lead to more workers being demanded at current wages or the same number at a higher wage. In the absence of increases in productivity the union is faced with the choice between current wage rates being maintained over the long term or higher wages resulting in fewer workers being employed.

In practice the position is rather more complicated. In some industries the monopoly power enjoyed by many firms means that they can absorb higher wage costs by a reduction in their level of super profits or can pass them on in the form of higher prices, especially when the demand for their products is inelastic. In these cases the union's ability to achieve higher wages may depend on the success of its negotiating strategy more than on any improvements in productivity by its members.

When we examine real, rather than money, earnings the situation is even more complex. Suppose that all workers receive a 5 per cent rise in wages without any change in productivity and all employers pass the pay rise on in the form of a 5 per cent price rise. There will then be a 5 per cent rise in money earnings but no change in real earnings. Because, however, some unions are more powerful than others and some industries enjoy a greater control over their market than others it may well happen that not all prices and earnings go up by a standard 5 per cent. Instead, some workers will achieve rises of more than 5 per cent and others less. This will result in a redistribution of income from the less powerful, less well-organised groups of workers to those with more bargaining power; the former suffering a fall in real incomes and the latter enjoying a gain.

Wage differentials

Neither marginal productivity theory nor the activities of trade unions are alone sufficient to explain the differences in pay between one job and another. Also important is the value placed by society as a whole on the various occupations performed in society. Such valuations feed through into the pay differentials between occupations. Some are recognised as relevant by trade unions or could be supported by reference to marginal productivity theory but others are based purely on the prejudices of society towards different occupational groups.

1   Skills and qualifications

The possession of rare skills or the attainment of stringent qualifications are generally recognised as being worthy of reward. Such a view is compatible with marginal productivity theory since skilled workers do contribute more to a firm's marginal revenue product than do unskilled workers. Sometimes technological change renders some jobs more skilled while deskilling others; yet the old differentials persist. Printing workers, for example, no longer require the skills that once warranted their being so highly paid.

2   Unique personal qualities

It is impossible to justify the large incomes received by some pop singers, professional sportsmen, film stars or media personalities on economic criteria. They receive such rewards partly because society accepts that they should and partly because of their uniqueness. These payments are therefore virtually pure economic rent since the person concerned would probably stay in the occupation at much lower incomes. It must be remembered that for every 'star' there are hundreds who fail and who will earn only a fraction of the rewards of those who have 'made it'.

3   Dangerous or hazardous occupations

The risks attached to working underground have rightly always been reflected in the pay of miners, yet agricultural workers, who experience a higher fatality rate through industrial injury than do miners, remain among the lowest paid workers in the country. Similarly, the hazards to health associated with certain kinds of factory work from cotton to chemicals have never been recognised in the pay of these groups of workers.

4   Vocations

Because people are attracted to certain occupations for reasons other than monetary reward it is assumed that they can be paid salaries which do not adequately reflect their qualifications and skills, e.g. nurses and teachers. This view is illogical since the chief executives of large companies apparently enjoy their work and yet still receive substantial remunerations.

Civil servants and other government workers also suffer the disadvantage that it is often impossible to identify a direct link between their work and a physical product. This also acts as a negative influence on pay in the private service sector. Even though long-established differentials may change over time there is a tendency for existing gaps in pay to be maintained by the practice of giving percentage increases. The low pay of nurses in the 1960s harked back to the days when nurses were either nuns or the unpaid daughters of the wealthy. Despite the large percentage increases given since then their pay has never caught up with comparable professional groups because of the low base from which it started. Similarly, traditional patterns of pay continue to leave women receiving lower wages than men for work requiring similar skills and experience.

REVISION TEST

1   Why is the closed shop regarded as such an important principle by trade unionists?

2   What action could a trade union take, short of a strike, in furtherance of their claim?

3   Under what circumstances might a firm secretly welcome a strike at its factory?

4   Explain why the basis for the salaries of politicians cannot be found either in market forces or in marginal productivity theory.

5   Explain the term 'demarcation dispute'.

6   What is the formula for the elasticity of demand for labour?

7   Outline three of the main factors which determine whether union action will be successful.

8   How is it possible for a group of workers to raise their real earnings without any improvement in productivity?

9   If money incomes rise by 10 per cent per year and prices rise by 12 per cent, what has happened to real incomes?

10   Why is the pay of train drivers higher than that of most signalmen, despite the fact that the latter are often more highly skilled?

Examination questions

1   a)   Explain the traditional economic theory of wage determination.
    b)   What factors can prevent wages being determined in this way?
                                                        (ABE1, December 1986)

2   Why do wage differentials between groups of workers persist over time?
                                                        (ABE1, June 1987)

3   Examine the supply and demand factors which determine wage rates.
                                                        (ABE1, June 1988)

4   Examine the view that a trade union is only able to raise the real wages of its members at the expense of reduced employed conditions for its members.
                                                        (LCCI Higher, November 1985)

5   a)   How does the marginal revenue productivity theory help to explain wage differentials?
    b)   What other factors may help to explain these?
                                                        (LCCI Higher, May 1986)

6   Examine the extent to which a trade union can secure wage increases for its members.
                                                        (LCCI Higher, November 1986)

7   The data in the following table refer to average gross weekly earnings of adult males in the United Kingdom in 1984.

	Males on adult rates 1984 £
Medical practitioners	381
University academic staff	297
Marketing and sales managers	282
Professional electrical/electronic engineers	245

	Males on adult rates 1984 £
Policemen (below sergeant)	228
Primary teachers	193
Locomotive drivers	172
Toolmakers, tool fitters	165
Postmen, mail sorters, messengers	155
Nurses and midwives	137
Costing and accounting clerks	134
Refuse collectors and dustmen	131
General labourers	127
General farm workers	108
All non-manual	209
All manual	153
All occupations	179

a) Calculate the percentage of manual to non-manual wages.

b) How do you account for the variation between manual and non-manual wages?

c) How do you account for the differences in wages within **either** the manual **or** the non-manual category?

(LCCI Third Level, May 1988)

8 a) How far can the marginal productivity theory of wages explain differences in earnings?

b) What additional factors may be relevant in explaining the differences?

(LCCI Intermediate, May 1986)

9 What are the factors which determine the ability of a trade union to raise the level of wages of its members without affecting the number of jobs available?

(LCCI Intermediate, December 1986)

10 a) How does the *marginal revenue productivity theory* explain the level of wages?

b) What factors determine a trade union's ability to raise the level of wages of its members?

(LCCI Intermediate, May 1987)

11 What effect would an increase in the marginal physical productivity of labour have on employment at the level of the firm or plant?

(ICSA, June 1987)

12 Will a firm operating under conditions of perfect competition necessarily reduce employment if wages increase and the price of the product remains constant?

(ICSA, December 1988)

13 To what extent can the marginal productivity theory account for actual earnings?

(ACCA, June 1988)

14   With reference to marginal productivity theory, explain what influence the existence of a trade union might have on employment and wages if its members worked for:
a)   many different employers?
b)   a single employer?

(ACCA, June 1989)

15   What economic facts must be considered by
a)   the employers, and
b)   the trade union representatives, when entering into negotiations on wages and conditions of employment?

(CIMA, November 1988)

16   The market for labour is highly imperfect. Clarify this statement, and comment on the effect of the market on wage rates.

(CIMA, May 1989)

17   To what extent would the imposition of a statutory minimum wage be likely to solve the problems of low pay in an industrial economy?

(CIMA, November 1989)

18   Why are some workers low paid? Give examples and reasons. Would a national minimum wage improve the position of the low paid in a country?

(Cert.M., June 1987)

19   a)   Define the term 'marginal revenue product'.
b)   Describe four reasons why marginal productivity theory breaks down in the real world.
c)   In simple economic theory, wage rates are the prices determined by the supply of and demand for labour. Explain how this theory needs to be modified to describe a developed economy in which wage inflation significantly exceeds price inflation at a time of historically high unemployment.

(I.Act., April 1987)

14 Investment and the rate of interest

- *How can firms evaluate the relative merits of alternative investment opportunities?*

- *What are the principal ways open to a firm to raise funds for investment purposes?*

The rate of interest

We have seen that the reward to capital is interest. If a firm is able to find all the funds it needs for investment in new capital from its own resources it will receive the interest payments itself (as implicit interest). If, however, it must borrow to finance new investment projects it will enter the market for investment funds and pay interest to those willing to provide funds. As with the rewards to other factors of production, the rate of interest is determined by the demand and supply of loanable funds.

The demand for investment funds

This comes from firms who wish to undertake an investment programme. In assessing the viability of such a programme the firm must either apply a discount to future cash flows or calculate an internal rate of return on the investment and compare it to the cost of capital. In either case the higher the current rate of interest the less attractive will be a particular planned investment. If the firm can borrow all the investment funds it wants at the current rate of interest it will go on borrowing until the rate of return on the last investment project, the marginal efficiency of capital (MEC), is equal to the cost of borrowing, i.e. the rate of interest. Any further investment at that rate of interest will not prove worthwhile. The firm's demand curve for investment funds is therefore the same as its MEC curve.

The firm's demand curve for investment funds will slope downwards from left to right. This is because a fall in the interest rate will make some investment projects previously not worth undertaking now viable. Put another way, the firm will undertake its most profitable investment programmes first and will be willing only to pay a lower rate of interest for less profitable programmes.

The supply of investment funds

This comes from those economic decision makers with funds available to lend to firms. Thus individual households may be willing to forego current consumption and make part of their incomes available for investment purposes in return for interest payments. Similarly, some firms may decide to lend funds to other firms if they are unable to identify investment projects of their own which will yield a comparable return. The higher the rate of interest the more likely are economic decision-makers to be willing to sacrifice liquidity in return for interest payments, so the supply curve for investment funds slopes upwards with the rate of interest.

The market for investment funds

The market MEC curve comprises the individual MECs of firms wishing to obtain investment funds. The market supply curve aggregates the supply curves of all those with funds available for investment. Classical economic theory predicts that the prevailing interest rate in the market will be determined by the interaction of the demand and supply of funds for investment purposes. For simplification it is assumed that there is only one market for investment funds. This is shown in Figure 14.1 where the intersection of demand and supply curves produces an interest rate I_1.

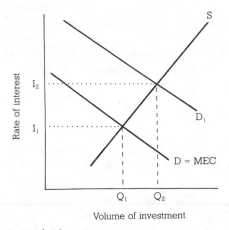

Figure 14.1 *Market for investment funds*

Changes in business expectations as to the likely return on investment will cause a shift in the demand for investment funds, irrespective of the current interest rate. So in Figure 14.1 a more optimistic business atmosphere leads to demand shifting from D to D_1, and when equilibrium is restored the quantity demanded and supplied of investment funds has expanded to Q_2 while the market interest rate has risen to I_2. Conversely, a less optimistic attitude among firms will lead to a reduction in the level of investment activity and a fall in the market interest rate.

Thus far we have treated the market for investment funds as a single, perfect market with one rate of interest. In fact, investment funds are relatively homogenous and very mobile between uses. In addition, the market for such funds is both highly competitive and well-informed. However, there are imperfections in the market and these account for the fact that there are always several interest rates in operation at any one time. The principal factors causing imperfections in the market include:

1 **Expectations** The difficulties associated with predicting the returns from a particular investment mean that the interest rate can only be one factor in the decision to invest. Confidence, or lack of it, in the firm's future and a particular project will often be the key factor in an investment decision.

2 **Necessity** A firm whose stock of capital equipment is nearing the end of its useful life will be likely to undertake planned replacement investment even if there is a sudden rise in interest rates.

3 **Time** Not all investment projects cover the same time period. In consequence suppliers of funds will expect a higher reward if their funds will be tied up for a number of years rather than for just a few months.

4 **Risk** Investment in a new company will probably be viewed as being more risky than in a long-established firm with a good reputation. The latter will therefore be able to borrow funds more cheaply and benefit from financial economies of scale.

5 **Attitudes to thrift** Consumption and savings patterns depend as much on social attitudes towards thrift as on the rate of interest. British society, for example, is much less committed to saving for its own sake than was the case 30 years ago.

6 **Monetary factors** Interest rates are influenced not only by the demand and supply of investment funds but also by the demand to hold money in liquid form. Furthermore, borrowing is not restricted to firms undertaking capital investment. Households also borrow in order to finance their consumption of goods and their needs must be met from the same pool of loanable funds.

These imperfections in the market have two consequences. First, instead of one market for capital there are several linked markets, each catering for particular groups of borrowers. Second, at any one time there will be many interest rates in operation. These will reflect the risk and/or inconvenience attached to the loan for the lender. Clearly, each of the linked markets referred to above will have its own competitive interest rate. The influence of other factors on the rate of interest will be examined in a later chapter.

The investment decision

Investment is undertaken by a company when it purchases capital in the form of buildings, equipment and tools to aid production. Such investment is likely to fall into one of three categories:

1 The direct replacement of capital items which have reached the end of their working lives.

2 The replacement of one of the other factors of production, e.g. labour.

3   To enable the firm to expand its productive capacity or diversify its operation.

4   The building up of stocks of finished goods.

By undertaking investment the firm is using resources that could have been diverted to current production, e.g. through the purchase of raw materials, or retained by the firm as profit. It must be assumed, therefore, that the aim of the investment will be to add to the firm's profitability. For this to be the case the projected increase in revenue resulting from the investment must be greater than the anticipated cost of that investment. Of course, much of the investment undertaken by the firm is replacement investment for those capital items which have worn out and here the expected costs and benefits will be easily gauged. Even then, the firm must be aware that by such investment it is foregoing alternative investment opportunities.

For new investment, in particular, the costs are substantial. In the short run they will include:

1   The revenue that would have been earned if the resources used had been allocated to working capital and used to aid current production.

2   The interest which must be paid on borrowed funds or, if the firm uses its own funds, the foregone interest which the firm would have earned had it invested the funds elsewhere.

3   The fact that the resources are tied up for the life of the capital item since many capital items have no alternative use.

The long-run cost is all those other capital investment possibilities that have had to be foregone. Furthermore, an investment project which failed and so wasted resources which could have been profitably used elsewhere, could have disastrous consequences for the firm.

Investment appraisal

Whether the planned investment is a replacement programme or a new departure for the company, the firm has at its disposal a number of techniques for appraising the worth of a particular investment and thus choosing between alternative investment projects. The underlying difficulty of investment appraisal is that uncertain future returns must be evaluated against present outlays. A taxi firm buying a new cab, for example, cannot know for certain how long the cab will be in service nor how many fares it will generate during that time. The problem is further complicated by changes in the value of money over time so that future receipts may not be equivalent in value to the same payment received today.

If, therefore, alternative investment projects will yield the same future returns over different time patterns it is necessary to devise a method of choosing the most pro-fitable. This is achieved by establishing the present value (PV) of a sum of money to be received in the future. Assuming that money will fall in value over a future time period the present value of anticipated future payments is calculated by applying a discount to them. In the absence of precise information concerning the future value of money this discount is related to the current rate of interest. So, if an interest rate of 10 per cent is assumed, £100 invested today will return £110 after one year but the PV of £100 received in one year's time will be equivalent only to that sum which will, invested today at 10 per cent give a return of £100 after one year, i.e. £90.91. As a rule the PV of a sum due in the future (S) based on the assumed interest rate (r) is:

$$PV = \frac{S}{(1 + r)^n}$$

where n is the number of years (or other time periods) before the sum becomes due.

Thus the present value of £100 received in one year when the interest rate is 10 per cent will be:

$$PV = \frac{£100}{(1 + 0.1)^1} = £90.91$$

Since the discount must be applied for each year that passes before the payment is received, the present value of this £100 received in two year's time would be:

$$PV = \frac{£100}{(1 + 0.1)^2} = \frac{£100}{(1 + 0.1) \times (1 + 0.1)} = £82.64$$

and so on.

Where a series of cash payments will be received over a number of years the present value will be:

$$PV = \frac{S_1}{(1 + r)^1} + \frac{S_2}{(1 + r)^2} + \frac{S_3}{(1 + r)^3} \text{ etc.}$$

Thus, if a firm undertakes an investment project which is expected to return £100 one year from now and £300 per annum for the following three years, the present value of the future returns (assuming an interest rate of 10 per cent) will be:

$$PV = \frac{£100}{(1 + 0.1)^1} + \frac{£300}{(1 + 0.1)^2} + \frac{£300}{(1 + 0.1)^3} + \frac{£300}{(1 + 0.1)^4}$$
$$= £90.91 + £247.93 + £225.39 + £204.90 = £769.13$$

Once the present value of the anticipated returns has been calculated it is possible to appraise the investment by deducting the cost of the project (C) from the present value to work out the net present value (NPV):

$$NPV = \frac{S}{(1 + r)^n} - C$$

If the NPV is greater than zero then the project is justified since it will repay the cost of the original investment and provide adequate compensation for the foregone use of the funds. Clearly if the firm is choosing between a number of possible investment projects it should select the one with the highest NPV.

The net present value method of discounting assumes a discount rate and applies it to the revenue received. An alternative method of discounting is the internal rate of return (IRR) or marginal efficiency of capital (MEC) method. This method treats the rate of discount as unknown and circulates that rate which will produce a present value of return equal to the cost of the project. The rate thus produced is the internal rate of return on the investment. If this rate is higher than the cost of acquiring capital, i.e. higher than the market rate of interest, the project will be rejected. If, for example, an outlay of £1 200 yields a return of £240, £576 and £1040 over the next three years a discount must be found which will reduce that total return of £1856 to a present value of £1200. Thus:

$$£1200 = \frac{£240}{(1+r)} + \frac{£576}{(1+r)^2} + \frac{£1040}{(1+r)^3}$$

which produces a discount rate of 20 per cent – the precise workings of this calculation need not concern us.

In practice, the two methods of discounting a cash flow produce the same indicator as to the viability of a particular investment. However, each method is claimed by its supporters to have a superior edge. The NPV method is claimed to be more accurate in ranking alternative projects in order of profitability and therefore to be superior on the grounds that the object of investment *is* profitability. On the other hand, the IRR method is said by its supporters to be more appropriate to the needs of managers used to the concept of a return on capital employed. It is also easier to compare the IRR with the cost of capital employed whereas the NPV method requires an estimate of present values for each possible cost.

While the debate about which of these methods is better may be inconclusive both are vastly superior to the various 'rule of thumb' methods of investment appraisal used by many businesses. These include the **pay-back** method which measures the period of time necessary to recoup sufficient profits to cover the initial outlay. The shorter the period involved the more attractive the project. Another is the **book rate of return** method which relates the rate of profit after depreciation to the initial capital outlay. If, therefore, an investment earns £500 over 10 years on an outlay of £250 the average rate of return is 20 per cent. This average rate of return is then compared to the cost of capital to see whether the project is worthwhile. Such methods take no account of the time element and the effect this has on the value of future receipts and can therefore be no more than rough guides to see whether a proposed project is worthy of more scientific analysis.

REVISION TEST

1   What would be the effect of a rightward shift in the demand for investment funds?

2   What are the main factors causing imperfections in the market for investment funds?

3   Name the main forms of investment by a firm.

4   For what reasons may replacement investment not be automatic?

5   Distinguish between the short-run and long-run costs of undertaking an investment project.

6   Why are even scientific methods of investment appraisal likely to be less accurate the longer the time period under consideration?

7 What is the present value of £200 received in three years' time when the current rate of interest is 10 per cent?

8 How is the net present value calculated?

9 What is the principal difference between the NPV and IRR methods of investment appraisal?

10 Name the two main 'rule of thumb' methods of investment appraisal.

Sources of finance

Internal funds

The funds for an investment project must either be generated from within the firm itself or be raised by borrowing from outside sources. Internal funds represent a less costly form of finance since there are no interest charges to be borne by the investment. However, the firm must take into account the opportunity cost of using its own resources in this way, i.e. the income which could be earned if the funds were lent out elsewhere.

The return on an investment, therefore, even from internal funds, needs to be considerably higher than the market rate of interest to make the investment worthwhile. Suppose a firm is contemplating whether to invest £5000 in new machinery or to lend the funds out on the market and receive an interest rate of 12 per cent. The return on the investment in machinery will have to be much more than 12 per cent to compensate for the depreciation of the capital asset and the provision of funds for its eventual replacement. If the life-expectancy of the machinery is 10 years the return on capital will need to be 22 per cent per annum to equal the earnings of a risk-free investment in the market for 10 years without loss of capital value. If the value of money is declining the return on capital invested could rise in the latter years of an asset's life but this will be offset by a rise in the replacement cost of the asset.

This requirement that the return on capital be sufficient to compensate both for risk and for replacement costs has another effect. During periods of low business confidence companies may well prefer to lend out accumulated profits, perhaps overseas, rather than increase their own productive capacity.

External funds

A firm which borrows to finance an investment project must earn enough from the investment to repay the interest due on the loan as well as the original funds. The rate of interest payable will, in addition, reflect the fact that capital equipment is not always good security against a loan because of the low resale value of most of it.

1 Long-term loans

The commonest form of loan capital is the **debenture**, a secured loan against one or more of the firm's assets. The debenture-holders receive a fixed-interest payment on their loans which must be paid before the firm can make any profit distribution. If it fails to meet these interest payments the debenture-holders have the right to put the company into liquidation and recover their funds from the sale of the assets pledged against the debenture.

The other main long-term loans available to the firm are the **mortgage**, usually linked to buildings, and the **unsecured loan stock** which is not redeemable against a particular asset but gives the holder similar rights to other creditors of the business.

2 Short and medium-term loans

Traditionally banks have been important sources of short-term finance for firms in the form of **overdrafts** and **bridging loans**. Bank credit represents a more significant source of funding for small firms than for large ones but for all firms it is a minor source of finance. In recent years, however, banks have played a greater role in the provision of long-term finance in the form of debentures and mortgages.

Two other forms of short-term finance for the small firm are *hire purchase* for the provision of capital equipment and *trade credit* to help spread the burden of finance for supplies and stocks.

3 Capital issues

The other principal source of capital funds is the part-sale of the business itself. For the small one-person business this may consist of forming a partnership while partnerships may expand by the addition of further partners. While such a move adds to the financial strength of the business it also results in shared control and perhaps a loss of cohesion of purpose. Instead the small firm may opt to become a limited company to facilitate the raising of capital without the need to relinquish control of the business.

Both private limited companies and public limited companies (PLCs) are able to make a share issue to raise capital. However, private limited companies are not able to make as much use of this facility as are PLCs since there are restrictions on their freedom to issue shares. Furthermore since they do not have a stock exchange quotation, as do PLCs, there is no secondary market in their shares.

Shareholders acquire part-ownership of the company in return for their purchase of shares. There are several types of share, the main ones being **ordinary shares** and **preference shares**. Ordinary shareholders are entitled to the distributed profits of the company, in the form of a dividend, after all other claims have been met, though there is no guarantee that a dividend will be paid. Each ordinary share carries a vote at the annual general meeting and the shareholders therefore have some control over the management of the company. In practice, the vast majority of shareholders rarely exercise these rights so control tends to remain with the directors who can rely on the support of the main shareholders. Preference shares rank before ordinary shares in the payment of dividends though normally the rate of return is fixed, however well the firm is doing and they do not normally carry a vote unless the company is unable to meet the annual dividends.

There are four principal ways in which capital issues may be made:

1   The company may make a **rights issue** whereby existing shareholders are given the option to buy additional shares in proportion to their existing holding.

2   It may sell shares direct to the public, either at a fixed price or by tender.

3   It may make an **offer for sale** by floating an issue of shares through an issuing house.

4   The shares may be issued via a **placing** whereby the shares are sold in large parcels to financial institutions such as pension funds and investment trusts.

In 1980 the Unlisted Securities Market (USM) was established to assist small to medium-sized companies which wished to obtain a quotation on the Stock Exchange but were deterred either by the cost of obtaining a quotation or by the requirement that 25 per cent of equity be held by the public. The USM enables such firms to float a share issue with only 10 per cent in public hands.

Gearing

The ratio of an individual company's loan capital and preference shares to ordinary shares is known as its 'gearing'. A newly floated public company may have difficulty in raising capital through the issue of ordinary shares. Instead it will have to offer investors the greater security afforded by debentures and preference shares. Companies with relatively little of their capital in the form of ordinary shares are termed 'highly geared'. The advantages of high gearing are that:

1   The management can retain control of the business by ensuring that they hold the voting capital.

2   If the firm is successful there will be relatively few ordinary shareholders to benefit from the high profits available for distribution.

On the other hand, high gearing carries some dangers:

1   As the interest on loans must be paid each year there is a considerable strain on the company during periods of financial difficulty when large interest payments only add to its problems.

2   High gearing makes the company a less attractive proposition to future investors when it wishes to raise further capital through the sale of ordinary shares since large interest payments will have to be made before ordinary shareholders can expect to receive a dividend.

As firms get larger their gearing tends to become lower and most public-quoted companies have a relatively low gearing.

Internal versus external funds

For most companies internal sources of funds are far more important than external sources and represent some 90 per cent of total finance. In the case of small firms there may be little choice as they often have difficulty raising all the funds they need from external sources. In the case of large firms the decision to use internal finance often reflects a desire to maintain control over its investment policy. For all firms there is the added attraction that internal funds can be used for more risky projects than could external funds. However, external sources of capital are vital to industry as a whole since few firms can rely entirely on their own resources for expansion. Since externally financed projects are likely to be costed more rigorously than internally financed ones they also help set a standard by which to judge the efficiency of internally generated investment.

TABLE 14.1
Industrial and Commercial Companies
Financial Liabilities 1985–1988

			£ billion	
	1985	1986	1987	1988
Bank borrowing:				
Sterling	5.2	8.4	9.8	21.3
Foreign Currency	2.4	1.0	3.2	8.3
Trade Credit	0.1	0.0	0.1	0.3
Other Loans	0.7	1.5	2.8	3.8
UK Capital Issues	4.3	5.9	13.7	5.8
Overseas Finance	0.6	4.4	6.7	6.6
Total	11.3	21.2	36.3	46.2

Source: Barclays Bank.

Government financial assistance

In addition to the capital market and financial institutions companies also have access to funds provided by the state or state-sponsored organisations.

In the UK 1945 saw the Industrial and Commercial Finance Corporation (ICFC) set up to provide long-term and permanent capital in amounts up to £200 000 (later £300 000) to small and medium-sized companies. Its capital was subscribed by the Bank of England and the principal deposit banks and it had borrowing powers of £30 million, solely through advances from the subscribing banks.

Also in 1945 the Finance Corporation for Industry (FCI) was formed with a capital of £25 million, again subscribed by the Bank of England and the main deposit banks. Its role was to invest in industries which were experiencing difficulties and therefore could not raise capital through more conventional means. In 1974 the FCI was merged with the ICFC to form Finance For Industry (FFI), both organisations retaining their autonomy. This organisation is now known as Investors in Industry (3i) and by the end of 1986 had invested over £3 billion in more than 8000 businesses.

In addition, the government makes a number of grants to individuals who are setting up in business, especially where they have been unemployed for a considerable period.

The location decision

One of the most important investment decisions made by a firm is that of choosing a site for its activities since this will have implications both for its costs of production and for the effectiveness of other investment undertaken. The theory of the firm predicts that the firm will seek a cost-minimising site so that the most important factors in the location decision will be:

1   The cost of transporting raw materials and the finished product to and from the site.

2   The rent and other costs related to each possible site.

In practice locational decisions are the result of a far greater number of factors, not all of which can be justified on economic grounds alone. Rather locational policy appears to confirm the behaviourist view that firms seek to find a suitable site which satisfies the minimum requirements of the various interests operating within the firm. The principal influences on location are:

1   Transport costs

The firm incurs transport costs, both in taking delivery of raw materials or semi-manufactures and in getting its finished product to the market. The cost-minimising location could therefore be near its source of raw materials, near its market or somewhere in between the two. In practice the last choice is likely to be the most costly. Transport costs per unit of distance fall as the distance is increased so a location involving short delivery distances for both raw materials and finished product will have higher transport costs than either of the alternatives.

In deciding whether to locate near the raw materials or the market the nature of the product itself is important. If the product loses weight during the production process transport costs will be kept down by locating near the source of raw materials. The fish curing industry, for example, is located near the ports rather than transport the bulky waste to market. The most extreme form of 'weight-losing' industry is an extractive industry like quarrying or mining which has no choice but to be located near its raw materials. If, on the other hand, the finished article is heavier than its essential raw materials the industry is 'weight-gaining' and transport costs will be minimised by locating at the market. So breweries add the bulkiest constituent of beer, water, at sites near the market.

The question of weight is less critical when the weight of the raw materials is small in relation to their value. Thus diamonds are transported from Africa to Europe for cutting and finishing while high-technology assembly plants can be located virtually anywhere.

The transport costs of fuel can also be a major influence on the location decision. A firm with high fuel demands may then be torn between a location site near the fuel and one near the raw materials. Since fuel is likely to lose a greater proportion of its weight in the productive process than most raw materials, the total weight of raw materials used will need to be greater than that of fuel to justify a location near the raw materials.

2   Markets

Most industries exhibit an increasing tendency to become 'footloose', i.e. their precise location has little bearing on their performance. This trend is due to several factors:

a) Alternative sources of fuel and a more efficient use of energy have released firms from the need to be sited near traditional sources of fuel.

b) The relative decline of transport costs and the greater flexibility of road transport has led to distance from raw materials or market being less of a limiting factor on location.

c) An increasing number of industrial processes involve the assembly of components from several different areas and no one site minimises transport costs.

This greater footlooseness has encouraged firms to locate nearer the market, particularly if the final product is weight-gaining. In the UK newer industries have tended, therefore, to gravitate towards the south-east, both because it is the largest and most prosperous market in the country and because it is near the even larger potential market of Europe. Other industries must, by their very nature, be sited near the market. These include the private and public service industries which are customer-oriented and whose location reflects the distribution of the population.

3   External economies of scale

Many industries remain concentrated in the areas in which they originated long after they become footloose. This concentration will be perpetuated by new firms being drawn to the area to benefit from such external economies as:

a) *A trained labour force*   A firm will reduce its training costs if it can recruit from a pool of labour already familiar with the tasks to be performed. In addition further education and training in the area is geared to providing support for the local dominant industries.

b) *Subsidiary and servicing industries*   As an industry grows in an area other firms providing components and maintenance facilities spring up around it. Such facilities are unlikely to be so developed elsewhere.

c) *Joint ventures*   Firms within the area may exchange technical expertise or develop complementary products. There may also be opportunities for the joint marketing of goods or joint purchase of materials.

d) *Prestige*   Once an area is associated with an industry firms will enhance their prestige by having an address in that area, e.g. diamond merchants in Hatton Garden or potters in Staffordshire.

4   Personal factors

The location of many a firm owes its origin simply to the personal preference of the founder. In long-established companies the personal preferences of managers and other key personnel continue to be important in determining location decisions. Managers will be reluctant to leave an area in which established business connections make marketing and the raising of finance an easier task than in a new location while family or social ties may be a disincentive to relocation. Firms which wish to move and to take key personnel with them must therefore choose an area which meets the expectations of such staff with regard to amenities. The research centres of most major industries, for example, are located in attractive parts of the country.

5   Government regional policy

Governments have often adopted policies which encourage firms to move their operations from one area to another or to direct their expansion into a new area. The aim of such policies is to stimulate the level of economic activity in particular parts of the country, especially those with high unemployment and traditional industries in decline. In the UK regional policy developed in response to the problems posed by the decline of several industries which were heavily concentrated in the North of England, Scotland and Wales; notably coal, steel, shipbuilding, heavy engineering and textiles. Principally, these problems were:

a) High unemployment, compounded by the occupational immobility of labour.
b) Wasted resources, whether unemployed labour, derelict land or abandoned factories.
c) Unbalanced growth in the economy which inhibits national planning and may result in inflation in prosperous areas while unemployment persists elsewhere.
d) Decline in social standards which manifests itself in depopulation (and congestion in more prosperous areas), and falling standards of health and education as local communities are unable to generate the wealth to maintain investment in the provision of such services.

Governments have responded by designating the worst affected areas as development areas and applying a variety of measures to alleviate the situation. The most important measures have been:

a) *Planning controls*   Until 1980 new factory and office space required an industrial development certificate (IDC) and the conditions under which these were issued were significantly less stringent for firms expanding in those areas designated as development areas.
b) *Industrial grants*   Firms in the development areas received more generous grants towards the purchase of plant and machinery.
c) *Tax allowances*   Firms in the development areas have received more generous tax relief on investment as well as a reduction in rates and development land taxes.
d) *Training allowances*   Firms have received support towards their training and retraining costs via the government's manpower and training strategy.

In the 1980s government policy has moved away from assistance to entire regions to help for those parts of the country where the problems are most serious. Between 1981 and 1984 25 enterprise zones were established to target assistance towards run-down city centres and other areas of severe decay. In 1988 development aid for larger companies was reduced to those projects which would not have taken place without government support. The funds so released are to be used to support small firms in the depressed areas and to encourage foreign firms to invest in the UK.

It is difficult to assess the effectiveness of development aid. The main form of regional assistance has always consisted of financial inducements for firms to move to the depressed areas. Such incentives are likely to appeal to footloose and capital-intensive industries and those which do not require a large pool of skilled labour. Thus regional aid has not always resulted in alleviating the root cause for intervention – high unemployment. Furthermore, regional policy has failed to tackle the problem of rigid wage structures. At least until the 1980s labour costs in the depressed areas were not sufficiently lower than elsewhere to attract new sources of employment.

The other major criticism of regional policy has been its emphasis on crisis measures rather than conscious planning for the regions. At no time has there been an attempt to reconstruct an area through the creation of an environment likely to give rise to spontaneous growth. Despite these failings regional policy has prevented greater economic waste and social unrest from arising in the depressed areas and has been responsible for the creation of some 900 000 jobs since 1960.

Changes in industrial location

There are, as we have seen considerable pressures keeping a firm in its current location. While change does occur the process is a slow one so that well under 1 per cent of total employment in manufacturing is affected by locational change in any year.

Much of the change that does occur is associated with expanding firms moving away from town centres to industrial estates on the outskirts. This is largely due to the fact that expansion is difficult in inner-city areas where land is at a premium, especially since the modern factory building operating on flow-line production methods needs more land than the old multi-storey factories. Fringe areas therefore provide a more practical outlet for expansion, especially as the greater available space enables them to provide car-parking, a sports and leisure centre and other facilities to keep key workers and attract new ones. Growing traffic congestion in city centres and greater restrictions on heavy goods vehicles coupled with stricter controls on pollution also combine to drive manufacturing firms out of city centres. Their places are taken by firms in the commercial and financial services sector who can use the space more effectively.

The inertia which pervades industrial location means that a location must become very unfavourable for a firm to seek a new location. The greatest pressure for movement is expansion so that relocation may be forced on the firm. Even then factors such as external economies of scale may lead a firm to seek relocation without having to leave the area entirely.

The impact of government policy is debatable. On the one hand it may stimulate firms to break out of their locational inertia into areas where the scope for expansion is greater. On the other hand firms may be dissuaded from siting their operations in the most efficient location, instead going elsewhere to take the benefit of government financial assistance. In the latter case the likelihood is that the firm will move away from the area once the financial incentives have been exhausted.

REVISION TEST

1 Why does the return on borrowed funds have to be so much greater than that on internally generated funds?

2 Why are internally generated funds by far the more important source of funding?

3 What is the difference between a share issue and a loan issue?

4 What are the main sources of short and medium-term loans?

5   How does a preference share differ from an ordinary share?

6   Explain the term 'gearing'.

7   What, if any, are the advantages of high gearing?

8   Explain the difference between a 'weight-gaining' and a 'weight-losing' industry.

9   What are the main external economies of scale which lead to the locational concentration of a particularly industry?

10 In what way may government policy on relocation conflict with economic efficiency?

_____ **Examination questions** _____

1   How can an enterprise raise finance?   (ABE1, June 1986)

2   What factors would a firm need to consider when deciding where to produce?
                                                                (ABE1, June 1988)

3   Study the following extract:
    'Cantector PLC is a company involved in selling computers and software pro-
    grammes. Such is the extent of the business that it wishes to expand into new areas
    and open several overseas branches. It needs £2 million for its expansion.
    a) Describe three ways the company may attempt to raise this £2 million.
    b) How might a government assist in this expansion?
    c) What special help may the company obtain in insuring its overseas sales
        against bad debts?
                                            (LCCI Intermediate, November 1987)

4   What effect does an increase in the level of investment have on the rate of interest?
                                                            (ICSA, December 1987)

5   What economic factors might a manufacturing company take into account in
    deciding whether or not to move to a new location.
                                                                (CIMA, May 1989)

6   Describe the ways in which a public limited company may finance its activities.
                                                            (CIMA, November 1989)

7   Firm X, located in your country, is a family-owned manufacturing business
    employing about 50 people. The firm wants to undertake long-term expansion.
    Compare the merits of the various sources of capital open to it.
                                                            (SCCA, November 1988)

8   Your organisation is considering moving to an area of above average unem-
    ployment. Examine what factors it should consider in determining whether such a
    move is in the interests of the organisation.
                                                            (IPS, November 1987)

9   'Regional policy – a half-hearted failure'.
    Discuss this statement with reference to the traditional determinants of industrial
    location.

    (IPS, May 1989)

10 Company XYZ PLC, which has both share capital and loan capital outstanding, is
    facing two main financing requirements:
    a) the building of a new factory which is expected to begin production in two
        years' time, and
    b) a cash flow problem due to late payment from debtors and a temporary surplus
        of stocks.
    Discuss:
    i) The types of finance that could be considered to meet each of the above
        requirements.
    ii) The advantages and disadvantages of each type of finance to the company, to
        its existing shareholders and to its loan stock-holders.

    (I.Act., September 1987)

11 a) State reasons why companies raise finance.
    b) Discuss reasons why companies should prefer to borrow in certain circum-
        stances rather than issue further share capital.

    (I.Act., April 1988)

12 a) A single investment of £20.95 million is expected to yield amounts as follows:

At end of year	Amount (£ million)
1	2
2	6
3	10
4	11

    Calculate the net present value (NPV) assuming an interest rate of 10 per cent
    and calculate the internal rate of return (IRR).
    b) Compare and contrast the NPV and IRR methods of evaluating yields bringing
        out clearly the advantages and disadvantages of each method.
    c) Describe two alternative 'rule of thumb' methods of evaluating yields.

    (I.Act., September 1989)

13 A United Kingdom company is seeking a Stock Exchange listing for the first time.
    Describe briefly four methods by which the company may make a new issue of
    ordinary shares.

    (I.Act., September 1989)

14 Identify the arguments for and against the government of a country intervening in
    the location decisions of business firms.

    (IFA, June 1989)

15 Money and the banking system

- *How do banks 'create' money?*
- *What distinguishes a bank from other financial institutions?*

Money

Money may be defined as:
Anything which is generally acceptable in settlement of debts.
In this context the term 'debts' includes not only loans or postponed payments but also payments required immediately in return for goods or services. Money confers on its holder an ability to purchase goods and services and other assets but has no direct use. Thus the possession of money is a means to an end, it is not wanted for its own sake.

The functions of money

Money can take many forms and each will be acceptable provided that it can fulfil the four functions of money:

1 Medium of exchange

In the absence of money the exchange of goods and services could take place only through barter. While many primitive societies have used barter as a basis for exchange such a system is fraught with difficulties. There is the rarity of the double coincidence of wants; if you have a telescope and wish to exchange it for a diamond ring how long will you search before you meet someone who is able and willing to take part in such an exchange. There is also the problem of agreeing a rate of exchange between, say, a carpet and eggs. The existence of money enables all goods to be exchanged against it and then used to obtain other goods. Without money the modern economic society based on specialisation and the division of labour could never have developed.

2 Unit of account or measure of value

Money simplifies the process of calculating the rate of exchange between commodities, i.e. it acts as a unit of account. Since all goods and services can be valued in terms of the unit of account, i.e. priced, it is possible to ascribe a relative value to them. The development of a price system makes it easier for households to choose how to allocate their incomes and for firms to compare the costs of alternative production methods.

177

3   *Standard for deferred payments*

Money enables loans and credit to be arranged since both borrower and lender can be sure of the precise sum due however long the time period involved. To perform this function adequately the value of money must be relatively stable or at least subject to predictable changes.

4   *Store of value*

Any commodity can be stored for future use but money has the advantage that it can be stored today without commitment as to how it will be allocated in the future. However, if it is to fulfil this function money must not lose its value while it is being stored. Clearly, the longer the period that money is held in this way the greater the risk involved.

Through history money has taken many forms, from shells to cattle and from salt to diamonds. Indeed, any commodity can perform the role of money provided that it possesses certain key qualities:

1   **Scarcity**   If very common commodities like sand in Egypt or blades of grass in Ireland are used they will command no confidence since they will be seen as worthless. Scarcity gives the appearance of value even if the commodity has no intrinsic value, e.g. paper money. Of course, until quite recently people expected money to have an intrinsic value as with gold or silver.

2   **Homogeneity**   Each unit must be the same, as near as makes no difference or else the commodity will not be able to serve as a unit of account. Salt is therefore suitable to act as money while an animal is less so.

3   **Durability**   The commodity must be sufficiently robust to circulate as a currency. Furthermore, it must not deteriorate if stored otherwise people will be unwilling to hold money for any length of time and it will be unable to perform the function of a store of wealth.

4   **Stable value**   Commodities which fluctuate wildly in supply are not suitable as money since their value is likely to fluctuate too. Thus mined metals like copper or nickel whose supply can be controlled serve as money better than agricultural products like corn or rice.

5   **Divisibility**   To act as a currency the commodity must be easily divisible into units, like grain or salt. Some commodities, such as precious stones, are divisible but lose part of their value if they are split up.

6   **Portability**   The value/weight ratio of the commodity must be sufficiently high that individuals can carry reasonbly high sums of money.

While many commodities have the qualities necessary to enable them to perform the functions of money, precious metals have been the dominant material of money in sophisticated societies until our own time. Apart from meeting all the requirements outlined above, gold, silver, copper and platinum all have intrinsic value. This adds to public confidence in the currency since if the monetary regime should collapse people would still be able to obtain goods and service in exchange for these precious metals.

Even then the value of precious metals could collapse if large new supplies came onto the market, as happened during the sixteenth century.

Modern forms of money

Modern paper money owes its origins to the growing realisation among traders that the transfer of a *claim* to gold or silver was both easier and safer than the transfer of the bullion itself. Increasingly, therefore, a receipt for gold from a reputable banking house was paid in settlement of a debt to be cashed by the recipient when desired. Soon these receipts were circulating without their ever being cashed at the issuing bank and it was a small step for banks to issue such receipts in convenient denominations as bank notes. By 1797 confidence in the use of paper money had become sufficiently wide-spread for it to be the only form of money in circulation until after the Napoleonic Wars. Since 1914 bank notes have ceased to be convertible into gold in the UK and we now have a paper money currency apart from the base metal coinage used as small change.

Most large transactions today are not, of course, made in any of the forms of money considered so far. Increasingly the discharge of debts has taken place without the use of cash by the payment of claims to money through the banking system, i.e. through cheques and other debits drawn on bank deposits. Note that a cheque is not money but the instrument by which bank deposits (which are money) are transferred from one person to another. Bank deposits now constitute over 80 per cent of money in the UK. The important part played by bank deposits subject to cheque within the total money supply is the reason for defining money as 'generally' rather than 'universally' accept-able in settlement of debts. Creditors do not have to accept a cheque but may insist on cash.

Near money

This is a liquid asset which performs some, if not all, of the functions of money but cannot be described as money because it is not generally acceptable in settlement of a debt. Savings accounts with banks and building societies count as near money as do credit cards and money orders. All these assets can quickly be converted into money and are virtually indistinguishable from money in the way they are used but technically cannot be counted as part of the total supply of money.

The measurement of the money supply

A strict interpretation of what constituted the money supply would include only bank notes and coins in circulation, together with non-interest bearing bank deposits subject to cheque. This limited definition is now officially entitled NIB M1 in monetary statistics and, although rather a narrow definition, it can be a useful economic indicator. For practical purposes it might well be considered appropriate to include the deposit accounts held with banks in the money supply. After all, while technically savings they can so easily be converted into cash that they are often used as a reserve to the customer's current account. Thus the measure M2 is used to describe NIB M1 together with interest-bearing deposit accounts of less than one month to maturity held by both commercial banks and building societies.

Yet even this wider definition may be considered inadequate. As we have seen, deposits with many other financial intermediaries, notably the building societies, perform some of the functions of money by acting as a good store of value and are highly liquid, but these can only be classed as near money. So still broader definitions of the money supply have been formulated. M4 includes all time deposits and M5 even more forms of near money. The range of monetary measures in use from June 1989 and their values are shown in Table 15.1.

TABLE 15.1
Monetary Measures: December 1989

			£m
1	Non-bank private sector's holdings of notes & coin	15 578	—
2	Non-bank private sector's holding of non-interest bearing (NIB) bank deposits	32 370	
3	NIB M1 (1+2)		47 948
4	Interest bearing bank deposits in M2	92 718	
5	Building society deposits in M2	96 222	
6	National Savings Bank ordinary account	1 576	
7	M2 (3+4+5+6)		238 464
8	M4 consisting of: Notes and coin	15 297	
	Banks' retail deposits	125 088	
	Building societies shares & deposits	142 115	
	Other interest-bearing bank deposits	135 985	
	Other building society deposits	4 441	
	Total (M4)		422 926
9	Foreign currency deposits	45 950	
10	M4c (8+9)		468 876
11	Money market instruments	5 164	
12	Certain national savings items	11 697	
13	M5 (8+11+12)		439 787

Source: Bank of England Quarterly Bulletin.

The variety of monetary measures now in force gives the government considerable choice in its setting of monetary targets. At the same time these many measures indicate the complexity of the modern monetary system with its thin dividing line between money and other liquid assets.

Banks and the creation of credit

The traditional functions of a bank are:

1 The receipt, transfer and encashment of deposits.

2 The provision of finance through loans to both business and private customers.

Banks therefore take deposits from economic decision-makers with funds surplus to their current requirements and lend them to those with insufficient means to meet current needs.

The function of lending grew out of the realisation by the early bankers of the seventeenth century that most of the funds deposited with them lay idle, waiting to be withdrawn by their owner. With prudence a bank could lend out a significant proportion of these funds without impairing its ability to meet the demands of depositors. It was the development of lending that brought with it the process of bank expansion of the money supply through the creation of credit.

This principle might best be illustrated by an example from a time when gold was the main ingredient of the money supply. An eighteenth century bank receives a deposit of £100 in gold for which a receipt is issued. The assets of the bank have risen by £100 in gold while its liabilities have also risen by £100 through the issue of a receipt promising to pay on demand the sum of £100. Suppose the bank decides that it can prudently make a loan of £10 of this deposit to a reputable customer. There is no change in total assets but £10 in gold has now been replaced by £10 in loans to customers; liabilities remain at the same level as before. The borrower now spends the £10 and it is redeposited with the bank by the eventual recipient, to whom a receipt is issued. The bank's assets now rise by £10 in gold while liabilities rise by £10 in deposits. Although the physical amount of extra gold lodged with the bank has not risen above £100 the total amount of money on deposit with the bank has risen to £110!

From the above example we see that bank lending expands the money supply by leading to an increase in bank deposits. Only if a loan is *not* redeposited with the banking system will no expansion of the money supply take place. Furthermore, even the fact that bank notes are redeemable against gold does not prevent the money supply exceeding the total amount of gold in the banking system. Under the modern monetary regime, of course, the absence of a gold standard means that bank lending policy does not have to be influenced by the need to hold enough gold to meet customers' demands. In consequence the banks can, by an active lending policy, increase the quantity of money in circulation almost indefinitely.

The significance of this may be demonstrated by another simple example. Let us assume that banks keep 10 per cent of all new deposits in reserve to meet demands from customers and other contingencies. If, therefore, a deposit of £100 is made at a bank only £10 will be kept in reserve, the other £90 being lent. This £90 will eventually be deposited with the same or another bank where £9 (10 per cent) will be held in reserve and the other £81 will be lent out. So the process continues until the effect of the initial lending is exhausted, as shown in Table 15.2.

TABLE 15.2
The multiple expansion of deposits

	Deposit (£)	New loan (£)	Reserves (£)
1st Bank	100	90	10
2nd Bank	90	81	9
3rd Bank	81	72.90	8.10
4th Bank	72.90	65.61	7.29
5th and subsequent banks	656.10	590.49	65.61
Total	1,000	900	100

It can be seen that the total increase in deposits from the original deposit of £100 is in this case £1000 or ten times as much. Clearly, the total expansion of deposits will depend on the reserve ratio operated by the banks. This expansion may be expressed as an equation:

$$\frac{£ \text{ initial deposit}}{\text{reserve ratio}} = \text{total expansion of credit}$$

So in this case:

$$\frac{£100}{10\%} = £1000$$

The factor by which the initial deposit grows to become the total expansion of credit is known as the **bank multiplier**, in this case 10. If the reserve ratio is 20 per cent the total expansion of credit arising out of an initial deposit of £100 will be £500 and the bank multiplier will be 5. It is the working of the bank multiplier which results in bank deposits being by far the most significant element of the money supply.

In theory if banks kept no reserve at all the bank multiplier would be infinity. In practice, however, there are three main limitations on the willingness of banks to expand credit indefinitely.

1 Prudence
Banks must keep some liquid reserves to meet withdrawal demands from depositors. This factor alone would indicate the need for a reserve ratio of at least 5 per cent. Banks must also provide for unpredictable demands for financing and for any interruptions to their predicted cash flow.

2 Profitability
Like any other business, a bank maximises its profits when MR = MC.

The marginal revenue from an extra loan is the amount of interest earned on that loan.

The marginal cost of an extra loan consists of:

a) The amount of interest paid on the deposits which are being lent out.
b) The administrative and marketing costs involved in attracting funds and in setting up the loan.
c) A provision for bad debts.

As the amount of credit is expanded the bank will find that its marginal costs rise. This is because it must offer higher interest rates to attract more funds while it will eventually exhaust the supply of low-risk customers and will find bad debts rising. At the same time marginal revenue will fall as firms will have already undertaken their priority investment projects and will only consider further investment at lower rates of interest. Once the optimum profit position is reached, therefore, there will be no gain by further credit expansion.

3 Government controls
In most countries the government or monetary authorities control the ability of the

banks to create credit, either by imposing a reserve ratio on the banks or taking other measures to control lending. This is because control of the money supply is seen as one of the methods open to the government to influence the working of the economy. These measures form the government's monetary policy and they will be examined at length in a later chapter.

REVISION TEST

1   What are the main characteristics required of a commodity for it to serve as money?

2   Name the four functions of money.

3   Give any examples of barter which still persist today, in your society.

4   Why is money '*generally* acceptable in settlement of a debt?'

5   How is it possible for the unit of account to be different to the unit of currency?

6   Why is a credit card not money?

7   Which forms of near money have grown in importance in recent years?

8   What is a reserve ratio?

9   How is the bank multiplier calculated?

10   What are the three limiting factors on the banks' ability to create credit?

The banking system

Financial intermediation

The principal functions of banks, outlined above, are to take deposits and make loans. In this they fulfil the role of **financial intermediaries**. The financial intermediary borrows from those with surplus funds and lends them to those with a shortage of funds. This role is a vital one because the needs of lender and borrower cannot always be matched through direct contact for several reasons.

1   The lender may wish to lend short while the borrower may wish to borrow long.

2   The lender may be willing to lend only a small sum while the borrower wants to borrow a large amount.

3   The lender may be unwilling to take the risk inherent in the borrower's project.

4   Lender and borrower may be unable to communicate directly due to distance or other factors.

The financial intermediary solves these problems by entering into two distinct and very different contracts; one with the lender and the other with the borrower. This enables the needs of both parties to be met. Thus the financial intermediary:

1 Borrows short and lends long, e.g. borrows on seven days' notice and lends on mortgage.

2 Borrows small sums and aggregates them to provide large loans.

3 Transforms risks. Lenders are spared the high risk of direct lending. Instead they enjoy the benefits of the risk-spreading activities of the financial intermediary, whereby losses are absorbed by the large number of loans undertaken.

There are many types of financial intermediary but central to the working of both the financial system and the economy as a whole are the banks.

Commercial banks

The 1979 Banking Act defines a bank as a deposit-taking business:

1 Having a long-established high reputation in the financial community;

2 Providing a wide range of banking services including the following:
   a) current and deposit facilities or the acceptance of funds on the wholesale money markets.
   b) overdraft or loan facilities or the lending of funds on the wholesale money markets,
   c) foreign exchange services,
   d) financing through bills of exchange and finance for foreign trade.
   e) investment advice and the purchase and sale of securities.

The reference to the wholesale money markets is necessary because of the unique role of the discount houses, discussed shortly.

Central to the activities of the major commercial banks is their role as clearing banks. This involves the operation of a money transfer service on behalf of customers and the maintenance of a national network of branches. Their other primary function remains the provision of finance to corporate and private customers. However, the clearing banks have steadily widened the range of services offered to customers and, in addition to those required by the Banking Act, they now provide cash dispensers, credit cards, executor and trustee services, investment management, unit trust management, insurance and property sales.

Some indication of the relative importance of the activities of the clearing banks can be gauged from their combined balance sheet, shown in Table 15.3. Note that, unlike other businesses, the banks list their assets in *descending* order of liquidity. The liabilities side speaks for itself. On the assets side 'Advances' constitute by far the largest proportion but some of the others are worthy of comment.

Certificates of deposit
These are negotiable fixed-term deposits which can easily be sold by the holder if the need arises. The banks both issue them (shown on the Liabilities side) and hold some issued by other banks.

TABLE 15.3
Combined balances of the clearing banks: December 1989

Liabilities	£m	Assets	£m
Capital etc.	61 797	Cash in hand	1 064
Sterling Deposits:		Balances with Bank of England	3 761
UK Banking Sector	25 158	Certificates of deposit	6 047
Other UK Residents	202 605	Balances with UK banks	29 396
Overseas Residents	23 060	Money at call	6 952
Certificates of Deposit	15 599	Treasury bills	1 631
Currency Deposits	63 482	Local Authority bills	293
		Other bills	9 359
		Overseas Market Loans	4 800
		Investments	13 846
		Loans to Local Authorities	370
		Advances	213 071
		Other Currency Assets	76 985
		Investment in subsidiaries and miscellaneous assets	24 126
	391 701		**391 701**

Source: Bank of England Quarterly Bulletin.

Cash in hand and balances with the Bank of England

These consist of cash balances at branches to meet the daily needs of customers and balances with the Bank of England to meet the daily settlement of cheques at the bankers' Clearing House.

Money at Call and Short Notice

As the names imply, these are funds lent to the Money Market, often on a day-to-day basis, which can be called back on demand.

Treasury bills

The government raises some of its finance by the issue of these short-term bearer securities with a life from the date of issue of 91 days. The clearing banks buy them through the money market and hold them as highly liquid assets.

Other bills

The banks also hold bills of exchange drawn on banks or other first-class companies which are purchased at a discount to their face value and are redeemed within periods of anything from 30 days to a year. They may be negotiated and turned into cash if necessary.

Special deposits

These are called for by the Bank of England when it wishes to restrict the expansion of credit, they are effectively frozen accounts at the Bank of England which earn interest at the Treasury Bill rate. Their importance will be examined in a later chapter.

Other commercial banks

The clearing banks are described as retail banks. They deal directly with the public, often in very small funds. The other major banks are the various types of wholesale bank who deal directly only with other financial intermediaries and corporate customers and only in relatively large transactions.

Merchant banks

As the name suggests most merchant banks began as trading firms who branched out into financial activities which in due course became their primary source of income. Their main functions today are:

1 **Bill acceptance**   This is their oldest function and arises out of their long-established links with and knowledge of the trading firms of other countries. It consists of accepting (i.e. guaranteeing) payment of bills of exchange drawn on trading companies in return for a commission. This facilitates international trade in that exporters will have confidence in selling to little-known companies if payment is guaranteed by a bank in the exporter's own country.

2 **Raising corporate finance**   In the late nineteenth century the merchant banks became specialists in raising loans for foreign and colonial governments, notably through the issue of bonds. Today, they specialise in raising capital for companies by floating new issues of share capital and loan stock and advise companies on such matters as dividend policy and takeover bids.

3 **Dealing in the markets**   They take large funds on deposit and invest these in marketable and non-marketable assets. Thus they have become involved in the management of unit trusts and pension funds through their dealings on the capital and money markets. They also operate in such specialist markets as the foreign exchange market, the gold market and the euro-currency markets.

Discount houses

The discount houses are the principal actors in the London money market, acting as banks to the other banks by taking funds at call or short notice and investing them in a slightly less liquid form. Their name comes from their main business of discounting, i.e. buying at less than face value, bills of exchange. They are also very active in tendering for Treasury Bills and in dealing in certificates of deposit and other short-term negotiable instruments.

The importance of the discount houses to the banking system as a whole lies in their relationship with the Bank of England which is discussed in the next chapter.

Foreign banks

These banks operate in London in much the same way as the merchant banks. However, they specialise in banking services for nationals of their country in the UK and in developing commercial links between British firms and those of their own nationality. International banks based in the UK perform a reciprocal function overseas.

The Bank of England

Today most countries have a central bank which supervises and underpins the rest of the banking system. In the UK this function is performed by the Bank of England. The Bank started as a private institution but gradually acquired a central bank role; this position eventually being regularised by it being nationalised in 1946.

Since the Bank Charter Act of 1844 the Bank of England has been divided into two departments; the Issue Department which is responsible for the note issue and the Banking Department which carries out the other functions of the bank. These functions can be grouped under three main headings:

1   Banker to the government

a) *Maintenance of the Exchequer Accounts*   The Bank keeps the central account of the government, together with several subsidiary accounts like those of the Inland Revenue and the National Debt Commissioners.

b) *Management of government borrowing*   The Bank arranges and administers the issue of Treasury Bills and longer term government borrowing, i.e. government stocks. This also involves the determination of interest rates and redemption dates to ensure that the annual turnover in government borrowing follows a smooth path. The Bank also acts as registrar of government stocks, keeping the register of stockholders and making interest payments on the due dates.

c) *Implementation of monetary policy*   The Bank intervenes in the money markets to influence the level of interest rates and lending activity to support the monetary policy of the government.

2   Banker to the banks

a) *Banker to the commercial banks*   Each of the London clearing banks has an account at the Bank of England and the banks settle clearing balances amongst themselves by transfers between these accounts.

b) *Maintenance of the note issue*   The Bank of England is the only English bank empowered to issue bank notes and, except for the first £4.3 million in circulation, the notes of Scottish and Northern Ireland banks must be backed by Bank of England notes. The note issue is, however, an administrative rather than a policy matter. If a bank needs notes it merely draws them from the Banking Department against its account with the Bank. This reflects the fact that it is not the note issue which determines the size of the money supply but the money supply, in the form of bank deposits subject to cheque, which determines the note issue.

c) *Lender of last resort*   Unlike other central banks, the Bank of England does not provide support to the banking system directly but through the discount houses. Each discount house has a loan account with the Bank and can always raise cash at the Bank, usually by rediscounting bills. The Bank of England chooses the method by which it provides support and can dictate the terms on which it will lend; but it never refuses to lend. Thus it gives support indirectly to the entire banking system.

d) *Supervision of the banking system*   Under the Banking Acts 1979 and 1987 the Bank of England exercises a supervisory role over the activities of the banks and other deposit takers. First, all institutions accepting deposits from the public must be authorised to do so by the Bank unless an exempted institution, e.g. a building society. Second, the Bank has powers to examine the capital adequacy and liquidity structure of any institution covered by the legislation. Third, the Bank administers the deposit protection scheme which compensates depositors in the event of a bank's failure.

3 *International financial participation*
   a) *Management of the exchange equalisation account* This account maintains the country's gold and foreign currency reserves. The Bank uses these funds to intervene in the foreign exchange markets to influence the value of the exchange rate.
   b) *Conduct of relations with monetary authorities* The Bank of England provides banking services for other central banks, such as holding and managing on their behalf their holdings of sterling, and vice versa. The Bank also maintains close contact with these banks over such issues as exchange rate fluctuations and joint action is frequently taken. The Bank is also a member of the Bank for International Settlements (BIS) which acts as a clearing house for the European central banks.

Other financial intermediaries

There is a whole range of other financial intermediaries which perform some of the functions of banks.

Building societies
These are deposit-receiving institutions which specialise in the provision of funds for private house purchase. The societies are non-profit making and therefore do not distribute profits as dividends. They have been very successful in attracting funds from personal savings despite being in competition with the retail banks due to certain advantages peculiar to their activities;

1 Their loans are secured against safe assets (housing).

2 Tax concessions are given on both the interest charged and distributed.

3 The turnover in mortgages ensures a regular flow of funds and most deposits tend to be long-term.

Since the 1970s there has been a progressive blurring of the differences between the various types of financial intermediary. Not only have the clearing banks taken on many of the functions previously performed by merchant banks but they have also entered the mortgage market. The building societies have responded by operating more like retail banks, a process accelerated by a number of mergers which created societies with national branch networks to rival those of the clearing banks. By the early 1980s they were offering customers cashpoint dispensers, cheque books, standing order facilities and other retail bank services. In addition they were offering a greater variety of deposit accounts, including high-interest accounts.

These developments were recognised in the Building Societies Act of 1986. This stipulates that 90 per cent of the assets of a building society must be in the form of loans for property purchase but gives building societies greater freedom to compete in a number of areas:

1   They can offer a greater variety of personal finance services, including personal loans.

2   They can offer a more comprehensive money transmission service with overdraft facilities, etc.

3   They can offer house sale and stockbroking facilities.

4   They can raise wholesale funds up to a limit of 20 per cent of total funds.

5   They may become public limited companies, as did the Abbey National in 1989.

Finance houses

Their main function is the provision of medium-term credit, mainly in the form of hire purchase, to private and commercial customers. Their funds are obtained through the money markets and by the issue of bills, though they do take some deposits.

Investment trusts and unit trusts

Investment trusts are public limited companies which raise capital through share issues and use these funds to buy the stocks and shares of other companies quoted on the Stock Exchange. Shareholders are thus able to spread their risk by buying shares in just one company.

Unit trusts perform a similar function except that the units cannot be sold on the Stock Exchange; they must be sold back to the unit trust. The purchase of units is often linked to an insurance policy or other savings scheme so that savers may achieve a greater return than is available from a savings account while minimising the risks attached to the purchase of shares.

Insurance companies

These offer savers a long-term savings scheme based on regular payments, usually coupled with a life policy. The massive funds so accumulated are placed on Stock Exchange and other markets to ensure a regular flow of income and long-term growth in the value of their assets. Pension funds operate in a similar way.

The financial markets

The financial intermediaries lend over longer periods than they borrow. In addition, only a very small proportion of the deposits lodged with them are kept in the form of money. In consequence, there is always the danger that they could find themselves short of liquidity. They can obtain this liquidity through the money markets.

The money markets

The **London money market** is a market for short-term funds in which all banks in London participate. Other financial intermediaries have access to it through their banks. The main business of the market is the buying and selling (discounting and rediscounting) of bills of exchange and Treasury bills and so it is often referred to as the London Discount Market. The market also deals in short-term government and local authority bonds, and certificates of deposit. So banks and other institutions know that they can always raise liquid funds by selling their holdings of these assets on the market. If as we have seen, the discount houses become short of liquidity themselves they can turn to the Bank of England for support.

Since the 1960s a number of 'secondary' or 'parallel' money markets have grown up. The markets provide both liquid assets and profitable lending opportunities for the participants who include the banks, local authorities and commercial companies. The most important secondary market is the **inter-bank market**. This is a market in which banks borrow exclusively from and lend exclusively to other banks, in the form of unsecured short-term loans. The market is particularly useful for merchant and international banks who use it to adjust their liquidity position and to support their on-lending to commercial borrowers. The interest rate operating in the market, the London Inter-Bank Offered Rate (LIBOR), is important in calculating the internal cost of funds charged to banks' branches by their head office and therefore in determining the interest rates charged to customers. Other secondary markets operate to provide liquidity for the local authorities and finance houses.

The capital market

Long-term investment also carries with it the problem of liquidity. Thus the willingness of both private individuals and financial intermediaries to purchase stocks and shares depends on the ability to liquidate their investment should the need arise. The capital market, i.e. the **Stock Exchange** meets this need by providing a market in long-term investments. It must be remembered that the Stock Exchange is a secondary market. The *primary* market for long-term investment funds is provided by the companies which float new issues of shares and loan stock and the government which issues loan stocks and Treasury bills.

That the capital market serves a useful purpose is undoubtedly true. However, the fact that it is a market in used securities leads to some activities which throw it open to criticism. First, much of the buying and selling activity that takes place is speculative and probably contributes no more to the economy than the speculative buying of rare stamps contributes to the development of postal services. Second, the speculative buying of shares in some companies may divert funds away from new investment opportunities without in any way benefitting the company whose share price has risen. Third, the market is dominated by large institutions who may use their power to sway the market or influence the policy-making of companies of which they are large shareholders. Fourth, the world's major stock exchanges are regarded as barometers of confidence in the economy of the country in which they operate. Severe fluctuations in the market can exaggerate trends in the economy and have an unsettling effect on potential investors.

REVISION TEST

1   What are the three functions of a financial intermediary?

2   Explain the difference between a retail bank and a wholesale bank.

3   What is the most important distinguishing characteristic of a clearing bank?

4   Name three of the most liquid assets of a bank, apart from cash.

5   What are the main activities of merchant banks?

6   In what ways does the Bank of England act as banker to the government?

7   What is meant by the 'lender of last resort' role of the Bank of England?

8   How are building societies able to compete so effectively with the banks for 'retail' customers?

9   How would the absence of a money market affect the behaviour of banks?

10 In what way does the capital market assist the process of investment by companies?

_____ **Examination questions** _____

1   In what sense is it true that the banking system can 'create money'? If the money supply can be increased in that way, why do banks face difficulties if too many of their customers withdraw their deposits as cash?

(ABE2, December 1985)

2   What do you regard as the main functions of the commercial banks? Why is it necessary for the activities of commercial banks to be controlled?

(LCCI Higher, November 1985)

3   The following table shows the items on the assets side of a commercial bank's Balance Sheet:

	£ million
Notes and Coins	150
Balance at Central Bank	250
Money at call or short notice	300
Treasury Bills discounted	200
Investments	800
Advances	2200
Special deposits	100
	4000

a) What do you understand by the term 'liquidity'?

b) What is the total value of the bank's holding of liquid assets?

c) Explain the meaning of the term 'special deposits'.

d) If the bank worked on a cash ratio of 10 per cent and it received a new deposit of £4000, what is the maximum amount of new credit it could create?

e) It is often said that banks try to reconcile the conflicting aims of liquidity and profitability.
    Explain what this means.

(LCCI Intermediate, May 1986)

4 a) How essential is money in a modern economy?
   b) It is said that banks can create money. How is this possible?

(ACCA, June 1989)

5 'Bank deposits . . . are largely created by the banks themselves.' (Hanson) Explain this statement, and describe how the power of the banks to create deposits is limited.

(CIMA, November 1988)

6 'The activities of the non-bank financial intermediaries (NBFIs) are important to the long-term financial market.' (Hanson) Who are the NBFIs, and what service do they provide, both as a group and as individual institutions?

(CIMA, May 1989)

7 Compare the functions of a country's Central Bank with the functions of its commercial banks.

(SCCA, November 1987)

8 Identify the major types of financial institutions in any *one* country with which you are familiar. To what extent is the conduct of each of these types of institution regulated by government?

(SCCA, May 1989)

9 What is meant by money? What is the purpose of the numerous measures of money supply that exist?

(Cert.M., December 1988)

10 Commercial banks reserve only a portion of their deposits received. Identify the reasons why we do not have panic runs on the banks. Describe what effect a higher reserve requirement would have on the banking system's ability to create money.

(IPS, May 1988)

11 'The Bank of England acts as "leader of the last resort".
    Explain:
    a) What is meant by this statement.
    b) How the Bank of England (or other central bank) is able to be responsible for implementing the Government's monetary policy.

(IPS, May 1989)

12 'Market making' is one of the major activities of the 'City (of London)'.
    a) List five other financial activities of the 'City'.
    b) Describe briefly how dealing in securities now differs from that which applied before 27 October 1986.

(I.Act., April 1989)

13 Outline the principal functions of a central bank.
Why is it so important for these functions to be carried out?

(IFA, June 1989)

14 What is the role of financial intermediaries within the economy?
What types of intermediary would business firms in your country be likely to deal with?

(IFA, December 1989)

16 National income

- *What is the purpose of calculating national income?*
- *What problems are encountered when attempting to compare the living standards in one country with those in another?*

The flow of national income

Until now we have been concerned with economic activities in so far as they relate to particular situations; the output of the firm, the demand for a particular product, the income of each factor of production, etc. In the remainder of the book we turn our attention to the working of the economy as a whole.

We begin by examining the ways in which the total economic activity of a society can be measured. Such activity results in the creation of economic wealth, i.e. the production of goods and services. The total flow of goods and services in society over a period of time is described by the term **national income**. There are three ways of looking at this flow of goods and services, depending on whether we view the economic decision-makers in society as consumers, income-earners or producers. As consumers they buy the goods and services produced by society. As providers of the factors of production they both produce these same goods and services and receive the incomes derived from the use of their factors. The result is a circular flow of income, as in Figure 16.1.

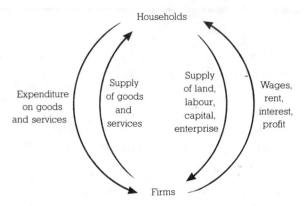

Figure 16.1 *The circular flow of national income*

In the circular flow of income firms pay incomes to households in the form of rent, wages, interest and profit. In return they have the use of factors of production owned by the households. These factors of production are used to produce goods and services which are then purchased by the households and so the cycle begins again. In this simple economy the total output of goods and services must be equal in value to the income paid to the various factors of production. Suppose that a boat is built and sold for £8000 and the total costs of using land (including raw materials), labour and capital amount to £7300; the residue of £700 will be profit retained by the entrepreneur. In the same way, output will also be equal in value to expenditure provided that all income is spent. Thus total expenditure = total income = total output.

The circular flow of income depicted in Figure 16.1 is a simplified model as it assumes a closed economy in which all income flows only between households and firms with no foreign trade. It also assumes no government economic activity. In fact income is lost from the circular flow in the form of **withdrawals** and enters the circular flow from outside the system in the form of **injections**.

The three withdrawals are:

1 **Savings** Households may refrain from spending part of their income, choosing instead to save it.

2 **Taxation** The government takes some household income in taxes, which cannot then be spent.

3 **Imports** When households buy goods from other countries the income leaves the circular flow since it goes to foreign companies.

The three injections are:

1 **Investment** Investment by firms in capital goods is additional to expenditure undertaken by households and thus increases the total income received by firms as a whole. Firms may also invest by building up their stocks of finished goods.

2 **Goverment expenditure** The government adds to the circular flow of income by expenditure with firms on goods and services and by giving subsidies to firms to assist the level of output.

3 **Exports** Exports result in income being received by firms from *foreign* households which is clearly an injection into the circular flow of income.

You will have noticed that these injections and withdrawals may be grouped together in three related pairs. Investment by firms takes place with funds obtained on the capital market from savings. Government expenditure is financed largely through taxation. Exports and imports are opposites but both result from trade between countries. Of course, the level of one has no direct influence on the level of the other.

When injections and withdrawals are introduced the circular flow of income resembles the situation in Figure 16.2.

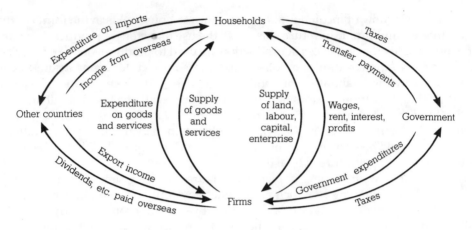

Figure 16.2 *The circular flow in an open economy*

The measurement of national income

We have seen that the flow of national income can be gauged by reference to the income, expenditure or output of an economic society. Similarly, the national income can be measured in three ways.

The income method

This measures the national income by adding together all the incomes earned by the factors of production, i.e. rent, wages, interest and profit. To this total must be added the surpluses earned by the public corporations and other public bodies. Included within income earned is **imputed rent**. This is a notional figure representing the payments which could be received by owner-occupiers if they were to let their houses. Thus owner-occupiers are regarded as paying a rent to themselves!

Not included, however, are **transfer payments**. These are incomes which are received by people without their contributing a factor of production to the creation of economic wealth. The majority of transfer payments are made by the government and consist of old-age pensions, social security payments and the like. However, gifts from one person to another are similarly excluded because they also involve a transfer of wealth rather than being payment for the creation of economic wealth itself.

When all factor incomes have been totalled a deduction is made for any appreciation in the value of stocks held by firms since such appreciation does not represent economic activity. The figure then obtained is the **gross domestic income (GDI)** or **gross domestic product (GDP)** at factor cost.

The expenditure method

This method of measurement adds together all the expenditure undertaken in the economy. Care must be taken here to exclude expenditure by firms on raw materials and transport otherwise double counting will result. So, in the case of a loaf of bread only the *final* expenditure of the consumer on the loaf must be counted, not the *intermediate* expenditure by the baker for his flour and yeast.

We begin therefore with the total expenditure of consumers on goods and services. This item excludes expenditure on housing; instead there is an amount for imputed rent, as discussed on page 196.

TABLE 16.1
Gross Domestic Income: 1988

	£m
Income from employment	249 775
Income from self employment	42 617
Gross trading profits of companies	70 242
Gross trading surplus of public corporations	7 286
Gross trading surplus of general government enterprise	−70
Rent	27 464
Imputed charge for consumption of non-trading capital	3 048
Total domestic income	400 722
less Stock appreciation	−6 116
Gross Domestic Product	394 606
Residual error	181
Gross Domestic Product at factor cost	394 787
Net property income from abroad	5 619
Gross National Product at factor cost	400 406
less Capital consumption	−54 769
Net National Product at factor cost	345 637

Source: Annual Abstract of Statistics.

Second, there is the current expenditure of all government bodies and public authorities. This includes expenditure on services which are provided 'free' to the public, such as education and the administration of justice.

Third, the investment expenditure of both the private and the public sector. The purchase of capital goods is shown under the item 'Gross domestic fixed capital formation'. Another item covers investment through the accumulation of stocks of goods by firms.

Fourth, the export of goods and services. Where overseas residents buy our goods and services the expenditure relates to economic activity that has taken place in this country and must be included. In the same way, the value of our imports of goods and services must be deducted since this relates to economic activity which took place outside this economy.

The total figure is the gross domestic expenditure at *market* prices. Market prices means that no allowance has been made for the distortional effects of taxation and subsidies. In the UK, for example, the price of a bottle of whisky is around £8, of which about £7 is tax. The consumer expediture involved in buying a bottle of whisky therefore bears little relationship to the economic activity involved in its production. In order for total expenditure to be aligned with the resources involved in production, therefore, taxes on expenditure must be deducted from and subsidies added to the gross domestic expenditure at market prices. The adjusted figure is the **gross domestic expenditure (GDE)** or **gross domestic product** at factor cost.

TABLE 16.2
Gross Domestic Expenditure: 1988

	£m
Consumers' expenditure	293 569
General government final consumption	91 847
Gross domestic fixed capital formation	88 751
Value of physical increase in stocks	4 371
Total domestic expenditure	478 538
Exports of goods and services	108 533
Total final expenditure	587 071
less Imports of goods and services	−125 194
Gross Domestic Product	461 877
Statistical discrepancy	2 056
Gross Domestic Product	463 933
less Taxes on Expenditure plus Subsidies	69 146
Gross Domestic Product at factor cost	394 787
Net property income from abroad	5 619
Gross National Product at factor cost	400 406

Source: Annual Abstract of Statistics.

The output method

This involves finding the total value of production of all private and public enterprises. Again there is a danger of double counting so it is important that only the **value added** by each firm in the production process is included. The value added is found by deducting from the total revenue of the firm payments to other firms for goods and services supplied. The value of the output of non-profit making government bodies is measured in terms of the incomes paid to employees of those bodies. After an adjustment is made for financial services (which facilitate but do not constitute production) the total figure obtained is the **gross domestic product** at factor cost.

The three measures of the gross domestic product should produce the same answer because they are measuring the same cycle of economic activity. The fact that they do not is due to the many errors and omissions in the data collected.

TABLE 16.3
Gross Domestic Output: 1988 (at constant factor cost: 1985 = 100)

	Weight per 1 000	1988
Agriculture, forestry and fishing	19	100.5
Energy and water supply	106	99.4
Manufacturing:		
metals	9	121.5
mineral products	12	117.2
chemicals	24	114.2
metal goods	13	110.4
engineering	63	112.7
motor vehicles	13	116.8
other transport equipment	13	107.1
food, drink and tobacco	31	105.5
textiles	8	102.7
clothing, footwear and leather	9	102.1
paper, printing and publishing	24	125.1
other manufacturing	19	128.0
Construction	59	117.0
Distribution, hotels and catering	134	118.0
Transport & communications	70	119.1
Banking, finance, insurance, etc.	155	134.0
Ownership of dwellings	59	103.0
Public administration, defence and social security	71	102.0
Education and health	85	107.0
Other services	59	119.0
Adjustment for financial services	−55·	138.0
Gross Domestic Product	1 000	113.1

Source: Annual Abstract of Statistics

Since the expenditure-based figures are regarded as the most reliable they are regarded as correct and 'residual error' items are inserted into the other two measures to bring them into line.

Thus far the three measures of national income have produced the GDP, i.e. the total value of production from economic activity within the UK. To produce a figure for National Income two further adjustments must be made. First, some of the income earned by residents of this country comes from overseas investment while some of the income generated within the UK is earned by overseas residents. The difference between these two sets of earnings is the **net property income from abroad** and this is added to (or subtracted from) the GDP to produce the **gross national product (GNP)**. Second, GNP is calculated without taking account of the fact that some of the nation's stock of capital goods will have worn out or depreciated during the period under consideration. So the item 'Capital consumption' is deducted from GNP to produce **net national product** or **national income**.

To summarise:

GDP + Net property income from abroad = GNP
GNP − Capital consumption = National income

Difficulties in measuring national income

The need to insert a residual error item in the measurement of national income indicates that there are difficulties in the production of accurate statistics. The difficulties fall into two groups.

1   Difficulties of assessment

These arise from the need to allocate a value to economic activity when only an estimate is possible:

a) **Capital consumption**   This figure can only be assessed because firms often use historical cost in assessing the depreciation while capital consumption must be based on current prices.

b) **Consumer durables**   Goods which have a serviceable life of several years, such as cars or washing machines, are included in the national income at their full value in the year in which they are purchased.

c) **Stock values**   An assessment must be made for increases in the value of stocks in the year in question.

d) **Imputed income**   The imputed rents ascribed to owner-occupied houses and similar other imputed incomes are inevitably just a broad estimate.

e) **Government services**   Those which are not paid for directly are included in national output at cost so their actual contribution to economic wealth is unlikely to be reflected in the figures.

2   Errors and omissions

These occur because of the sheer difficulties involved in collecting all the required data.

a) **Double counting**   Despite the adoption of a value-added method of measuring expenditure and output errors are inevitable and some production is likely to be duplicated in the statistics.

b) **Work involving no monetary reward**   A considerable amount of economic activity is never recorded because it consists of work done by members of the household for themselves, e.g. housework, gardening, etc. The greater the proportion of production in the economy taking this form, the more inaccurate will be national income statistics. A subsistence farmer, for example, may not figure in the national income at all!

c) **The 'Black Economy'**   This term refers to those economic activities which are never recorded because they are not declared to the authorities. These include untaxed cash payments to individuals for casual work and payments in cash to firms to avoid VAT. In some countries the black economy covers a high proportion of total economic activity.

d) **Illegal trading**   A considerable amount of economic activity takes place which cannot be declared because it is illegal, e.g. sale of harmful drugs, smuggling, etc.

e) **Inaccurate returns**   Whether by accident or design many income tax and other returns are likely to contain errors and omissions.

f) **International transfer payments**   Whereas transfer payments within the country are not counted for national income purposes, those from overseas do add to national income. However, such payments as gifts from relatives abroad rarely find their way into the statistics.

REVISION TEST

1 Explain the term 'injection' as applied to the circular flow of national income.
2 Which are the withdrawals from the circular flow of national income?
3 What are transfer payments?
4 How are market prices converted to factor prices?
5 Which of the measures of national income is considered to be the most accurate by the authorities and why?
6 What is the difference between GDP and GNP?
7 Explain what is meant by the 'Value-added method of measuring output'.
8 What are imputed payments and why are they used?
9 Given the figures for GDP at market prices, what steps would you take to convert these to net national product?
10 What are the principal areas of omission from the national income statistics?

The use of national income statistics

Despite the difficulties of measurement and the undoubted inaccuracies which follow, national income statistics are essential as a basis for a number of exercises.

1 To measure the total wealth, and therefore the standard of living of a country.
2 To measure the rate of economic growth of the country.
3 To assist in the process of government planning for the economy.
4 To compare the rate of economic change and living standards of different countries.

National income changes within a country

Growth in national income can be measured by how one year compares with past years, i.e. whether it has increased and by how much. However, in order to measure the rate of growth and any consequent changes in living standards with any degree of accuracy certain adjustments will be necessary.

1 Changes in the price level

Any comparison of national income figures from one year to another must take into account the effect of changes in the value of money. Suppose that next year the monetary measure of national income rises by 10 per cent but the prices of all goods and services produced also rises by 10 per cent, i.e. the rate of **inflation** is 10 per cent. What has been the change in economic wealth in society? – none. So money national income has risen by 10 per cent while *real* national income has not changed. Between 1929 and 1932, for example, the national income of the United States actually fell due to the Great

Depression but because the value of money rose during this period money national income fell even more dramatically.

To compare one year with another, therefore, the figures must be adjusted so that we are using a common price level. Thus we can compare the national income of 1989 with that of 1990 at 1989 prices, 1990 prices or any other common basis.

2   The size of the population

When considering the question of living standards the per capita income, i.e. economic wealth per person, is of more value that the total national income. If the population is growing, for example, national income must grow at the same rate just to maintain average living standards. Put another way, population growth reduces the improvement in living standards of a given rise in national income.

3   Quality of life

National income statistics are unable to measure changes in living standards which involve no changes in the level of income. An obvious example is leisure time. Comparisons of living standards over long periods are bedevilled by the reduction in the working week and the hours worked per day over the past 150 years. That shorter working weeks and longer holidays represent improvements in living standards is beyond doubt but such changes cannot show up in the national income statistics.

In the same way, no account can be taken in the statistics of reductions in the quality of life through overcrowding, stress or greater levels of pollution.

4   Capital versus consumer goods

National income growth may not be accompanied by rising living standards, at least in the short run, if the growth is concentrated in capital goods. Where the capital goods consist of defence equipment there may be no tangible improvements in living standards even in the long run.

On the other hand, the contribution of past capital investment to current living standards may be underestimated in the statistics. Thus the construction of a new reservoir is counted only in the year it occurs through it contributes to the water supply of the population from then on.

Comparisons between countries

It is useful to compare national income changes in one country with those of another as a guide to economic performance and changes in relative living standards. Unfortunately international comparisons are made extremely difficult by the diversity of factors affecting the national incomes of different countries.

1   Level of development

Mention has already been made of the fact that work done for oneself does not get included in national income statistics. A similar problem occurs if the economy functions to a substantial extent on barter. In developing countries a much larger share of GDP will consist of subsistence farming and similar economic activities which do not get recorded. Thus economic activity is under-estimated when compared to a developed country.

Countries with a large black economy will also tend to under-estimate their national incomes. Italy, for example, is believed to have a proportionately much larger black economy than other members of the European Economic Community.

2   The cost of living

It is usual to convert the money national incomes of countries into a common currency, like the US dollar, for purposes of comparison. We then find that many developing countries have annual per capita incomes which would not prove sufficient for one month in an advanced country. However, the price level is usually much lower in those countries so that living standards are not as low as they would be on the same income in Europe. In this sense converting all currencies into a standard unit is misleading because a US dollar, for example, actually buys more in Korea than it does in America.

3   The size of population

Countries vary greatly in terms of population size and this must be taken into account when comparing one with another. The national income of the USA, for example, is six times that of the UK. But this does not mean that the average American has a standard of living six times as great as that of the average Briton. The population of the USA is 4½ times that of the UK so the average American enjoys a living standard roughly 1.3 times as great as the average Briton.

4   Differences of measurement

There is no internationally agreed method of measuring national income so not every country uses the same basis for their figures. Some countries, for example, use market prices for expenditure rather than factor cost. Thus we are frequently not comparing like with like.

5   Economic/political systems

The objectives of the government will affect the allocation of scarce resources and thus influence living standards. Some totalitarian regimes, for example, embark on major capital investment programmes, especially in prestige building projects and armaments which result in substantial increases in national income while leaving living standards unchanged, or even falling.

Furthermore, in countries where economic wealth is concentrated in the hands of a small proportion of the population per capita income may be high while most people have very low living standards.

6   State of development

Relative growth rates are misleading unless account is taken of the base from which each country has progressed. The growth rates of developing countries frequently outstrip those of advanced countries without their making the same economic progress. Suppose that Country A has an annual per capita income of $25 000 while Country B has one of $250. In the next year the national income of Country A increases by 4 per cent while that of Country B increases by 10 per cent. Their respective per capita incomes are now $26 000 and $275 so while Country B is growing faster its population is falling further behind that of Country A, even if it has gained in relative terms.

7 Geographical factors

Even if two countries have the same per capita income we cannot say that they enjoy the same living standards. The harshness of the climate may require that one country uses more resources on irrigation or flood production while the other is free to concentrate on direct benefits to the population. One country may already have a well-developed infrastructure of communications and essential services that no longer shows in national income statistics while the other is still installing these. One country may have a very high population density and the stress that goes with it.

Because of the severe difficulties attached to comparing the national incomes of different countries, living standards are often compared by more simple criteria. Thus the proportion of the population with a car or how many weeks' wages it costs the average worker to buy a washing machine may be used as an indication of relative living standards. Even here statisticians must tread warily. Societies have different cultural values and material expectations and the lack of a car does not represent as heavy a burden in some cultures as it might in the USA.

REVISION TEST

1 Define the term 'per capita income'.

2 What are the four main uses of national income statistics?

3 If money national income has risen by 50 per cent and the value of money has fallen by 20 per cent, what is the real percentage change in national income?

4 In the case above, what would be the effect on real national income if the value of money has *risen* by 10 per cent?

5 Give three examples of economic transactions which are often left out of national income calculations, especially in developing countries.

6 Under what circumstances could living standards rise while national income fell?

7 Why is it easier to compare the national income statistics of the UK with those of Sweden or France than with those of Peru or Nigeria?

8 Give three of the factors deterimental to living standards in Hong Kong which cannot be reflected in its national income figures.

9 Give two reasons for wishing to compare national income statistics between countries.

10 Why is it difficult to compare living standards between different cultures?

Examination questions

1 a) Calculate the per capita income in the following two situations:
      i) Country A has a national income of £250 000 million and a population of 50 million.
      ii) Country B has a national income of £8000 million and a population of 10 million.
   b) Explain why a per capita income figure may not always be a good indicator of a country's economic well being.
   c) Why is a mere comparison of per capita income of two countries not an accurate assessment of their respective wealth?

(LCCI Intermediate, May 1986)

2 Explain how we obtain estimates of national income from figures of gross domestic product at factor cost.

(ICSA, June 1986)

3 If the national income of a country doubles between two years, does it mean that everyone is twice as well off? Explain your answer.

(ICSA, December 1986)

4 How will estimates of national income be affected by
   a) an increase in the physical amount of stocks and work in progress from one year to another, *and*
   b) an increase in the value from one year to another of a given quantity of stocks?

(ICSA, June 1987)

5 Explain the importance of capital consumption in national income accounts and discuss the problems involved in quantifying it.

(ICSA, December 1987)

6 What are the difficulties involved in comparing changes in the average standard of living in different countries at the same point in time and in one country at different points in time?

(ICSA, December 1988)

7 To what extent do national income figures accurately reflect changes in the standard of living of a country over a period of years?

(ACCA, December 1988)

8 However the national income is calculated, the resulting figures are not a reliable guide with which to compare changes in the standard of living over a period of years. Discuss this statement.

(CIMA, May 1989)

9 Explain what value added is and show how in a closed economy with no government the sum of the value added (GDP) equals the sum of the factor incomes (GDI) equals the total of final expenditure (GDE).

(Cert.M., June 1986)

10   What are the three broad identities used to obtain a figure for national income? Explain how each is measured.

(Cert.M., November 1986)

11   a)   Explain the meaning of circular flow of national income.
      b)   Critically comment on the problems encountered in calculating the national income.

(IPS, November 1987)

12   a)   Compare and contrast the expenditure and income approaches to measuring the gross domestic product.
      b)   If a country's national income at constant prices has risen, explain why it is not necessarily true that a rise in the economic welfare of its people has occurred.

(IPS, May 1988)

13   For what purposes do governments collect national income data and what other information is needed and why in order to have a clearer understanding of a country's living standards?

(IPS, May 1989)

14   What do you understand by the term 'gross national product'?
      Analyse any problems which might exist when GNP statistics are used for interpretative purposes.

(IFA, December 1988)

17 The Keynesian model of national income

- *What is the relationship between investment and savings in the national income?*

- *Why do changes in the level of aggregate demand have a greater effect on national income than the amount of the original change?*

Keynesian theory

Such is the contribution of John Maynard Keynes to the development of economic theory that his model of national income is still the starting point for macro-economic analysis over 50 years after his major work 'The General Theory of Employment, Interest and Money' was first published.

In the early twentieth century economists believed that the economy was self-regulating and would naturally move towards an equilibrium level of national income where economic resources are fully employed. If, for example, there were unemployed labour in the economy, the price mechanism would operate to push down the price of labour (the wage rate) and so increase the quantity of labour demanded and eventually restore full employment. Unemployment was thus seen as a temporary side-effect of economic change. Here, as elsewhere, classical theory was disproved by the events of the 1930s when unemployment proved to be both substantial and prolonged.

Keynes addressed the problems posed by the economic upheavals of the 1930s by showing that, while it is perfectly possible to establish the equilibrium level of national income, there is no reason why this equilibrium should not be accompanied by a high and persistent level of unemployment. He began with the premise that demand and supply analysis could be applied as much to the whole economy as to the microeconomic activity of the consumer and the firm. Thus the equilibrium level of national income would be found where total demand for goods and services in the economy (**aggregate demand**) is equal to the total supply of goods and services in the economy (**aggregate supply**). This coincides with the principle underlying the measurement of national income whereby expenditure is equal to output. Indeed, *satisfied* aggregate demand is the same as total national expenditure, i.e. national income.

Aggregate demand

The Keynesian model is primarily concerned with aggregate demand for two reasons.

In the first place Keynes was concerned with short run variations in the level of national income whereas fundamental alterations in the supply side of income involve long run decisions. In the second place the supply side of national income presented no pressing problems during the excess capacity and high unemployment period between the two world wars.

Keynesian analysis starts from the premise that, if aggregate demand is maintained at the same level through successive time periods, the national income is in equilibrium in that it will show no tendency to deviate from its present level. It follows that any reduction in aggregate demand will, to restore equilibrium, require a compensatory fall in the level of aggregate supply. The level of aggregate demand would fall, for example, if consumers switched from home-produced to imported goods. Again, consumers might decide to reduce consumption and withhold a greater proportion of their income as savings. Such savings will result in a fall in the aggregate demand unless they find their way back into the circular flow of income via the capital market.

A fall in aggregate demand will, all things being equal, result in disequilibrium in the national income. Aggregate supply now exceeds aggregate demand and firms find themselves with unsold production and increased stocks. In the next time period firms must either make up the shortfall in aggregate demand themselves by building up stocks further or respond by reducing output to the level which can be supported by aggregate demand. Similarly, a rise in aggregate demand will stimulate a rise in aggregate supply provided that there are still unemployed resources in the economy.

Savings and investment

Central to Keynesian analysis of equilibrium national income is the relationship between savings(S) and investment(I). Let us assume a closed economy with no foreign trade and no government activity in the economy. If the national income is in equilibrium all income must either be spent on consumption goods or saved, i.e.

National Income (Y) = Consumption (C) + Savings (S)

At the same time output in the economy must consist either of consumer goods or investment goods, i.e.

National Output (O) = Consumption (C) + Investment (I)

So we have:

$$Y = C + S$$
$$O = C + I$$

Since the national income is assumed to be in equilibrium national income and national output will be identical so, if $Y = O$ and C is common to both equations $I \equiv S$.

That savings should be equal to investment under conditions of national income equilibrium seems rather a coincidence. Indeed, it is far-fetched to suggest that savers and investors should independently decide to allocate exactly the same amount of resources to their activities. This is not what Keynesian theory predicts. It accepts that *intended* saving is different to *intended* investment but that these differences can only exist under temporary conditions of disequilibrium. Once equilibrium is restored, *actual* savings and investment will be equal. That this is so can be shown by a simple example. Suppose that, out of a national income of 100 units, consumers wish to save 10 units; firms, on the other hand, only wish to undertake investment projects totalling 5 units. Since there are excess savings of 5 units this represents a net withdrawal from the circular flow of income. At the same time, all things being equal, aggregate demand in the economy has now fallen to 95 units. In the next time period firms will reduce output to match aggregate demand so national income falls to 95 units. If consumer expenditure stays at 90 units savings will fall to 5. So actual investment equals actual saving even though planned investment and planned saving were different.

Another important point to emerge from the above discussion is that it is the level of investment which determines the level of saving, rather than the other way round. Firms will not decide to invest in new machinery just because consumers have decided to make more of their incomes available for investment. If, on the other hand, firms decide to allocate more of the resources to investment and less to current production consumers will have less to buy and will be forced to save more.

Savings as financial investment

Savings are sometimes confused with investment because the words 'investment' and 'capital' are not always used in their economic sense. Investment, as we have seen, is the allocation of funds to the purchase of capital goods. The act of saving is essentially the act of non-consumption. The saver may make his or her savings available to potential borrowers but there is no guarantee that such funds will be wanted and therefore be able to receive interest. However, accumulated savings are often referred to as 'capital' and when they are lent to financial intermediaries are termed 'investments', both by the saver and by the financial intermediary.

This use of the words 'investment' and 'capital' to describe two different economic activities stems from the separation of the functions of producer and consumer in our modern economic society. In a subsistence economy saving and investment are inextricably linked since the act of non-consumption leads directly to the accumulation of resources for investment, e.g. seedcorn for future crops. This close relationship is much rarer in a complex economic system but even here it is possible to reconcile these different meanings of investment. Firms undertake investment in capital goods to produce a stream of future income and the decision to invest is made on the basis of whether or not the income earned will compensate for the cost of the investment. The private individual chooses to forego current consumption in order to save. He or she lends the funds to those who wish to invest them, either directly or via a financial intermediary, and receives a stream of future income which may be used to pay for subsequent purchases of consumption goods. In both cases the income earned is **interest** on the investment made; the firm and the individual sharing the return on the investment. However, the purchase of shares or opening of an account with a bank is not itself investment. It is the allocation of savings to a **financial investment**, which funds can then be used for investment in capital goods.

Injections and withdrawals

It has been shown that, in a closed economy, savings must equal investment when the national income is in equilibrium. In an open economy with government economic activity we know that, when the national income is in equilibrium, total expenditure (aggregate demand) will consist of consumption by domestic consumers, expenditure on investment, government expenditure and consumption of our goods by overseas residents, i.e.

$$\text{Expenditure (E)} = \text{Consumption (C)} + \text{Investment (I)} + \text{Government Expenditure (G)} + \text{Exports (X)}$$

Which is the same as:

$$\text{Expenditure (E)} = \text{Consumption (C)} + \text{Injections (J)}$$

At the same time all income must be spent on consumption of domestically produced goods, saved, paid in taxes or spent on foreign goods (imports), i.e.

$$\text{Income (Y)} = \text{Consumption (C)} + \text{Savings (S)} + \text{Taxation (T)} + \text{Imports (M)}$$

Which is the same as:

$$\text{Income (Y)} = \text{Consumption (C)} + \text{Withdrawals (W)}$$

So we have:

$$E = C + J(I + G + X)$$
$$Y = C + W(S + T + M)$$

As the national income is assumed to be in equilibrium national expenditure and national income will be identical so, if $E = Y$ and C is common to both equations:

$$J(I + G + X) = W(S + T + M)$$

Thus Injections = Withdrawals
We can go further and say that, as $I = S$,

$$G + X = T + M$$

To summarise, if the national income is in equilibrium total injections into the circular flow of income will equal total withdrawals from the circular flow. Furthermore savings will equal investment and government expenditure plus exports will equal taxation plus imports. Of course, *intended* injections may differ from *intended* withdrawals and result in national income disequilibrium. Once equilibrium is restored, however, injections and withdrawals will once again be equal.

As, when national income is in equilibrium, injections are equal to withdrawals, the level of national income can be determined by the intersection of the injection and withdrawal schedules, as in Figure 17.1. Here the level of injections is assumed to be constant since they are the result of independent decisions taken by firms, the government and foreign residents, irrespective of the level of national income. Withdrawals, on the other hand, are assumed to rise with national income as the higher the level of income the more likely it is that some income will be saved, paid in taxes or spent on imported goods. If withdrawals become negative the national income has fallen to a point where imports and taxes are falling towards zero while dis-saving (the spending of past savings) is taking place.

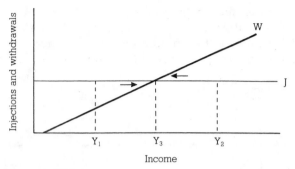

Figure 17.1 *National income equilibrium*

In Figure 17.1 the equilibrium level of national income is at Y_3. At any point to the left of Y_3, say at Y_1, injections are greater than withdrawals so that there is unsatisfied demand in the economy, with firms experiencing falling stocks, rising prices and increased profits. Firms will respond by using what spare capacity there is in the economy to increase output; this process continuing until the level of national income has risen sufficiently for withdrawals to match the level of injections. Alternatively if income is to the right of Y_3, say at Y_2, withdrawals are greater than injections so that there is insufficient demand in the economy. This leads to rising stocks, falling prices and declining profits. Firms will react by cutting production and using less resources so that output, and thus income, fall to the point where injections and withdrawals are once again in equilibrium. So the only sustainable level of national income is one where injections and withdrawals are equal.

Shifts in injections and withdrawals

On the basis of the foregoing discussion of national income equilibrium it is possible to predict the effect of changes in the level of either injections or withdrawals. Changes in the injections schedule are shown in Figure 17.2. In Figure 17.2 (a) the level of injections rises from J to J_1, so increasing the level of aggregate demand in the economy. The level of national income eventually rises from Y to Y_1, and with it total withdrawals, until injections and withdrawals are once again in equilibrium. In Figure 17.2 (b) the level of injections falls from J to J_1 and equilibrium is restored at a lower level of national income, i.e. Y_1 instead of Y. By this time withdrawals have fallen sufficiently for them to once again equal injections.

Figure 17.3 illustrates shifts in the withdrawals schedule. In Figure 17.3 (a) there is an upward shift in withdrawals, from W to W_1, so that aggregate demand contracts. This results in a fall in the level of national income from Y to Y_1 with withdrawals and injections restored to equilibrium at this lower level of income. A fall in the level of withdrawals, as in Figure 17.3 (b) from W to W_1, will lead to national income rising from Y to Y_1 and actual withdrawals being restored to their former level.

You will note that, as with investment and savings, it is injections which determine the level of withdrawals rather than the other way round.

It might be useful at this stage to recap on the national income 'alphabet' as it will be used a great deal in this and future chapters.

C = Consumption
E = Expenditure
G = Government Expenditure
I = Investment
J = Injections
Y = Income

M = Imports
O = Output
S = Savings
T = Taxation
W = Withdrawals

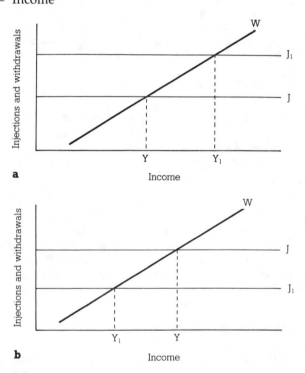

Figure 17.2 *Injection shifts*

REVISION TEST

1 What is the principal difference between the Classical and the Keynesian view of national income equilibrium?

2 How is the equilibrium level of national income determined?

3 Explain how it is that Savings = Investment under conditions of national income equilibrium.

4 Which determines which, savings or investment?

5 What is the difference between investment and financial investment?

6 If S and I are unchanged what are the possible effects of an increase in G?

7 What is the relationship between G + X and T + M?

8 Explain the difference between expenditure and consumption.

9 Define the term 'dis-saving'.

10 Follow the effect on national income, step-by-step, of a rise in the level of imports.

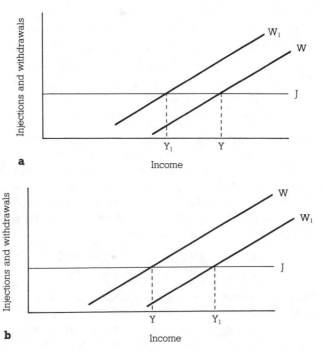

Figure 17.3 *Withdrawal shifts*

Consumption

In the last section we saw that the national income is in equilibrium when injections are equal to withdrawals. The other critical factor in determining national income is the level of consumption. You will recall that:

$$Y = C + S + T + M \text{ and}$$
$$E = C + I + G + X.$$

Since $Y = E$ when the national income is in equilibrium we can also illustrate equilibrium by reference to these two measures. This is shown in Figure 17.4 where the 45° line represents those situations where $Y = E$ and the national income is in equilibrium. Points above or to the left of the 45° line result in E being greater than Y while points below or to the right indicate a situation where Y is greater than E. The equilibrium level of national income will therefore be found where the $E (C + I + G + X)$ line crosses the 45° line and is therefore equal to Y. At this level of national income injections must also equal withdrawals.

Since Y and E are two ways of measuring national income and C is common to both equations an increase in the value of C will result in a rise in the level of national income, all things being equal. This may be shown by ascribing values to the above equations. Suppose we begin with the following situation:

$$40(Y) = 30(C) + 3(S) + 5(T) + 2(M)$$
$$40(E) = 30(C) + 3(I) + 6(G) + 1(X)$$

If, due to a cut in taxes to 2, total consumption rises to 33, withdrawals will now be less than injections with national income no longer in equilibrium. With unsatisfied demand in the economy firms will expand output and the level of national income will rise until withdrawals once again match injections. For example, a new equilibrium may be established where:

$$45(Y) = 35(C) + 3(S) + 3(T) + 4(M)$$
$$45(E) = 35(C) + 3(I) + 6(G) + 1(X)$$

It will be noticed that, when equilibrium is restored, consumption has risen again, to 35. Why should this have occurred? We must return to the circular flow of income to answer this question. Let us assume, quite logically, that the original rise in consumption led to firms increasing output by three to meet the new level of aggregate expenditure. This in turn would lead to higher income, in the form of increased factor payments, flowing into households. If this extra income were spent on imported goods the new equilibrium position would be as follows:

$$43(Y) = 33(C) + 3(S) + 2(T) + 5(M)$$
$$43(E) = 33(C) + 3(I) + 6(G) + 1(X)$$

Withdrawals would once again be equal to injections at a higher level of national income. If, however, the households decide to spend some of their extra income on further consumption the level of expenditure flowing into firms would rise again. The result would be another round of income generation for households, some of which is consumed and some spent on imports. This cycle will be repeated until the process of income generation is exhausted and withdrawals are once again equal to injections. The effect is that national income has risen by more than the original increase in income available to households. Such will be the result of any reduction in withdrawals or increase in injections provided that the change leads to some increase in consumption. Since this is always the case for society as a whole, even if not for every individual, we

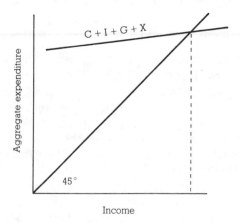

Figure 17.4 *Expenditure–income equilibrium*

can say that consumption is a *function* of income in that consumption increases with income, though not necessarily at the same rate.

The marginal propensity to consume

The rate at which consumption increases as income rises is known as the **marginal propensity to consume (MPC)**. So if every pound of income results in a rise of consumption of 70 pence, the marginal propensity to consume will be 0.7. The remainder of this extra income must have been saved, paid in taxes or spent on imports, i.e. withdrawn from the circular flow of income. The proportion of extra income saved is the **marginal propensity to save (MPS)**. Similarly there is a **marginal propensity to pay taxes (MPT)** and a **marginal propensity to import (MPM)**. Together, these three make up the **propensity to make withdrawals (MPW)**. Since the extra unit of income must have been used for consumption, or saved, or paid in taxes or spent on imports:

$$1 = MPC + MPS + MPT + MPM$$
$$Or\ 1 = MPC + MPW.$$

Let us assume in this case that, of the extra pound of income received, 4 pence is saved, 20 pence is paid in taxes and 6 pence is spent on imports. We then have a marginal propensity to save of 0.04, a marginal propensity to pay taxes of 0.2 and a marginal propensity to import of 0.06. We then have:

$$£1 = 0.7 + 0.04 + 0.2 + 0.06$$
$$Or\ £1 = 0.7 + 0.30$$

The MPC in this case is 0.7. But can it be assumed that the MPC will remain 0.7 with every extra unit of income received? The answer is no for a number of reasons.

1   As an individual's income rises the pattern of consumption changes. The higher the income the greater the diversity of goods consumed and thus the more likely that part of extra income will be spent on imports.

2   The higher a person's income the more likely it is that extra income will be taxed. Furthermore luxury goods are more likely to incur taxes than necessities. As a person's income rises it is likely that extra income will involve expenditure on goods on which tax will be paid.

3   The higher the income the more likely it is that some of the extra income will be saved.

4   Even if income is constant the MPC will be affected by changes in interest rates which make saving more or less attractive; by changes in the pattern of expenditure which affect the level of imported goods bought and by changes in tax levels.

However, for the purpose of this analysis we will simplify matters by assuming that the MPC and the constituent parts of the MPW are constant.

The multiplier

Earlier in this module we saw that an increase in consumption may lead eventually to a rise in national income greater than the original increase in consumption. Indeed, this will always be the case provided that some of the extra income generated by the initial increase in consumption is used by its recipients for another round of consumption.

Similar to the effect of an increase in consumption will be that of a rise in aggregate expenditure caused by an increase in the level of injections. Suppose that the level of investment in the economy rises by £1 million due to a new factory being built. This will result in the owners of the factors of production receiving income of £1 million for their part in building the factory. Provided that some of this income is used for consumption further income will be generated for those supplying these goods and services and the process will begin again.

This tendency for a rise in the level of aggregate expenditure to produce a magnified rise in the level of national income is due to the **multiplier** effect. The multiplier will have a numerical value based on the equation:

$$\text{Multiplier} = \frac{\text{Total increase in national income}}{\text{Initial increase in national income}}$$

If, therefore, an initial increase in national income of £5 million leads to a total increase in national income of £10 million the value of the multiplier will be 2.

The size of the multiplier depends on the extent to which, at each round of income generation, income leaks from the circular flow in the form of withdrawals; the greater the proportion withdrawn (MPW) the smaller the multiplier effect. Let us take the example of an extra injection of £2 million in investment where the MPC is 0.6 and the MPW is 0.4. The effect is shown in Table 17.1.

TABLE 17.1
Multiplied growth of national income

	Increase in Income (£)	Consumption (£)	Withdrawals (£)
Injection	2 000 000	1 200 000	800 000
1st regeneration	1 200 000	720 000	480 000
2nd regeneration	720 000	432 000	288 000
3rd regeneration	432 000	259 200	172 800
4th regeneration	259 200	155 520	103 680
5th regeneration	155 520	93 312	62 208
etc.			
Total	5 000 000	3 000 000	2 000 000

After the multiplier effect has been exhausted the total increase in national income resulting from an injection of £2 million will be £5 million, giving a multiplier value of 2½. At the same time consumption will have grown by £3 million and withdrawals by £2 million. Thus national income equilibrium is restored when withdrawals have risen by the same amount as the new injection, i.e. when total injections are equal to total withdrawals.

Rather than going through the lengthy process described above to calculate the value of the multiplier we can find the answer more quickly by use of a simple formula:

$$\text{Change in income} = \text{Injection} \times \frac{1}{1 - \text{MPC}}$$

Which is the same as:

$$\text{Change in income} = \text{Injection} \times \frac{1}{\text{MPW}}$$

In the example quoted above, therefore,

$$\text{Change in income} = \text{\pounds 2 million} \times \frac{1}{1 - 0.6}$$

$$= \text{\pounds 2 million} \times \frac{1}{0.4} = \text{\pounds 5 million}.$$

Since the value of the multiplier is 2½ it is the reciprocal of the MPW. In this example only a change in investment has been examined but a similar effect will occur through an increase in any of the three injections or a reduction in any of the three withdrawals. The multiplier will also operate downwards so that a decrease in exports or a rise in savings will lead to a greater decline in national income than the amount by which injections have fallen or withdrawals risen.

Inflationary and deflationary gaps

Thus far we have seen how the Keynesian model predicts that national income will always return to equilibrium. Keynes went on to show that the classical economists were wrong to assume that equilibrium was sufficient to produce a healthy economy. He argued that, on the contrary, national income equilibrium is perfectly consistent with high unemployment and wasted resources.

Deflationary gap

Let us assume that the national income is in equilibrium and all resources are fully employed. Exports then fall by £1 million so that total injections are now less than total withdrawals. Producers will find that aggregate demand has dropped and will reduce output, laying off workers and reducing expenditure on raw materials and investment goods in the process. This contraction in national income will go on until national income has fallen by the amount necessary for total withdrawals to decrease by £1 million and bring the national income back into equilibrium. The multiplier effect will ensure that the final decrease in national income is greater than the original reduction in injections. The economy is now producing below its optimum level with unused resources, notably unemployed labour.

This principle is illustrated in Figure 17.5 where, at the full employment level of national income (F), withdrawals are greater than injections. This gap between full employment income and expenditure is known as a **deflationary gap** and is shown by the distance between F and G. Since aggregate expenditure is insufficient to sustain the full employment level of national income the national income will fall to its equilibrium level E. The fall in the level of national income is greater than the original deflationary gap due to the action of the multiplier.

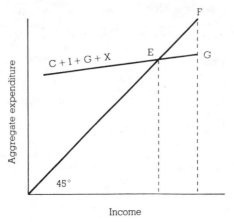

Figure 17.5 *Deflationary gap*

Two important points follow from this analysis.

1   The national income can be in equilibrium without the economy operating any-where near its full potential.

2   There is no guarantee that, in a situation of declining aggregate demand, injections will remain constant. Firms may well lose confidence and reduce investment plans, so opening another deflationary gap and leading to a further contraction of the equilibrium level of national income.

There is, however, an equilibrium level below which the national income will not sink. No matter how low confidence may fall, economic activity will never cease entirely.

Inflationary gap

We have seen that an increase in injections leads to a multiplied growth in national income. Once full employment equilibrium is attained, however, any further increase in aggregate demand will not result in a growth in national income since there are no resources available to enable such growth to occur. In such circumstances a rise in injections will result in an **inflationary gap**. The higher aggregate demand will lead firms to raise prices to choke off excess demand. At the same time the prospect of increased profits leads them to seek to increase output by employing more resources. Since there are no resources available they will have to raise the rewards paid to the factors of production to attract resources from other producers, whose own output will fall. In consequence there is an upward spiral of prices without any increase in total output or of *real* national income. In Figure 17.6 aggregate demand is greater than the full employment level of national income (F). The equilibrium level of national income is at E but this is unattainable since it is beyond the full employment level. There is thus an inflationary gap between F and G. Unlike the deflationary gap, the inflationary gap will persist indefinitely. It can only be reduced by a reduction in injections or a rise in withdrawals.

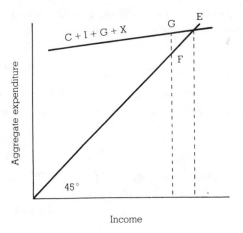

Figure 17.6 *Inflationary gap*

REVISION TEST

1   What is the significance of the 45° line in Figure 17.4?
2   How is consumption a function of income?
3   Explain the term 'marginal propensity to pay taxes'.
4   For what reasons is the MPC of an individual unlikely to stay constant as income rises?
5   If the MPC is 0.8 what is the MPW?
6   MPS + MPT + MPM = ?
7   If the multiplier is 6 what is the MPW?
8   £5000 is injected into the national income. If the multiplier is 3 by how much will consumption have risen when equilibrium in the national income is restored?
9   What equation describes the numerical value of the multiplier?
10 If the MPC were 1 what would be the effect on national income of an injection of an extra £1 million into the national income flow?

_____ **Examination questions** _____

1   Students are often confused about financial versus real investment. What do you think are the differences between these two concepts?

(ABE2, June 1986)

2   Define the marginal propensity to consume concept (MPC) and use it to show how the impact of a change in the level of investment–spending can be determined; illustrate your explanation with a numerical example showing how in principle investment appears to create its own finance.

(ABE2, June 1987)

3 Examine the probable effects of a rise in the rate of interest on business activity. In your answer take care to distinguish financial assets from real investment in goods and services.

(ABE2, December 1987)

4 What economic grounds are there for business people to fear that a government policy of allowing free markets to find their own level will lead to ever-deepening domestic recession?

(ABE2, June 1988)

5 Distinguish the *equilibrium level of national income* from the *full employment level of national income* and explain why they may differ.

(LCCI Higher, November 1986)

6 The following data refer to a hypothetical closed economy:

National Income £m	Consumption £m	Savings £m	Investment £m
3 750	3 250	500	1 400
4 500	3 700	800	1 400
5 250	4 150	1 100	1 400
6 000	4 600	1 400	1 400
6 750	5 050	1 700	1 400
7 500	5 500	2 000	1 400
8 250	5 950	2 300	1 400
9 000	6 400	2 600	1 400

a) What is the equilibrium level of national income?
b) What is the value of the marginal propensity to save?
c) Why is a knowledge of the MPS of value to government economists?
d) What is the multiplier?
e) What is the consumption function?

(LCCI Higher, May 1987)

7 a) Assume a closed economy in which equilibrium output is £2000 m., consumption is £1600m. and investment is £80m. (Ignore the effect of taxation.) What is the level of government expenditure?
b) The level of investment is increased to £130m. and the marginal propensity to consume (MPC) = 0.8. What is the new level of national income?
c) Given the changes in (b), what is the new level of consumption and government expenditure?
d) Assume that the economy is opened to international trade. What will be the effect on national income if, in the short term, demand for imports exceeds the demand for exports?
e) What would be the effect if imports exceeded exports in the long term?

(LCCI Higher, November 1987)

8 What is the multiplier and how would it be affected if income were to become more equally distributed?

(ICSA, December 1986)

9 What effect will an increase in the marginal propensity to save from a given level of income have on the marginal efficiency of capital?

(ICSA, June 1987)

10 How does an increase in investment affect the level of consumption and how does an increase in consumption affect the level of investment?

(ICSA, June 1988)

11 How will an increase in the propensity to consume with a given level of aggregate income affect the level of investment of a firm?

(ICSA, December 1988)

12 What factors are most likely to influence the aggregate level of consumer spending?

(ACCA, June 1989)

13 a) Distinguish planned saving from actual saving and planned investment from actual investment.
   b) The Japanese economy is characterised by high levels of savings, investment and growth. If the citizens of competitor countries were to increase their level of savings, would this guarantee them higher levels of investment and growth?

(ACCA, December 1989)

14 Discuss the factors which, according to Keynesian theory, determine the amount of saving by private households.

(CIMA, November 1988)

15 Explain why a national economy will be in equilibrium when savings equal investment.

(Cert.M., June 1986)

16 What are the main injections and withdrawals from the circular flow of income? What are the effects of these injections and withdrawals?

(Cert.M., June 1988)

17 In a hypothetical closed economy that does not trade with other nations, each of
   a) the marginal propensity to consume,
   b) the marginal propensity to save,
   c) the marginal propensity to pay taxes.
   is constant throughout the community.

Total national income has been £100 000 per annum for a number of years and the economy is in equilibrium.

i) If the marginal propensity to consume is 0.4 and the marginal propensity to save is 0.15, explain how to calculate the total taxes collected each year from the data given and perform the calculation.

ii) If an outside developer establishes a new factory, thus injecting a once and for all further £50 000 into the economy but otherwise leaving other factors unchanged, explain how to calculate the amount to which the national consumption will rise and perform the calculation.

(I.Act., April 1988)

18   What do you understand by the circular flow of income?
What is the significance of injections to and withdrawals from this flow?

(IFA, December 1989)

18 Changes in national income

- *Is the trade cycle inevitable?*
- *What is the relationship between population change and changes in the level of economic activity?*

In discussing changes in national income it is important to distinguish between short-term fluctuations in the level of economic activity and long-term changes in national income which result from economic growth.

The trade cycle

We saw in the last chapter that there is no guarantee that national income equilibrium will result in full employment and stable prices. It is just as likely that equilibrium will be accompanied by a deflationary gap with the economy producing less than its capacity output and resources under-employed. Alternatively, there may be an inflationary gap with a spiral of rising commodity and factor prices and no truly attainable equilibrium. Once one of these conditions is obtained it could, theoretically, persist for an indefinite period. In practice, a given equilibrium position will eventually break down and, after a process of adjustment has taken place, a new equilibrium will be established. Thus an inflationary gap may be closed by a rise in withdrawals and a fall in the level of aggregate demand. Or a deflationary gap may be closed by a rise in the level of injections.

   The sequence of events through which the economy moves from deflationary gap and recession through full employment to inflationary gap and excessive demand and back again is described as the **trade cycle**. The existence of the trade cycle poses the important question of why the economy should break out of an established equilibrium. Why, in fact, should the level of aggregate demand change? In the modern economy it is government action which immediately springs to mind as the likely source of such a change but trade cycle patterns can be traced back to periods long before there was conscious government intervention in the working of the economy. For the origin of the trade cycle we must look, therefore, to those factors which operate autonomously to disturb the level of economic activity.

1 Natural forces

In an economy based principally on agriculture a good harvest will enable exports to be increased, so raising the level of injections into the national income and stimulating expansion of the economy. A poor harvest will have the opposite effect. Thus the trade cycle may be based on fluctuations in the level of agricultural output.

2 The interest rate

As a depression deepens the demand for loanable funds falls and with it the cost of borrowing. Eventually the interest rate will be low enough for some businesses to decide that, even in a depression, the increased potential profits justify the risk of undertaking a particular investment project. Other firms will decide that the time is right to replace old capital equipment.

3 The price level

A deflationary gap will tend to depress prices and, provided that not all other countries are going through a similar depression, will lead to exports becoming more competitive, thereby increasing overseas sales and raising aggregate demand in the economy. An inflationary gap, on the other hand, will lead to the country's goods being too expensive so that exports fall and imports rise, thereby reducing aggregate demand in the economy.

4 Business confidence

When firms are confident about the future they are more likely to undertake new investment than when they believe that the economy is about to enter a period of recession. If enough firms believe that a recession is likely they will cut investment plans and so help bring about the recession they feared. So the business community can 'talk itself into recession'. Similarly business confidence may generate economic expansion.

From the above discussion on business confidence you will see that the trade cycle may be perpetuated through a kind of self-fulfilling prophecy. If they know from past experience that after a depression has lasted three years economic activity picks up again, firms will behave accordingly. Once a recession has lasted three years they will anticipate its end by expanding production and investment, thus bringing the recession to an end! An opposite phenomenon will be observed at the reverse phase of the trade cycle when the economy is enjoying boom conditions. So, once established, the trade cycle will behave with predictable regularity. The four phases of the trade cycle are shown in Figure 18.1. In the first phase, a depression or slump, there is a deflationary gap with high unemployment, low investment and declining national income, or at best zero growth. The second phase, expansion, signifies growing confidence and economic activity. The rate of growth accelerates and there is falling unemployment as slack in the economy is taken up. The third phase, boom, is that period when the economy is operating at or near its full capacity, i.e. on its production

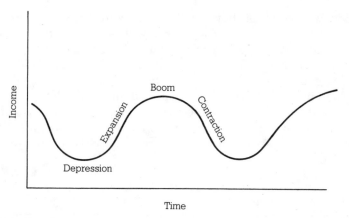

Figure 18.1 *The trade cycle*

possibility curve. It may well be overheating and running an inflationary gap. In the last phase, contraction, any inflationary gap has closed and declining aggregate demand is leading to a slowing growth rate and rising unemployment.

Note that, if the economy exhibits a tendency to long-term growth, each successive peak will be higher than the last. In fact, the existence of boom periods is an incentive to firms to innovate and push the production possibility curve outwards.

The accelerator

Suppose that firms try to resist the pattern of the trade cycle and refuse to cut output when a boom period should be coming to an end. Such activity will be unable to counter the trade cycle completely because of the effect of the **accelerator** on investment behaviour.

Accelerator theory relates changes in investment not only to changes in the level of national income but also to the rate of change of national income. Suppose that the national income is rising steadily and investment is increased to provide the extra capacity needed to meet the anticipated future higher demand for consumer goods. Then national income stops growing so that no more *extra* capacity is required. Net investment will now fall so that those firms supplying investment goods experience a recession. This will reduce employment and affect aggregate demand so spreading the recession to the consumer goods industries. Three conclusions follow:

1   Capital goods industries experience greater fluctuations in demand than do consumer goods industries.
2   Cyclical demand fluctuations for capital goods are inevitable. These will result in alternating periods of growth and decline which will be felt throughout the economy when the industries involved are major contributors to the national income.
3   A stable, buoyant economy is still liable to go into recession unless consumption is capable of continuous expansion.

The working of the accelerator is shown in Table 18.1 where a company making a consumer good, say shoes, is shown with initial aggregate sales of £100 million. Its capital stock consists of 20 machines of varying ages valued at £30 million and one machine is replaced each year as it wears out. Gross investment is therefore £1.5 million per annum while net investment (gross investment minus depreciation) is zero. Over the next few years consumer sales grow by between 11 and 25 per cent before levelling off at £200 million in Year 6. Over the same period, however, the firm's investment in machinery, i.e. its demand for capital goods, changed by amounts between 500 per cent and −80 per cent. When, in the seventh year, consumer sales fall by just 2½ per cent the firm does not need to replace the machine wearing out so its demand for capital goods falls by 100 per cent.

TABLE 18.1
The accelerator

Year	Sales of shoes (£m.)	Stock of machines (£m.)	Investment Gross (£m.)	Net (£m.)	Change in shoe sales (%)	Change in Gross Inv (%)
1	100	30	1.5	–	–	–
2	120	36	7.5	6	20	500
3	150	45	10.5	9	25	40
4	180	54	10.5	9	20	0
5	200	60	7.5	6	11	−29
6	200	60	1.5	0	–	−80
7	195	58.5	0	−10	−2½	−100

If the pattern represented in Table 18.1 is repeated throughout the shoe industry the mild fluctuations in demand for shoes will have resulted in major swings in the demand for machinery. If now the sales of shoes remain static for a long period there will be some years when shoe manufacturers need to buy several machines at once and others when no replacements are necessary, resulting in a cycle of boom and slump in the machine goods industry. So capital goods industries can go into recession even when consumer sales are still buoyant. On the other hand the capital goods industries may lead the economy out of a depression as some new investment is required, however low the level of consumer output. Thus the accelerator helps ensure that neither a boom nor a slump will persist indefinitely.

The impact of the accelerator is magnified by the multiplier effect. So a relatively small increase in net investment will have a multiplied effect in its increase in the level of national income. Similarly, a relatively small fall in net investment will lead through the downward multiplier effect to a much larger fall in national income.

While a valuable theory, the accelerator alone cannot explain the cyclical pattern of investment since it ignores a number of important factors in investment decisions:

1   There is a time-lag in most new investment decisions as firms wait to see if an increase in demand is sustained before committing themselves to a new capital programme. In the meantime they will use existing capital more intensively. Thus an increase in investment may well come after income has already been rising for some time.

2   It ignores the importance of the marginal efficiency of investment. The need for profitability will ensure that the cost of borrowing has a significant effect on the investment decisions of firms.

3   The accelerator views new investment as a response to changes in demand. In reality, firms often embark on new investment to improve efficiency or to anticipate increases in demand.

Cycles of different length

The typical business cycle lasts from three to five years and is associated with business confidence and the other variables outlined earlier; interest rates, price levels, etc. For the capital goods industries, however, the trade cycle is longer and varies between industries according to the frequency with which capital goods of different types are replaced. Thus the trade cycle for the shipbuilding industry is much longer than that for the machine tools trade. The longer the cycle the greater the impact on the national income as a whole and major recessions are associated with a crisis in a key industry such as energy or construction.

From the above it can be seen that, at any one time, there are many overlapping cycles in operation. At times these will be in conflict so that when the economy is going through a deep, prolonged slump there will still be minor upswings as some industries experience peaks in demand. Clearly the greatest problems are posed when almost all cycles, whatever their length, are moving in the same direction.

REVISION TEST

1   Why, in theory, is an inflationary gap unlikely to persist indefinitely?
2   Name three factors which influence the business cycle.
3   How might a fall in the price level help pull the economy out of a depression?
4   What are the four phases of the trade cycle?
5   What economic characteristics would you expect to find in each of these phases?
6   Explain the basis of the accelerator theory.
7   Show how the accelerator predicts that capital goods may be in recession while the consumer goods industry it supplies is buoyant.
8   What are the weaknesses of accelerator theory?
9   Why would you expect the trade cycle of oil-tanker builders to be longer than that of knitting-machine manufacturers?
10   Why is the trade cycle for consumer goods shorter than that for capital goods?

Economic growth

When considering long-term changes in national income we find that we are dealing almost exclusively with growth. Very few countries experience a decline in national income which lasts for more than a decade. Even when such cases occur the country in question is usually beset by some continuing drain on its resources such as civil war or prolonged famine. Thus we shall be concerned here with economic growth and the conditions which foster it.

Short-run changes in national income are associated with changes in the utilisation of existing productive capacity. In the upward phase of the trade cycle output expands until productive capacity is fully used and any further expansion of aggregate demand results in an inflationary gap. In other words real increases in national income are limited by the extent of the production possibility curve. In the long run national income grows through an expansion of the productive capacity of the economy, i.e. the rightward shift of the production possibility curve. These two situations are illustrated in Figure 18.2. With a production possibility curve of AB point X represents a deflationary gap and Y an inflationary gap. Only when the production possibility curve shifts to CD is a real income of Y attainable.

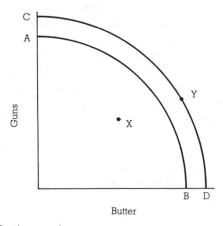

Figure 18.2 *Growth in productive capacity*

The expansion of productive capacity, and with it economic growth, is a natural consequence of the evolution of an economy. Even the apparently modest growth rate in national income of 3 per cent per annum will lead to a doubling of national income in a quarter of a century. This growth brings with it rising living standards for those who share in the greater production of goods and services which occurs.

Causes of economic growth

Increases in the productive capacity of the economy are associated with a number of key factors, of which the most important are:

1 Population growth

The growth of population has, in the past, provided a stimulus to economic growth both by enlarging the potential market for goods and services and by increasing the supply of labour available to produce these goods and services. So a larger population raises both the aggregate demand and the aggregate supply of goods in the economy. In most advanced economies the population grows slowly, if at all, and increased labour adds only marginally to the productive capacity of the economy. Thus population growth is today a relatively unimportant source of economic growth.

2   Invention and innovation

Invention is the discovery of new products and processes and innovation is the process by which such discoveries are put to economic use. Without a continuous stream of innovative ideas awaiting application society would soon exhaust all its investment projects and reach a plateau of economic progress beyond which it could not advance. Innovation provides constant sources of new growth through the better use of existing resources and the opening up of new outlets for the profitable exploitation of investment funds generated by the economy. Essential to continued economic growth, therefore, is the presence in society of those willing to perform the entrepreneurial functions of innovation and risk-taking, whether in the private or the public sector.

3   The accumulation of capital

Greater use of capital is essential to economic growth since the supply of land is largely fixed and, as we have seen, an increase in the supply of labour adds only marginally to the productive capacity of the economy. Where production has been labour-intensive a greater use of capital enables the costs of production to be reduced as expensive labour is replaced by machinery. Furthermore, a greater use of capital in one industry releases labour for other sectors. The ability of firms to add to their stock of capital depends, however, on their having access to adequate supplies of investment funds. Two important conclusions follow:

1   Society must generate sufficient savings to fund the investment requirements of the industrial sector.

2   There must be well-developed capital and money markets to facilitate the process by which the pool of funds available for investment are channelled to their ultimate users.

4   Human capital

The successful introduction of many new products and technical processes depends on the ability of labour to undertake the more complex tasks required of it. Thus economic growth requires that technological progress is matched by an improvement in the quality of labour. By improvement is not meant a marginal increase in physical quality; rather we mean that the technical expertise of labour is developed. This development takes place through education and training and the abilities possessed by labour as a result are referred to as human capital since they do not derive from innate abilities such as strength or manual dexterity. The rate of economic growth will clearly be retarded if there are not enough people in society qualified to make full use of the technology available; a computerised system cannot be introduced unless there are sufficient skilled workers to operate the system.

5   *Demand conditions*

Most investment decisions are based on the medium to long-term expectations of the firm and the entrepreneur will only undertake a particular investment project if future demand patterns appear to justify the cost of the investment. In a modern economy based on mass markets this usually requires both that living standards will rise and that there will be a reasonably equitable distribution of income so that new products can be offered to the public as a whole and not just to a small group of very wealthy customers. Buoyant demand conditions help to stimulate a cycle of economic growth since they encourage the expansion of productive capacity. In turn this increases employment opportunities and sets off a further bout of economic growth.

6   *External factors*

Foreign trade enables countries to solve the problems posed by domestic resource shortages through the purchase of capital goods and technical expertise from abroad. Foreign trade also enables a country to develop areas of activity which require world markets to become viable such as aircraft production or offshore oil development. A healthy export market also stimulates demand and helps create a confident environment for future investment.

Population problems

Since labour is one of the factors of production, it follows that population growth should contribute to economic growth since it increases the supply of labour available to take part in the productive process. In order to add to national well-being, in the form of higher living standards, it is not sufficient for the extra population to increase the total supply of goods and services; each extra unit of labour must contribute as much in terms of output as it takes in terms of consumption. All population problems centre on this one issue of whether changes in the structure of the population add to or subtract from the economic well-being of the nation. Three main problems can be identified:

1   *Over-population*

Here there are insufficient supplies of the other factors of production to combine with the amount of labour available. In consequence the law of diminishing returns sets in and eventually average product per unit of labour employed falls. The law of diminishing returns underlay the theories of Thomas Malthus, the nineteenth century economist who argued that population growth would always be faster than the growth of the food supply so that the mass of the population would be condemned to live at subsistence levels. Malthus's fears were not confirmed by events. In Britain and other European countries a rise in population was accompanied by increasing living standards. Malthus did not foresee that there would be improvements in farming techniques and other production methods while at the same time the average family size would diminish.

The ideas of Malthus do, however, have some relevance to the developing countries, especially where some countries are experiencing a population explosion so that the amount of labour increases without any accompanying rise in the amount of land or capital with which that labour can work. Provided, however, that the population does not grow overnight the increased demand will stimulate production growth and innovation in production techniques to increase output. None the less steady population growth is to be preferred to a rapid growth of population since it enables the economy to absorb the extra supply of labour more effectively.

Under-population is less of a problem since the country can confine its economic activities to the amount of land appropriate to its needs. However, it is possible for the population to be too small for the country to exploit the technical knowledge available or to realise economies of scale in its production levels.

For any country there must be an **optimum population** which enables it to achieve its full potential without lowering the living standards of its people. Of course, that optimum level will vary over time so that the optimum population of the United States today, with its high degree of technological progress, is significantly higher than it was a hundred years ago.

2   Young population

When the population grows rapidly it is quite likely that the population will be a young one so that a disproportionately high percentage of the population is below the working age and therefore economically dependent on a relatively small workforce. Once, however, population growth in a country stabilises a young population tends to augur well for future economic development, provided the other ingredients of economic growth are present. This is because the young population will eventually feed through into an expanded workforce and higher aggregate demand.

3   Ageing population

Most western countries now have an ageing population, a phenomenon associated with two developments this century:

a)   There has been a long-term tendency for the birthrate to decline; a trend broken in the UK only during the decade 1955–65.
b)   There has been a long-term decline in the death rate, resulting in a larger proportion of the population living to retirement age and long beyond that.

Since the birth rate has fallen more rapidly than the death rate population growth in the UK has slowed considerably since the 1960s and it is projected that it will grow only slowly for the foreseeable future. However, changes in the structure of the population this century have been much more dramatic as Figure 18.3 shows.

In 1901 the UK exhibited the profile of a young population with over half the population under the age of 14 and a relatively small dependent population over retirement age. By 1931 the base of the age distribution pyramid has begun to shrink and by 1981 the profile of an ageing population has been established. The proportion of the population aged under fifteen fell from a third in 1901 to a fifth by 1981. Over the same period the retired population grew from 6 per cent of the population to nearly 20 per cent. So, while the proportion of the population which is economically inactive has remained almost constant this century, the elderly have become an increasingly more significant section of the dependent population. The economic implications of an ageing population are as follows:

a) Since older people are generally more restrained in their expenditure patterns, an ageing population is likely to offer more limited market potential for consumer goods than a young population.

b) Among demands for public goods, there will be pressure for more health care and social services at the expense of education and nursery facilities.

c) There will be reduced demand for family housing but a call for more dwellings for one or two persons, especially sheltered accommodation.

d) There may be a shortage of labour, unless automation progresses sufficiently to meet the shortfall. In the early 1990s, for example, the UK is expected to suffer from a serious shortage of labour because of the decline in the 16–19 age group. The government is therefore expected to pursue ever more vigorously policies which aim to increase economic activity rates among women.

e) In the long term the rise in the dependent population may impose a severe burden on a relatively smaller working population, forced to pay higher taxes to fund the ever-increasing cost of providing services for the elderly. This could curtail the process by which the retirement age has been progressively reduced as people are persuaded to stay on at work longer.

Generally, an ageing population is regarded as being less likely to stimulate economic growth. However, improved pension and savings opportunities mean that the elderly will continue to become more affluent and influence consumption patterns in the economy to a far greater extent than hitherto.

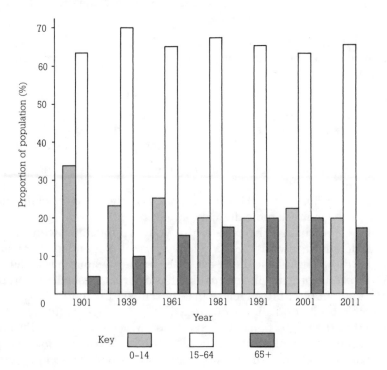

Figure 18.3 *Population change – UK*

REVISION TEST

1 Distinguish between short and long-run changes in the level of national income.

2 Which are the factors of production principally connected with economic growth?

3 Define the term 'human capital'.

4 Why is population growth a two-edged sword with regard to economic development?

5 How do demand factors influence the rate of economic growth?

6 Why are the theories of Malthus more relevant today in parts of the Third World than they were in nineteenth-century England?

7 What is meant by the term 'optimum population'?

8 Why may the optimum population for a country change over time?

9 Under what circumstances could the population be both shrinking and yet getting younger?

10 What are the main economic problems associated with an ageing population?

_____ **Examination questions** _____

1 a) The size of a country's population is a matter of concern to its government. Why is this?
   b) What policies can a government use to influence the rate of growth of the population?

(ABE1, June 1986)

2 Outline the major factors that determine the rate of change in the size of a country's population.

(ABE1, December 1987)

3 Explain the typical course of a business cycle and indicate its effects on business development.

(ABE2, December 1985)

4 'The theory can be summed up by saying that given the psychology of the public, the level of output and employment as a whole depends on the amount of investment. I put it this way not because investment is the only factor on which aggregate output depends, but because it is the factor most prone to sudden and wide fluctuations.'

(J. M. Keynes)

Give as careful an explanation of this statement as you can in the time available. It might be useful to present diagrams in support of your arguments.

(ABE2, June 1986)

5   a)   What are business cycles?
    b)   Why do business cycles take place?

(ACCA, December 1987)

6   a)   To what extent is the precise measurement of economic growth possible?
    b)   What factors are responsible for economic growth?

(ACCA, June 1988)

7   What is the relationship between inflation and unemployment?

(ACCA, December 1988)

8   'According to the accelerator theory, investment is a function of change in income.'
    Explain.

(Cert.M., November 1986)

9   a)   Describe three methods of measuring national income. Why will the answers
          produced by each of these methods be different?
    b)   It has been said that two causes of economic growth are an increase in
          population and the accumulation of capital.
          i) Write brief notes on how each of these factors may lead to economic growth.
          ii) Write brief notes on four other factors that can lead to economic growth.

(I.Act., April 1987)

10 Discuss the factors that cause the level of national income to fluctuate in a modern
    mixed economy.

(I.Act., April 1988)

19 Inflation and unemployment

- *Is excess demand the cause or the consequence of growth in the money supply?*

- *What factors, other than a deflationary gap, lead to unemployment?*

Inflation

In previous chapters we have seen that an inflationary gap occurs when full employment output in the economy is unable to satisfy full employment aggregate demand. This results in a perpetual cycle of excess demand, rising prices, rising profits, rising factor incomes and excess demand. So an inflationary gap is typified by a situation in which prices of both goods and factors tend to rise without leading to an increase in output. This tendency for prices to rise throughout the economy is referred to as **inflation**, and must not be confused with price rises which result from market forces and which may lead to changes in demand and supply conditions.

Inflation is often defined as 'too much money chasing too few goods'. While something of a simplification, this definition does at least refer to the fact that inflation is the result of excess demand in the economy. In addition, it raises the question of the role of money in the inflationary process. Do increases in the money supply act as the primary cause of inflation or does growth in the money supply simply follow the needs of economic decision-makers in carrying out their transactions?

The role of money in the economy

In Chapter 15 we saw that the primary function of money is to facilitate economic transactions by acting as a medium of exchange and unit of account. As such, money neither constitutes wealth in the economic sense nor does it relate directly to the level of economic activity in society. However, the rapid inflation experienced in Europe following the influx of gold and silver from the New World in the seventeenth century led economists to seek a causal relationship between the two events. In consequence, the **quantity theory of money** was developed to show that the price level is directly related to the stock of money. Thus an increase in the money supply, all things being equal, would lead to a rise in the price level by the same proportion.

This theory was further refined at the beginning of the twentieth century by the American economist Irving Fisher in his 'Quantity Equation of Exchange'. This states that:

$$MV \equiv PT$$

The symbol $\equiv$ means 'necessarily equal' and is used because, as we shall see in a moment, the two sides of the equation are different expressions of the same process.

M is the quantity of money, i.e. the stock of money in the economy.

V is the velocity of circulation, i.e. the number of times that each unit of money is used during a given period.

P is the price level, i.e. the average price of all goods and services exchanged.

T is the volume of transactions in the economy during a given period.

Thus the equation states that the quantity of money multiplied by the number of times that each unit of money is used is necessarily equal to the price level of goods and services multiplied by the volume of goods and services bought during a given period.

In effect, the equation is a truism since MV and PT are two ways of expressing total expenditure in the economy over a given period of time. MV regards the members of society as consumers; their total expenditure being equal to the amount of money at their disposal (M) multiplied by the number of times each unit of money is used (V). PT sees the members of society as producers; the total receipts from their output being equal to the number of goods and services exchanged (T) multiplied by the price at which these transactions take place (P). It follows that if we know the value of any three of the variables in the equation we can calculate the fourth. So, if P is 15 and T is 20 million (PT = 300 million), while M is 150 million, then V must be 2 (MV = 300 million).

There are various versions of the quantity theory of money but all start from the Fisher equation and all seek to explain the effect of changes in the quantity of money on the price level. The quantity theory espoused by economists in the early part of this century was based on the premise that money is essentially neutral in its impact on the level of economic activity. So changes in the quantity of money lead directly to changes in the price level. This premise was based on a number of assumptions concerning the working of the economy.

1 Full employment is the natural state of the economy so that a change in M is unable to influence the level of economic activity and T is therefore constant.

2 Both factor prices and the prices of goods are able to adjust in line with changes in the quantity of money so that a change in M translates directly into a change in P.

3 The distribution of real income is unaffected by changes in M.

4 V is independent of changes in M. This is because the amount of money held by people against a given level of income and expenditure is determined by institutional factors in making and receiving payments and this does not change in the short run.

On the basis of these assumptions both T and V are held to be constant so that changes in M must lead directly to changes in P.

In practice the assumptions underlying the quantity theory do not stand up to close scrutiny:

1 It is likely that prices will not be able to adjust as fast as the quantity of money changes. Thus a change in M giving rise to a change in demand will be felt not only

in the price level but will also affect the level of economic activity. So even if there is full employment firms may use overtime and other methods of increasing output.

2   Changes in M will almost certainly have an effect on the distribution of income. An increase in M which leads to a rise in the price level will benefit debtors at the expense of creditors, so redistributing wealth and affecting the level and pattern of expenditure.

3   Rising factor incomes may lead people to respond to changes in money income even when real income is unaffected. In this case the effect of higher money incomes in stimulating expenditure will not be matched by the effect of higher prices in discouraging expenditure.

4   Changes in the price level may lead people to anticipate further changes. If prices are rising they may try to get rid of money quickly before its value falls further. This will increase the velocity of circulation and so V will not be unaffected by changes in M.

5   The theory assumes that the price level changes uniformly whereas the prices of different goods change at different rates and some prices may even be falling while the general price level is rising. Thus there is no evidence to support the view that a rise in M will have proportionately the same effect on P.

Keynesian theory of money

The quantity theory of money was largely discredited by the experience of the UK and other economies during the 1920s. Then, the operation of a gold standard, with a monetary regime closely linked to it, failed to ensure that prices moved smoothly in line with changes in the quantity of money and a falling price level was accompanied by sluggish economic activity and persistent unemployment.

An alternative view of the role of money in the economy was propounded by Keynes. He saw money as not only a medium of exchange but also an asset which people may choose to hold in preference to other assets. Once it is accepted that money may be held for its own sake, it will be subject to the principles of supply and demand analysis. The supply of money is determined by the banking system through the process of credit creation. The demand for money means the demand to hold money in preference to other assets, i.e. **liquidity preference**. Keynes identified three motives for liquidity preference:

1   *Transactions motive*
This arises from the need for both households and businesses to hold money for current expenditure.

a) **Households**   These hold money to ensure that they have funds available for expenditure throughout the period from one receipt of income to the next. The importance of this motive will depend firstly on the length of time which elapses between income receipts. A weekly-paid person receiving £300 per week who spends all his or her income will hold £300 at the start of the week and nothing at the end of it, resulting in an average holding of £150. If the same person is now paid monthly he or she will receive £1300 each month, resulting in an average holding of £650.

The size of a person's income will also affect the amount of money held under the transactions motive. Suppose that one person has an income of £2000 per month while another has an income of £1000 per month. Provided that both spend all the income received the former person will have an average holding of £1000 while the latter will have an average holding of £500. Thus as income rises there will be a greater demand for money due to the transactions motive.

b) **Firms** Money is held by businesses to meet necessary expenditure during that period when costs of production have been incurred but sale proceeds have not yet been received. The size of the firm's transaction holding will depend on the length of the period between the incurring of costs and the receipt of income. It will also depend on the turnover of the firm; generally, the larger the turnover the greater the amount of money needed to meet current expenses.

The transactions motive for holding money was recognised by the quantity theorists. It is the second and third motives for holding money which distinguishes Keynesian theory from that of the classical economists.

2   Precautionary motive

Money held under the transactions motive is intended to meet known expenditure. However, individuals may choose to hold money balances to provide for unforeseen contingencies such as unexpected domestic bills, sickness, unemployment or other misfortunes. The amount held to satisfy this motive varies with the temperament of the individual and his or her economic circumstances. In the case of temperament some people are naturally prudent and will try to set money aside in case of future difficulties; others make little or no provision for the future and trust to luck or charity if things go wrong. With regard to economic circumstances it is clearly easier for the wealthy individual to put money aside for unexpected misfortune since this will involve little or no sacrifice of current expenditure plans. Poor people may be unable to meet current expenditure needs, let alone save for a rainy day.

The precautionary motive also depends on the nature of the economic society within which individuals live. The existence of a state welfare scheme or free health service is likely to reduce the need to hold money under the precautionary motive. Similarly, access to a range of pension and insurance schemes, whether private or public, reduces the need for the individual to operate his or her own precautionary balances.

Firms may also hold precautionary balances, especially if they experience considerable fluctuations in expenditure or receipt patterns and do not wish to find themselves temporary illiquid.

3   Speculative motive

If the precautionary motive arises out of the need for some caution in the allocation of expenditure, the speculative motive is prompted by opportunism and the chance to make profits from future uncertainties. Money held for this motive consists mainly of funds which would normally be placed on the capital or money markets but which are being kept liquid in the expectation that more profitable opportunities will arise in the future. The speculative holding of money results in a cost – the foregone interest that would have been received had the money been invested. There is therefore a direct relationship between the rate of interest and the willingness to hold money for specu-lative purposes; the higher the interest rate the greater will be the interest foregone by holding money and the lower will be the willingness to do so.

The relationship between the rate of interest and the amount of money held for speculative purposes is straightforward. The interest rate is a price and the higher the price offered to sacrifice liquidity the greater the incentive to make that sacrifice. Given the sacrifice involved in holding money for speculative purposes the only logical reason for holding such balances is the expectation that the interest rate will rise in the *future*. A rise in the interest rate will bring down the prices of alternative assets and enable the speculator to make capital gains. To understand this point it must be remembered how the prices of stocks are determined. Once a stock is issued the interest on it is fixed. If interest rates rise that stock may then be giving a lower return than a new stock. This will make it less attractive and cause its price to fall until the **yield** is equivalent to that earned on the new stock.

Suppose that the prevailing rate of interest is 10 per cent and a new stock is issued carrying a rate of 12½ per cent. Investors will be keen to sell existing stocks and buy the new one and market forces will drive down the price of existing stocks until they yield 12½ per cent. Thus a £100 stock carrying a nominal interest rate of 10 per cent would fall in price to £80, at which point it would yield a return of 12½ per cent, i.e.

$$\frac{\text{Price of new bond}}{\text{Price of old bond}} = \frac{\text{Interest rate on new bond}}{\text{Interest rate on old bond}}$$

In this case:

$$\frac{100}{80} = \frac{12½}{10}$$

It is therefore possible for individuals to make profits by buying stocks when they are cheap (because of high interest rates) and selling them when they are dear (when the interest rate has fallen). The speculative demand for money will therefore be high when interest rates are expected to rise and low when interest rates are expected to fall.

Together these three motives, transaction, precaution and speculation, determine the demand for money and the individual's liquidity preference. From the analysis of the speculative motive we see that the demand to hold money rises when the interest rate is low. This must also be true of both the other motives for holding money since the lower the interest rate the lower the cost of holding money, i.e. the foregone interest. This is shown in the downward sloping liquidity preference curve in Figure 19.1.

The interest rate can be equated with the price of money. The higher the price (the rate of interest) the less attractive it will be to hold money in preference to interest-bearing assets. The interest rate itself will be determined by the intersection of the

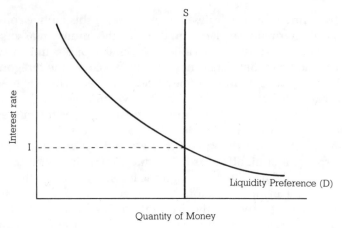

Figure 19.1 *Liquidity preference*

demand and supply of money. An increase in the demand for money will raise interest rates as people sell stocks to increase cash balances and so force down the price of stocks.

Modern monetarism

The persistent inflation of the 1950s led to a revival of interest in the quantity theory of money, notably among the Chicago School of economists led by Milton Friedman. The modern monetarists accept that only when real output is constant, as when there is a situation of full employment, are M and P directly related. Then changes in M will result in changes in PT, provided that V is constant, or at least subject only to predictable change. Controlling M will control the money level of national income (PT) which can be expected to move in the same direction as M.

Money and inflation

The most significant difference between monetarist and Keynesian theories of money centres on the effect that changes in the money supply have on the economy, in particular with regard to inflation. Briefly, their contrasting views are:

Monetarism
1 An increase in the money supply will, in the short run, lower interest rates and raise prices. If there are unused resources there may also be an increase in output.
    In the long run both unemployment and output will settle at their 'natural' level. An excessive money supply will lead to attempted increases in consumption but will result inevitably in higher prices.

2 Inflation is the result of excess demand in the economy. This in turn is due to growth in the money supply.

3 An increase in the money supply will result in higher interest rates following a rise in the price level.

Keynesianism

1 An increase in the money supply will result in lower interest rates. This will stimulate investment as well as demand and result in increased output in the short run and economic growth in the long run.

2 Inflation is the result of excess demand in the economy. This is due especially to fluctuations in the level of investment at the full employment level which may produce inflation without any increase in the money supply.

3 An increase in the money supply will lead to lower interest rates as people use the extra money to buy stocks rather than increase their liquidity holdings.

These differences result in monetarists and Keynesians advocating very different policies, especially to combat inflation. These alternatives will be considered in the next chapter.

REVISION TEST

1 Define 'inflation'.

2 Explain the meaning of the equation $MV = PT$.

3 Given that $MV = PT$, what possible results would follow to the other components if the value of V halved?

4 What does the 'speculative motive' mean in Keynesian theory?

5 Why do firms have a precautionary motive?

6 Explain why stocks with an interest rate of 6 per cent can still command a market price when the current market rate of interest is 10 per cent.

7 If the 'normal' interest rate is 10 per cent what price will £100 of 4 per cent undated stock command in the market?

8 Why is the quantity theory of money regarded as unrealistic?

9 Explain how market forces operate in determining a 'price' for money? To what extent does money differ from goods when applying the principles of supply and demand theory?

10 According to modern monetarists, what condition is necessary for increases in the money supply to lead directly to higher prices?

Types of inflation

We have seen that monetarists and supporters of Keynes differ as to the precise cause of inflation. Monetarists see growth in the money supply as the principal factor while Keynesians believe that inflationary forces can be in operation without any change in the money supply. Both agree, however, that inflation is the result of excess demand in the economy as described by the term **demand–pull inflation**.

However, events in the UK and other Western economies in the period after 1960 led to modern supporters of Keynesianism, the neo-Keynesians, revising their view of inflation. They observed that inflationary pressures could be generated by rises in costs which occur outside the flow of national income. The initial rise in costs leads to a rise in the price level which prompts workers to press for higher wages to restore living standards. These higher wages constitute an increased cost for the industries in which they work so that another round of price and wage rises commences. This inflation is described as **cost–push inflation**. Examples of events which set off cost–push spirals in the UK include the devaluation of sterling in 1967 and the oil-price rises of 1973 and 1979, both of which led to costs rising through higher prices of imported raw materials.

Demand–pull and cost–push inflations are compared in Figure 19.2. In Figure 19.2(a) an increase in aggregate demand from D_1 to D_2 results in excess demand in the economy. Since there is full employment the aggregate supply of goods and services is unable to respond so prices rise as a way of removing the excess demand. Firms then attempt to attract more factors of production by raising the rewards paid to them so that the supply shifts from S_1 to S_2. The increased factor earnings give another boost to aggregate demand which now rises from D_2 to D_3 and so the process is repeated with rises in *money* aggregate demand and supply but no change in *real* national income. In Figure 19.2(b) a rise in the costs of production leads aggregate supply to shift to the left from S_1 to S_2. The higher prices which follow will, in theory, lead to a fall in aggregate demand. In practice, workers and other groups in receipt of factor earnings demand higher rewards to maintain their living standards so that aggregate demand shifts from D_1 to D_2. These increased factor rewards represent a rise in costs to producers so that supply once more shifts to the left, to S_3. Again there are rises in *money* aggregate demand and supply but no change in real national income.

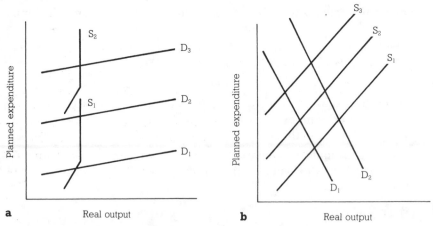

Figure 19.2 *Types of inflation compared*

Whether initiated by demand–pull or cost–push pressures, an inflationary spiral, once in operation, follows a similar pattern; factor earnings increasing in response to rising prices. One important distinction between demand–pull and cost–push inflation surrounds the state of the economy within which they occur. The former is synonymous with an inflationary gap and is therefore associated with full employment and a buoyant economy. The latter can occur whatever the state of the economy since it is a response to a rise in costs rather than a rise in demand. Indeed, cost–push inflation is more likely to be associated with contraction in the economy. If costs have risen there has been a downward pressure on real national income and any price rises which follow represent a fall in real living standards rather than booming demand conditions.

The concept of cost–push inflation is not accepted by most monetarists. They believe that all inflation stems from excess demand and that rises in costs will only lead to a price-wage spiral if demand conditions are sufficiently buoyant to support this spiral, strengthened if necessary by growth in the money supply. If they are not unemployment will rise until demand conditions respond to the new situation imposed by higher costs and reducing living standards.

Effects of inflation

Whatever its cause, inflation poses a number of problems for the smooth working of the economy.

1 Redistribution of income
It is extremely unlikely that all sections of the community will be equally affected by inflation. Those on fixed incomes will suffer a fall in real incomes in line with inflation. Borrowers gain by being able to repay loans in money which is reduced in value while creditors, on the other hand, see their savings reduced in real terms. There is also a redistribution of income from those in weak bargaining positions to those who can negotiate from strength. Finally, cost-push inflation affects different groups unevenly; a rise in energy prices is likely to affect the old most since they spend a high proportion of their income on heating.

2 Effects on business activity
An inflationary gap results from boom conditions in the economy so that firms enjoy good trading conditions and are encouraged to expand both output and investment. Furthermore, inflation boosts profits since it adds value to raw materials and goods held in stock between the time they are processed and the point when they are sold.

However, if the inflation rate rises much above 5 per cent per annum it becomes difficult to plan for the future because of uncertainties surrounding costings and profitability. With cost–push inflation the same problems may arise or the economy may be in recession so that inflation is yet another cause of uncertainty and doubt in future planning.

3 Persistent inflation
The longer that the economy is beset by inflation the more used society becomes to rising prices. Further inflation is then anticipated and this may lead to product and factor prices rising faster than the current rate of inflation, so accelerating the rate still more. The faster that prices rise the less resistant are customers to higher prices. Firms may exploit this situation by raising prices by a larger amount than is necessary to keep pace with inflation, thereby adding to their profits and producing **price–push inflation**.

Inflation may eventually become so embedded in the economy that even with deflation and rising unemployment prices continue to rise steadily. Sometimes it may even get out of hand so that a country experiences runaway or hyper-inflation of the type experienced by Germany in 1923, Hungary in 1946 and, to a lesser extent, a number of developing countries at the present time.

4 The external position

If a country's inflation rate is higher than that of its trading competitors it will find that exports fall and imports rise as it prices itself out of its markets. Where there is an inflationary gap this may help to reduce inflation since aggregate demand in the economy will fall relative to aggregate supply. If, however, the economy is operating below full capacity with cost–push inflationary pressures a deterioration in the country's trading position will result in a growth in unemployment and a decline in national output.

The measurement of inflation

Changes in the value of money must be taken into account when comparing economic data from one year to another. So the fact that money wages have doubled tells us nothing about living standards unless we also know how much prices have gone up over the same period. It is customary to measure changes in the value of money by the use of a **price index** which is calculated as follows:

1   A base year is selected.

2   A 'basket' of goods is made up and the prices of all the goods in it are added to determine the basket's value.

3   The value so obtained is given the index value of 100.

4   The same basket is valued at current prices.

5   The current value is expressed as a percentage of the base year and this becomes the index value for the current year. So if the basket of goods has risen to 1.3 times its base year value, the price index now stands at 130. It is, of course, possible for the index to fall below 100 if prices have fallen so that the value of money has actually risen.

Unfortunately, the construction and use of an accurate price index is beset by problems, the main ones of which are:

1   **Which goods to include**   The goods to be included must depend on the type of index being constructed. A retail price index, for example, should include goods like food, clothing and heating, on which the average household spends its income. Clearly the inclusion of luxury goods which only the very rich can afford would distort the index and weaken its value. In the UK the most recent debate has centred around whether the cost of mortgage payments should be included. Their current inclusion leads to dramatic changes in the retail price index every time the mortgage interest rate is changed.

2   **Weightings**   To avoid distortion each good or service included in the index must be given a weighting to reflect the relative expenditure on the good. Thus the price of a

radio may be 40 times that of a cabbage but allowance must be made for the fact that the typical household may buy a radio only once every three years while it may buy a cabbage every two weeks.

3   **Changes in consumption patterns**   These change over time so the content and weighting of the basket must be constantly reviewed if it is to retain its application to current expenditure patterns.

4   **Different consumption patterns**   The index is necessarily the representation of the 'average' household. As such it does not truly reflect the effect of changes in the value of money on particular groups in society. If energy costs comprise only a small part of the basket a sharp rise in energy prices may affect the index only slightly but for some sections of the community this may represent a substantial fall in the real value of their income.

To get round some of these problems governments often use more than one price index to enable comparisons to be made within fairly limited areas, e.g. import prices, raw material prices, wholesale prices, output prices, etc.

Source: Barclays Bank

Figure 19.3 *UK and international inflation trends: consumer prices, annual percentage changes*

Unemployment

Inflation is associated with one phase of the trade cycle when there are boom conditions and an inflationary gap. At the other end of the cycle the recession phase produces a deflationary gap and unemployment. However, just as the inflationary gap is not the sole root of inflation, the downward phase of the trade cycle is not the only cause of unemployment. The main forms of unemployment can be categorised as:

1   Frictional unemployment

A situation of full employment is generally regarded as one in which less than 3 per cent of the potential workforce is unemployed. The absence of unemployment entirely is due to the existence of frictional unemployment, i.e. short-term unemployment which results from the fact that workers cannot always move smoothly from one employment to another. Frictional unemployment includes those who voluntarily leave one job without going directly to the next; those who are made redundant but then find another job; those who are laid off temporarily due to strikes or other disruptions in their industry and those who leave one job and then retrain to gain work in another occupation. Together these groups account for 1 per cent of the workforce being unemployed at any one time.

Frictional unemployment is inevitable in a healthy economic society where industrial and economic change leads to some industries contracting and others growing. The greater the mobility of labour the faster the process by which the frictionally unemployed are re-absorbed into the workforce. During the late 1950s and early 1960s the number of unemployed in the UK was around 300 000, less than 2 per cent of the workforce.

2   Cyclical unemployment

This is that unemployment which is the direct result of the downward phase of the trade cycle and is thus associated with a deflationary gap. This is potentially the most serious form of unemployment and, during a major slump, may result in millions being thrown out of work. During the typical trade cycle it may still lead to large numbers losing their jobs in those industries which are particularly susceptible to cyclical demand patterns such as construction and engineering.

3   Structural unemployment

This is the consequence of a permanent change in demand conditions which results in an industry contracting rapidly. Because of the occupational immobility of labour, workers who are laid off continue to seek employment in the industry even though their chances of finding work are very slim and they thus become structurally unemployed.

In the UK structural unemployment has been aggravated in the past by the decline of several major industries, such as coal, steel, shipbuilding and textiles, which were heavily concentrated in certain regions. The term **regional unemployment** was used to describe the high unemployment in those areas of the UK where the problems of structural unemployment were most heavily concentrated, i.e. Scotland, Wales, Northern Ireland and the northern regions of England. The persistence of higher unemployment levels in these areas is illustrated in Table 19.1.

The decline in UK manufacturing generally has added to the problem with more than 1.75 million jobs disappearing from manufacturing between 1975 and 1986. Even cyclical unemployment, which begins with deficient demand, may develop into structural unemployment if industries suffer a downturn due to a slump in world trade but lose ground to overseas competitors in the subsequent recovery.

4   Technological unemployment

Contraction of employment opportunities in an industry also occurs when technological change enables labour to be replaced by capital. Thus employment in the industry may decline even though the industry itself is continuing to grow. The problems of technological unemployment have been known since at least the time of the industrial revolution when mechanisation led to widespread unemployment in

TABLE 19.1
Regional unemployment (%)

	1978	1982	1985	1988
North	6.4	13.3	15.4	11.9
Yorkshire & Humberside	4.2	10.4	12.0	9.5
East Midlands	3.6	8.4	9.9	7.2
East Anglia	3.5	7.4	8.0	4.8
South East	3.0	6.7	8.0	5.2
South West	4.6	7.8	9.3	6.3
West Midlands	4.0	11.9	12.7	8.5
North West	5.3	12.1	13.8	10.7
Wales	5.7	12.1	13.8	10.5
Scotland	5.9	11.3	12.9	11.2
Great Britain	4.3	9.4	10.8	7.8
Northern Ireland	8.1	14.4	16.1	16.4
United Kingdom	4.3	9.5	10.9	8.0

Source: Annual Abstract of Statistics.

many craft occupations. Generally, however, these problems have been shortlived during the last hundred years as technical progress has brought greater employment opportunities. Furthermore economic growth has enabled any tendencies towards an excess supply of labour to be offset by reductions in the available pool of labour by reductions in the working week, education for the young and pensioned retirement for the old. In 1950, for example, the British economy had a shortage of labour despite the introduction of labour-saving innovations throughout industry and a fivefold increase in population since 1800.

Provided that workers who lose their jobs through technological unemployment quickly rejoin the workforce, their position is similar to that of the frictionally unemployed. However, the continued acceleration of technical progress since 1980 has raised increasing doubts as to whether, in the future, the employment opportunities created by technological progress will compensate for the jobs lost through it. In these circumstances the effects of technological unemployment may more closely resemble that of structural unemployment. Such is the pace of technological innovation that even employment in some service industries is now being affected so that this sector may not provide the long-term solution to the employment needs of those displaced from the manufacturing sector.

5 Disguised unemployment

At best, technological unemployment presents short-term difficulties for those workers displaced by technology. It is more difficult to accept for older workers who may not gain from any long-term benefits which follow later. So fear of technological unemployment has led many workers to resist the introduction of new technical processes or to accept them only if current manning levels are maintained. This results in disguised unemployment whereby the workforce contains units of labour which are not actually contributing to production. This form of unemployment also occurs if firms do not lay off skilled workers during a minor recession for fear of being unable to recruit suitable replacements when demand recovers.

Disguised unemployment retards economic efficiency through the wastage of resources and it inhibits growth by preventing the release of resources which could be used more effectively elsewhere. It is thus likely to be damaging to the long-term progress of both the industry and the economy as a whole.

6   Seasonal unemployment

Government unemployment figures are adjusted to take account of seasonal fluc-tuations in unemployment and although the factors causing such fluctuations have declined in importance in recent years their influence is still strong in some industries. In particular, the construction and other industries affected by weather conditions traditionally provide greater employment opportunities in the spring and summer months while some agricultural sectors are still in greatest need of workers in the late summer and early autumn. However, in all these industries the impact of technological change has reduced the demand for labour so lessening the numbers affected by seasonal unemployment. In recent years the greatest growth in seasonal employment patterns has been in the leisure and entertainment industries.

Supply side economics

Monetarists see the control of the money supply as the way of curbing excess demand in the economy. They also see output and employment as supply-determined rather than determined by demand as Keynesian analysis suggests. Thus supply conditions are seen as initiating changes in prices and output and determining the long-run equilibrium level of output and employment. This is illustrated in Figure 19.4.

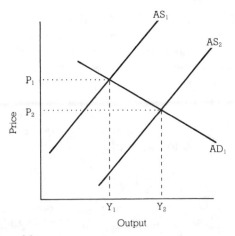

Figure 19.4 *The supply side model*

This model of national income equilibrium sees increases in aggregate supply as the foundation for the expansion of economic activity. A shift in aggregate supply from AS_1 to AS_2 will lead to higher output and employment and serve to push prices downwards. So supply side economics stresses the importance of those factors which influence productive capacity, and thus economic growth, like the level of investment, the degree of mobility of labour, the rate of introduction of new technology rather than the factors which affect short-run aggregate demand conditions.

Supply side economists predict that if markets operate efficiently there will be no demand–deficient unemployment in the long run since unemployment will bring down wages and lead to firms taking on new workers. By the same token excess pay rises do not lead to cost-push inflation but to higher unemployment. The only unemployment which persists in the long run is the 'natural' rate of unemployment, including frictional, technological and voluntary unemployment. The first two categories are inevitable in a healthy economic society while the third is the consequence of people preferring not to work because the income they would receive employed is not sufficiently greater than they receive through state benefits. So the first two categories should be minimised by measures to improve the mobility of labour while the third should be dealt with through the tax and benefits system.

REVISION TEST

1 How does demand–pull inflation occur?

2 What are the main differences between demand-pull and cost-push inflation?

3 Which school of economic thought does not recognise the existence of cost-push inflation?

4 Name three effects of inflation on the economy.

5 Define price-push inflation.

6 What proportion of the workforce is likely to be frictionally unemployed at any one time?

7 Explain how structural unemployment can develop into regional unemployment.

8 Which type of unemployment is likely to produce the largest number of unemployed?

9 What sort of unemployment is experienced by a school-leaver who takes six weeks to find employment after leaving school?

10 What is meant by the 'natural' rate of unemployment by supply-siders?

_____ Examination questions _____

1 Explain what is meant by a high rate of inflation and discuss the good and bad effects it may have on a country's economic life.
   Given that government, business and households purchase different baskets of goods, can a national inflation rate be calculated? Explain your reply.
   (ABE2, June 1987)

2   Define 'inflation', and examine critically at least two economic arguments in favour of keeping the rate of inflation low, compared to the supposed costs of allowing inflation to rise.

(ABE2, June 1988)

3   Explain what you understand by the *quantity theory of money*. How far does this theory provide a satisfactory explanation of price inflation?

(LCCI Higher, November 1985)

4   Explain the quantity theory of money and comment on its relevance as an explanation of inflation.

(LCCI Higher, May 1986)

5   a)   Explain the various causes of inflation.
      b)   What are the major economic effects of inflation?

(LCCI Higher, November 1986)

6   What do you consider to be the main economic effects of inflation in your country?

(LCCI Intermediate, May 1986)

7   Why will people hold more or less money if the rate of interest rises?

(ICSA, June 1986)

8   Does an increase in the supply of money affect the level of employment or the level of prices?

(ICSA, June 1986)

9   Explain carefully what is meant by 'money'. Why is it thought important to control the amount of money?

(ICSA, December 1986)

10   Under what conditions would an increase in the quantity of money lead to an exactly proportional increase in average prices?

(ICSA, June 1987)

11   How does an increase in investment affect the demand for money?

(ICSA, June 1987)

12   Can there ever be too little money in an economy?

(ICSA, December 1987)

13   Why do some countries have more than one retail price index? Is it possible for the different price indices in one country to move in different directions?

(ICSA, June 1988)

14 a) Define money and indicate its functions.
   b) Examine the monetarist view that an increase in the supply of money above the
      rate of increase of real output will lead to rising prices.

(ACCA, June 1987)

15 Explain the liquidity preference theory of interest rate determination.

(ACCA, June 1987)

16 What factors determine the demand for money? How are changes in the supply of
   money linked with the demand for goods and services?
   a) From a Keynesian point of view.
   b) From a monetarist's viewpoint.

(ACCA, December 1987)

17 Compare and contrast the monetarist and Keynesian view of inflation.

(Cert.M., June 1987)

18 How might you classify different types of unemployment?
   Which is likely to be the most serious?

(IFA, June 1989)

20 Government management of the economy

- *To what extent do the macro-economic objectives of the government conflict with one another?*

- *Why cannot all inflation be cured by the same policy measures?*

The government's objectives for the economy

All governments, whatever their political complexion, claim to work for the economic good of the nation as a whole. In so doing they usually identify the following objectives for their policies:

1 Economic growth

The expansion of the productive capacity of the economy enables it to support a growing population and to improve the living standards of the people. Against a background of economic growth it is more likely that the government will be able to pursue policies of change without any one section of society losing in the process. This in turn means that the government is more likely to receive the national support necessary to ensure success for its policies.

2 An equitable distribution of income

The concentration of wealth and income in the hands of a small minority is detrimental to the development of consumer industries and other economic activities which depend on large markets. Thus some movement towards greater equality of income will benefit the economy as a whole. How far this process is taken by the government is a political decision but most governments seek to achieve sufficient equality for there to be a broad demand base and for poverty to be eliminated without destroying the incentive to succeed in society.

3   Full employment

Unemployment results not only in unused human resources but also, except in the case of technological unemployment, in unused capital and other productive resources as well. The economy is therefore operating within its production possibility frontier. Unemployment also leads to social deprivation and may cause political unrest in those areas in which it is most serious. This in turn will make it more difficult for the government to carry out the successful conduct of the economy. All governments therefore attach great importance to its minimisation.

4   Stable prices

We saw in the last chapter that inflation distorts economic activity, causes uncertainty in the conduct of business and affects some groups in society more than others. The resultant distortional effects in the economy may well inhibit the attainment of other economic objectives. The containment of inflation to acceptably low levels is thus a primary aim of government. The eradication of inflation entirely is rarely an aim of government since, as we shall see, this achievement would hinder the attainment of other objectives.

5   Balance of payments equilibrium

The subject of international trade will be dealt with in later chapters. For the moment it is sufficient to note that when imports are greater than exports, i.e. M>X, the level of aggregate demand is insufficient to maintain the national income at its current level and the national income will therefore contract. Thus the government will endeavour to ensure that, over a number of years, the level of imports and other overseas payments is financed by earnings through exports and other income from overseas. Note also that a permanent surplus of exports over imports is no more attractive since this may mean that national output is insufficient to meet aggregate demand so resulting in a shortage of goods for domestic consumption and demand-pull pressures in the economy.

Conflicting objectives

All of the objectives outlined above are inter-related so efforts to achieve one objective will have repercussions for the achievement of one or more of the others.

In theory, this should present no difficulties for a government as it could aim to moderate the effects of the trade cycle to produce a situation of full employment and low inflation. With the resultant strong, buoyant economy the government could then go on to promote economic growth and rising living standards. It would also be in a position to undertake some redistribution of income without the need to reduce the living standards of any one section of the population. Lastly, a healthy, growing economy is more likely to provide an environment conducive to the expansion of trade and the elimination of balance of payments problems.

In practice, governments find their task made more difficult by the frictional pressures which operate within the economy. In particular, the fact that policies are uneven in their impact means that policies to lower inflation will cause unemployment to rise in some parts of the economy while inflationary pressures persist elsewhere. Similarly, policies to combat unemployment will result in some sectors experiencing rising prices before unemployment has been wiped out everywhere. This trade-off between inflation and unemployment is illustrated in the **Phillips curve**, devised by A. W. Phillips in the 1950s.

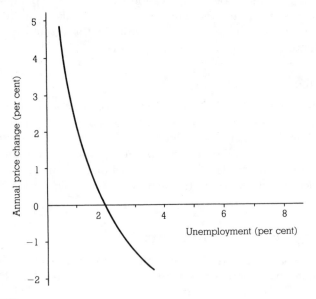

Figure 20.1 *The Phillips curve*

When the Phillips Curve was first projected for the UK an unemployment rate of 2 per cent was sufficient to eradicate inflation. Since then the Phillips curve appears to have moved progressively upwards and to the right as a higher and higher rate of unemployment appears to be necessary to reduce a given rate of inflation. In 1989, for example, an unemployment rate of 6 per cent was accompanied by an inflation rate of 7 per cent. This rightward shift of the Phillips curve points to inflation being less responsive to the downward phase of the trade cycle than in the past. This conclusion is compatible with at least some inflationary pressures being the result of cost-push rather than demand-pull factors. Thus the situation frequently referred to as 'stagflation' has often been in evidence since 1970 whereby both unemployment and inflation are at relatively high levels.

Other objectives which may conflict with each other include balance of payments equilibrium and full employment. This is because policies to stimulate consumption and raise aggregate demand may result instead in higher expenditure on imported goods. In the same way, economic growth could conflict with rising living standards as policies which aim to increase the nation's capital stock may require short-term sacrifices by consumers.

In the following sections the various measures adopted by governments to achieve the objectives outlined above will be examined. We begin with measures which affect the level of economic activity.

Demand management

This term is used to describe the manipulation of aggregate demand, and thus aggregate expenditure, in the economy to counter the effects of the trade cycle and so eliminate inflationary and deflationary gaps. Such activities also affect, indirectly, the standard of living, the long-term growth rate and the balance of payments.

You will recall that it is quite possible for national income equilibrium to be accompanied by either an inflationary or a deflationary gap. Furthermore there is no guarantee that, left to themselves, natural economic forces will eventually operate to close such gaps. It may therefore be necessary for the government to intervene to reduce aggregate demand and close an inflationary gap or increase aggregate demand and close a deflationary gap. Even if natural economic forces would eventually restore the economy to a healthy equilibrium position government action would still be justified to speed up the process of natural correction.

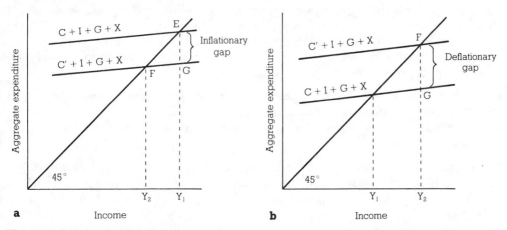

Figure 20.2 *Demand management*

In Figure 20.2(a) there is an inflationary gap (E–G) and the equilibrium level of national income is at the unattainable point Y_1. Government action to reduce the level of aggregate expenditure from C+I+G+X to C'+I+G+X will bring the equilibrium national income into line with full employment at Y_2.

In Figure 20.2(b) there is a deflationary gap (F–G) so that the equilibrium level of national income Y_1 is below that necessary to sustain full employment. Government action to increase the level of aggregate expenditure will raise the equilibrium level of national income to the full employment level of Y_2.

Government action to alter the level of aggregate expenditure may take several forms. Since, however, all action must affect C+I+G+X it must alter either the level of injections or the level of consumption (and thus the level of withdrawals). Such measures may be classified according to which pair of injections and withdrawals are the subject of government policy:

Trade policy	—	Exports and imports
Monetary policy	—	Investment and savings
Fiscal policy	—	Government exports and taxation

Trade policy

This is now a little used government weapon. The days are gone when imperial powers could force subject colonies to take their exports and so boost aggregate demand. Most governments do, however, encourage exports by giving exporting firms financial, insurance or other back-up support. The ability of governments to act directly on the level of imports is also severely limited. Most countries are party to free trade and other agreements which prevent their prohibiting or artificially restricting the flow of overseas goods into the country.

Monetary policy

Monetary policy is the regulation of aggregate expenditure through measures which change the volume and cost of credit and level of liquidity in the economy. It thus involves influencing expenditure decisions by the manipulation of the money supply rather than the government intervening directly to alter the level of economic activity. Monetary policy must aim for one of two outcomes:

● Either it aims to expand aggregate demand by encouraging consumption and creating an environment conducive to increased investment;
● Or it aims to reduce aggregate demand by discouraging consumption and the expansion of credit.

In the former case the result will be an expansion of aggregate expenditure and such a policy would be appropriate when there is a deflationary gap. The latter policy will lead to a contraction in aggregate expenditure and so would be appropriate when there is an inflationary gap.

Monetary policy is determined by the government but its execution is left to the central bank which is in the key position of being banker both to the government and to the banks. In the UK, for example, monetary policy is mapped out by the Treasury but is implemented by the Bank of England.

In determining monetary policy the government is constrained by its monopolistic control of the money supply. Like all monopolies the government can control either the price of money (the rate of interest) or the supply (the amount of money generated by the banking system) but must leave the other to find its own level. The principal measures available to the authorities in the implementation of monetary policy are:

1   Interest rates
Through its operations in the money markets the central bank can exert an immediate impact on short-term interest rates. It can trigger a rise in short-term rates by raising the

rate at which it will lend to the discount houses or equivalent operators in the market. This rise in short-term rates will cause long-term rates to move upwards and so raise the cost of new funds for capital investment.

Higher interest rates reduce the profitability of businesses by raising the cost of credit to finance current activities and they deter the borrowing of funds for new investment. Furthermore the higher cost of credit deters some consumers from borrowing to finance consumer spending. Both firms and households will therefore reduce demand and this will result in a fall in aggregate expenditure and a reduction in inflationary pressures. This was the policy adopted by the UK government in 1989/90 to reduce the rate of inflation in Britain.

The reverse should happen if there is a fall in interest rates. So in a recession the government could engineer a fall in interest rates to encourage borrowing by both businesses and consumers. This would stimulate aggregate demand and help close the deflationary gap.

2 Reserve ratio

In Chapter 15 we saw that the total amount of credit creation by the banking system from a given deposit depends on the size of the banks' reserve ratio. Thus an increase in the reserve ratio over and above that proportion of their assets which the banks would choose to keep in liquid form will restrict their ability to create credit and so slow growth of the money supply.

In the UK the reserve ratio has taken a number of forms in the last 25 years. Between 1971 and 1981 the banks were required to maintain 12½ per cent of their sterling deposits in the form of liquid assets other than cash, e.g. Treasury bills, bills of exchange, money at call with the discount market, etc. This was to enable banks to use these funds profitably but not to expand the level of credit. Since 1981 this strict ratio has been abolished but banks undertake to discuss with the Bank of England any proposed changes in their liquidity arrangements.

Raising the reserve ratio to slow the expansion of credit is effective only if the banks always keep the minimum reserve ratio permitted. If they have surplus liquidity a raising of the reserve ratio may not affect them at all. In any case altering the reserve ratio is a cumbersome method of squeezing credit creation; open market operations or special deposits are more effective, and more flexible, ways of reducing surplus liquidity.

3 Open market operations

These consist of intervention in either the money market or the stock market by the Bank of England or other central bank to make changes in interest rates more effective.

a) **The Money Market** If the Bank of England wishes to raise short-term interest rates it may lower the price at which it will buy, i.e. rediscount bills of exchange, from the discount houses. This will both squeeze the funds available to the market and force up interest rates via the higher discount rate.

b) **The Stock Market** The Bank of England may sell government securities to the public on the open market. The buyers will pay for these securities by withdrawals from their bank accounts, resulting in a fall in bank deposits. In order to maintain an adequate liquidity ratio banks will have to reduce their advances and this will lead to a multiplied contraction of bank lending. This process is shown in Table 20.1.

TABLE 20.1
Open market operations

Bank of England				
Assets		*Liabilities*		
Government securities	−£1m	Clearing bank deposits		−£1m
	−£1m			−£1m
Clearing bank				
Assets		*Liabilities*		
Reserves	−£1m			
Loans and Investments	−9m	Demand deposits		−£10m
	−£10m			−£10m

If the deposit banks maintain a reserve ratio of 10 per cent an open market sale of £1 million will reduce deposit bank reserves by £1 million and result, through the downward bank multiplier, in demand deposits contracting by £10 million as the banks seek to restore the required reserve ratio. Conversely, the Bank of England could buy securities on the open market and stimulate a multiple expansion of credit.

The sale of securities on the open market affects interest rates in two ways:

1 The multiple contraction of deposits outlined above results in an excess demand for loans over the amount available so banks will raise interest rates to choke off excess demand.

2 By selling more securities on the open market the government increases the supply of stocks and this will push down their price. If a £100 stock paying an interest rate of 10 per cent falls in price to £90 the effective interest rate is now 11 per cent.

Clearly the purchase of securities by the government will lead to a fall in interest rates.

4   Special deposits

These were introduced in 1960 as a way of reducing surplus liquidity in the banking system. By calling for special deposits the Bank of England requires the deposit banks to place a specified proportion of their total deposits on deposit with the Bank. Such deposits carry two penalties. First, the interest received on these deposits is Treasury Bill rate, significantly lower than the rate the banks would charge on advances. Second, these deposits must be found by the banks converting their liquid assets into cash, thus leaving the banks short of liquidity. To rectify the position the banks will cut back on advances and bid more actively for deposits, so pushing up interest rates in the market.

5   Quantitative controls

The monetary authorities may choose to limit credit expansion by placing controls on the total level of bank advances. In the 1970s, for example, the Bank of England placed a limit on the growth of interest-bearing eligible liabilities. Banks which exceeded the limit would have to place a proportion of the excess on interest-free deposit with the Bank of England.

The government may also consider other quantitative controls such as raising the minimum deposit on a purchase by credit or insisting that credit card balances are repaid over a shorter time scale. Such controls were commonly used until the 1980s but have been largely neglected by the British government since then.

6   Qualitative controls

Since the 1950s the Bank of England has instructed the deposit banks to give priority to certain categories of borrower, especially during periods of credit restraint. Thus the banks are expected to give a higher priority to industrial borrowers, notably exporters, small businesses and growth industries, than to private customers. Since banks are much more likely to be guided by their own self-interest in determining their lending policy the priority categories of the government will tend to be favoured less than mortgage business and small personal loans. So to make qualitative controls successful the government may have to consider accompanying them with inducements to the deposit banks.

The effectiveness of monetary policy

There is no real consensus as to the effectiveness of monetary policy. The failure of an expansionary monetary policy to bring the economy out of recession in the 1930s led to doubts concerning its usefulness. Indeed post-war governments largely ignored monetary policy, the bank rate being unchanged from 1932 until 1951. Throughout the 1950s and 1960s monetary policy was used mainly as a back-up to fiscal policy and consisted usually of hire purchase and other quantitative controls. The use of monetary policy reflected the views of the Radcliffe Committee which in 1958 concluded that 'Monetary measures alone cannot be relied upon to keep in nice balance an economy subject to major strains both from without and from within. Montetary measures can help, but that is all'.

In the 1970s there was renewed interest in monetary policy. This followed the emergence of modern monetarist economists for whom monetary policy was at the centre of economic policy, control of the money supply being essential to any counter-inflationary strategy. Governments were also attracted to monetary policy by the failure of traditional fiscal policies to control inflation. In 1976 the British government, for example, began announcing targets for money supply growth. The Conservative government elected in 1979 was very committed to monetarist measures as a way of curing inflation and the control of the money supply was at the centre of government economic policy throughout the 1980s.

Despite the relative success of monetary policy in controlling UK inflation in the 1980s a number of question marks remain over its effectiveness. This applies whether we examine control of the price of money, i.e. interest rates, or the supply of money.

Interest rates

In the 1980s interest rates were frequently used as the main, often the only, measure to control the growth of credit and thus aggregate demand in the fight against inflation. Yet changes in interest rates have only a limited effect on the borrowing decisions of both consumers and firms.

Consumers tend to make their borrowing decisions by reference to whether they can afford the repayments rather than the interest rate itself, as evidenced by the punitive interest rates charged on borrowing by credit card or in-house store card. Thus higher interest rates only deter consumer borrowing to the extent that they raise the payments due.

We have already seen that firms make their investment decisions on the basis of confidence and the expected rate of return. So high interest rates may not dissuade firms from investing when the economy is booming. Indeed, higher interest rates may add to inflationary pressure if firms are able to pass on higher borrowing costs to the consumer in the form of higher prices. During a depression, on the other hand, low interest rates may do little to stimulate investment activity among depressed industries. It would appear, however, that high interest rates are more effective in dampening investment activity than are low rates in stimulating it.

When they were used as the sole policy instrument, as in 1989/90, interest rates had to rise to very high *real* rates before they began to affect consumer demand. By this time, however they were seriously affecting the willingness of industry to invest.

A further limitation on the effectiveness of interest rates stems from the growth in money movements between countries. So while higher interest rates may reduce the expansion of credit from internal sources, they will attract overseas funds into the domestic banking system which will eventually lead to expansion of the money supply.

Money supply

Until 1980 direct methods of controlling the money supply consisted principally of a reserve ratio to limit credit expansion, open market operations and special deposits to reduce bank liquidity and quantitative controls to impose a ceiling on bank lending. They would be used to create a credit squeeze to reduce the availability of credit and so push up the cost of borrowing.

The effectiveness of such measures depends on there being no surplus liquidity in the banking system. If there is, a credit squeeze may just lead to the slack in the system being taken up. A further problem is that ways may be found round the controls. In the 1970s, for example, the 'corset' was frequently used to set monthly targets for the growth of bank lending; the exceeding of which resulted in the banks incurring penalties. When the corset was pulled tight in 1979 both companies and banks soon found loopholes which they could exploit. A particular problem was that of **disintermediation**, i.e. the substitution of direct lending for financial intermediation. Examples of disintermediation include:

1   The inter-company market which enables firms with surplus funds to lend them to those short of funds without going through financial intermediaries.

2   The sterling commercial paper market established in London in 1986 on which companies issue bearer loans of between 7 and 364 days.

3   The use of the Eurobond market by banks to raise international loans for companies.

4   Rate arbitrage whereby companies borrow from banks and lend the funds out at higher rates so stimulating monetary expansion.

In 1981 the UK government introduced a new strategy referred to as the 'monetary base system'. Instead of controlling the creation of credit, the monetary base system concentrates on the control of cash held by the banks, i.e. notes, coins and balances with the Bank of England, since this is the part of the money supply which the Bank of England can control. At various times over the next ten years the government set targets for a whole range of monetary measures, from the narrow M1 to the wide M5. The distortion of M1 by the existence of large volatile interest bearing balances led to its being replaced by M0 as the narrow monetary aggregate in 1984.

Whatever the monetary measure it proved almost impossible to keep within the target set and some measures often reached levels well above the target, as when M4 reached an annual rate of growth of 18 per cent in June 1989. In consequence the inflation rate proved difficult to hold below around 4–5 per cent. Nor was the relationship between money supply growth and the inflation rate always straightforward. Between 1982 and 1986, for example, Sterling M3 (now M3) grew at a higher rate than in previous years while the inflation rate was falling. Even when the government succeeded in keeping within its narrow monetary targets the growth of credit continued unabated through the expansion of the use of credit cards and other forms of instant credit.

The monetary base system has also led to more volatile and higher interest rates which have had a detrimental effect on the level of investment and attracted inflows of deposits from overseas which leak into the domestic money supply and stimulate further credit creation.

There are also question marks over the effectiveness of monetary policy as a whole.

1   Monetary measures are not precise instruments. Thus increases in interest rates hit depressed sectors of the economy just as hard as those which are overheated.

2   Expansionary monetary measures have had little success in promoting economic activity though a tight monetary policy does seem to affect business activity, if only because of the negative impact on business confidence.

3   The time-lag between implementation and impact of monetary measures means that the government may have difficulty in gauging what effect particular measures are having, so risking the possibility that new measures will be introduced which go further than is necessary.

4   Where monetary policy results from the espousal of a strict monetarist stance by the government it may be used to the exclusion of all other policies and this certainly limits the government's freedom of action.

REVISION TEST

1   What are the main objectives of government macro-economic policy?

2   Give two examples of where government objectives may be in conflict.

3 What is the nature of the relationship referred to as the 'Phillips curve'?

4 On which injection and which withdrawal is monetary policy intended to act?

5 Name three types of monetary policy which the government may use to influence economic activity.

6 Which items of aggregate demand are likely to be sensitive to changes in interest rates?

7 What is a central bank trying to achieve when it sells stocks on the open market?

8 What limitations are there on the effectiveness of interest rate changes as a monetary measure?

9 If the reserve ratio were abolished what would be the likely effect on the money supply?

10 What is disintermediation?

Fiscal policy

Prior to the development of Keynesian theory fiscal policy was seen primarily in accounting terms; the object of the government being to balance expenditure and revenue or perhaps even achieve a budget surplus. During a recession the government would encounter falling tax revenues and would therefore cut its expenditure in order to balance its budget. The effect would be a reduction in aggregate demand and a worsening of the recession, which monetary policy proved unable to reverse.

To an extent the existing fiscal structure does moderate inflationary or deflationary effects when left to itself because of its **built-in stabilisers**. So in a recession rising unemployment and falling consumer demand will reduce automatically receipts from taxation while increasing government expenditure on unemployment and social security benefits. Similarly, inflation, by raising incomes, will lead to more households paying taxes and reduce the numbers eligible for social security.

Discretionary fiscal policy

While built-in stabilisers reduce the extent of the fluctuations of the trade cycle, they are not of themselves sufficient to eliminate them entirely, even when supported by an appropriate monetary policy. The failure of such a policy strategy in the 1930s led Keynes to argue that the government should intervene directly in the economy during a depression, by increasing its own expenditure *without* increasing taxes to pay for this extra activity. This would raise aggregate demand and stimulate the level of economic activity generally. Clearly, opposite measures would need to be taken when the economy was suffering from an inflationary gap. Fiscal policy which is directed at influencing the level of economic activity rather than at balancing the government's budget is known as discretionary fiscal policy.

Discretionary fiscal policy involves the acceptance by the government that it must abandon the principle of always seeking to balance its budget. Instead it must be prepared to budget for either a deficit or a surplus. In the case of a deficit this means that the government will finance some of its expenditure by borrowing. In the case of a surplus this means that it will be able to allocate some of its revenue to repay past borrowing.

By incurring a budget deficit the government effects an upward shift in C + I + G + X. This will involve either an increase in government expenditure or a reduction in taxation. In either case the multiplier will come into play so that the growth in aggregate expenditure from a given increase in government expenditure or cut in taxation will be greater than the original increase in aggregate demand. If, therefore, the multiplier has a value of 2 an increase in government expenditure of £5 billion would be sufficient to close a deflationary gap of £10 billion.

A budget surplus results from either a reduction in government expenditure or an increase in taxation and leads to a multiplied downward shift in C + I + G + X which will help to reduce an inflationary gap.

The implementation of a discretionary fiscal policy is complicated by the fact that the multiplier effect of different courses of action varies from one to another. This is true both in the way a deficit is financed or a surplus disposed of and whether the government alters the level of government expenditure or the level of taxation. A deficit financed by borrowing from the banking system will increase the banks' holding of liquid assets and enable them to expand credit. This will have a stronger multiplier effect than if the deficit is financed by borrowing from private individuals which merely transfers spending power from individuals to the government. Even in this latter case there is still a multiplier effect since those individuals might have spent some of this income on imports or saved it while the government can direct the entire amount into the circular flow of income. Similarly, in disposing of a surplus, the government's deflationary measures would be better supported by repaying debts held by the banking system rather than by private individuals.

The multiplier effect of increased government expenditure is greater than that of reduced taxation. Whereas all increased government expenditure goes into the circular flow of income, some of income retained through lower taxes will leak out of the flow by being saved or spent on imported goods. So to achieve a given increase in aggregate expenditure through cuts in taxation a bigger budget deficit will be required than if the deficit resulted from increased government expenditure. Similarly, cuts in government expenditure are more effective in reducing demand than are increases in taxation as some of the extra tax paid would have been withdrawn from the circular flow anyway.

The multiplier process will ensure that a final deficit or surplus is smaller than that initially introduced. A budget deficit will lead to higher incomes and expenditure throughout the economy and result in increased tax receipts. Similarly, a budget surplus will be reduced by the consequent reduction in national income lowering tax revenue.

It is also possible for the government to maintain a balanced budget and yet address the problems posed by a deflationary or inflationary gap. This is because of the **balanced budget multiplier**. If there is an increase in government expenditure and taxation by the same amount the upward multiplier effect of the increase in govern-ment expenditure will be greater than the downward multiplier effect of the increase in taxation so there will be a rise in national income. A reduction in both variables will result in a fall in national income. Clearly the use of a balanced budget to manage demand requires much greater increases in the level of government intervention to achieve a given target.

Fiscal and monetary measures

While monetary and fiscal policy have been examined individually there are clearly many links between them:

1   Monetary measures aimed at altering the money supply will affect incomes and this will have implications for the government's budget.

2   The way a government finances a deficit or disposes of a surplus may have an effect on bank creation of credit, as outlined above.

3   An increase in government expenditure will lead to a rise in income which in turn will enable a growth in bank deposits and a multiplied creation of credit.

4   Typically monetary policy would be used in support of fiscal policy or vice versa. However, the government may choose to stimulate investment by relaxing monetary policy yet maintain a tight fiscal policy to prevent the emergence of inflationary pressures.

5   Fiscal policy can be more precisely targeted than monetary policy since the government can decide in which sectors of the economy to stimulate economic activity.

The effectiveness of fiscal policy

The Keynesian development of a discretionary fiscal policy assumed that the government's role would develop into the '**fine tuning**' of the economy. Thus the government would intervene to stimulate demand during a recession and act to dampen demand if the economy became overheated. This would moderate the effects of the trade cycle and enable the government to achieve its aims of full employment and stable prices. At the same time a stable, healthy economic environment would be created within which economic growth would be stimulated and the government could pursue this and its other economic objectives.

In practice the use of discretionary fiscal policy has proved less successful than was originally hoped. While its use has averted the worst problems of the 1930s, attempts to fine tune the economy have failed to eradicate the trade cycle or enable the government to achieve its macro-economic objectives. A number of factors account for this.

1   To be effective fine tuning requires that the government takes action at exactly the right time. If not it may expand demand too late to avert a recession or expand it when the economy is about to turn out of recession so causing it to overheat.

2   There may be conflict between the needs of the domestic situation and those of the external position. Thus the domestic situation may require expansionary measures to combat a recession while balance of payments problems demand deflationary measures to reduce demand, and thus imports.

3   **Fiscal drag**: this is the tendency for discretionary fiscal policy to be rendered less

effective by the workings of the existing fiscal system. So cuts in taxation to stimulate demand and increase expenditure will be partly offset by the increased payment of taxes on expenditure.

4 Fiscal policy is unable to solve the problems of regional and technological unemployment which require specific remedies applied to particular sectors of the economy.

5 Counter-inflationary policies may be frustrated by **structural rigidity**. This is the tendency for wages and prices to be upwardly mobile but resistant to downward pressures. Thus deflationary periods are not accompanied by falling wage rates or, to a lesser extent, falling prices.

6 Fiscal policy is unable to deal with the problem of cost-push inflation since the problem is not one of excess demand but attempts to maintain real incomes in the face of rising costs. Higher taxes on expenditure or income serve merely to raise the cost of living and lead to demands for higher incomes, so fuelling cost-push inflation.

Prices and incomes policies

It was the failure of discretionary fiscal policy to solve the problem of inflation during the 1960s which led British governments to seek alternative policies. This resulted in the prices and incomes policies of the late 1960s and 1970s and, as we have seen, the revival of monetarist policies in the 1980s.

The problem of cost-push inflation was symptomatic of the fact that western economic societies, and particularly British society, had become resistant to falling living standards, however temporary or illusory. Traditional methods to deal with inflation actually exacerbated the situation by raising prices in the shops. Even higher unemployment had little impact on this kind of inflation as those workers with jobs continued to push for wage rises which would maintain their living standards. So inflation persisted during periods of recession and the term **stagflation** was coined to describe a situation in which a recession was accompanied by rising prices.

In the 1960s and 1970s successive British governments sought to control cost-push inflation by limiting increases in costs, primarily wage costs. These incomes policies set a target for wage rises over a given period and were often, but not always, accompanied by limits on price rises. It was hoped thereby to reduce inflation without affecting the level of aggregate demand. The course of each policy followed a similar pattern. The policy would in most cases be voluntary and would be accepted at first, perhaps grudgingly. It would encounter growing opposition from the unions as distortions in its application worsened and would finally be abandoned against a background of industrial unrest. The period following the incomes policy would be one of rapidly rising wage levels and an accelerating rate of inflation which would eventually result in the introduction of another incomes policy.

Despite the variety of policies tried a number of conclusions apply to most or all of them.

1 Firm, particularly statutory, wage controls do keep wage rises lower than they would otherwise have been.

2   Price rises prove extremely difficult to control because of external pressures on raw material prices and thus of internal costs involving imported materials.

3   The failure to control prices is a significant factor in weakening the success of controls on incomes.

4   Pay controls distort previously established differentials, usually at the expense of skilled workers or public sector employees.

5   Pay policy is difficult to enforce on workers with high fringe benefits such as managerial staff who can evade controls by increasing perks or regrading posts. This causes resentment among groups who are bound rigidly by pay controls, particularly those in the public sector.

6   The acquiescence of the trade unions is vital to a prolonged period of income restraint and within three years the difficulties outlined above have usually become sufficiently serious for the policy to crumble.

7   When the policy is relaxed or abandoned wage increases tend to accelerate to make up for lost ground. This is particularly a problem when, during the life of the policy, external factors cause prices to rise rapidly.

Both management and unions tended to oppose incomes policies because of their interference with the process of free collective bargaining. They were also opposed by monetarists who rejected the notion of cost-push inflation. Instead, they argued, tight monetary controls ensure that excessive pay claims lead to higher unemployment rather than higher prices as workers price themselves out of jobs. This would occur either because employers would seek alternative, cheaper methods of production or they would give the pay rise and go under as their prices ceased to be competitive.

The Conservative government elected in 1979 adopted the monetarist position and rejected the introduction of an incomes policy. During the 1980s, however, the government frequently imposed limits on public sector pay and exhorted restraint in the private sector. As the trade unions continued to link pay claims to the retail price index and firms were still able to pass high pay awards on to the consumer the argument that cost-push inflation does not exist is difficult to sustain.

Supply side measures

In modern times all governments have engaged in measures to improve aggregate supply whether by direct involvement through public investment or by policies which encourage an expansion of output. In recent times, however, supply side economics, as outlined in the last module, has been dominated by monetarists and others concerned to reduce the 'interference' of government in economic activity. They stress the need for markets to operate properly to ensure that there is full employment and economic growth with stable prices.

Supply side policies concentrate on measures which improve the working of markets and thus tend to be micro- rather than macro-economic in their nature.

1   Manpower policy

This includes measures which aim to improve the occupational and geographical mobility of labour such as training schemes, job information, relocation allowances, etc.

2   Taxation and social security policy

Measures would be taken to ensure that voluntary unemployment was reduced by making it more attractive to take employment than remain unemployed. Thus the level of income at which tax is paid would be raised while social security benefits would be kept at a level which discouraged people staying out of work until they found a job which suited them. Lower tax rates could also be expected to stimulate the incentive to work and thus increase output.

3   Government economic activity

Modern free market economists argue that obstacles to the operation of free markets should be removed, including direct government activity in the economy. They thus support the privatisation of the nationalised industries and many public services. Government action should be limited to ensuring that restrictive practices and monopoly power are kept to a minimum.

Of course supply side policies could equally involve state planning and investment by the government in specific industries. Thus all command and most mixed economies have intervened to support vital industries which require extra capital investment or structural reorganisation.

REVISION TEST

1   Fiscal policy is concerned with which injection into and which withdrawal from the circular flow of income?

2   Under what circumstances should a government aim for a budget deficit?

3   How does a government finance a budget deficit?

4   If the multiplier is 3 what reduction in government expenditure would close an inflationary gap of £180 million?

5   Why might governments tend to put taxes on all luxury goods at the same time?

6   Explain what is meant by the balanced budget multiplier.

7   Why is the government expenditure multiplier greater than the taxation multiplier?

8   Explain the term 'fine tuning' in relation to demand management.

9   Give three of the reasons why discretionary fiscal policy is unable to solve all the problems of demand management.

10   What is structural rigidity?

_____ Examination questions _____

1 'The existence of *involuntary* unemployment makes nonsense of current monerarist attacks on fiscal policy, since in such circumstances higher government expenditure *must* lead to greater output at almost constant cost.' Analyse and comment on the argument in this statement.

(ABE2, December 1986)

2 Can a country cure a recession by cutting interest rates and expanding the money supply? Set out your reasoning carefully.

(ABE2, December 1986)

3 'Taxation transfers purchasing power from the consumers to the Government and so affects neither the value of the national product nor the national income.' Review this statement critically in terms of national income determination, analysing the effect on a country's level of economic activity if its Goverment
   a) collections more taxation than it spends
   b) exactly balances taxation against total Government spending.

(ABE2, December 1986)

4 'Jobs come from customers and from nowhere else. That simple and enduring truth must underlie any useful discussion of employment.'

(HMSO: Cmnd 9474:1986)

Discuss this statement in the light of the possible influence of government spending and taxation on business prosperity.

(ABE2, June 1987)

5 'Slow growth and unemployment are not cures for inflation. They are the side effects of a successful cure.' (Milton Friedman)

What is the cure for inflation monetarists suggest and why should it have such side effects?

(ABE2, June 1987)

6 'A 1 per cent government expenditure increase might add 0.3 per cent to the growth of gross domestic product (GDP); and a 1 per cent rise in GDP might reduce government expenditure by 0.15 per cent because of welfare benefits saved. More important, GDP growth reduces public spending as a proportion of national income, and generates extra tax revenue to pay for it.'
   (Lloyds Bank Economic Bulletin UK)

Explain the economic analysis that justifies this defence of higher government spending and comment briefly on its advantages (or disadvantages) from a profit-seeking businessman's point of view.

(ABE2, December 1987)

7 Monetarists have argued that to control inflation a slow-down in the growth of the money supply is both simpler to achieve and less harmful to business than a prices and incomes policy.

Examine the economic arguments monetarists could use to justify their view and discuss its applicability in practice.

(ABE2, December 1987)

8   If a country is facing recession, should business people urge the government to increase taxes and cut government spending programmes, including welfare and social security spending?
Your answer should be based on your understanding of macro-economic analysis.

(ABE2, June 1988)

9   How can the money supply be controlled? Can business people expect that a government policy to expand the growth of the money supply will lead to higher prices for their products?

(ABE2, June 1988)

10   A central part of the monetarist argument is that control of the money supply is essential if inflation is to be controlled.
a)   Define the money supply.
b)   Consider how the money supply can be controlled.

(LCCI Higher, May 1987)

11   'Unemployment can be reduced by increasing aggregate demand.' Discuss.

(LCCI Third Level, May 1988)

12   In a closed economy with no government expenditure or taxation, total consumption expenditure is always 2/3 of disposable income and planned investment expenditure is initially £40bn.
a)   Calculate the original equilibrium level of national income and explain the effect of an increase in planned investment of £10bn.
b)   If in the original situation a tax on all incomes had been introduced at a rate of 25p in the £ (¼) for all incomes, together with planned government expenditure of £20bn, what would have been the effect on:
i) The equilibrium level of national income
ii) The multiplier?
c)   Given the economy in part (b), examine the effect of the introduction of international trade, when expenditure on imports is ⅖ of total consumption expenditure and export spending is £10bn.
d)   Explain the importance of the multiplier concept in economic management.

(LCCI Third Level, May 1988)

13   a)   'Too much money chasing too few goods.' By reference to this definition, explain the various causes of inflation.
b)   Briefly identify the major effects of inflation.
c)   What steps might a government take to deal with inflation?

(LCCI Intermediate, December 1986)

14 a) Explain the major causes of unemployment.
   b) How might a government seek to remedy the problem of high levels of unemployment?

(LCCI Intermediate, May 1987)

15 What effects will the imposition of income tax have on the level of wages and the level of employment?

(ICSA, June 1986)

16 How should a government decide whether to use fiscal or monetary policy when it is seeking to expand economic activity?

(ICSA, June 1987)

17 How should a government decide the appropriate combination of fiscal and monetary policy measures it introduces?

(ICSA, June 1988)

18 A government wishes to reduce unemployment. Which course of action is likely to be most effective in achieving this objective – a cut in taxation, or an equivalent increase in government expenditure?

(ACCA, June 1987)

19 a) List the main functions of the central bank of a country.
   b) Describe the means which are available to the central bank for regulating the demand for, and the supply of, money and credit.

(ACCA, June 1988)

20 Are supply side economic measures the answer to long-term unemployment?

(ACCA, December 1989)

21 You are required to
   a) state the basic objectives of governmental economic policy
   b) discuss the practicability of achieving these aims by relying mainly on monetary policy.

(CIMA, May 1989)

22 How can central monetary authorities control the supply of money?

(Cert.M., June 1986)

23 What are the economic goals of a national government and what instruments are available to achieve them?

(Cert.M., November 1986)

24 What are the causes of unemployment? What policies can be applied to cure unemployment?

(Cert.M., June 1987)

25   How may a government seek to control money supply in a country?
                                                      (Cert.M., June 1988)

26   a)   Explain what is meant by 'demand-pull inflation' and 'cost-push inflation'. To
          what extent is it possible to identify the cause of inflation in practice?
     b)   Discuss how inflation may be controlled by government policy.
                                                      (IPS, November 1987)

27   a)   Explain why stable price levels and full employment are regarded as being
          desirable objectives of government policy.
     b)   Suggest why governments in recent years have not generally succeeded in
          attaining both these objectives simultaneously.
                                                      (IPS, November 1988)

28   a)   State with reasons why the prices and incomes policies of successive United
          Kingdom governments in the 1970s did not generally find favour with
          economists.
     b)   Describe the methods available to United Kingdom governments to manipu-
          late aggregate demand in the United Kingdom economy.
                                                      (I.Act., April 1989)

29   How might a government use monetary policy and fiscal policy in order to
     influence the level of aggregate demand and economic activity within the
     economy?
     Provide an analysis of the effectiveness of each as a policy technique.
                                                      (IFA, December 1988)

30   Discuss the sort of economic policy objectives which a present day government is
     likely to follow. Why is it difficult for a government to achieve these objectives
     simultaneously?
                                                      (IFA, December 1989)

21 Public finance

- *Why does the effect of government borrowing depend on the way that borrowing is financed?*

- *To what extent is the National Debt a burden?*

Government expenditure must normally be financed either by taxation or by borrowing, though in recent years the UK government has augmented its income by the sale of public assets through its privatisation programme. It is the purpose of this module to examine the raising of government revenue and the management of government borrowing.

Taxation

Until this century governments aimed to meet all their expenditure by the raising of taxation. A budget deficit would occur only during a war when a vastly increased government expenditure would necessitate borrowing from the financial institutions and the public. The return of peace would be accompanied by the government aiming for a budget surplus in order to pay off the accumulated national debt. Today, almost all government expenditure is still financed by taxation in most countries. In levying taxes the government must have regard to the **principles of taxation** first enunciated by Adam Smith in the 'Wealth of Nations':

1 **Certainty** It should be clear to taxpayers how much tax they are required to pay and when they have to pay it.

2 **Cost** The cost of assessing and raising taxes should be kept to a minimum.

3 **Convenience** Within reason, taxes due should be paid at times most convenient to the taxpayer.

4 **Equality** Members of the community should pay taxes in proportion to their income.

It is difficult to quarrel with the first three but Smith was at pains to spell them out because the British system of taxation in the late eighteenth century fell short of these in many respects. Today, the tax system meets the criteria of certainty and convenience, by and large, but questions remain as to its cost effectiveness. The tax system is so complex that thousands of experts are employed by taxpayers to find loopholes in the system and by the Inland Revenue to close them. Furthermore political considerations may outweigh those of efficiency when introducing a new tax. In 1990 the British government introduced the community charge to finance local government activity in place of the rates system, despite the fact that the community charge is more expensive to administer.

Smith's fourth principle was an attempt to find a just basis for the taxation of individuals at a time when tax liabilities in most countries bore little relationship to a person's income or wealth. While few would argue with Smith's principle, the issue of 'equality' is a contentious one. Although Smith argued for equality based on a proportion of income, it is also possible to argue for equality based on the same amount paid or for equality of burden so that the impact felt by each taxpayer is the same, regardless of income. These three views of equality give rise to a classification of taxes as to whether they are proportional, regressive or progressive.

Proportional taxes

These are based on the premise that every taxpayer should pay the same percentage of his or her income in the tax. Thus the rich pay more taxes than the poor in absolute terms but the same in proportion to their income. Such a tax may seem eminently fair at first sight but it cannot be argued that the impact of the tax is felt equally. Suppose that a proportionate income tax of 50 per cent is introduced so that a person with an income of £100 pays £50 in tax and a person with an income of £1000 pays £500 in tax. While both pay the same proportion of their income in tax the lower-paid person will feel the impact of the tax more because of the **diminishing marginal utility** of income. This results in lower utility being derived from each extra unit of income as first essential and then luxury wants are satisfied. So a pound paid in tax by the poorer person results in greater foregone utility than does the pound paid in tax by the person on a high income.

It is rare to find a truly proportional tax but most taxes on income are proportional over certain ranges of income.

Regressive taxes

These are taxes which take a higher proportion of income, the lower the taxpayer's income. The most regressive tax of all is the poll tax under which every person pays the same amount in tax, irrespective of the person's income. The community charge introduced in Scotland in 1989 and in the rest of the UK in 1990 is often referred to as a poll tax. This is not strictly correct since certain sections of the population pay a reduced tax due to low incomes. It is, however, still an extremely regressive tax since very wealthy people have the same tax liability as those on average incomes.

Taxes on expenditure are regressive taxes since they are either a flat fee or based on the value of the item rather than on the income of the purchaser. While the burden of such taxes is clearly greater for those members of society on lower incomes there is a case for their retention in that people do have some choice in buying the goods and therefore paying the tax. Indeed, if regressive taxes were abolished it would be difficult to tax expenditure, even on luxuries.

Progressive taxes

These are based on the principle that, the higher the income, the higher the proportion of that income is paid in tax. The purpose of such taxes is to achieve 'vertical equality' in that the burden of taxation is felt equally, regardless of each individual's income. This form of taxation may also aim for 'horizontal equality' in that taxpayers with similar incomes and similar circumstances should pay the same amount of tax.

Most income tax systems are progressive in that the rate of taxes rises with income. Furthermore allowances against tax are given to ensure some degree of horizontal equality. Even then anomalies are inevitable; the system of allowances in Britain favours the self-employed rather than employees.

The impact of three types of taxation as income changes are illustrated in Figure 21.1.

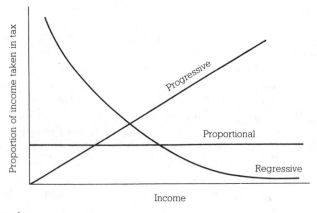

Figure 21.1 *Impact of taxes*

Direct taxes

These are taxes on the individual and may consist of a tax on income or a tax on wealth. In the UK the former includes income tax and national insurance while the latter includes capital transfer tax and capital gains tax. All such taxes are usually progressive, the tax rate rising in percentage terms as income or wealth increases. The justification for such progressive taxes rests on three arguments:

1   Progressive taxes are related to the ability to pay. This argument is based on the theory of the diminishing marginal utility of income whereby higher tax rates are levied on those who derive the least economic satisfaction from their income or wealth.

2   Progressive taxes lead to a more equitable distribution of income. This is one of the objectives of government economic policy in most modern economic societies for two reasons:

a) Such are the economic advantages possessed by the wealthy and those on high incomes that progressive taxes are necessary to prevent the distribution of income and wealth becoming ever more concentrated in the hands of a small proportion of the population.

b) A more equitable distribution of income leads to a broader base of economic demand which is essential to the development of consumer industries and balanced economic growth. This in turn provides greater investment and consumer opportunities for the wealthy in society.

3   Progressive taxes are the only way of reducing the large economic rent payments enjoyed by certain groups, such as highly paid entertainers.

Despite their attractions, highly progressive systems of direct taxation are subject to a number of criticisms based on the distortional effects they have on the working of the economy:

1   Such a system may have disincentive effects. Where, as in 1979, high-income UK taxpayers could be liable to a marginal tax rate of 83 per cent, there may be little incentive for them to seek promotion or new responsibilities. This view led the British government to reduce the top rate of income tax in stages to 40 per cent in 1988.

   The disincentive effect of income tax is, ironically, felt acutely among those on low incomes because of the complex interaction of tax thresholds, national insurance payments and social security benefits. Thus an increase in pay of £1 may bring the recipient over the tax threshold and lead him to lose certain social security benefits, resulting in his being better off by only 10 pence per week. The effective marginal rate of tax for this person is therefore 90 per cent.

2   Highly progressive taxes are an inducement to high earners to seek non-taxable forms of income or 'perks' such as free medical insurance, credit cards, subsidised mortgages, etc. This leads to inequalities between those who receive such perks and those who receive only salaries subject to direct taxation.

3   Substantial resources of time and money may be expended non-productively on ways of avoiding taxes. If the tax system is perceived as too oppressive or unfair in the way it is applied some taxpayers may even evade taxation entirely by non-declaration of income.

Indirect taxes

These are taxes on expenditure and include value added tax (VAT) and other types of purchase tax, customs and excise duties and licence fees. Such taxes are, by their nature, regressive since they are related, not to the taxpayer's income, but to his or her willingness to purchase the good or service. Despite their regressive nature the imposition of indirect taxes can be justified on a number of grounds:

1   They admit an element of choice which does not apply to direct taxes since people may avoid the tax by not buying the item on which it is levied. This argument only holds provided indirect taxes are not placed on necessities like food or heating.

2   Indirect taxes represent a significant source of government revenue. In their absence income and other direct taxes would be much higher, reducing the proportion of income over which the individual retains control.

3   Many of the goods on which indirect taxes are levied are luxuries or potentially harmful, or both, so that taxation may deter too many economic resources being directed to their production and consumption, e.g. tobacco or alcoholic drinks.

4   Indirect taxes are very simple to collect and are difficult to evade. They thus tend to be an efficient way of raising government revenue.

General Government Receipts: £206.4 bn

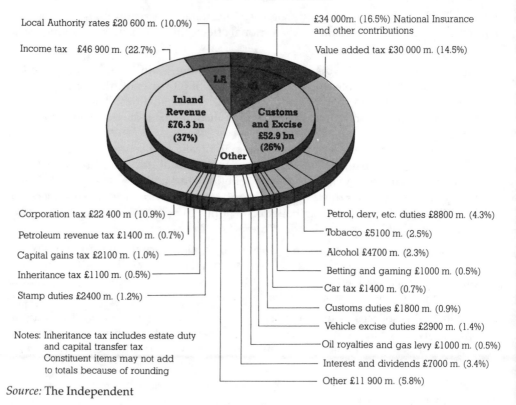

Local Authority rates £20 600 m. (10.0%)

Income tax   £46 900 m. (22.7%)

£34 000m. (16.5%) National Insurance and other contributions

Value added tax £30 000 m. (14.5%)

Inland Revenue £76.3 bn (37%)

Customs and Excise £52.9 bn (26%)

Other

Corporation tax £22 400 m (10.9%)

Petroleum revenue tax £1400 m. (0.7%)

Capital gains tax £2100 m. (1.0%)

Inheritance tax £1100 m. (0.5%)

Stamp duties £2400 m. (1.2%)

Petrol, derv, etc. duties £8800 m. (4.3%)

Tobacco £5100 m. (2.5%)

Alcohol £4700 m. (2.3%)

Betting and gaming £1000 m. (0.5%)

Car tax £1400 m. (0.7%)

Customs duties £1800 m. (0.9%)

Vehicle excise duties £2900 m. (1.4%)

Oil royalties and gas levy £1000 m. (0.5%)

Interest and dividends £7000 m. (3.4%)

Other £11 900 m. (5.8%)

Notes: Inheritance tax includes estate duty and capital transfer tax
Constituent items may not add to totals because of rounding

Source: The Independent

Figure 21.2 *Sources of revenue 1989–90*

REVISION TEST

1   What are Adam Smith's four principles of taxation?

2   How far does the excise duty on a bottle of whisky meet Smith's criteria?

3   Explain how a proportionate tax with allowances against tax is actually progressive.

4   Give an example of a direct regressive tax.

5   Why do all indirect taxes tend to be regressive?

6   Give three arguments against progressive taxation.

7   A person's income rises from £80 to £90 per week. The rate of income tax is 25 per cent and he loses social security benefits totalling £5 per week. What is the effective marginal rate of tax?

8   How do you think that the abolition of all indirect taxes, while government revenue remained the same, would affect economic activity?

9   Which is the most regressive form of indirect taxation?

10   On what grounds would you justify a wealth tax being more steeply progressive than an income tax?

Government borrowing

Originally, as we have seen, the government aimed always to achieve a balanced budget, its revenue being sufficient to meet its expenditure. Indeed a successful Chancellor of the Exchequer was one who could achieve a budget surplus and repay some of the public debts incurred in financing past wars. With the development of discretionary fiscal policy, however, governments ceased to aim for a balanced budget and were prepared to operate with a budget deficit in order to pursue expansionary economic policies. Yet despite the fact that budget deficits have become more common they are still managed in much the same way as in former times through the government's borrowing activities. It should also be remembered that, at most, government borrowing finances a relatively small part of total government expenditure.

Budget deficits

The effect of any budget deficit will be to stimulate an increase in aggregate demand via the multiplier. If, however, the government finances the deficit by borrowing from the private sector there may also be a downward multiplier effect on demand which partially cancels the upward multiplier effect of increased government expenditure or reduced taxation. This is because the government will have attracted funds which would have been used for private consumption or investment. In practice, this downward multiplier effect is mitigated in two ways.

1   Much of the funding attracted for public investment and consumption would have been withdrawn from the circular flow of income anyway through investment overseas or import expenditure. In this case there would be no net downward multiplier effect.

2   The source of the government's borrowing will be very important in determining both the overall multiplier effect and the impact on the money supply. The government may finance the Public Sector Borrowing Requirement (PSBR) in four ways:

     a)   The government may increase the note issue by exchanging interest-bearing securities with the Bank of England. Here there will be no downward multiplier effect since the government is financing its activities by a direct increase in the money supply.

b)   The government may borrow from the deposit banks and other financial institutions through the sale of government securities, either government stocks or Treasury bills. In this case there is no reduction in bank deposits or the money supply to counter the expansion which occurs through the government's increased expenditure. Instead, if the government borrowing takes the form of Treasury bills, the banks' liquidity will be increased and they will be able to expand the money supply through the credit creation multiplier.

c)   The government may borrow from the UK non-bank private sector by selling stocks to individuals and firms. The effect of this is to reduce private sector liquidity and potential expenditure but this downward multiplier effect should be exceeded by the upward multiplier effect of increased government expenditure in areas where it will do most to stimulate aggregate demand. The major disadvantage of financing the PSBR in this way is that the public sector may draw resources away from growing areas of the private sector. Furthermore, if the borrowing is large enough it will push up market interest rates and deter natural recovery in the economy.

d)   The government may borrow from overseas account holders. Since there is no reduction in domestic bank deposits to finance this deficit the effect will be more expansionary than a deficit financed by the UK private sector.

Typically, the budget deficit will be financed by a combination of some or all of these. While it is not possible to predict exactly what the effect of government borrowing will be, it is likely to increase the money supply to some extent. Thus government borrowing to finance a budget deficit will have an expansionary effect on the economy additional to that produced by the direct fiscal effects. So if the government calculates only the fiscal impact of its measures it will under-estimate the overall effect on the economy of a budget deficit.

Budget surpluses

A budget surplus is one method available to the government to control aggregate demand and reduce inflationary pressures in the economy. Because it results in government revenue being greater than expenditure, a surplus involves net borrowing, i.e. the repayment of past government borrowing. As with a deficit, the precise impact of a budget surplus depends on the form that repayment of loans takes.

1   The government may redeem loans held by the Bank of England by the payment of cash to the Bank. This will lead to a contraction of the money supply as the cash paid ceases to form a part of it.

2   The government may make a net repayment of loans to the banks and other financial institutions. The commercial banks are now forced into holding less liquid assets and this will reduce the extent to which they can create credit.

3   The government may make a net repayment of loans to the UK non-bank private

sector. This will have the least deflationary effect on the economy as the reduction in government expenditure will be partly offset by the extra spending generated by increase in bank deposits following the repayment of the stock.

4   The government may make a net repayment of overseas debt. Since there is no repayment to domestic bank deposits there will be no compensatory expansion of spending potential to offset the reduction in domestic money following redemption of the loan.

Again, the fact that the repayment of debt will have the effect of contracting the money supply means that a budget surplus will have a greater deflationary impact on the economy than that predicted by the purely fiscal calculation.

For most of the period between the Second World War and the mid-1980s the UK had an annual budget deficit and PSBR. The late 1980s, however, saw a series of budget surpluses and thus a Public Sector Debt Repayment (PSDR), as shown in Figure 21.3. To a large extent this was due to receipts from the sale of public assets through the government's privatisation programme but it did result in a series of net repayments of the accumulated public indebtedness – the National Debt.

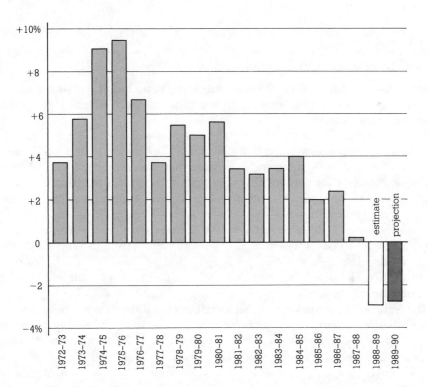

Figure 21.3 *Public sector borrowing requirement*

The National Debt

The modern National Debt originated in 1694 with a loan of £1.2 million by the newly-formed Bank of England to William III to help him finance a war. Apart from the last 30 years the National Debt has always grown most rapidly during war-time. Then borrowing offers a way of meeting part of the rapid increase in government expenditure which would have to be met otherwise by a massive increase in tax rates. In recent years much of the growth in the Debt has resulted from the investment programmes of local authorities and the nationalised industries.

Repayment of the Debt?

Throughout the eighteenth and nineteenth centuries the view of peacetime governments was that every effort should be made to repay the Debt. This ambition sprang from three distinct motives.

1   Public debt was regarded as similar to a private debt incurred for consumption in that it was not balanced by the holding of a profitable asset. This followed from the growth of the Debt to finance wars which destroyed rather than created capital assets.

2   Governments were afraid that the existence of a large public debt might hinder future borrowing. This was a common argument in the eighteenth century as governments were not seen as the most reliable of debtors.

3   There was the fear that a general fall in prices and consequent rise in the value of money would lead to a real increase in the value of the National Debt and the interest payments due on it.

In the present century repayment of the National Debt ceased to be a live issue. To begin with, the cost of wars rose to such an extent that the very size of the Debt made thoughts of repayment over a reasonable time scale impossible. Furthermore, most of the recent growth in the Debt has been to finance investment in the nationalised industries and local authorities and so has been backed by tangible assets. Finally the existence of a National Debt is essential to the management of the economy. If the government were resolved always to finance its expenditure from its revenue it would be unable to stimulate demand by operating a budget deficit or control demand through a surplus. Fiscal policy could then only be conducted by the effects of the balanced budget multiplier.

Even if it were decided to pay off the National Debt it is difficult to see how this could be achieved without posing some problems for the economy. The only practicable method would be through a series of huge budget surpluses. Thus the economy would suffer a protracted period of induced deflation which would seriously hamper the ability of the government to achieve its macro-economic objectives and would outweigh any stimulus to economic growth promoted by the release of investment funds to the private sector.

The burden of the National Debt

The only possible justification for paying off, or at least reducing, the National Debt is that it has become a serious burden on society. To the extent that the Debt is held domestically it cannot be a burden on society as a whole. The annual interest payments merely represent a transfer from taxpayers to stockholders and there is obviously an overlap between the two groups.

Nor is it true that the National Debt is a burden for future generations resulting from the excessive borrowing of the current generation. The real cost of government activity, whether it is building a road network or sending a task force to the Falklands, lies in the use of real resources which would otherwise have been used elsewhere. This opportunity cost of public expenditure is the same whether it is financed by taxation, the sale of public assets or public borrowing. If the government borrows to finance its activities those who provide the loan surrender current consumption in favour of the general taxpayers who would otherwise have borne the burden. In the future holders of the loans will receive interest payments paid for by future taxpayers. Thus the burden is not passed from one generation to another. Rather the bondholders of one generation sacrifice purchasing power to the taxpayers while the taxpayers of subsequent generations sacrifice purchasing power to the bondholders of that generation. In each generation the debt cancels out.

It is also the case that the real value of the National Debt falls with time because of inflation. Only if the Debt rises faster than the rate of inflation will this not be the case.

There are, however, a number of ways in which the National Debt can be a real burden to society.

1   Interest costs
If the interest payments on the debt were such that tax rates were very high to meet them this could have a deflationary effect on the economy if the receivers of interest payments withdrew these from the circular flow of income. Such a situation could also lead to a growing inequity in the distribution of income. In fact, since the interest payments are subject to tax a substantial part of the cost of servicing the debt is borne by the debt-holders themselves. In the UK the interest costs of the debt are such that they take up less than 10 per cent of government revenue compared to 22 per cent in 1938.

2   Monetary policy
A substantial body of public marketable debt is essential to the conduct of open market operations and therefore to the execution of monetary policy. However, the larger the Debt the greater the continuing flow of maturities and the need continuously to refinance maturing debt may lead the central bank permanently to support the market in government securities in order to make it receptive to funding operations. On balance, therefore, the existence of a very large national debt may well prove a hindrance to monetary policy.

3   Private investment
If the government is forced to borrow to meet its commitments it may force up interest rates in the capital market. This will make it more costly for the private sector to embark

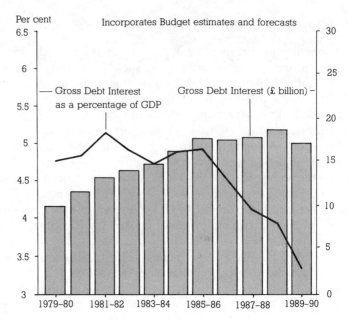

Figure 21.4 *Government debt interest payments*

on capital investment and may deter some companies from doing so. If private sector investment is more conducive to economic growth than public sector investment this may have an adverse effect on economic development.

4   External debt

Interest paid to overseas holders of the Debt must be financed by export earnings or other payments from abroad. These interest payments will therefore place a strain on the country's balance of payments unless the loan on which they are paid finances an increase in the productive capacity of the country sufficient to more than pay for these overseas interest costs. The burden of external debt has been a major problem for many developing countries since they have found that an excessive proportion of their overseas earnings is used to meet the interest charges on their external debt.

REVISION TEST

1 Outline the four ways in which the government may finance its borrowing requirement.
2 Which of these will have the least expansionary effect?
3 What is the PSDR?
4 If the government repays debt to the Bank of England, how does this reduce the money supply?
5 What were the three traditional arguments for redeeming the National Debt?
6 If government expenditure is financed by borrowing which group in society is required to contribute less to public finance?

7   Why would redemption of the National Debt be detrimental to the conduct of government economic policy?

8   In what way may a large National Debt militate against private sector investment?

9   In what ways may the National Debt be a burden?

10 If the National Debt stays constant why will its importance tend to diminish over time?

—————— **Examination questions** ——————————————————

1   Define 'national debt' and briefly outline the methods available to a Government for financing it. Government borrowing is often said to cut private investment in industry by causing shortages of loanable funds and higher interest rates. Can that possibly be true if the investment multiplier analysis is correct? Explain your reasoning.

(ABE2, December 1986)

2   a) What criteria should be used in assessing a country's tax system?
    b) By reference to any one country, examine the major aims and objectives of its taxation policy.

(LCCI Higher, November 1986)

3   a) Discuss the structure and importance of the tax system in any economy with which you are familiar.
    b) Discuss the possible disadvantages of a progressive income tax system.

(LCCI Higher, November 1987)

4   a) Distinguish between a progressive, a proportional and a regressive tax giving suitable numerical examples to illustrate your answer.
    b) If the government were to increase income tax by 12½ per cent, describe the likely affects upon:
       i) Income distribution
       ii) Inflation
       iii) Balance of payments
       iv) Employment.

(LCCI Intermediate, May 1986)

5   How will an increase in the average rate of income tax affect the demand for
    a) luxuries and
    b) necessities?

(ICSA, June 1988)

6   In the last few years the national debt of the USA has reached a record level whilst at the same time some of the developing countries, such as Mexico, have run up huge external debts.

a) Explain the difference between national debt and external debt.
b) Compare and contrast the problems of a developed country, such as the USA, which has a large national debt, with the problems of a developing country, such as Mexico, which has a large external debt.

(ACCA, December 1987)

7   What methods may a government use to finance its expenditure?
What are the likely economic consequences of each method?

(CIMA., November 1988)

8   What are the relative advantages and disadvantages of indirect and direct taxation?

(Cert.M., November 1986)

9   Same question as above.

(Cert.M., November 1987)

10   To what extent, if at all, has your country's taxation system achieved the following particular outcomes:
a)   to raise revenue to fund public expenditure;
b)   to redistribute wealth on a more equitable basis;
c)   to discourage the consumption of harmful substances;
d)   to help conserve scarce resources?

(IPS, May 1988)

11   Adam Smith first outlined the principles of taxation and suggested that the principle of equality should be interpreted to mean that members of the community should pay taxes in proportion to their income. Others have since argued in favour of regressive indirect taxes and progressive direct taxes. Discuss the economic arguments for and against each of these methods of taxation in the United Kingdom.

(I.Act., April 1988)

12   Identify and evaluate the main criteria which may be used to assess taxes.

(IFA, June 1989)

22 International trade

- *How can countries gain by importing goods they could produce more efficiently themselves?*

- *Are there any circumstances under which completely free trade might be harmful to a country's economy?*

International trade

Many countries have, at one time or another, sought to be self-sufficient and provide their basic economic needs independently of other nations. It is now generally accepted, however, that no country is capable of providing all the resources it requires to develop its full economic potential and to satisfy the demands of its domestic economy. International trade enables a country to specialise in the production of those goods and services in which it is economically efficient and to trade these for goods and services which either it cannot produce or cannot produce efficiently. This international specialisation gives rise to the development of economies of scale and a better utilisation of resources. In consequence, the populations of trading countries enjoy higher living standards both through a greater variety of goods and services and lower prices than would otherwise be the case.

Comparative advantage

It is obvious that if two countries each produce the same two goods (A & B) and one has an absolute cost advantage in A while the other has an absolute cost advantage in B the two countries will benefit by specialisation and trade. Each country can specialise in the good it produces more efficiently and trade some of this production for the good it produces less efficiently.

Less obvious but more important is the principle of **comparative advantage** developed in the nineteenth century by David Ricardo. He pointed out that even if one country is able to produce *all* goods more cheaply than another, there will still be differences in the extent of this absolute advantage from product to product. The efficient country thus has a comparative advantage in those products where its absolute advantage is greatest while the inefficient country has a comparative advantage in those products where its absolute *disadvantage* is least. Ricardo claimed that this was the basis on which countries should trade. So each country should specialise in the production of those goods in which it has a comparative advantage and buy from others the goods in which it has a comparative disadvantage.

Ricardo illustrated his argument by reference to trade between England and Portugal in wine and cloth. In Table 22.1(a) both England and Portugal produce wine and cloth. The Portuguese have an absolute advantage in both products since they can produce either 1X units of wine or 1Y units of cloth using less resources (labour) than the English. England's absolute disadvantage is less in the case of cloth, however, because only 11 per cent more labour (100 units instead of 90) are required to produce the same amount of cloth, whereas 50 per cent more labour (120 units instead of 80) are needed to produce the same amount of wine. Thus Portugal has a comparative advantage in the production of wine while England has a comparative advantage in the production of cloth.

When the comparative advantage of both countries is exploited through specialisation, as in Table 22.1(b), the total production of both wine and cloth is increased. Ricardo did not consider the rate at which the two goods might be exchanged but a possible exchange rate is shown in Table 22.1(c) where IX barrels of wine for IY yarns of cloth leaves both countries better off after trade.

TABLE 22.1
Production of wine and cloth in Portugal and England

	Country	Units of labour used	Barrels of wine	Yarns of cloth
a) Before specialisation	England	100		1Y
		120	1X	
	Portugal	80	1X	
		90		1Y
	Total		2X	2Y
b) After specialisation	England	220		2.2Y
	Portugal	170	2.125X	
	Total		2.125X	2.2Y
c) After trade:		Consumption of wine and cloth		
1 barrel of wine for 1 yarn of cloth	England		1X	1.2Y
	Portugal		1.125X	1Y
	Total		2.125X	2.2Y

It is also possible to describe the principle of comparative advantage in terms of opportunity cost, as shown in Table 22.2. A country has a comparative advantage in the production of a good when it has a lower opportunity cost in producing that good than has another country. The opportunity cost of producing one extra unit of cloth in England is 5/6 unit of wine, i.e. the wine which could have been produced using the same resources. As the opportunity cost of cloth is lower (5/6 X wine) for England than for Portugal (9/8 X wine) England has a comparative advantage in cloth production while Portugal has a comparative advantage in wine.

TABLE 22.2
Opportunity cost ratios

	Barrels of wine	Yarns of cloth	Opportunity cost of producing one extra unit of:	
			cloth	wine
England: alternative production using 100 units of labour	$5/6$X	1Y	$5/6$ barrel of wine	$6/5$ yarns of cloth
Portugal: alternative production using 80 units of labour	1X	$8/9$Y	9/8 barrels of wine	$8/9$ yarns of cloth

Criticisms of comparative advantage theory

The weakness of comparative advantage theory is that it is based on a number of assumptions which do not stand up to close scrutiny.

1   Factor mobility

The theory assumes complete mobility of factors of production within countries and total immobility of factors between countries. In the case of factor mobility within countries there is a limit to the process by which factors of production can be transferred from one use to another and thus to the extent to which a country can specialise. If a country has a comparative advantage in coal-mining, for example, it cannot turn over all land to coal production.

2   Constant costs

Comparative advantage theory assumes that average costs do not change with output, so ignoring the impact of economies and diseconomies of scale. Specialisation is likely to yield economies of scale but taken beyond a certain point this may lead to over-specialisation and diseconomies of scale. This is the problem encountered by many developing countries which have one-crop economies.

3   Static economies

The decision to specialise in one group of goods and services to the exclusion of others assumes that current comparative advantages will persist into the foreseeable future. So no allowance is made for the changes in technology or supply of factors which could alter existing comparative advantages. England largely abandoned attempts to grow its own food in the mid-nineteenth century yet found it had a comparative advantage in food production again by the middle of the twentieth century.

4   Demand factors

These tend to be ignored by comparative advantage theory as it is assumed that demand patterns are able to adjust to the increased volume of production which will follow greater specialisation. If a country has a comparative advantage in paper flowers, electric light bulbs and shuttlecocks it cannot assume that world demand for these goods will match increases in supply of them.

5 Transport costs
Again, transport costs are largely ignored, despite their importance. Many developing countries are unable to exploit their comparative advantage in cheap bulk goods because of the high transport costs of sending their production to the European and North American markets.

6 Free trade
In order for countries to enjoy fully the benefits of comparative advantage they must have unrestricted access to the markets of other countries. In reality, trade is often subject to barriers such as tariffs and quotas while countries enter trade agreements which favour parties to the agreement at the expense of others. Such practices distort or even cancel out comparative advantages.

7 Interdependence
Specialisation inevitably leads countries to abandon ideas of self-sufficiency and rely more on other countries. For political reasons, or to retain some degree of self-sufficiency, countries will not abandon key industries such as agriculture or energy entirely merely for the sake of comparative advantage. Nor will they wish to risk the problems associated with over-specialisation. Interdependence of the kind envisaged by comparative advantage theory is likely to be fully achieved only by an imperial power and its colonies where economic policy decisions can be imposed on the colonies by the "mother" country. The post-colonial period has seen a number of developing countries faced with economic problems which stem from a reliance on one industry or crop introduced during the colonial era.

Despite its inherent weaknesses comparative advantage theory does show that countries benefit from international trade because of their relative efficiencies. Even in the extremely unlikely case of two countries having identical relative efficiencies in every product, international trade would enable them to specialise and so achieve a more efficient use of resources.

Terms of trade

The theory of comparative advantage points to the circumstances under which trade might advantageously take place but it cannot predict how much of one good will exchange for another, i.e. the **terms of trade**. In Ricardo's original illustration of comparative advantage both countries are able to benefit from trade provided the terms of trade are within the ranges:
  a) $1X = 1.2Y$ (where there is no gain to England)
  b) $1.125X = 1Y$ (where there is no gain to Portugal).
The terms of trade which emerge in practice depend on the demand and supply conditions in each country for the products in question.

1   **Price elasticity of demand for exports**   The terms of trade will favour countries the demand for whose exports are price inelastic. Thus oil-producing countries enjoy a stronger terms of trade than do producers of other primary products.

2   **Price elasticity of supply of exports**   The more price elastic the supply of exports the more easily will increased export demand be satisfied and the smaller will be the improvement in a country's terms of trade.

3   **Changes in world patterns of demand or supply**   Where changes in the pattern of demand favour a country's products its terms of trade will improve, as when increased industrial demand for mineral supplies in the present century led to improvements in the terms of trade of countries with large reserves of these.

Similarly the decision by European countries to grow most of their own sugar since 1950 has led to a glut on the world market and seriously affected the terms of trade of traditional sugar producers in the West Indies.

The terms of trade index

Although the terms of trade may be measured in other ways the principal and most widely used measurement is the **barter terms of trade** which is:

The ratio of the export price index to the import price index over the same time period.

This ratio can be expressed as an index number, using the formula:

$$\text{Index of terms of trade} = \frac{\text{Export price index}}{\text{Import price index}} \times 100$$

Starting from a base of 100, a rise in the index to 110 signifies an 'improvement' in the terms of trade; fewer units of exports need be sold to pay for a given quantity of imports. Note, however, that such an improvement does not necessarily indicate a rise in export earnings since the price of exports relative to imports will have risen rather than the quantity of exports themselves.

The effect of a rise in the terms of trade index depends on the cause of that rise. If, for example, this relative rise in export prices is due to a rise in the costs of producing export goods the volume of exports will almost certainly fall. The impact of this fall on export revenue will depend on the price elasticity of demand of exports. Only where demand is inelastic will higher export prices result in higher export revenue. In the 1960s the UK terms of trade improved but only because the high UK inflation rate meant that UK export prices rose relative to those of her competitors. The result was that export volumes rose much slower than import volumes. If, however, the relative rise in export prices is the consequence of increased demand for the country's goods, a rise in the terms of trade will be accompanied by a rise in the value of exports. This is the position achieved by Japan over most of the period since 1950.

The same principles apply to a fall in the terms of trade index. Where a relative fall in export prices is due to a fall in the costs of production the volume of export goods will probably rise. But only if the demand for exports is price elastic will this lead to a rise in export revenue. Where, on the other hand, the relative fall in export prices is due to a fall in demand for the country's goods the effect of a deterioration in the terms of trade will be a fall in the value of exports. This was a problem encountered by many of the developing countries during the 1970s when western industrial countries adopted deflationary measures which resulted in falls in both world demand and world prices for the products of many developing economies.

REVISION TEST

1 What is the difference between 'absolute advantage' and 'comparative advantage'?

2 How would you use the principle of opportunity cost to illustrate the theory of comparative advantage?

3 Why was the theory of comparative advantage more appropriate to the British Empire of 1900 than the modern trading community?

4 Name three of the assumptions on which comparative advantage theory is based.

5 In country A it costs 10 units of labour to produce 2 units of X or 5 of Y. In country B it costs 10 units of labour to produce 1 unit of X or 4 of Y. In which product does country B have a comparative advantage?

6 In the above example give a terms of trade which would benefit both countries.

7 Define 'terms of trade'.

8 How is the terms of trade index calculated?

9 If the terms of trade double what does this say about the relationship between exports and imports?

10 If import prices are constant and the terms of trade index rises from 105 to 110 what has happened to export prices?

Barriers to trade

That countries benefit through trade is indisputable. Yet most countries still erect some barriers to trade to restrict the import and export of goods. These trade barriers take several forms but the most common are tariffs, quotas and exchange control.

Tariffs

A tariff is a tax imposed on an imported good. Usually it is levied on the good to raise its price, thereby reducing its competitiveness against domestically produced goods. This is illustrated in Figure 22.1 where before the imposition of the tariff the market supply curve is S and the market price is £5. The imposition of a tariff of £1 per unit has the same effect as the imposition of any other tax on a commodity. Suppliers must now raise their prices to earn the same net revenue as before so the market supply curve shifts left to S_1 and a new equilibrium market price of £5.80 is established. This means that part of the tariff has been absorbed by the suppliers themselves; only if demand is totally inelastic will the supplier be able to pass the whole tariff onto the consumer.

Tariffs are most successful in reducing demand for an imported good when demand is elastic as when there are close substitutes available from domestic suppliers or where profit margins are too narrow to enable suppliers to absorb the tariff. Tariffs are sometimes imposed on goods with inelastic demand but this is usually for the purpose of raising revenue as in the case of customs duties on wine, spirits and tobacco.

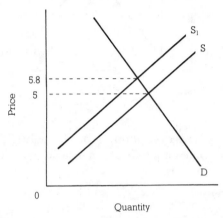

Figure 22.1 *Effect of a tariff*

Quotas

A quota is a limit placed on the number of units of a particular good which may be imported. As Figure 22.2 shows, the effect of the quota is to shift supply from S to S_1 so that, however much buyers bid up prices, no more can be made available by suppliers. Quotas are commonly used by industrialised countries to restrict the importation of cheap goods from developing countries, notably in the Far East. In addition, some of the Newly Industrialising Countries (NICs) and Japan have agreed to limit their export of cars and electrical goods to the EEC in a series of voluntary quotas known as Voluntary Export Restraints (VERs).

Exchange control

Importers must be able to obtain foreign currency in order to pay for the purchase of overseas goods. Many countries control the level of imports by making it extremely difficult for their nationals to obtain foreign currency or to hold foreign currency accounts; a policy adopted by Eastern European regimes prior to the collapse of the communist monopoly of power in 1989 and 1990.

Counter trading

This term is now used to describe barter trade whereby imports are tied directly to an agreement to buy goods from the importing country. The logical outcome of counter

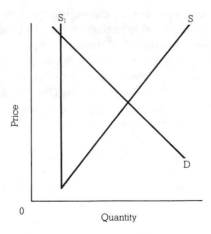

Figure 22.2 *Effect of a quota*

trading is that each country buys from another country only to the extent that it can sell to that country. It therefore encourages bilateral instead of multilateral trade.

Other non-tariff barriers

The extent to which countries can use the barriers to trade outlined above is limited by their trade agreements with other countries. So many have developed more subtle forms of trade barrier such as complex customs formalities to delay import entry, sudden changes in health and safety regulations with which foreign goods cannot immediately comply and technical specifications which only domestically produced goods can meet. It is also the case that in some cultures there is a natural aversion to buying imported goods and even government exhortation to buy foreign goods has little effect. Japan is perhaps the strongest example of this 'cultural protectionism'.

Arguments for protection

Governments adopt protectionist measures for a variety of reasons, many of them not based on reasoned economic argument. Among the commonest are:

1 **To protect a declining industry**   Formerly very powerful industries may use their residual influence to pressure the government into introducing trade barriers to protect their declining market. Such protectionism cannot be defended on purely economic grounds since, if it has lost its comparative advantage, perhaps it should make way for more efficient overseas rivals. This would release the resources currently used in the industry for more productive uses. It has been argued that there is a case for giving an industry short-term support during a period of modernisation although even here investment support might be more appropriate than a tariff.

2 **To protect employment**   This heading encompasses two distinct arguments.
    a)   That where the world market is shrinking imports should be prohibited to

prevent excess capacity in the domestic industry. This argument was used by industrialised countries in the 1930s and resulted in a trade war which left all countries with lower trade and employment levels.

b) That domestic industries are subjected to the unfair competition of those based in developing countries which have access to very cheap labour. Against this it is argued that in the long term the higher profits enjoyed by Third World producers will lead to their workers demanding and receiving higher wages, so removing their competitive edge. The evidence does not support this optimistic view, however. The profits made out of the cheap labour of the developing countries do not necessarily go to local employers; often they go to the multinational companies which distribute the goods. While tariffs may not solve the problem it is pointless to ignore the fact that unemployment in such industries as textiles and electrical goods is directly related to the importation of cheap foreign goods.

3   **To correct the balance of payments**   Tariffs have often been used as a policy measure to reduce imports and close a trade deficit. The success of this policy depends on the country's exports being resilient to rising prices since other countries are almost certain to retaliate. The trade war which follows is likely to result in reduced national output and income.

4   **To protect domestic industry against 'dumping'**   Countries frequently attempt to control the level of cheap imports when they feel these lower prices are the result of unfair competition rather than arising from a comparative advantage. Thus several western governments have taken action against East European countries dumping excess production on their markets at prices well below cost. The imposition of tariffs on these very cheap goods still leaves them much cheaper than domestic substitutes so they are usually subjected to a quota.

Another example of unfair competition is the practice of giving large subsidies to exporting industries to enable them to penetrate new markets. In 1985 the US government imposed higher tariffs on British steel products because of subsidisation of the UK export price by the UK government. In addition to subsidies some governments give assisted finance and preferential insurance to exporters, services in the UK provided by the Export Credit Guarantee Department (ECGD). Tariffs and quotas against unfair competition are generally regarded as acceptable since dumping and similar practices impede rather than assist free trade.

5   **To protect infant industries**   According to this argument some countries are prevented from specialising in those industries in which they would have a comparative advantage. This is because the industries do not grow sufficiently to develop economies of scale before they wither in the face of foreign competition. Protection would give the industry the breathing space necessary for it to achieve technical efficiency and scale production and could be removed once this stage is reached.

6   **The infant economy argument**   Developing countries in the early stages of industrialisation might argue that all their industries are infant ones and therefore warrant protection. Import controls would assist the process by which domestically produced goods are substituted for imports.

7 **Self-sufficiency** While most countries have abandoned the aim of satisfying all their needs from the domestic economy, few would wish to rely entirely on other countries for food, energy and other vital products in case supplies were interrupted through political or military events. Thus agriculture, munitions and other strategic industries are often protected, or at least favoured by government aid.

International trade agreements

Although most countries have adopted protectionist policies at one time or another this does not alter the fact that protectionism, by damaging trade, inhibits the development of the world economy and thus eventually harms those countries which erect trade barriers. Indeed, of the arguments for protection outlined above only the infant industry one is totally convincing, though a strong case can be made for both the infant economy argument and that to prevent dumping.

Since 1945 protectionism has been much less in evidence than during the 1930s and freer trade between countries has been promoted through growth in trade agreements. Such agreements have taken two forms:

1 There are agreements which aim to promote freer world trade. The most important of these is the General Agreement on Tariffs and Trade (GATT) which came into force in 1948. It provides a framework for the conduct of international trade and sets out a number of guidelines on fair trade practice:
   a) All trade must be conducted on the basis of non-discrimination. This means that a change in the tariff applied to imports from one GATT member must be applied to all other GATT members, except where the change emanates from a trade preference agreement in operation before GATT was established or where the country is making the change under its obligations as a member of a customs union or free trade area.
   b) Trade barriers other than tariffs are barred. In practice this regulation has proved impossible to enforce.
   c) GATT provides a framework within which negotiations for reductions in tariff barriers can take place. Under its auspices there have been seven tariff reduction agreements, the most recent being the Tokyo Round from 1973 to 1979. These reductions had led, by 1980, to all the major industrial countries operating a single figure percentage tariff.

2 Countries with close economic, political and geographical ties may join to form a trading bloc. These take two principal forms:
   a) **Customs union** This is an arrangement whereby tariffs between the member countries are abolished and a common external tariff is established. A supranational agency is established to administer the customs union and member states surrender some control over trade matters to this body. The European Economic Community (EEC) is an example of a customs union which has subsequently widened the scope of its activities to include the regulation of agriculture, monopoly and restrictive practices, consumer protection and trading matters within the EEC. By the end of 1922 it is anticipated that all barriers to the movement of goods, services and the factors of production

between member states will have been removed. This establishment of a single European market will lead, it is anticipated, to eventual economic union with some form of federal political structure.

b) **Free trade area** These are weaker arrangements in that the members bind themselves only to free trade with their partners. Each state retains the right to determine its own external tariff. Examples of free trade areas include the European Free Trade Association (EFTA) and the Association of South-East Asian Nations (ASEAN).

The formation of trading blocs does not imply a move towards worldwide free trade since their policies frequently discourage trade with non-members. Rather they signify a movement towards regional self-sufficiency.

REVISION TEST

1 Name three main forms of trade barrier.

2 When might a tariff be levied to raise revenue rather than to limit imports?

3 What is counter trading?

4 Give examples of two types of product where a quota would be more effective at limiting imports than a tariff.

5 Why is the self-sufficiency argument for protection a political, rather than an economic, argument?

6 What is the difference between the 'infant industry' and 'infant economy' arguments for protection?

7 Explain the term 'dumping'.

8 What is the principal difference between a customs union and a free trade area?

9 Give an example of each of the above.

10 Outline the work of GATT.

Examination questions

1 In order to reduce unemployment some policy-makers argue in favour of protectionism, others in favour of export promotion. Examine arguments in favour of **one** of these choices critically, and explain its likely effects on local business bearing in mind possible membership of GATT.

(ABE2, June 1986)

2 What problems may arise for members of the General Agreement on Tariffs and Trade if its free-trade principles are to be extended to (a) agriculture, (b) services such as banking, tourism and building construction at present excluded and (c) infant industries in the developing countries?

(ABE2 December 1986)

3 Explain the case either for or against the imposition of sanctions on exports from Japan by America and Europe.

(ABE2, December 1987)

4 a) Explain the benefits to be obtained from the application of the principle of comparative advantage in international trade.
   b) Under what circumstances could a country be justified in restricting its imports or exports?

(LCCI Higher, November 1986)

5 a) Using a numerical example, explain the theory of comparative costs in relation to foreign trade.
   b) What do you understand by 'terms of trade'?
   c) Using your example in (a), show the relationship between comparative costs theory and terms of trade.

(LCCI Intermediate, December 1986)

6 a) Explain *comparative advantage* in international trade.
   b) In view of the advantages accruing to countries engaged in foreign trade, why do they sometimes practice policies of protection?

(LCCI Intermediate, November 1987)

7 Demonstrate that international trade can lead to the production of greater amounts of *both* commodities when one country is relatively more efficient at producing both of them.

(ICSA, June 1986)

8 Why is a worsening of its terms of trade sometimes good for a country?

(ICSA, December 1986)

9 Why might a government decide to impose an indirect tax on goods which are subject to import controls which restrict the quantity of those goods which can be imported?

(ICSA, June 1987)

10 Demonstrate how transport costs can negate the apparent advantages from specialisation and international trade.

(ICSA, June 1987)

11 When is it desirable and when is it undesirable to protect domestic industries from foreign competition?

(ICSA, December 1987)

12 Demonstrate that specialisation and international trade can lead to an increase in the output of every commodity even if one country has absolute advantage in the production of all commodities. What are the important assumptions made in arriving at these conclusions?

(ICSA, December 1988)

13 One consequence of the world recession has been a renewed call by some writers for a period of 'protectionism', in respect of their own economies. With this in mind, explain:
    a) The case for protectionism.
    b) The case against protectionism
                                                        (ACCA, December 1987)

14 Account for the advantages which countries derive from trade with each other.
                                                        (ACCA, December 1988)

15 In what circumstances may an improvement in a country's terms of trade not be advantageous?
                                                        (CIMA, November 1988)

16 Given that the Law of Comparative Advantage is valid, why should any country wish to adopt a protectionist policy?
                                                        (CIMA, May 1989)

17 Evaluate the case for the elimination of all possible barriers to international trade.
                                                        (SCCA, November 1987)

18 Evaluate the case for the United Kingdom introducing a 'protectionist' trade policy.
                                                        (SCCA, May 1988)

19 What is meant by comparative advantage and explain its relevance to foreign trade?
                                                        (Cert.M., June 1986)

20 Give reasons as to why an improvement in a country's terms of trade may not be advantageous.
                                                        (Cert.M., November 1986)

21 Using your knowledge of economic theory, what are the gains from trade?
                                                        (Cert.M., June 1988)

22 What are the main barriers to trade and why are they erected?
                                                        (Cert.M, December 1988)

23 Government subsidies to firms are normally regarded as unfair under international agreements. Identify other methods a government may adopt to protect the domestic economy and analyse the appropriateness of such protective measures.
                                                        (IPS, May 1989)

24 a) Describe the three fundamental problems that society faces in deciding how to allocate its scarce resources.

b) Explain what is meant by the term 'opportunity cost'.

c) The opportunity cost of producing bananas in an equatorial country is lower than it is in a non-equatorial country but the opposite situation applies to the opportunity cost of producing computer equipment. Illustrating your answer by a simple numerical example, explain how these two countries could both benefit from trade in bananas and computer equipment.

(I.Act., April 1989)

23 The balance of payments

- *Does the balance of payments always balance?*
- *Why should a country wish to eliminate a balance of payments surplus?*

Balance of payments accounts

The balance of payments of a country is a record of all economic transactions between its residents and those of all other countries over a given period. Economic transactions in this context include not only the exchange of goods and services but also the transfer of money or assets in the form of gifts or pensions. Such transactions are usually settled by the exchange of currency but also includes trade conducted under barter arrangements.

The balance of payments are recorded in the form of a series of credits (+) and debits (−):

- Credits arise from economic transactions which result in the **receipt** of foreign currency from abroad.
- Debits arise from economic transactions which result in the **payment** of foreign currency abroad.

The balance of payments accounts are divided into three sections:

1 Current account

This is the record of trade in goods and services and the payment of pensions and similar transactions. It is broken down into:

    a) *The balance of trade* This is the difference between the value of goods exported (+) and the value of goods imported (−). It is also referred to as the visible trade balance.

    b) *The balance of invisibles* This is so-called because it covers those transactions and transfers which result in the movement of foreign exchange but not in the physical movement of goods. It is made up of several parts.

      i) Receipts and payments of currency for the provision of services such as banking, tourism, shipping, insurance, etc.

      ii) Receipts and payments arising out of rent, interest and dividends on the property holdings of domestic residents overseas and overseas residents in the recording country.

iii) The receipt and payment of gifts, pensions and similar transfers.

iv) Government payments overseas for the maintenance of diplomatic representation and military bases.

When the various receipts and payments are netted out the result is the balance of invisibles.

When the balance of trade and balance of invisibles are added together they produce the **balance on current account**.

2 Investment and other capital flows

This section records capital flows into (+) and out of (−) the country. This is broken down into:

a) *The short-term capital account* This consists of movements on accounts held by overseas residents in domestic banks and vice versa which involve inward or outward flows of currency. This section also includes foreign currency dealing by banks and trade credit on exports and imports. Many of these short-term movements are motivated by the speculative activity in currencies and interest-bearing securities which gives rise to the term 'hot money'.

b) *Long-term capital movements* These consist of:

i) Private capital movements. These include the purchase and sale of stocks and shares in foreign governments and companies by individuals and institutions, i.e. **portfolio investment**. They also include the purchase by companies of controlling interests in firms based in other countries, i.e. **direct investment**.

ii) Public capital movements. These consist of long-term loans by one government to another.

In all cases investment in the recording country from overseas is a credit while investment by the recording country overseas is a debit to the balance of payments.

When they are netted out the result is the **balance on capital account**.

When the balances on current account and capital account are added together they should yield a figure equal to the net receipt or payment of foreign currency over a given period, i.e. the **balance for official financing**. If this balance is positive the country has a balance of payments surplus while if it is negative the country has a balance of payments deficit.

3 Official financing

This third section is the other side of the balance sheet and shows how a balance of payments surplus is utilised or a deficit financed. Its main items are:

a) Changes in the country's gold and foreign currency holdings.

b) Foreign currency borrowing.

c) Loans or repayments of loans with international monetary authorities.

A surplus will result in the repayment of foreign currency debts and/or an increase in foreign currency reserves. A deficit will result in increased borrowing and/or a reduction in the country's foreign currency reserves. Note that in this section a positive figure signifies an outflow of foreign currency while a negative figure signifies an inflow of foreign currency. The use of this device ensures that the two sides of the balance of payments cancel each other out. If, therefore, the balance for official financing is +£1 bn. the official financing section should total −£1 bn.

Balancing item

When you look at the balance of payments for the UK, in Table 23.1 you will see that there is also a balancing item. This arises from the fact that it is impossible to reach an accurate figure for the balance of payments because of errors and omissions which occur in the gathering of data. The 'official financing' section is assumed to be correct because there are relatively accurate records of gold and foreign currency movements. The far less accurate balance for official financing is then brought into line by the addition or subtraction of the balancing item.

The balance of payments in practice

The structure of a country's balance of payments reflects both its stage of economic development and the pattern of economic activity within the country. Several types of structure may be identified.

1   The developing country

The balance of trade consists of the export of one or two, usually low-value, products the earnings of which are frequently inadequate to finance the importation of essential industrial and capital goods. The balance of trade is therefore often in deficit, as is the balance of invisibles, and this deficit on current account is supported by borrowing which shows up as a surplus on the long-term capital account. Many of the countries of Africa and Asia fall into this category.

2   The newly industrialising country (NIC)

These countries have a number of recently established industries which enjoy a competitive edge due to low wage costs. The success of their export industries results in a surplus on the balance of trade which is used to finance a deficit of invisibles and to finance capital borrowings for further industrial development. The NICs include Taiwan, Singapore and South Korea.

3   The developed creditor country

Eventually a developed country may find that continued growth of export earnings results in a very large surplus on the balance of trade. In addition, the growth of its own service industries reduces any deficit on invisibles so that the current account as a whole is in surplus. This surplus can be used to finance a deficit on capital account as

TABLE 23.1
UK Balance of Payments: 1988

	£ million
Current Account	
Visibles:	
Exports	80 602
Imports	101 428
Balance of Trade	−20 826
Invisibles:	
Services balance	4 165
Interest, profits and dividends balance	5 619
Transfers balance	−3 575
Balance of Invisibles	6 209
CURRENT BALANCE	−14 617
Investment & Other Capital Flows	
Net foreign currency transactions of UK banks	5 608
Net sterling transactions of UK banks	8 987
Deposits with and lending to banks abroad by UK non-bank private sector	−3 035
Borrowing from banks abroad by:	
UK non-bank private sector	3 830
Public corporations	−253
General government	−10
Investment overseas by UK residents:	
Direct	−15 219
Portfolio	−9 718
Investment in the UK by overseas residents:	
Direct	7 346
Portfolio	4 639
Net change in external assets and liabilities of:	
UK non-bank private sector and public corporations	2 901
General government	21
CAPITAL BALANCE	5 097
BALANCING ITEM	12 283
Total For Official Financing	2 763
Official Financing	
Additions to official reserves	−2 761

Note: Figures do not quite balance because of rounding up.

the country begins to build up its portfolio and direct investment overseas. Japan is presently the most successful country of this type.

4   The mature creditor country

Over a long period the developed creditor country will build up substantial overseas capital interests. It will then enjoy a growing surplus on invisibles as these investments yield rent, interest and dividend payments. The surplus on invisibles will be sufficient to counter a deterioration in the balance of trade as the country's exports are faced with growing competition from the NICs.

5   The ageing debtor country

Eventually a mature creditor country's balance of trade may worsen to the point where invisible earnings are no longer sufficient to finance the deficit. A persistent deficit on current account will require corrective measures from the government since no reliance can be placed on future spontaneous improvements. Great Britain and the United States are two countries which have reached this phase and consequently governments have found that the balance of payments acts as a constraint on their ability to pursue other objectives.

Progression from one phase to another is by no means inevitable. West Germany, for example, has been able to enjoy the advantages of a mature creditor country while maintaining a surplus on the balance of trade. Other countries, like India, seem unable to become major industrial exporters despite well-established cultural and trading practices. Even when two countries have reached similar stages of development their balance of payments positions may diverge because of the nature of their exports, the stability of their economies and patterns of world demand. Thus countries whose exports are based on essential raw materials such as oil or metals or advanced technological equipment tend to be in a stronger position than those dependent on cheap manufactures or foodstuffs like textiles, rice or sugar.

The UK balance of payments

The structure of the UK balance of payments has passed through all the phases outlined above during the past 200 years. In 1900 the UK was a mature creditor country. The balance of trade was usually in deficit but this was offset by the large surplus on invisibles produced by income on past investment abroad. The decline into ageing debtor country status in the first half of the twentieth century was accelerated by the sale of capital assets overseas to finance the two world wars. In the 1950s the country had a virtually permanent deficit on the balance of trade but this was matched by an invisible balance surplus earned through services like shipping, banking and insurance. So the balance of payments remained more or less in balance over this period.

Yet under the UK balance of payments was a time bomb. This was the poor rate of growth of exports compared to imports. Throughout the 1960s and 1970s the volume of exports of UK manufactures grew at a much slower rate than that of the rest of the world and Britain's share of world exports of manufactures fell from 17 per cent in 1960 to less than 7 per cent in 1988. While exports were growing slowly (and actually falling during the early 1980s) imports of manufactures were growing much faster; at twice the rate of exports. In the 1960s and early 1970s the balance of payments went through a series of crises and acted as a constraint on government action in other areas of the economy.

From the late 1970s to the late 1980s the impending crisis was obscured by the contribution of North Sea oil to the balance of payments. Britain moved from being a net importer of oil to a net exporter and the visible oil balance went from −£3839 m. in 1974 to +£8163 m. in 1985. The oil surplus began to decline in the late 1980s but even if this had not been the case the balance of payments was bound to go into deficit again because of the changing pattern of trade in manufactures. In 1983 the total value of manufactured imports exceeded that of manufactured exports for the first time in 200 years. Once established the gap between the two widened dramatically, especially during periods of rapid growth in domestic consumer expenditure. By 1988 the UK had a large deficit which was being financed by overseas borrowing and in 1989 the government was forced to take measures to deal with a deficit which threatened to reach £20 bn. over a full year. The decline in the UK balance of payments during the 1980s is shown in Figure 23.1.

REVISION TEST

1   What are the three sections into which the balance of payments is divided?
2   Define the 'balance of trade'.
3   Name the four groups of items which make up the balance of invisibles.
4   A Nigerian company exports goods to France in a Liberian ship insured by Lloyds of London. What will be the entries to the various countries' balance of payments?
5   What is the difference between portfolio and direct investment?
6   If the balance of trade is +200, the balance of invisibles is −140, the capital account balance is +30 and there is a balancing item of +10 what is:
    a)   The balance on current account
    b)   The balance for official financing?
7   What is hot money?
8   What relationships are apparent between the current account and the capital account of the balance of payments?
9   Explain the difference between a developed creditor country and a mature creditor country in terms of their balance of payments.
10   In what sense did the balance of payments of the UK resemble that of a developing country in the mid-1980s?

Balance of payments disequilibrium

The balance of payments always balances in the sense that a surplus or deficit on the balance for official financing will be equalled by an appropriate adjustment in the official financing section. However, a country's balance of payments is said to be in fundamental equilibrium when autonomous income and expenditure balance out over a given period without interference by government. A country which alternates between small surpluses and small deficits over a number of years is thus in equilibrium. Most countries, however, tend to a condition of fundamental

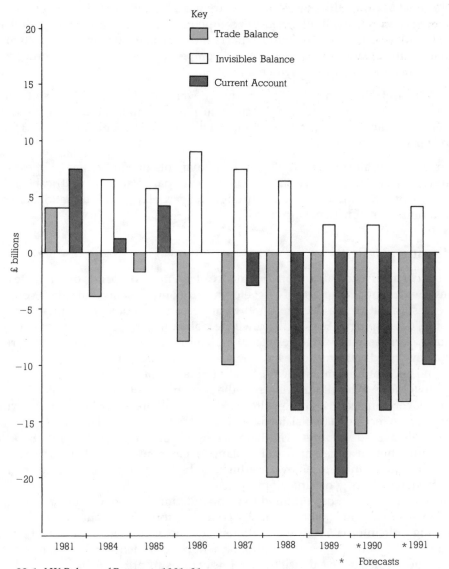

Figure 23.1 *UK Balance of Payments 1981–91*

disequilibrium with long periods of balance of payments surplus or deficit. There are three main causes of fundamental disequilibrium:

1 **The level of domestic demand** If there is excessive domestic demand in the economy so that domestic expenditure is greater than domestic output, imports will be sucked in to meet this excess demand so leading to a balance of trade deficit. Whether the balance of payments as a whole is also in deficit depends on the balance of invisibles and the balance on capital account. Similarly deficient demand will tend to create a balance of payments surplus.

2 **The level of competitiveness** If a country has a higher rate of inflation than other trading countries it will suffer a loss of competitiveness. This loss of competitiveness will result in a fall in the volume of exports and a rise in the volume of imports and so weaken the balance of trade. Increased competitiveness will, on the other hand, strengthen the balance of payments position.

3 **Excess capital movements** Speculative movements of short-term capital to, or from, a country may lead to a deficit or surplus on capital account. These movements usually reflect current or anticipated economic events and may, in turn, trigger such events themselves.

Governments aim to keep the balance of payments in equilibrium as one of their macro-economic objectives. This is because the external position is inextricably related to the state of the domestic economy through the part played by international trade in the determination of national income.

Rectifying a deficit

The effect of a persistent deficit on the balance of payments depends on the state of the domestic economy. In the case of a developing economy the deficit may be a conscious policy arising out of the need to import both essential goods and capital funds for industrial development. Such a deficit will be maintained in the short run as part of the country's overall strategy in the expectation that it will not persist over the long run.

In a developed country, however, a deficit is likely to be a cause for concern. Starting from a position of full employment equilibrium, a deficit on the balance of payments means that the level of withdrawals from the circular flow of national income is greater than the level of injections. This results in a downward foreign trade multiplier with its deflationary effect on national income. Where there is an inflationary gap in the economy increased imports will help to bring the national income back into equilibrium, though at the expense of a balance of payments deficit. In this case a deficit will enable the country to enjoy an artificially high standard of living through the consumption of more goods than it produces.

Such deficits cannot be permitted to go on indefinitely. A deficit must be financed either by running down the country's gold and foreign currency reserves or by borrowing from international organisations and other countries. If the deficit persists, year after year, both the reserves and international confidence will be exhausted. In taking action to deal with a deficit three kinds of measure are available:

1 Direct controls

These are measures which act directly on the level of imports or the movement of foreign currency. They include tariffs, quotas, exchange control and restrictions on overseas travel or investment. Direct controls do not tackle the underlying cause of a deficit; they merely bring imports down to an artificially low level. They are also potentially dangerous since they invite retaliation from other countries which could lead in turn to a trade war. The result would be a contraction of world trade and recession in all the countries involved, as occurred during the 1930s.

A further restriction on the use of direct controls for most trading nations arises out of their membership of GATT and of free trade associations like the EEC and ASEAN. As an alternative to controlling imports a government may seek to encourage exports through subsidies, tax incentives, cheap export credit and other services to exporters. Even here, trade agreements usually limit the extent to which exports may be subsidised.

2   Deflationary measures

We have seen that lack of competitiveness is a principal cause of balance of payments deficits. If the prices of domestically produced goods are high relative to those of other countries exports will fall and imports rise. Such a situation will occur when inflation is higher in one country than in that of its competitors. In these circumstances the government may adopt counter-inflationary measures to reduce the rate of inflation and the level of domestic demand. *Monetary measures* can be introduced to reduce domestic demand by restricting the availability of credit. Such measures will assist the current account of the balance of payments in a number of ways:

a)   Reduced demand for goods and services in general should reduce the demand for imports.

b)   Reduced demand for domestically-produced goods may encourage domestic producers to seek out new export markets.

c)   By slowing the rate of inflation such measures will help to restore the competitiveness of domestically produced goods.

The capital account will also benefit from a tighter monetary policy as higher interest rates attract both short-term and long-term funds into the country. *Fiscal measures* can also be used to reduce demand by cutting government expenditure and increasing taxes. Fiscal measures carry the additional advantage that they can be applied selectively to create the most impact on the external position, e.g. government expenditure overseas.

The use of deflationary measures to deal with a deficit has its unpleasant side-effects. Reductions in aggregate demand will slow economic growth and lead to higher unemployment. Furthermore such measures are unlikely to be entirely successful when inflationary pressures in the economy stem from cost-push rather than demand-pull factors. Then, higher interest rates or increased taxes may lead to claims for higher wages and so increase production costs and ultimately prices. In these circumstances direct control of prices and incomes may be more effective in improving the current account position.

3   Currency depreciation

The government may choose to lower the value of the country's currency against other currencies. This will have the effect of making imports dearer and exports cheaper, so helping to restore the price competitiveness of domestic industry. Where the country has a fixed exchange rate this can be achieved by a formal **devaluation** of the currency. If the country has a floating exchange rate which fluctuates with market forces the monetary authorities can withhold support of the currency in the foreign exchange markets to encourage depreciation. The effect of such a depreciation is shown in Table 23.2, which illustrates the changes in the prices of goods wholly produced in the UK and the USA following the 1967 devaluation.

TABLE 23.2
Effect of 1967 Devaluation

Before devaluation (£ = $2.80)
British good priced at £200 = $560
American good priced at $560 = £200
After devaluation (£ = $2.40)
British good priced at £200 = $480
American good priced at $560 = £234

While a fall in the value of the currency will make a country's goods more price competitive, the impact on both the volume of trade and the balance of trade is less certain. Goods produced partly or wholly from imported materials will not fall in price by the same proportion as the original depreciation so the degree of increased price competitiveness is unpredictable. Furthermore, the extent to which exports can grow is dependent upon the productive capacity available. The one certainty is that the terms of trade have deteriorated and a greater volume of exports is needed to pay for a given level of imports. If there were no change in the volume of trade export earnings would fall and the national import bill rise.

The success of a currency depreciation depends on the demand elasticity of exports and imports and the supply elasticity of exports. According to the Marshall–Lerner elasticity condition a devaluation will improve the balance of trade provided that the sum of the elasticity of domestic demand for imports and the elasticity of foreign demand for exports is greater than unity. Suppose that the elasticity of foreign demand for a country's exports is zero so that a cut in export prices has no effect on demand. The effect of a devaluation will be to leave export earnings, measured in local currency, unchanged. In order for the sum of elasticities to be greater than unity the elasticity of domestic demand for imports must also be greater than unity so higher import prices will lead to the value of imports, measured in local currency, falling. While foreign currency earnings have fallen by the same percentage as the devaluation, foreign currency expenditure on imports has fallen by more than the percentage devaluation. There will thus be an improvement in the balance of trade.

TABLE 23.3
Effect of 20 per cent devaluation on initial export value of 400 and import value of 500: selected elasticities

Demand elasticity		Post devaluation (local currency)		Post devaluation (foreign currency)	
exports	imports	Export value	Import value	Export value	Import value
2	0	560	600	448	500
0	2	400	360	320	300
½	1	440	480	352	400
1	¼	480	570	384	475
¾	¾	460	510	368	425
½	¼	440	570	352	475

In Table 23.3 the impact of a currency depreciation in various combinations of export and import demand elasticities is shown. Only in one case, where the two demand elasticities add up to less than one, would the country not improve its balance of trade by devaluing. Clearly, the greater the sum of demand elasticities for exports and imports, the greater the improvement in the balance of trade.

The nature of a country's exports and imports will determine the demand elasticity for them. Generally, the demand for services is more elastic than that for manufactures while the demand for manufactures is more elastic than the demand for primary products. Thus an oil-exporting country which imports most of its food and essential manufactures might well find that devaluation reduced export earnings and raised its import bill. Such a country would improve its balance of trade by **revaluation**, i.e. by increasing the value of its currency against other currencies. Even where demand elasticities are favourable to a devaluation, the supply of domestically produced goods must be sufficiently elastic to enable the country to gain from its increased competitiveness. Since elasticity of supply is greater in the long run than in the short run there is usually a time lag between devaluation and its full impact on the balance of trade. This phenomenon is termed the 'J' curve effect and is illustrated in Figure 23.2.

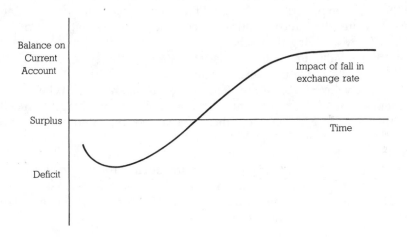

Figure 23.2 *'J' curve*

Ultimately the success of a devaluation or depreciation of the currency strategy depends on the responsiveness of the domestic economy to the changed conditions. The immediate effect of higher import prices will be higher prices of essential imported goods and a drop in living standards until higher export demand boosts national income in the long run. It is essential in the short run that incomes do not rise to compensate for higher prices and set off a cost-push inflationary cycle which will undo the benefits of the devaluation. It may be necessary, therefore, for the devaluation to be accompanied by deflationary measures and perhaps a prices and incomes policy. The other threat to the success of a devaluation is that, if supply elasticity is low, manufacturers may let their prices creep higher so raising profits rather than output.

Rectifying a surplus

At first sight a surplus on the balance of payments seems to be highly desirable, leading as it does to a net injection into the circular flow of national income and so higher output and employment opportunities. However, a persistent surplus does present the government with two main problems:

1   The domestic population is unable to purchase the goods and services its income would support. While this will act as a stimulus to commercial and industrial expansion, there is a likelihood that the economy will experience demand-pull inflationary pressures, especially if there is full employment.

2   A series of surpluses will result in the country building up its gold and foreign currency reserves at the expense of permanent deficit countries. Eventually, these deficit countries will be forced to reduce current levels of demand as they attempt to rectify their external position. Should this result in an increase in trade barriers the surplus country will itself suffer through the consequent downturn in world trade.

The cures for a surplus are the opposite to those for a deficit. Thus the government could relax import controls, discourage exports or introduce fiscal and monetary policies aimed at expanding domestic demand and raising living standards. Imports should then rise, exports fall and capital flow out of the country. Alternatively the country could alter the external value of its currency upwards, either through a formal revaluation or by allowing the exchange rate to rise on the currency markets. Note, however, that revaluation will only assist matters if the sum of the elasticities of demand for exports and imports exceeds unity.

Unfortunately surpluses are as difficult as deficits to eradicate. When a country has a permanent surplus the government can pursue policies aimed at growth without fear of the effect of these policies on the external position and higher investment, productivity and incomes follow. If the country reduces its surplus by investing more overseas the long-term effect will be increased interest and dividend earnings to boost the surplus on the balance of invisibles. Measures such as revaluation lower the price of imports, reduce inflationary pressures and raise living standards, making it even more likely that the economic environment will be favourable to increased economic efficiency and a healthy balance of payments.

REVISION TEST

1   Define fundamental equilibrium in the balance of payments.

2   What advantages, if any, are attached to a balance of payments deficit?

3   Why must action be taken to deal with a persistent balance of payments deficit?

4   What are the main measures available to a country to cure a long-term balance of payments deficit?

5   Which particular measures would be likely to produce a surplus on capital account?

6   How may a balance of payments deficit be financed?

7   Explain how borrowing may assist in curing a deficit in the short term but not in the long term.

8   When will devaluation of a currency be most effective in dealing with a balance of payments deficit?

9   What is the Marshall–Lerner condition?

10   What are the two principal reasons for wishing to cure a balance of payments surplus?

Examination questions

1   Why do policy-makers sometimes discover that a government's decision to reduce unemployment results in a growing balance of payments deficit? What policies might they adopt in this situation?

(ABE2, December 1985)

2   Using the concept of the nation's 'propensity to import' explain how economic expansion might be stopped by the resulting balance of payments problems. Review policies governments might adopt when faced with this crisis, stating the reasons for the choice you would consider most beneficial for local business.

(ABE2, June 1986)

3   Define 'terms of trade' in international trade and explain the probable effects of a devaluation of a country's currency on its international trading position and domestic production.
How would such a devaluation affect the development of a country already dependent on the export of one main primary product such as sugar?

(ABE2, December 1986)

4   Outline the most likely global impact of a continued and determined effort by America to end its balance of payments international deficit.

(ABE2, June 1988)

5   A deficit on the balance of payments on current account may have favourable short run but unfavourable long run consequences. Explain and assess the validity of this statement.

(LCCI Higher, November 1985)

6   The national income of a country would be £1000 million if the working population were fully employed. The inhabitants habitually spend ⅘ of their disposable incomes on consumption. Companies are forbidden to retain undistributed profits.
The government levies an income tax of ⅛ on all personal income, but raises no other form of taxation. It does not pay out any unemployment benefits, pensions or other transfer incomes. Government expenditure on goods and services is currently £80 million. Investment amounts to £140 million and export earnings are

currently £100 million. The country's expenditure on imports is always equal to ¹⁄₁₀ of its national income. Unfortunately the country is currently suffering from unemployment.

From the information given:

a) What is the present level of national income and the state of the balance of payments?

b) Calculate the increase in government expenditure necessary to achieve full employment.

c) What would be the effects of this on the budgetary balance and the balance of payments?

(LCCI Higher, May 1986)

7 How does a depreciation of the rate of exchange of a currency affect a country's balance of trade?

(ICSA, June 1986)

8 What effect will an increase in interest rates have on a country's balance of payments?

(ICSA, December 1986)

9 When will a devaluation or decline in its exchange rate help a country's balance of payments on current account?

(ICSA, June 1987)

10 Can an increase in the cost of domestically-produced goods ever lead to an improvement in the balance of trade?

(ICSA, December 1987)

11 How is the balance of trade affected by a worsening of the terms of trade?

(ICSA, December 1988)

12 If the USA has a balance of payments deficit,

a) What measures might it adopt to cure the deficit?

b) What are the problems associated with each of the available policy options?

(ACCA, December 1988)

13 In the 1980s both Britain and the USA experienced worryingly high foreign trade deficits.

With reference to one or other of the above examples discuss:

a) The possible causes of these trade deficits;

b) The effects of a major trade deficit.

(ACCA, June 1989)

14 You are required to

a) State what information is provided by the UK Balance of Payments on Current Account.

b) Describe, and explain the relative importance of, the invisible items on this account.

(CIMA, November 1989)

15 Explain the term 'balance of payments' in the context of a country's international accounts.

(SCCA, November 1988)

16 Does an imbalance of a nation's balance of payments really matter? Justify your answer.

(Cert.M., November 1986)

17 What courses of action may be open to a country wishing to correct a deficit on its balance of payments?

(Cert.M., June 1987)

18 Distinguish between the concepts of balance of trade and terms of trade. Explain how changes in the terms of trade help to determine a country's balance of trade.

(Cert.M., November 1987)

19 Explain the main determinants of a country's balance of payments deficit or surplus.

(Cert.M., June 1988)

20 Explain the following terms, and comment on any relationships there may be between them.
a) Balance of trade.
b) Terms of trade.
c) Balance of payments.

(IPS, November 1987)

21 Define the following terms and explain how they are connected, if at all.
a) Balance of trade,
b) Terms of trade.
c) Balance of payments.
d) Exchange rates.

(IPS, November 1988)

22 What methods are available to a country when it attempts to correct a balance of payments deficit? Comment on the effectiveness of each method which you identify.

(IFA, June 1989)

23 Distinguish between the balance of payments, the balance of trade, and the terms of trade.

(IFA, December 1989)

24 Exchange rates

- *Why do exchange rates not always reflect the relative purchasing powers of the currencies concerned?*

- *If we have floating exchange rates why do governments still intervene in the foreign exchange markets?*

Financing international trade

The settlement of domestic economic transactions is a relatively straightforward matter. Payment is made via a medium of exchange, the unit of currency, which is generally accepted throughout society. International transactions, on the other hand, are rather more complicated because of the absence of an international currency to perform a similar function. Instead international trade transactions must be conducted via one of three means:

- By exchanging goods for other goods, i.e. barter, *or*
- By establishing an external standard by which all currencies may be valued, e.g. the gold standard, *or*
- By establishing appropriate exchange rates for the various currencies in which trade is conducted.

Barter

Barter or counter trade has survived in international trade to a much greater extent than in domestic trade. This is due largely to two factors.

1 For political reasons a number of communist countries have been reluctant to use currency to pay for imports for fear of running down their limited gold and foreign currency reserves. In particular a trade deficit could force them to borrow from the western industrialised countries to finance such a deficit. Thus most of the east European countries insisted on barter arrangements for trading with the West until the late 1980s.

2 Many developing countries are often so short of foreign currency that barter presents the only way of financing essential imports without adding to their already high international debts. Thus it has become quite common for western companies

to find that trade deals are dependent upon their accepting payment in locally produced goods, most often commodities or agricultural goods.

Despite its attractions to countries short of foreign currency, barter trade is not conducive to the long-term development of world trade for three reasons.

1 As there is unlikely to be a double coincidence of wants it is a device for unloading excess production rather than satisfying mutual needs.

2 The recipient of the bartered goods is likely to be forced into complicated transactions to unload them. Barter trade may therefore require far more organisation than conventional trade and be less efficient to operate as a result.

3 Since barter trade imposes conditions on trade it acts as a barrier to the free movement of goods and services. This has led GATT to express concern at its growth in recent years.

The gold standard

Historically gold has been the most important external standard to which currencies have been linked though silver and other metals have at times performed a similar role. Under a gold or other external standard countries keep the value of their monetary units equal to a defined weight of gold or other metal. When Britain was on the gold standard, for example, an Act of 1870 set the weight of £1 at 123.27447 grains troy, so one ounce of gold was priced at £3.17.10½ (£3.89). The exchange rate between two currencies on the gold standard was thus based on the gold content of each currency. An exchange rate of £1 = $4.6867, for example, meant that £1 weighed 4.6867 times $1. Traders would therefore be prepared to take payment in any currency provided they were sure of its gold content so that gold was effectively an international currency.

Under the gold standard most trade payments were met without moving gold physically from one place to another. Instead, payment was usually made through the use of paper currency, bills of exchange and other claims to gold. However, underpinning the entire trading system was the security that a trader could convert a payment for exports into gold should he so wish. Yet even with the use of paper currency the gold standard was beset by the problem that growth in world trade depended on gold supplies expanding sufficiently to maintain an adequate supply of international liquidity. The shortage of gold supplies in the early twentieth century meant that world liquidity did not grow fast enough for the needs of world trade.

The other main weakness of the gold standard arose from the direct link between the domestic money supply and the country's gold reserves. If gold reserves fell the government would have to introduce deflationary monetary measures to reduce bank deposits in line with the new level of gold holdings. Thus a balance of payments deficit would be followed by deflationary measures whatever the state of the domestic economy. In theory, the balance of payments was self-correcting under the gold standard since deflation would lead to falls in both commodity and factor prices and eventually a rise in exports and fall in imports. In fact, as Britain found in the 1920s, factor prices were resilient to downward pressure, and the economy was subject to sustained deflationary pressure without the balance of payments problem resolving itself.

Exchange rates

International trade transactions may also be settled in the currencies of the countries concerned, provided that a suitable exchange rate between the currencies can be found. In the absence of an external standard, such as gold, by which to gauge the relative values of the currencies, exchange rates must be determined either by market forces alone or by market forces subject to some degree of government intervention. In the former case exchange rates are said to be **floating** and in the latter **fixed**. Before going on to consider both systems in some detail we shall examine the forces which operate in the foreign exchange markets.

Exchange rate determination

Where the exchange rate is determined purely by market forces the price of one currency in terms of another (i.e. the exchange rate) occurs at the intersection of the demand and supply curves for that currency on the foreign exchange market. The exchange rate of the pound sterling against the US dollar is shown in Figure 24.1.

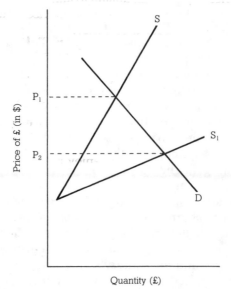

Figure 24.1 *Exchange rate determination*

In Figure 24.1 the initial equilibrium rate is at P_1 where the demand for pounds from holders of dollars and the supply of pounds from those wishing to obtain dollars are in equilibrium.

The demand for pounds consists of dollars exchanged for pounds by:

1 US importers of British goods and services.
2 US residents transferring capital funds to the United Kingdom.
3 British and other non-American holders of dollars converting their funds into sterling.

The supply of pounds consists of pounds exchanged for dollars by:

1 UK importers of American goods and services.
2 UK residents transferring capital funds to the United States.
3 Oversea holders of pounds converting their funds into dollars.

A mirror image market for dollars priced in pounds also operates with the reverse demand and supply factors to those listed above. In addition there are foreign exchange rate markets for all the major currencies priced in all other major currencies.

A change in the demand or supply conditions operating in the market will result in a new equilibrium exchange rate. If, therefore, there is a substantial movement of capital funds from Britain to the United States, this would be shown in Figure 24.1 as a shift in supply from S to S_1, resulting in a fall in the value of the pound against the dollar from P_1 to P_2. Simultaneously, the market for dollars priced in pounds will show a rightward shift in the demand for dollars and raise the price of dollars against the pound. Similarly, a deficit in the UK balance of trade with the USA means that the supply of pounds from British importers will exceed the demand for pounds by American importers causing the price of pounds in dollars to fall.

We have established that exchange rates are determined by the forces of supply and demand operating in the market for a currency. Changes in supply and demand conditions are a response to the various influences which operate on the market for a currency.

1 **Relative inflation rates** Where one country has a higher rate of inflation than another its products will become less competitive. This will lead to a fall in exports and a rise in imports, resulting in downward pressure on the exchange rate.

2 **Demand elasticity of exports** Countries which export goods which are inelastic in demand and essential to other countries enjoy a strong external position which strengthens the exchange rate.

3 **Interest rates** Since short-term capital movements are highly responsive to changes in interest rates, a rise in a country's interest rate will draw in overseas funds and strengthen the exchange rate.

4 **State of the economy** A strong economy with a healthy external position will attract foreign funds and this will exert an upward pressure on the exchange rate. Economic instability or doubts about future prosperity will probably lead to funds leaving the country, thereby lowering the exchange rate.

5 **Political factors** Uncertainties about the political situation may be expected to damage confidence, leading to an exodus of capital and a fall in the exchange rate. This is especially likely if there is the possibility that a government unsympathetic to foreign capital will take power.

6 **Speculation**   Uncertainties about future movements of the exchange rate enable speculators to gain by buying and selling currencies. Such speculation may be self-fulfilling in that if enough buyers enter the market in expectation of a rise in the rate the rate will indeed rise.

The purchasing power parity theory

The factors outlined above indicate the way in which exchange rates can be expected to move. The purchasing power parity theory, however, attempts to predict the exact exchange rate between two currencies. It is based on the premise that the exchange rate between two currencies will be determined by their relative domestic values. If, for example, a basket of goods is priced at £100 in the UK and F1000 in France the exchange rate will be £1 = F10. Thus the exchange rate ensures purchasing power parity between the two countries.

There is clearly a certain logic in the theory. If there were no relationship between the exchange rate and the domestic purchasing power of each currency we might see a UK resident converting £5 into Lire 10 000 and travelling to Italy to buy a car! However, the theory is rather simplistic as a foundation for exchange rate determination. Let us go back to the exchange rate between the pound and the franc of £1 = F10 and assume that the basket of goods still costs £100 in Britain but only F900 in France. Britons should now convert their pounds into francs and buy French goods, thereby saving £1 in every 10. The UK balance of payments will deteriorate and the increased demand for francs will push the pound down against the franc. Eventually, a new equilibrium exchange rate of £1 = F9 will be established. In practice, however, the relative purchasing powers of currencies can deviate from their exchange rate because of the imperfections of international trade.

1 **Transport costs**   The cost of transporting goods from one country to another means that prices in two countries can deviate from the purchasing power parity without it being economically viable for the residents of either country to travel to the other to buy goods.

2 **Trade barriers**   Wine is cheaper in France and relatively easy to transport to the UK but customs duties wipe out much of the saving made. Import quotas may also enable the prices of domestically-produced goods to be higher than those of foreign imports since the shortage of imports will force some consumers to buy domestically-produced goods despite the higher price.

3 **Production and supply conditions**   Price levels tend to be higher in developed than in developing countries but the latter may be unable to take advantage of this because of limited productive capacity.

4 **Currency restrictions**   The fact that many currencies are not freely convertible means that the official exchange rate bears little or no relationship to the internal purchasing power of the currency.

Despite its limitations, the purchasing power parity theory does have its uses. First, it provides a rule of thumb guide for an appropriate exchange rate when normal international relations are resumed following wars and other disruptive events. Second, it acts as a guide to exchange rate disequilibrium when there are significant variations in inflation rates between countries.

REVISION TEST

1   What is the alternative name for barter trade?

2   An exporter of machine goods receives payment in rice from a developing country. What are the likely disadvantages to the exporter and the developing country in this arrangement?

3   What is meant by 'an external standard' when applied to exchange rates?

4   How did the existence of the gold standard (a) encourage and (b) inhibit the growth of world trade?

5   What are the principal determinants of supply and demand for a currency?

6   Give recent examples of where political events have affected a country's exchange rate.

7   State three factors which might lead to a currency's exchange rate falling.

8   Give two factors which would lead to the demand for a currency shifting to the right.

9   Explain the principle underlying the purchasing power parity theory.

10 To what extent is the purchasing power parity theory based on the assumption of a perfect market?

Fixed and floating exchange rates

We have seen that, when exchange rates are determined by market forces, the distinction between fixed and floating rates refers to whether or not the government intervenes to influence the action of market forces.

Fixed rates

A fixed exchange rate requires the setting of a designated par value for a currency against other currencies together with an undertaking by the monetary authorities to intervene in the foreign exchange markets to maintain that rate. In theory a government could adhere to a rigidly fixed rate and act to prevent any deviation from that rate. In practice, governments are content to ensure that the rate does not deviate excessively from the established parity.

In the period of fixed exchange rates between the end of the Second World War and the early 1970s countries undertook to ensure that exchange rates did not deviate by more than 1 per cent either side of parity. For most of this period, for example, the exchange rate between the pound sterling and the US dollar was £1 = $2.80 so the exchange rate was permitted to range between an upper limit or 'peg' of £1 = $2.828 and a lower limit of £1 = $2.772. This situation is illustrated in Figure 24.2.

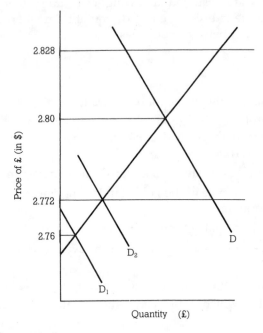

Figure 24.2 *Fixed exchange rates I*

In Figure 24.2 the par rate of exchange of sterling against the dollar is £1 = $2.80. Provided that the exchange rate moves only between the upper and lower pegs there will be no interference by the monetary authorities in the working of the market. Suppose, however, there is a fall in demand for pounds resulting in a leftward shift in the demand curve from D to D_1. The equilibrium exchange rate for sterling is now, at $2.76, below the lower permitted limit. The Bank of England would now intervene in the market to support sterling by buying pounds and selling dollars held in the Exchange Equalisation Account. The aim of this intervention would be to shift the demand curve for sterling rightward from D_1 to D_2 so that once again the exchange rate is within the accepted limits. If the pound threatened to break through the upper limit the Bank of England would sell pounds so shifting the **supply** of pounds to the right and bringing the equilibrium rate back within the accepted limits, as in Figure 24.3.

There is a limit to the extent to which a fixed exchange rate can be maintained by government intervention. If a country has a permanent balance of payments deficit there will be continuous downward pressure on the exchange rate. This will lead to the country's gold and foreign currency reserves being run down, both to finance the deficit and to support the currency on the foreign exchange markets. Eventually the monetary authorities will have no choice but to devalue the currency to a rate sustainable by market forces. Where the exchange rate is constantly threatening to breach the upper peg the country will find its gold and foreign currency reserves rising steadily as it intervenes to hold the rate down. By revaluing its currency it may be able to stop upward pressure on the exchange rate and enable its residents to enjoy cheaper imports and a higher standard of living.

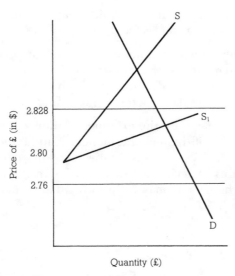

Figure 24.3 *Fixed exchange rates II*

Advantages of fixed rates

The principal claim made for fixed exchange rates is that, by promoting stability in the international financial system, they help create an environment conducive to the development of the world economy. Thus they:

1   **Promote the expansion of world trade**   Fixed exchange rates enable traders to predict with greater certainty both prices and profits, so encouraging firms to enter overseas markets. In practice, even under a system of floating exchange rates, individual traders can be sure of the value of an overseas transaction by taking out a forward exchange contract guaranteeing a particular rate of exchange when they either buy or sell foreign currency.

2   **Promote stability in the international capital markets**   Investors are more likely to feel confident about investing overseas if they can be sure that their investments will hold their value in terms of their own currency. At the same time speculators will be able to make only limited gains from exchange dealings unless they are able to force a major revaluation or devaluation.

3   **Discipline on domestic economic policies**   In order to avoid pressure on the exchange rate the government must ensure that its domestic economic policies do not lead to high inflation or a persistent balance of payment deficit.

Disadvantages of fixed rates

The main objection to fixed exchange rates is that they act as a severe restraint on the government's freedom of action in executing its economic policies.

1   **They require substantial official reserves**   The monetary authorities must maintain a large pool of reserves to enable a prolonged period of intervention to support the exchange rate, should this prove necessary. Large reserves are also required to

finance balance of payments deficits which may be a persistent feature of the
economy when the exchange rate is fixed.

2   **They lead to exchange rate misalignment**   Over a long period there is a tendency
for exchange rates to move out of alignment and require substantial readjustment
through either revaluation or devaluation. Such changes may themselves be a
source of disruption to international trade and finance.

3   **Economic policy is dictated by the external position**   Pressures on the external
value of the currency will require the monetary authorities to take appropriate
action, even if this runs counter to the needs of the domestic economy. Thus
deflationary measures to rectify a balance of payments deficit and downward
pressure on the exchange rate may be introduced at a time of recession and high
unemployment

Floating rates

We have seen that the determination of floating exchange rates is left to market forces.
So the principal arguments advanced in their favour centre on the greater freedom they
give to the working of market forces and to the operation of government policy.

Advantages of floating rates

1   **They automatically adjust the balance of payments**   When a freely floating
exchange rate is in operation the balance for official financing should be zero since
the exchange rate will move to equate the demand and supply for the currency. A
drop in exports will reduce demand for a country's currency and so lower the price
of that currency. This in turn will make it cheaper for foreign investors to buy capital
assets in the country and increase inward capital flows. Thus a deficit on current
account will be offset by a surplus on capital account. A surplus on current account
will have the opposite effect. In both cases the position on capital account should
cancel out the current account balance.

The current account will also be self-adjusting to some extent. A deficit leads,
through a lower exchange rate, to an increase in demand for the country's cheaper
exports and a decrease in domestic demand for the now dearer imports. The precise
effect of this development depends on the price elasticity of demand for exports and
imports but provided the Marshall-Lerner elasticity condition holds the lower
exchange rate will help to improve the balance on current account.

2   **They eliminate the need for large official reserves**   As the balance of payments is
self-adjusting countries need not maintain levels of reserves sufficient to support a
series of deficits nor to support the exchange rate on the markets. Furthermore,
there should be a more even spread of world liquidity with no country accumulating
massive reserves from a series of balance of payments surpluses.

3   **They free domestic policy from external restraints**   Since the exchange rate
operates to maintain balance of payments equilibrium the government has no need
to adopt measures to cure a deficit. Thus domestic economic policies can be tailored

to the needs of the domestic situation without undue concern for the external position.

4 **They provide for smooth exchange rate changes** Natural movements in the exchange rate, whether up or down, prevent the exchange rate from getting out of line with its true market value. This helps avoid the need for dramatic adjustments in rates through devaluation or revaluation and the potential damage these do both internally and externally.

5 **They may reduce speculation** Smoother movements of the exchange rate should reduce the scope for speculation and the instability this promotes. This follows from the fact that under a fixed rate system it is obvious in which direction, if any, a country will have to change its rate; a deficit country's rate can only stay as it is or move downwards. A speculator moving out of a deficit country's currency, therefore, will either break even or win, he cannot lose. With a floating system the exchange rate *can* move by small amounts in both directions so that a loss becomes possible.

Disadvantages of floating rates

The arguments against floating exchange rates stem from the greater uncertainties attached to international trade by less stable currency values.

1 **They increase uncertainty** Because trade contracts often take a long time to complete both exporters and importers wish to be able to predict future currency values. With floating rates predictions become very difficult and trade uncertain. However, firms may make use of the forward exchange market to eliminate all but the very long-term uncertainties.

2 **They contribute to price instability** If exchange rates are prone to short-term volatility, import prices and, consequently, domestic costs are also liable to fluctuate. In particular, a downward floating exchange rate will make imports more expensive and this will increase the inflationary pressures operating within the economy.

3 **They may increase speculation** Though floating rates avoid the possibility of speculators piling pressure on a currency until it is forced into a major correction, they may allow a steady decline or rise to produce a significant change in the rate over a relatively short period. Indeed there is evidence to support this view in the dramatic fluctuations in the value of sterling in 1976/77 and again in 1984/85.

In considering the relative merits of fixed and floating exchange rates it is clear that the advantages of the former tend to be the disadvantages of the latter and vice versa. In practice the fixed exchange rate system which operated between 1945 and the early 1970s sought to obtain some of the flexibility of floating rates by allowing rates to deviate by up to 1 per cent either side of parity. Similarly, in the floating exchange rate system of today few governments are willing to allow their currency to float without a degree of intervention for fear that a violent movement in the rate will have undesirable consequences for the internal economy. Most governments have therefore tended to operate a system of managed or 'dirty' floating whereby the exchange rate is theoretically free to float but where the government intervenes to prevent too dramatic a movement, especially if it feels that the rate is being driven too far out of line with its 'natural' rate.

Managed floating

Major difficulties arose for the system of floating exchange rates in the 1980s because of the wide fluctuations in foreign exchange rates for all the main currencies. This volatility seems to have arisen from the fact that much of the growth in foreign currency trading was linked to the movement of capital rather than for the settlement of international trade transactions. The situation was exacerbated by the over-valuation of the US dollar due to high American interest rates.

In 1985 the USA, Japan, West Germany, France and the UK joined in the Plaza agreement to co-operate in the managed floating of their currencies' exchange rates and to secure an orderly fall in the value of the US dollar. The success of this co-operation led to the Louvre accord of 1987 in which the Group of Seven (the Plaza Five plus Canada and Italy) agreed to continue to manage exchange rates with the objective of achieving greater exchange rate stability.

Although the current international financial system is characterised by managed floating some countries have entered into more formal arrangements, most notably the European Monetary System (EMS) of the EEC. The EMS ties the exchange rates of the member countries to each other through an adjustable peg system similar to that which prevailed internationally prior to 1971. At the centre of the EMS is the European Currency Unit (ECU), the value and composition of which are defined in terms of a basket of currencies. Each member currency has an ECU-related central rate and fluctuations of exchange rates between currencies are limited to 2¼ per cent either side of the central rate, except in the case of countries with floating rates which are allowed margins of up to 6 per cent. There are also divergence thresholds which are fixed at 75 per cent of the maximum spread of divergence. When a currency crosses this threshold the authorities of the member state concerned must take appropriate measures to correct the divergence; if necessary this may require an adjustment of central rates, i.e. a revaluation or devaluation.

The International Monetary Fund (IMF)

The IMF was established in 1945 under United Nations plans to establish an international financial regime which would be conducive to the growth of world trade through the provision of stable exchange rates and the free convertibility of currencies. General agreement of the need to avoid the chaotic floating exchange rate era of the 1930s resulted in an attempt to create a well-ordered structure of international liquidity involving an international monetary institution, an international currency and a direct link between the exchange rate structure and gold. This resulted in:

a) The system of fixed exchange rates outlined above;
b) The establishment of the US dollar as a reserve currency to which all other currencies party to the system would be linked;
c) The US dollar going into the gold standard, so providing a link between all currencies and gold.

d)   The establishment of the IMF as an international monetary institution.

The IMF began operating in 1947 and today most of the countries of the world are members, apart from Switzerland and some communist countries.

The formal objectives of the IMF are specified in the Articles of Agreement as follows:

1   To promote international monetary co-operation.

2   To facilitate the expansion of trade and so promote and maintain high levels of employment and real income.

3   To promote exchange rate stability and avoid competitive exchange depreciation.

4   To assist in the establishment of a multilateral system of payments and the elimination of foreign exchange restrictions.

5   To make the IMF's resources available to members and so enable them to correct balance of payments maladjustments.

6   To shorten the duration and lessen the degree of disequilibrium in the international balances of member countries.

In attempting to fulfil these objectives the IMF has acted like an international bank. Each member is a given a **quota** based roughly on its importance as a trading nation and is required to subscribe that quota to the Fund. Originally a quarter of the quota had to be subscribed in gold, with the remainder in the member's currency but the so-called 'gold tranche' has now been replaced by a reserve tranche of foreign currency. The subscriptions from members enable the IMF to honour members' drawing rights which are themselves based on each member's quota. A member with a shortage of a particular currency can draw that currency from the IMF and pay for it with its own currency. If, therefore, the UK were short of the currency to meet a debt denominated in French francs it could buy francs from the IMF and pay for them in sterling. Thus a drawing leads to an increase in the Fund's holdings of the drawing member's currency and a decrease in the holdings of the currency purchased.

The system of drawing rights and other credit facilities enabled the IMF to assist members over temporary balance of payments difficulties, shortages of international liquidity and pressures on the par values of their currencies. Over the first 20 years or so this regime worked well but by the early 1970s the weakness of the dollar led to increasing doubts as to its ability to continue the role of a reserve currency. In 1971 the US dollar ceased to be convertible into gold but this did not halt speculation and in 1973 the other major currencies detached themselves from the dollar, thus ushering in the era of floating exchange rates with which we are now familiar.

Since the late 1960s the IMF has adapted its role to address the various pressing issues with which the international financial community has been faced.

1   Special drawing rights (SDRs)

Throughout the 1960s the growth of world liquidity lagged behind that of world trade. To alleviate this shortage SDRs were introduced in 1967. SDRs are, in effect, non-repayable credits issued to each member of the IMF in proportion to its IMF quota.

When a country needs to finance a balance of payments deficit or meet some other liquidity problem it may use its allocation of SDRs to obtain currencies from other countries, subject to the limitation that it maintains an average of 30 per cent of its allocation. Thus 70 per cent of the SDR allocation is unconditional extra liquidity while the other 30 per cent is a short-term borrowing facility. The SDR unit, which is composed of a basket of currencies, is now the official unit of the IMF.

2   Demonetisation of gold
In 1976 the IMF agreed to the demonetisation of gold. While gold remains acceptable in settlement of international debts it no longer performs a central role in the determination of exchange rates. The IMF has since sold off most of its gold holdings, using the proceeds to assist the liquidity position of the developing countries.

3   Assistance to developing countries.
Increasingly the IMF has taken on the role of guiding and supporting developing countries. Apart from the provision of credit facilities the IMF has also played a leading role in the rescheduling of the debts of the developing countries by working with the international banking community and the countries themselves to produce a solution to the threatened insolvency of such countries.

REVISION TEST

1   Why, theoretically, would a country with a floating exchange rate never have to adopt deflationary policies?

2   Why is entirely free floating not allowed by most governments?

3   Under a fixed exchange rate regime what action should a government take to prevent the exchange rate falling below its established lower limit?

4   Give three main advantages of fixed exchange rates.

5   Why were floating exchange rates unpopular during the period of reconstruction after the Second World War?

6   What is an IMF quota?

7   What is the purpose of the Exchange Equalisation Account of the Bank of England?

8   If gold has been demonetised why do most countries continue to maintain some gold reserves?

9   What is the purpose of the forward exchange market?

10   Define Special Drawing Rights (SDRs) and outline their usefulness.

———— **Examination questions** ————

1   Floating exchange rates are often criticised by students of economics on the grounds that they create business uncertainty. How could a Central Bank stabilise its rate and what problems might it meet in the process? What are the likely effects on trade if the rate is set too high?   (ABE2, June 1986)

2   Trading nations are attempting to stabilise international exchange rates in a 'partnership for growth'. What benefits could be hoped for, and what difficulties might prevent such a stabilisation being achieved?

(ABE2, December 1987)

3   Why has the flexible exchange rate system of the 1980s apparently failed to end world exchange rate instability and balance of payments surpluses and deficits?

(ABE2, June 1988)

4   Discuss the arguments for and against the adoption of (a) fixed and (b) floating rates of exchange.

(LCCI Higher, May 1987)

5   What are the arguments for and against the adoption of (a) floating and (b) fixed rates of exchange?

(ACCA, June 1987)

6   a)   How under a system of 'dirty' floating exchange rates is the rate of a particular currency determined?
    b)   What are the likely effects of an appreciation of the Japanese yen on:
         i) the Japanese economy?
         ii) the economies of Japan's trading partners?

(ACCA, June 1988)

7   By use of appropriate examples illustrate the ways in which exchange rates are determined.

(ACCA, December 1989)

8   To what extent is it true that floating exchange rates prevent countries suffering long term balance of trade deficits?

(SCCA, May 1988)

9   The UK's exchange rate with the currencies of its major trading partners is currently (1988) considerably higher than it has been for many years. What effect is that relatively high exchange rate likely to be having on the UK economy?

(SCCA, May 1989)

10 In the absence of official intervention in the foreign exchange market, what factors are likely to influence changes in a country's exchange rate?

(Cert.M., November 1987)

11 Discuss how each of the following are affected by a fall in the value of the £ sterling on the foreign exchange market:
    a)   the British economy, and
    b)   the work of a purchasing department.

(IPS, May 1988)

12 Discuss the arguments for and against fixed exchange rates.

(I.Act., April 1989)

13 What are the advantages of a floating exchange rate system?
    Have these advantages been witnessed by the widespread application of such
    exchange rate systems over the last decade or so?

(IFA, December 1988)

25 Trade and economic development

- *What factors prevent many developing countries achieving the conditions necessary for rapid economic growth?*

- *Why have so many developing countries accumulated vast external debts?*

Economic development

Although international trade is only one of the factors contributing to economic growth within a country it occupies a central role in the economic development of Third World countries. To see why we need only compare the economy of a developing country today with that of a developing country 200 years ago.

By modern standards Great Britain was a developing country in the late eighteenth century. It was then transformed into an industrial society enjoying a high rate of economic growth within a relatively short period. This success arose out of several coincidental factors;

1   There was an accumulated supply of investment funds available for the innovating entrepreneur.

2   The rapid population growth of the period provided both a pool of cheap labour for the new factories and a market for the goods they produced.

3   Advances in agriculture and medicine improved the health of the population and thus the quality of the workforce.

4   The existence of the British Empire meant that overseas trade with the colonies could be directed to promoting economic growth in the UK itself.

One after another the other western countries followed the pattern of rapid economic growth set by Britain and in this century many third world countries have achieved striking rates of progress. In much of Africa, Asia and South America, however, poorer countries remain much as they did decades ago and some, like Ethiopia or Haiti, appear to have gone backwards.

Currently, developing countries are categorised as:

1   **Oil-producing countries**   These countries are usually members of the Organisation of Petroleum Exporting Countries (OPEC). Their development has been based

on a product vital for world economic development and this has therefore brought great prosperity to many of them.

2   **Lesser developed countries (LDCs)**   These are the non-oil developing countries whose exportable resources have generally been of low value so that they can finance only a limited amount of capital accumulation. These countries have consequently enjoyed much lower levels of economic development than those in the previous category.

3   **Newly industrialising countries (NICs)**   This group is distinguished by the fact that its members are passing through the transitional stage from developing country to industrial nation, as indicated in their quite rapid industrialisation and high rate of economic growth. Their economies are thus comparable to that of Britain in the early nineteenth century. The Organisation for Economic Co-operation and Development (OECD) identifies the NICs as: Argentina, Brazil, Greece, Hong Kong, Mexico, Portugal, Singapore, South Korea, Spain, Taiwan and Yugoslavia. The average annual growth rate of South Korea between 1983 and 1987 was 9.5 per cent and that of Hong Kong was 8 per cent while Taiwan was, by 1989, the thirteenth largest trading nation in the world.

TABLE 25.1
Developing countries' key statistics

	GDP/Capita (1988: US$)	Real GDP Growth (%) (1984–88 average)	(US$m: 1988) Trade balance	Current Acc. balance
Selected LDCs				
Cote d'Ivoire	750	−0.2	816	−1335
Egypt	640	2.3	−6751	−1856
Zambia	360	0.9	497	−229
India	330	5.9	−6375	−7250
Philippines	670	0.5	−1085	−661
Thailand	890	6.7	−2074	−1858
Colombia	1290	4.3	648	−467
Ecuador	1010	3.6	589	−597
Selected NICs				
Argentina	2890	0.4	4043	−1812
Brazil	2450	4.8	19089	4426
Hong Kong	9550	8.4	−734	2842
Mexico	2120	0.8	1752	−2905
Singapore	8840	5.6	−2346	1683
South Korea	4080	10.4	11445	14117
Taiwan	6150	9.9	13834	10180
Yugoslavia	2390	0.6	−264	2200

Source: Barclays Bank

The plight of many LDCs is that they seem unable to reach that stage of development where sustained economic growth occurs. Often this is due to the fact that some of the conditions necessary for growth are present while others are lacking. In such circumstances those conditions which are present may actually be detrimental to the country's attempts to achieve economic growth. Improvements in medicine and hygiene have led to rapid population growth in many developing countries. However, this population growth has added little to total output since, in the absence of an industrial base and pool of capital to develop it, the extra labour has been forced to stay on the land and rely on subsistence farming. There is thus a danger that the law of diminishing returns will come into play as more and more labour is added to a fixed amount of land. This results in a reduction in per capita income since each person coming into the labour force adds less to national output than he or she consumes.

That so many developing countries suffer the lack of a capital base follows from the nature of their economic structure. As they are subsistence economies the vast majority of the population are unable to save so that there is no accumulation of savings available for investment. In consequence there is no progress in the introduction of capital goods into agriculture nor are there funds available to support the development of new industries. In order to progress along the path of economic development such countries must therefore seek injections of capital from overseas. These funds may be obtained through trade, through borrowing or through aid.

Trade

A developing country may adopt one of two trade strategies.

1 Specialisation

The country may specialise in the product(s) in which it has a comparative advantage and use the receipts obtained from the export of these goods to finance the importation of capital and other goods. For most of the developing countries this would mean specialising in agricultural or other primary products and herein lies a problem. Since most of these products are low in value the country finds that the terms of trade are against it. Furthermore, the long-term trend is for the prices of agricultural goods to fall relative to those of manufactured goods so worsening the terms of trade of economies based on primary products. Thus the developing country may find it has to export more and more of its own product to finance a given level of imports.

There are of course some developing countries whose products command a relatively high world price and they have progressed quite rapidly through specialisation, most notably the oil-producing countries such as Saudi Arabia and Kuwait. All countries which choose specialisation, however, are exposed to the dangers which arise from fluctuations in world trade and changes in technology and taste, all of which may affect demand for their products.

2 Income substitution

The developing country may seek to be more self-sufficient. This option involves the process of income substitution whereby local industries such as bicycle assembly or brewing are set up to produce goods previously imported. Although initially development is likely to be slower than under a regime of specialisation this alternative can be supported on two grounds:

1 Continued specialisation in agricultural goods could result in the economy encountering the law of diminishing returns, in addition to the terms of trade constraint.

2 Import substitution enables the developing country to achieve more balanced growth and move into areas of activity which will yield a comparative advantage in the future. In order to get local industries off the ground a policy of import substitution may need to be accompanied by import controls, using the infant industry/economy arguments.

Borrowing

Economic development may also be financed by borrowing from other countries and some recourse to such funds is essential for most developing countries which are trying to establish new industries. In the past many developing countries have been able to finance their industrial development and consequent economic growth by the issue of government-backed loans on the world's stock markets. For developing colonial territories this process was made easier by the fact that their issues were underwritten by the imperial government. But even the railways of South America were built with finance raised on the European stock markets.

Foreign investment is advantageous in that funds are raised more quickly than through the indigenous accumulation of capital while the risk is borne by the lending country. On the other hand this inflow of capital will result in a future outflow of profits and interest. As these payments, as well as repayment of loan, will be made in foreign currency it is important that such injections of capital are used to finance activities which will either earn or save the expenditure of foreign currency.

Aid

Unfortunately not all developing countries are able to finance their development either by trade or by investment financed from overseas. In these circumstances developing countries may well be dependent on aid as a source of investment funds. Aid may take the form of gifts but there is also an element of aid in loans which are given with interest-free or reduced interest terms. Other aid takes the form of the loan of skilled workers or the gift of items of capital. Aid has the advantage that it promises more rapid development than does trade without the high interest and repayment costs associated with borrowing.

Despite its obvious attractions aid may be less of an unmixed blessing than is apparent at first sight. Capital is likely to have strings attached in that the assisting country will expect to sell capital goods or technical expertise to the developing country as part of the deal. Where skilled workers are seconded to the developing country they may know little of local conditions and could be a liability to the country as much as an asset. The capital goods are usually given without reference to the need for investment planning and the country often has a bewildering array of different types of equipment which it cannot service and for which spares are no longer available. Finally, there is the problem that aid will not foster the country's economic development if it does nothing to develop local industry or stimulate its trade. At its worst aid may be likened to charitable gifts to a beggar which solve an immediate problem but which do nothing to improve his prospects of employment.

Among the most important sources of aid for developing countries has been the International Bank for Reconstruction and Development (IBRD) and its subsidiary agencies. The IBRD, commonly known as the World Bank, was established in 1944 to help finance the renewal of areas devastated during the Second World War and to aid the development of the world's poorer nations. Its funds are raised through the subscriptions of member countries and from loan issues floated on the international capital markets. Since 1950 its activities have been exclusively devoted to assisting the developing countries through the provision of loans to governmental bodies to finance the foreign exchange costs of capital projects.

Stringent criteria are applied to loan applications; criteria which the LDCS find it very difficult to satisfy and thus to obtain assistance. For this reason the International Development Association (IDA) was set up in 1960 to finance projects which assist the process of development but which are not revenue-producing. The IDA is financed by the wealthier members of the IBRD and gives interest-free loans for up to 50 years, repayments to start after ten years. Another subsidiary organisation of the IBRD is the International Finance Corporation (IFC) which invests, in partnership with private investors, in private enterprise in the developing countries.

REVISION TEST

1   What economic factors were present in the developing countries of western Europe in the nineteenth century but which are not present in the LDCs of today?

2   Describe the three main types of developing country.

3   What trading disadvantage is common to most LDCs?

4   How would you compare the production possibility curve of an LDC to that of an NIC?

5   What are the three main methods of financing economic growth in a developing country?

6   Which injection into the circular flow of national income is affected by each of the above methods?

7   What is meant by 'import substitution'?

8   What are the advantages and disadvantages of a developing country seeking to grow through the exploitation of a comparative advantage?

9   Name two of the problems which may arise for a country using aid to promote industrial development.

10   What is the role of the IFC?

The international debt problem

Whether a developing country persistently imports more than it exports or borrows on the international capital markets for specific capital programmes, the effect will be that it accumulates a growing international debt. Not only will this debt have to be repaid at some time in the future but the country will have to meet annual interest charges from its overseas earnings.

During the 1980s the combined international indebtedness of the developing countries grew to a level which threatened difficulties not only for these countries but for the international banking community. The crisis had its origins in the oil price rises of 1973–74 and 1979–80; the immediate consequence of both events being a severe worsening of the balance of payments of the LDCs. This situation was exacerbated by the industrial countries responding to higher oil prices by adopting deflationary measures which reduced their demand for the products of the LDCs. Though the oil-producing countries built up large balance of payments surpluses these were invested in the major industrial countries rather than used to buy imports from the LDCs. This latter group thus had no choice but to turn to the major banking centres of the United States, Western Europe and Japan for funds to finance their deficits. So began the process whereby oil surpluses were recycled to debtor developing countries by the international banking system through the mechanism of eurocurrency credits.

A further cause of indebtedness among the developing countries was the growing demand for investment funds by the NICs. These countries were enjoying rapid rates of growth in the 1970s but were unable to supply indigenously all the capital funds required to maintain this growth.

By 1980 a growing number of these debtor countries were slipping into arrears, both on making interest payments and on repaying debts. The reasons for this were threefold:

1 **Unregulated bank lending** The banks had considered default by governments unthinkable and so had not applied normal loan criteria to their lending. In consequence many of the developing countries had run up debts of over 40 per cent of the value of their GDP.

2 **Interest rates** Real interest rates in the 1970s and 1980s were much higher than in the past. Since many of the debts were not repaid on maturity but were rolled forward on a short-term basis to avoid default, they now attracted high short-term interest rates. Furthermore much of the long-term debt carried short-term rates. For these reasons every hike in interest rates led to increased debt service costs. By the early 1980s it was estimated that every 1 per cent on interest rates cost the LDCs $2.5 bn. per annum.

3 **World rececession** There were world recessions following each oil price rise which were aggravated by the adoption of deflationary measures by the industrial nations. Reduced demand for their products led to a worsening of the terms of trade of the LDCs, cut their export earnings and increased their dependence on borrowing to finance their imports.

The extent of the problem by the mid-1980s is shown in Figure 25.1. The situation was such that there was a possibility that some of the largest debtors might default on their debts. In 1983 the total outstanding external debt of the LDCs stood at $669 bn. Of this over $300 bn. was owed by Latin American countries and it was feared that from

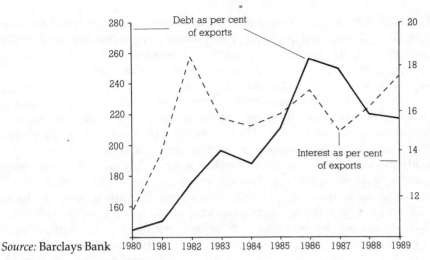

Source: Barclays Bank

Figure 25.1 *33 LDCs – key debt indicators*

these the first defaulter would come. Indeed, in 1982, Mexico had been unable to repay her scheduled debts following a fall in oil revenues. A crisis here had been averted by over 50 international banks raising $10 bn. of new credit, so enabling the rescheduling of Mexico's debts.

The willingness of so many banks to assist in the Mexican rescue operation reflected the concern of the banking world of the consequences of a default. The great danger was that this would be followed by other defaults which would place an excessive strain on the banking system, bringing the collapse of some banks. Many of the banks were now owed so much already that, rather than let a default occur, they were prepared to go on lending debtor countries the finance to meet interest payments due on earlier loans. These further loans would, of course, create their own problems at a later date. Thus the banks were in a cleft stick. They did not wish to increase their lending for fear of a default but to stop lending would bring a default that much nearer. The immediate crisis was eased by the rescheduling of debts.

Debt rescheduling

Rescheduling involves a reduction in the level of capital repayments and a consequent lengthening of the repayment period. This reduces the debtor country's burden of servicing its debts while increasing the likelihood that the debts will eventually be repaid. The work of co-ordinating rescheduling operations was undertaken by the IMF which also made some advances to the largest borrowers. However, the IMF imposed austerity packages on many of the debtor countries as a condition of arranging rescheduling. Under these arrangements rescheduling jumped from $10 bn. in 1982 to over $100 bn. in 1983, some 15 per cent of all LDC debt. However, this was not the end of the crisis. The austerity programmes imposed on the debtor countries were often so harsh as to be almost unacceptable and by 1984 some of the Latin American countries were once again threatening to default rather than subject their peoples to further economic hardship.

In its 1984 annual report the World Bank argued that current policies were too negative since the rescheduling packages had pushed repayment further into the distance while slowing the long-term growth rates necessary to make repayment possible. It recommended a greater emphasis on export and industrial growth, supported by aid, rather than a policy of restraint.

Without the question of the debt being resolved, the situation has improved somewhat since 1984. The austerity programmes of the IMF coupled with internal economic reform enabled many of the LDCs to improve their external positions and encourage exports. This was especially so as western deflationary policies were eased and commodity prices revived to help their terms of trade. The balance of payments current account position of the leading 25 non-oil LDCs improved from a deficit of $30.2 bn. in 1983 to a surplus of over $5 bn. in 1989. At the same time the burden of interest payments was reduced by a fall in interest rates through most of the 1980s. The US money market interest rate, for example, fell from an average of 10.4 per cent in 1984 to an average of 6.9 per cent in 1987. Finally, a number of banks accepted the inevitable and wrote off large proportions of their outstanding debt; action reflected in the reduced profits of the British clearing banks in 1989 and 1990.

Multinationals and the developing countries

Instead of trying to establish its own industries, whether financed from its own economy or through overseas borrowing, a developing country may encourage multinational companies to set up operations within its borders. There are three main benefits to a country receiving investment from a multinational company:

1   **Technology**   The advent of a multinational will bring with it increased training and skills for the local workforce. There should also be spin-off benefits for those home-based industries able to make use of the new technological skills introduced.

2   **Employment**   The multinational is likely to employ considerable numbers of local workers in its plants or factories. This in turn will increase aggregate demand and, via the multiplier effect, will lead to more jobs being created throughout the economy.

3   **The external position**   Where the multinational produces raw materials for processing in its manufacturing plants elsewhere the country will enjoy increased export earnings. If the multinational produces manufactured goods there may be a saving on imports as these goods replace goods previously bought abroad.
There are, however, also disadvantages to multinational investment within a country. These disadvantages weigh particularly heavily on the LCDs.

1   The multinational is likely to be less interested in the technological development of the country than a local firm. It will probably bring in its own nationals as managers and may be reluctant to allow local employees to take part in the research and development function. There is thus the danger that neither local technology nor local labour will benefit from the technical progress initiated by the multinational, the country being seen only as a provider of cheap labour.

2   There is the danger that a small developing country could become economically dependent on a multinational company which could then use its power to obtain favourable treatment from the government in terms of location, tax concessions, the movement of capital and legal controls. It may even use the threat of withdrawal to ensure government support for its objectives.

3   There may be little direct benefit to the host country's economy. A highly capital-intensive operation would create little local employment and would probably rely mainly on professional and managerial staff from the company's home country. If it seeks to raise capital locally the company may well attract funds away from more risky infant industries and retard their development. Finally, it may repatriate most of its profits, ploughing little or nothing back into the developing country's economy.

4   The multinational may prove too powerful a competitor for local industry in a number of ways, so inhibiting its growth:
    a) *Economies of scale* By making use of cheap labour, internationally-based marketing strategies and financial and taxation economies, the multinational can maintain a competitive edge over its national rivals.
    b) *Market leadership* The multinational can establish market dominance and dictate output and pricing policies. Once dominant, it may force up prices and standardise products to suit its international marketing strategy, irrespective of local needs.
    c) *Labour market dominance* Because it is able to use resources more efficiently the multinational may be able to offer higher pay rates and so attract the best qualified workers. It also has the resources to resist strike action longer than a local firm and so may also pose a threat to the aims of organised labour.

Despite these drawbacks most developing countries extend a cautious welcome to investment from multinationals. In particular the NICs have grown in confidence in their dealings with the multinationals and have used the increased investment and copied the improved technology to establish their own industries. Indeed some NICs have since produced their own multinational companies.

REVISION TEST

1   At which point does external borrowing by a developing country become a problem?

2   How does the debt problem for the NICs differ to that of the non-oil producing LDCs?

3   Which events precipitated the onset of the international debt problem?

4   What role did the eurocurrency markets play in the growth of international debt?

5   What was the dilemma facing the banks in the early 1980s?

6   Explain what is meant by a rescheduling package.

7   What factors alleviated the international debt crisis in the mid-1980s?

8   Why is a multinational company more of a threat to a developing country than to an industrialised one?

9   What are the main advantages of multinational investment in a developing country?

10 In what ways do multinationals inhibit the development of indigenous industry?

_____ **Examination questions** _____

1   'It is not shortage of international liquidity that has caused the modern debt-crisis but excessive lending to Third World governments that permitted them to avoid structural changes to their economies that are needed for long-term survival'. Explain and assess this statement.

(ABE2, December 1985)

2   What is the international debt crisis and how has it come about?
Could debtor nations benefit by switching part of their trade to direct barter arrangements? State your reasoning.

(ABE2, June 1987)

3   Is development best achieved by export-led growth, or should countries hope for industrialisation through import-substitution (ISI)? Base your answer on economic analysis illustrated by reference to any country with which you are familiar.

(ABE2, June 1988)

4   Is aid or trade a better way to promote economic development?

(LCCI Higher, November 1985)

5   Many nations' economies are heavily dependent upon primary production. Explain the economic problems which might result from this dependence.

(LCCI Higher, May 1986)

6   'Trade, not aid, is the best solution to the problems of developing countries.' Discuss.

(LCCI Third, May 1988)

7   Explain some of the problems which might arise when a country is heavily dependent upon primary production.

(LCCI Intermediate, May 1986)

8   'Multinational corporations pose a threat to host countries.' Discuss.

(SCCA, November 1987)

9   'All that multinational corporations bring to developing countries is the capital intensive production of goods that the indigenous population neither want nor can afford.' Evaluate this statement.

(SCCA, November 1988)

10 What are the likely costs and benefits for the host country of inward foreign investment?

(SCCA, May 1989)

CHAPTER

26 Revision

You have now completed your course and should have covered all the areas likely to be tested in your examination paper. When you are ready to commence your revision programme it is important to use the resources available to their full effectiveness. In the case of this book have regard to:

1 Those areas which are listed at the front of the book as being relevant to your own particular syllabus.

2 The past examination questions at the end of each chapter. These are useful for a number of reasons:
   a) They show which areas are most popular with examiners generally since each chapter is drawing on the same number of examination papers.
   b) They indicate which areas of the syllabus particular examining boards choose to set questions on.
   c) They give a clue to the style of question likely to be posed by an examining board.

You will wish to take note of all these factors when preparing your revision strategy. Note, however, that while some areas are less frequently used as a source for questions they must not be neglected in your revision since they lay foundations for development in the chapters which follow, e.g. Chapter 2 or Chapter 12. Economics is a subject in which the areas interlock and it would be extremely dangerous to assume that parts of the subject can be understood without reference to other key topics.

Examination styles

The 'building blocks' nature of the subject results in many examination questions drawing on material from more than one chapter. In this book a question which relates to two consecutive chapters is included after the latter chapter. But sometimes a question draws on material from several chapters and sometimes one relates to an economic principle which recurs throughout the book.

In the first category come questions which ask for short answers on a variety of areas such as:

1 Explain any **two** of the following as fully as time allows:
   a) Control of the money supply.
   b) The structure of the balance of payments accounts.
   c) Liquidity preference and the level of interest rates.

340

d) The current work of the International Monetary Fund (IMF).
e) The gains from international trade.

(ABE2, December 1986)

2 Explain any TWO of the following as fully as time allows:
a) International money.
b) The work of the Central Bank.
c) The measurement of a nation's money supply.
d) The accelerator principle in economic theory.
e) The possible effects of taxation on the supply of labour.

(ABE2, December 1987)

3 Comment on any TWO of the following, explaining them briefly:
a) The work of a stock exchange.
b) The foreign trade multiplier.
c) Non-interest banking systems.
d) 'Real' and 'nominal' GDP.
e) The quantity theory of money.
f) IMF.
g) The EEC.

(ABE2, June 1988)

4 Write brief notes on:
a) Stock Exchange Automated Quotes.
b) Bearer stocks.
c) Industrial leasing.
d) Bills of exchange.

(I.Act., September 1989)

Also in the first category are questions which draw on related material from several chapters. These include:

1 It has been suggested that National Income statistics tell us nothing about social welfare. Explain what an observer needs to know about wealth and income distribution, the nature of taxation and inflation, and the value of the pound, to objectively assess the standard of living of ordinary working people.

(IPS, November 1988)

2 As the purchasing officer for a large publishing company, consider the effects on your organisation of the following tax changes:
a) The introduction of VAT on books.
b) A substantial reduction in income tax.
c) The imposition of a new tax on imported timber.
d) An increase in the tax allowances for capital expenditure.

(IPS, November 1988)

3   For an industry with which you are familiar, comment on the main factors affecting:
    a)   The demand for the product.
    b)   The market structure of the industry.

(IPS, May 1989)

4   a)   Describe five advantages that small firms enjoy over large firms in a developed
         economy.
    b)   Explain why the Stock Exchange found it necessary to set up the Unlisted
         Securities Market (USM) in 1980. Discuss the attractions of the USM to a small
         company compared with obtaining a full listing, mentioning any disadvan-
         tages.

(I.Act., September 1988)

5   Describe briefly how the United Kingdom government has sought to give direct
    assistance to industry, including reference to:
    a)   Industrial and Commercial Finance Corporation.
    b)   National Enterprise Board.
    c)   Industrial Development Certificates.
    d)   Manpower Services Commission.
    e)   Youth Training Scheme.

(I.Act., April 1989)

6   Describe the following statistics which are published regularly in the United
    Kingdom:
    a)   Earnings indices,
    b)   Index of Producer Prices,
    c)   Tax and Price Index,
    d)   Index of Retail Prices.

(I.Act., September 1989)

Questions dealing with general economic principles include:

1   Discuss the general problems which the government of an industrial economy
    might face in attempting to implement a new economic policy.

(CIMA, November 1989)

2   The concept of the 'margin' (e.g. marginal cost, marginal revenue, marginal
    returns) occurs frequently in economic analysis. Why? It is a legitimate tool of
    analysis if, in fact, economic agents (e.g. firms, consumers, workers) do not actually
    think in those terms?

(SCCA, May 1989)

3   Purchasing strategies involve forecasting both prices and availability of supplies
    and services. How might a knowledge of economics lead to a better purchasing
    decision?

(IPS, November 1987)

4 Analyse the relationship between the following factors:
  a) The rate of interest.
  b) Investment.
  c) Consumer demand.
  d) Balance of payments.

(IPS, May 1989)

5 Explain what you understand by the concept of 'opportunity cost'.

Does it have any practical applications?

(IFA, December 1989)

From the foregoing sample it is clear that questions of the types outlined tend to be set most frequently by a few of the examining bodies. Other types of question set include:
1 Multiple choice (ACCA)
2 Calculation questions (LCCI)
3 Compulsory short answer questions (LCCI)

In addition, the Institute of Actuaries requires that all questions are answered.

Examination technique

Whatever examination you are attempting the following good practices will assist you in being successful.

1 Before the examination ensure that you are familiar with the type of examination paper set by your own examining body. Practise on past papers and buy and read the examiner's reports to ensure that you are up to the standard expected of a candidate.

2 Do not enter the examination room without ensuring you have all the equipment you could possibly need, including a calculator if permissible.

3 Do not enter the examination room with any papers or books which might lead the invigilator to suspect your motives, however unfounded those suspicions might be.

4 Make sure you read and follow the instructions carefully. The examination format may have changed since the last sitting.

5 Ensure that you answer the correct number of questions. If you answer one too many the last answer will probably be discounted and that could be your best answer. If you answer one too few you will lose a substantial proportion of the total marks available.

6 Decide the questions you will answer and do them in the order which suits you best but make sure that each answer is on a separate sheet of paper so they can be put in the right order at the end.

7   Do not spend too long on your 'best' question. Remember it is easier to get the first ten marks on your next question than the last five on your present question and you must leave enough time to answer the correct number of questions.

8   When answering each question make sure that you identify the key issues raised and that you address those points; many students fail by giving a good answer to the wrong question. It may profit you to map out the form your answer will take in a few lines before attempting the answer proper but make sure that such roughwork is scored through and handed in.

9   Make life as easy as possible for the examiner by:
   - writing clearly,
   - sticking to the point,
   - giving a full but not padded answer,
   - completing any particulars required on the answer book,
   - putting your papers neatly in numbered order at the end of the examination.

   Examiners are only human; they mark hundreds of scripts and will have to try very hard to be generous to someone who meets few if any of these criteria.

10 Ensure that you have time at the end of the examination to read through the paper and correct any glaring errors. Lastly, Good Luck.

Index

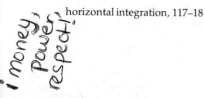
i money,
Power
respect?